Urantia 2025 Part 1

Urantia 2025 Part 1

The Central and Superuniverses

A Revised Urantia Book

Joel F. Covey

Joel F Covey
Urantia 2025 Part 1

Published by Spines
ISBN 979-8-89383-731-5

Spines

The Parts of the Urantia 2025 Book

PART 1

THE CENTRAL AND SUPERUNIVERSES

Sponsored by a Uversa Corps of Superuniverse Personalities acting by authority of the Orvonton Ancients of Days

PART 2

THE LOCAL UNIVERSE

Sponsored by a Nebadon Corps of Local Universe Personalities acting by authority of Gabriel of Salvington

PART 3

THE HISTORY OF URANTIA

These papers were sponsored by a Corps of Local Universe Personalities acting by authority of Gabriel of Salvington

PART 4

THE LIFE AND TEACHINGS OF JESUS

This group of papers was sponsored by a commission of twelve Urantia midwayers acting under the supervision of a Melchizedek revelatory director.

The basis of this narrative was supplied by the superhuman watchcare of the Apostle Andrew.

The Titles of the Papers

Paper	Author
Foreword	Divine Counselor

PART I. THE CENTRAL AND SUPERUNIVERSES

1. The Universal Father	Divine Counselor
2. The Nature of God	Divine Counselor
3. The Attributes of God	Divine Counselor
4. God's Relation to the Universe	Divine Counselor
5. God's Relation to the Individual	Divine Counselor
6. The Eternal Son	Divine Counselor
7. Relation of the Eternal Son to the Universe	Divine Counselor
8. The Infinite Spirit	Divine Counselor
9. Relation of the Infinite Spirit to the Universe	Divine Counselor
10. The Paradise Trinity	Universal Censor
11. The Eternal Isle of Paradise .	Perfector of Wisdom
12. The Universe of Universes	Perfector of Wisdom
13. The Sacred Spheres of Paradise	Perfector of Wisdom
14. The Central and Divine Universe	Perfector of Wisdom
15. The Seven Superuniverses	Universal Censor
16. The Seven Master Spirits	Universal Censor
17. The Seven Supreme Spirit Groups	Divine Counselor
18. The Supreme Trinity Personalities	Divine Counselor
19. The Coordinate Trinityorigin Beings	Divine Counselor
20. The Paradise Sons of God	Perfector of Wisdom
21. The Paradise Creator Sons	Perfector of Wisdom
22. The Trinitized Sons of God	Mighty Messenger
23. The Solitary Messengers	Divine Counselor
24. Higher Personalities of the Infinite Spirit	Divine Counselor
25. The Messenger Hosts of Space	One High in Authority
26. Ministering Spirits of the Central Universe	Perfector of Wisdom

PART II. THE LOCAL UNIVERSE

PART III. THE HISTORY OF URANTIA

PART IV. THE LIFE AND TEACHINGS OF JESUS

Contents

Preface

I first read the Urantia Book in the early 1970's and in Part IV, I found a portrayal of the Jesus I knew from my early childhood religious experiences. I fell in love with the Urantia Book, even with its many scientific flaws, errors, and by today's standards, occasional politically incorrect attitudes. I have read and studied the Urantia Book for almost 50 years, and when the copy-write was lost in 2006, and the whole book became available for download in an editable format online, I was overjoyed. I was now free to fix the book and make it better.

The Urantia Book cosmology was created in the 1930's and had to conform to what the established ideas were about society and the universe at that time. Today (2025) we have tremendously increased our knowledge of the universe. Advances in physics have made most of the original descriptions of scientific concepts obsolete; particularly in Part III on the history of our planet, and these I have corrected or deleted. Also new discoveries in Physics such as String Theory have provided new cosmologies that can be used to improve the concepts contained in the Urantia Book. I take one such approach in my revision. There were also a number of now discredited ideas of the 1930's that were bound into the teachings that needed to be deleted or modified: such as Social Darwinism, Eugenics, and Evolutionary Saltation (the old hypothesis emphasizing sudden drastic evolutionary changes). In addition, there was still existent in the 1930's much sexism and racism that crept into the teachings. All of these old ideas have now been removed or replaced with more modern concepts.

I have been a spiritual seeker for most of my life and I have tried to be guided by the Spirit of Truth, accepting books based on my perception of their spiritual value even if they apparently conflicted with each other intellectually. Thus, there are several key areas in the Urantia Book which, I believe, are improved by bringing in concepts from other "New Age" sources such as the books of Alice A. Bailey (A.A.B.), The Agni Yoga Society, A Course in Miracles, etc.

The original cosmology of the Urantia Book identified the 7th Superuniverse with our Milky Way Galaxy, and had our "local universe" of Nebadon be a small subsection of this galaxy. I believe this identification was a great over-simplification made in the 1930's and grossly belittles the extent of things. I view our "local universe" of Nebadon to be the entire observable universe that we can see with our modern instruments, i.e. our entire 4 dimensional space-time. If String Theory (or some variant of it) proves to be true, then there are many more than 4 dimensions and there are structures (called hypersurfaces or M-branes) that exist in these higher dimensional spaces. It's in this more extended String Theory type of framework that I believe the cosmology of the Urantia Book belongs. Each local universe is a 4-Dimensional M-brane and the superuniverse exists in the larger 10 (or more) dimensions and is constructed from, or made up of, countless M-brane universes of various dimensions. Then in this higher dimensional arena, there are 7 superuniverses "surrounding" the central divine universe which exists outside of any space or time, i.e. outside of the 10 (or more) dimensions in which the 7 superuniverses exist.

The above changes to the concept of a universe also required adding a new organizational level for galaxies, and then changing what the definitions were for a minor and major sector. Now the new organization goes local systems, constellations, galaxies, minor sectors of the universe, major sectors of the universe, and finally the entire local universe. However, even with all of these changes, and numerous small minor updates, many of the papers in the Urantia Book still required no, or only a little, editing (or deletions), sometimes just a few words here or there. As one example in particular, I have replaced or deleted the words "race" and "racial" as much as possible and have changed or removed the whole genesis, meaning, and use of the "colored" races concept, by making this a subjective coloring based on the Seven Rays idea from the books by A.A.B. This coloring now no longer relates to physical skin pigmentation at all, but to a spiritual or esoteric color, only seen with spirit vision. I think this fixes the single biggest problem from the original book.

WHY do I feel that it is acceptable for me to make these deletions and changes? See the quotes from the Urantia Book below:

From Paper 101 section 4: The Limits of Revelation, gives one explanation on why the science of the Urantia Book must be updated from time to time:

"Because your world is generally ignorant of origins, even of physical origins, it has appeared to be wise from time to time to provide instruction in cosmology. And always has this made trouble for the future. The laws of revelation hamper us greatly by their proscription of the impartation of unearned or premature knowledge. Any cosmology presented as a part of revealed religion is destined to be outgrown in a very short time. Accordingly, future students of such a revelation are tempted to discard any element of genuine religious truth it may contain because they discover errors on the face of the associated cosmologies therein presented.

Mankind should understand that we who participate in the revelation of truth are very rigorously limited by the instructions of our superiors. We are not at liberty to anticipate the scientific discoveries of a thousand years. Revelators must act in accordance with the instructions which form a part of the revelation mandate. We see no way of overcoming this difficulty, either now or at any future time. We full well know that, while the historic facts and religious truths of this series of revelatory presentations will stand on the records of the ages to come, within a few short years many of our statements regarding the physical sciences will stand in need of revision in consequence of additional scientific developments and new discoveries. These new developments we even now foresee, but we are forbidden to include such humanly undiscovered facts in the revelatory records. Let it be made clear that revelations are not necessarily inspired. The cosmology of these revelations is not inspired. It is limited by our permission for the co-ordination and sorting of present-day knowledge. While divine or spiritual insight is a gift, human wisdom must evolve."

From Paper 102 section 1:

"Owing to the isolation of rebellion, the revelation of truth on Urantia has all too often been mixed up with the statements of partial and transient cosmologies. Truth remains unchanged from generation to generation, but the associated teachings about the physical world vary from day to day and from year to year. Eternal truth should not be slighted because it chances to be found in company with obsolete ideas regarding the material world. The more of science you know, the less sure you can be; the more of religion you have, the more certain you are.

The certainties of science proceed entirely from the intellect; the certitudes of religion spring from the very foundations of the entire personality. Science appeals to the understanding of the mind; religion appeals to the loyalty and devotion of the body, mind, and spirit, even to the whole personality."

From Paper 176 section 3:

"Truth is living; the Spirit of Truth is ever leading the children of light into new realms of spiritual reality and divine service. You are not given truth to crystallize into settled, safe, and honored forms. Your revelation of truth must be so enhanced by passing through your personal experience that new beauty and actual spiritual gains will be disclosed to all who behold your spiritual fruits and in consequence thereof are led to glorify the Father who is in heaven. Only those faithful servants who thus grow in the knowledge of the truth, and who thereby develop the capacity for divine appreciation of spiritual realities, can ever hope to "enter fully into the joy of their Lord." What a sorry sight for successive generations of the professed followers of Jesus to say, regarding their stewardship of divine truth: "Here, Master, is the truth you committed to us a hundred or a thousand years ago. We have lost nothing; we have faithfully preserved all you gave us; we have allowed no changes to be made in that which you taught us; here is the truth you gave us." But such a plea concerning spiritual indolence will not justify the barren steward of truth in the presence of the Master. In accordance with the truth committed to your hands will the Master of truth require a reckoning."

And from Paper 178 section 1 (on my attempts to update the Book and add interpretations of String Theory and a new more expansive concept of what a superuniverse is):

"This gospel of the kingdom is a living truth. I have told you it is like the leaven in the dough, like the grain of mustard seed; and now I declare that it is like the seed of the living being, which, from generation to generation, while it remains the same living seed, unfailingly unfolds itself in new manifestations and grows acceptably in channels of new adaptation to the peculiar needs and conditions of each successive generation. The revelation I have made to you is a living revelation, and I desire that it shall bear appropriate fruits in each individual and in each generation in accordance with the laws of spiritual growth, increase, and adaptative development. From generation to generation this gospel must show increasing vitality and exhibit greater depth of spiritual power. It must not be permitted to become merely a sacred memory, a mere tradition about me and the times in which we now live."

Also, I believe the original Urantia Book was "diluted" and intentionally made imperfect so that it would be more acceptable to the average people of the 1930's with a mixture of the racism, sexism, etc. then prevalent. See paper 28 section 5:

"And if it becomes desirable to "incarnate" this philosophy of perfection, so to dilute it as to make it practical of application to, and assimilation by, the lowly peoples of the lower worlds, these living mirrors have only to turn their faces downward to reflect the standards and needs of another world or universe.

By these very techniques do the Perfectors of Wisdom adapt decisions and recommendations to the real needs and actual status of the peoples and worlds under consideration…"

I believe that I have removed the shackles that have imprisoned the Urantia Book to the past, and have given it new wings into the future, so that it's spiritual message can be read and accepted in today's world. At the same time making the bare minimum changes necessary for a cleaner, clearer and more perfect book: a revised Urantia Book, URANTIA 2025.

Joel F. Covey

This revision is dedicated with love and gratitude to all of my spiritual teachers, they are too numerous to acknowledge all of them here, but I would like to thank the following in particular: my first teacher Helena P. Blavatsky, without her books I would never have read the Urantia Book; Alice A. Bailey and the Arcane School; Helena Roerich and the Agni Yoga series; Sri Aurobindo author of the epic 700+ page poem "Savitri", Pir Vilayat Inayat Khan author of "Toward the One", and last but not least, to Ram Dass and his book "Be Here Now". I look forward to seeing them, and all of you on the inward journey to the infinite.

URANTIA 2025: A Revised Urantia Book

Foreword

In the minds of the mortals of Urantia — that being the name of your world — there exists great confusion respecting the meaning of such terms as God, divinity, and deity. Human beings are still more confused and uncertain about the relationships of the divine personalities designated by these numerous appellations. Because of this conceptual poverty associated with so much ideational confusion, I have been directed to formulate this introductory statement in explanation of the meanings which should be attached to certain word symbols as they may be hereinafter used in those papers which the Orvonton corps of truth revealers have been authorized to translate into the English language of Urantia.

It is exceedingly difficult to present enlarged concepts and advanced truth, in our endeavor to expand cosmic consciousness and enhance spiritual perception, when we are restricted to the use of a circumscribed language of the realm. But our mandate admonishes us to make every effort to convey our meanings by using the word symbols of the English tongue. We have been instructed to introduce new terms only when the concept to be portrayed finds no terminology in English which can be employed to convey such a new concept partially or even with more or less distortion of meaning.

In the hope of facilitating comprehension and of preventing confusion on the part of every mortal who may peruse these papers, we deem it wise to present in this initial statement an outline of the meanings to be attached to numerous English words which are to be employed in designation of Deity and certain associated concepts of the things, meanings, and values of universal reality.

But in order to formulate this Foreword of definitions and limitations of terminology, it is necessary to anticipate the usage of these terms in the subsequent presentations. This Foreword is not, therefore, a finished statement within itself; it is only a definitive guide designed to assist those who shall read the accompanying papers dealing with Deity and the universe of universes which have been formulated by an Orvonton commission sent to Urantia for this purpose.

Your world, Urantia, is one of the many millions of similar inhabited planets contained within your Milky Way galaxy. Your galaxy, along with billions of other galaxies, comprises the local universe of *Nebadon*. This universe, your entire observable universe, can be thought of as a four dimensional membrane existing within a much higher dimensional space-time. Your universe together with many similar creations makes up the superuniverse of *Orvonton*, from whose capital, Uversa, our commission hails. Orvonton is one of the seven evolutionary superuniverses of time and space which exist outside of your observable universe; with each superuniverse being composed of large numbers of four (or higher) dimensional membrane universes. Think of a superuniverse as somewhat like a flower existing within a ten or more dimensional space-time where each petal is a four dimensional universe. These seven superuniverses circle the never-beginning, never-ending creation of divine perfection — the central universe of *Havona* which exists outside of all space and time dimensions. At the heart of this eternal and central universe is the stationary Isle of Paradise, the geographic center of infinity and the dwelling place of the eternal God.

The seven evolving superuniverses in association with the central and divine universe, we commonly refer to as the grand universe; these are the now organized and inhabited creations. They are all a part of the *master universe*, which also embraces the uninhabited but mobilizing universes of outer space. These "outer space" universes exist in new regions of space-time out beyond the seven superuniverses.

I. DEITY AND DIVINITY

The universe of universes presents phenomena of deity activities on diverse levels of cosmic realities, mind meanings, and spirit values, but all of these ministrations — personal or otherwise — are divinely co-ordinated.

DEITY is personalizable as God, is prepersonal and superpersonal in ways not altogether comprehensible by man. Deity is characterized by the quality of unity — actual or potential — on all supermaterial levels of reality; and this unifying quality is best comprehended by creatures as divinity.

Deity functions on personal, prepersonal, and superpersonal levels. Total Deity is functional on the following seven levels:

1. *Static* — self-contained and self-existent Deity.
2. *Potential* — self-willed and self-purposive Deity.
3. *Associative* — self-personalized and divinely fraternal Deity.
4. *Creative* — self-distributive and divinely revealed Deity.
5. *Evolutional* — self-expansive and creature-identified Deity.
6. *Supreme* — self-experiential and creature-Creator-unifying Deity. Deity functioning on the first creature-identificational level as time-space overcontrollers of the grand universe, sometimes designated the Supremacy of Deity.
7. *Ultimate* — self-projected and time-space-transcending Deity. Deity omnipotent, omniscient, and omnipresent. Deity functioning on the second level of unifying divinity expression as effective overcontrollers and absonite upholders of the master universe. As compared with the ministry of the Deities to the grand universe, this absonite function in the master universe is tantamount to universal overcontrol and supersustenance, sometimes called the Ultimacy of Deity.

The *finite level* of reality is characterized by creature life and time-space limitations. Finite realities may not have endings, but they always have beginnings — they are created. The Deity level of Supremacy may be conceived as a function in relation to finite existences.

The *absonite level* of reality is characterized by things and beings without beginnings or endings and by the transcendence of time and space. Absoniters are not created; they are eventuated — they simply are. The

Deity level of Ultimacy connotes a function in relation to absonite realities. No matter in what part of the master universe, whenever time and space are transcended, such an absonite phenomenon is an act of the Ultimacy of Deity.

The *absolute level* is beginningless, endless, timeless, and spaceless. For example: On Paradise, time and space are nonexistent; the time-space status of Paradise is absolute. This level is Trinity attained, existentially, by the Paradise Deities, but this third level of unifying Deity expression is not fully unified experientially. Whenever, wherever, and however the absolute level of Deity functions, Paradise-absolute values and meanings are manifest.

Deity may be existential, as in the Eternal Son; experiential, as in the Supreme Being; associative, as in God the Sevenfold; undivided, as in the Paradise Trinity.

Deity is the source of all that which is divine. Deity is characteristically and invariably divine, but all that which is divine is not necessarily Deity, though it will be co-ordinated with Deity and will tend towards some phase of unity with Deity — spiritual, mindal, or personal.

DIVINITY is the characteristic, unifying, and co-ordinating quality of Deity.

Divinity is creature comprehensible as truth, beauty, and goodness; correlated in personality as love, mercy, and ministry; disclosed on impersonal levels as justice, power, and sovereignty.

Divinity may be perfect — complete — as on existential and creator levels of Paradise perfection; it may be imperfect, as on experiential and creature levels of time-space evolution; or it may be relative, neither perfect nor imperfect, as on certain Havona levels of existential-experiential relationships.

When we attempt to conceive of perfection in all phases and forms of relativity, we encounter seven conceivable types:

1. Absolute perfection in all aspects.

2. Absolute perfection in some phases and relative perfection in all other aspects.

3. Absolute, relative, and imperfect aspects in varied association.

4. Absolute perfection in some respects, imperfection in all others.

5. Absolute perfection in no direction, relative perfection in all other manifestations.

6. Absolute perfection in no phase, relative in some, imperfect in others.

7. Absolute perfection in no attribute, imperfection in all.

II. GOD

Evolving mortal creatures experience an irresistible urge to symbolize their finite concepts of God. Man's consciousness of moral duty and his spiritual idealism represent a value level — an experiential reality — which is difficult of symbolization.

Cosmic consciousness implies the recognition of a First Cause, the one and only uncaused reality. God, the Universal Father, functions on three Deity-personality levels of subinfinite value and relative divinity expression:

1. *Prepersonal* — as in the ministry of the Father fragments, such as the Thought Adjusters.

2. *Personal* — as in the evolutionary experience of created and procreated beings.

3. *Superpersonal* — as in the eventuated existences of certain absonite and associated beings.

GOD is a word symbol designating all personalizations of Deity. The term requires a different definition on each personal level of Deity function and must be still further redefined within each of these levels, as this term may be used to designate the diverse co-ordinate and subordinate personalizations of Deity; for example: the Paradise Creator Sons — the local universe fathers.

The term God, as we make use of it, may be understood:

By designation — as God the Father.

By context — as when used in the discussion of some one deity level or association. When in doubt as to the exact interpretation of the word God, it would be advisable to refer it to the person of the Universal Father.

The term God always denotes personality. Deity may, or may not, refer to divinity personalities.

The word GOD is used, in these papers, with the following meanings:

1. *God the Father* — Creator, Controller, and Upholder. The Universal Father, the First Person of Deity.

2. *God the Son* — Co-ordinate Creator, Spirit Controller, and Spiritual Administrator. The Eternal Son, the Second Person of Deity.

3. *God the Spirit* — Conjoint Actor, Universal Integrator, and Mind Bestower. The Infinite Spirit, the Third Person of Deity.

4. *God the Supreme* — the actualizing or evolving God of time and space. Personal Deity associatively realizing the time-space experiential achievement of creature-Creator identity. The Supreme Being is personally experiencing the achievement of Deity unity as the evolving and experiential God of the evolutionary creatures of time and space.

5. *God the Sevenfold* — Deity personality anywhere actually functioning in time and space. The personal Paradise Deities and their creative associates functioning in and beyond the borders of the central universe and power-personalizing as the Supreme Being on the first creature level of unifying Deity revelation in time and space. This level, the grand universe, is the sphere of the time-space descension of Paradise personalities in reciprocal association with the time-space ascension of evolutionary creatures.

6. *God the Ultimate* — the eventuating God of supertime and transcended space. The second experiential level of unifying Deity manifestation. God the Ultimate implies the attained realization of the synthesized absonite-superpersonal, time-space-transcended, and eventuated-experiential values, co-ordinated on final creative levels of Deity reality.

7. *God the Absolute* — the experientializing God of transcended superpersonal values and divinity meanings, now existential as the *Deity Absolute*. This is the third level of unifying Deity expression and expansion. On this supercreative level, Deity experiences exhaustion of personalizable potential, encounters completion of divinity, and undergoes depletion of capacity for self-revelation to successive and progressive levels of other-personalization. Deity now encounters, impinges upon, and experiences identity with, the *Unqualified Absolute*.

III. THE FIRST SOURCE AND CENTER

Total, infinite reality is existential in seven phases and as seven co-ordinate Absolutes:

1. The First Source and Center.
2. The Second Source and Center.
3. The Third Source and Center.
4. The Isle of Paradise.
5. The Deity Absolute.
6. The Universal Absolute.
7. The Unqualified Absolute.

God, as the First Source and Center, is primal in relation to total reality — unqualifiedly. The First Source and Center is infinite as well as eternal and is therefore limited or conditioned only by volition.

God — the Universal Father — is the personality of the First Source and Center and as such maintains personal relations of infinite control over all co-ordinate and subordinate sources and centers. Such control is personal and infinite in *potential*, even though it may never actually function owing to the perfection of the function of such co-ordinate and subordinate sources and centers and personalities.

The First Source and Center is, therefore, primal in all domains: deified or undeified, personal or impersonal, actual or potential, finite or infinite. No thing or being, no relativity or finality, exists except in direct or indirect relation to, and dependence on, the primacy of the First Source and Center.

The First Source and Center is related to the universe as:

1. The gravity forces of the material universes are convergent in the gravity center of nether Paradise. The gravity forces we speak of here are those that exist outside of your four dimensional space-time, which connect and hold together the many universes which make up the seven superuniverses. This is why the geographic location of his person is eternally fixed in absolute relation to the force-energy center of the nether or material plane of

Paradise. But the absolute personality of Deity exists on the upper or spiritual plane of Paradise.

2. The mind forces are convergent in the Infinite Spirit; the differential and divergent cosmic mind in the Seven Master Spirits; the factualizing mind of the Supreme as a time-space experience in Majeston.

3. The universe spirit forces are convergent in the Eternal Son.

4. The unlimited capacity for deity action resides in the Deity Absolute.

5. The unlimited capacity for infinity response exists in the Unqualified Absolute.

6. The two Absolutes — Qualified and Unqualified — are co-ordinated and unified in and by the Universal Absolute.

7. The potential personality of an evolutionary moral being or of any other moral being is centered in the personality of the Universal Father.

REALITY, as comprehended by finite beings, is partial, relative, and shadowy. The maximum Deity reality fully comprehensible by evolutionary finite creatures is embraced within the Supreme Being. Nevertheless there are antecedent and eternal realities, superfinite realities, which are ancestral to this Supreme Deity of evolutionary time-space creatures. In attempting to portray the origin and nature of universal reality, we are forced to employ the technique of time-space reasoning in order to reach the level of the finite mind. Therefore must many of the simultaneous events of eternity be presented as sequential transactions.

As a time-space creature would view the origin and differentiation of Reality, the eternal and infinite I AM achieved Deity liberation from the fetters of unqualified infinity through the exercise of inherent and eternal free will, and this divorcement from unqualified infinity produced the first absolute divinity-tension. This tension of infinity differential is resolved by the Universal Absolute, which functions to unify and co-ordinate the dynamic infinity of Total Deity and the static infinity of the Unqualified Absolute.

In this original transaction the theoretical I AM achieved the realization of personality by becoming the Eternal Father of the Original Son simultaneously with becoming the Eternal Source of the Isle of Paradise. Coexistent with the differentiation of the Son from the Father, and in the presence of Paradise, there appeared the person of the Infinite Spirit and the central universe of Havona. With the appearance of coexistent personal Deity, the Eternal Son and the Infinite Spirit, the Father escaped, as a personality, from otherwise inevitable diffusion throughout the potential of Total Deity. Thenceforth it is only in Trinity association with his two Deity equals that the Father fills all Deity potential, while increasingly experiential Deity is being actualized on the divinity levels of Supremacy, Ultimacy, and Absoluteness.

The concept of the I AM is a philosophic concession which we make to the time-bound, space-fettered, finite mind of man, to the impossibility of creature comprehension of eternity existences — nonbeginning, nonending realities and relationships. To the time-space creature, all things must have a beginning save only the ONE UNCAUSED — the primeval cause of causes. Therefore do we conceptualize this philosophic value-level as the I AM, at the same time instructing all creatures that the Eternal Son and the Infinite Spirit are coeternal with the I AM; in other words, that there never was a time when the I AM was not the Father of the Son and, with him, of the Spirit.

The Infinite is used to denote the fullness — the finality — implied by the primacy of the First Source and Center. The theoretical I AM is a creature-philosophic extension of the "infinity of will," but the Infinite is an *actual* value-level representing the eternity-intension of the true infinity of the absolute and unfettered free will of the Universal Father. This concept is sometimes designated the Father-Infinite.

Much of the confusion of all orders of beings, high and low, in their efforts to discover the Father-Infinite, is inherent in their limitations of comprehension. The absolute primacy of the Universal Father is not apparent on subinfinite levels; therefore is it probable that only the Eternal Son and the Infinite Spirit truly know the Father as an infinity; to all other personalities such a concept represents the exercise of faith.

IV. UNIVERSE REALITY

Reality differentially actualizes on diverse universe levels; reality originates in and by the infinite volition of the Universal Father and is realizable in three primal phases on many different levels of universe actualization:

1. *Undeified reality* ranges from the energy domains of the nonpersonal to the reality realms of the nonpersonalizable values of universal existence, even to the presence of the Unqualified Absolute.

2. Deified *reality* embraces all of infinite Deity potentials ranging upward through all realms of personality from the lowest finite to the highest infinite, thus encompassing the domain of all that which is personalizable and more — even to the presence of the Deity Absolute.

3. *Interassociated reality.* Universe reality is supposedly either deified or undeified, but to subdeified beings there exists a vast domain of interassociated reality, potential and actualizing, which is difficult of identification. Much of this co-ordinate reality is embraced within the realms of the Universal Absolute.

This is the primal concept of original reality: The Father initiates and maintains Reality. The primal *differentials* of reality are the deified and the undeified — the Deity Absolute and the Unqualified Absolute. The primal *relationship* is the tension between them. This Father-initiated divinity-tension is perfectly resolved by, and eternalizes as, the Universal Absolute.

From the viewpoint of time and space, reality is further divisible as:

1. *Actual and Potential.* Realities existing in fullness of expression in contrast to those which carry undisclosed capacity for growth. The Eternal Son is an absolute spiritual actuality; mortal man is very largely an unrealized spiritual potentiality.

2. *Absolute and Subabsolute.* Absolute realities are eternity existences. Subabsolute realities are projected on two levels: Absonites — realities which are relative with respect to both time and eternity. Finites — realities which are projected in space and are actualized in time.

3. *Existential and Experiential.* Paradise Deity is existential, but the emerging Supreme and Ultimate are experiential.

4. *Personal and Impersonal.* Deity expansion, personality expression, and universe evolution are forever conditioned by the Father's freewill act which forever separated the mind-spirit-personal meanings and values of actuality and potentiality centering in the Eternal Son from those things which center and inhere in the eternal Isle of Paradise.

PARADISE is a term inclusive of the personal and the nonpersonal focal Absolutes of all phases of universe reality. Paradise, properly qualified, may connote any and all forms of reality, Deity, divinity, personality, and energy — spiritual, mindal, or material. All share Paradise as the place of origin, function, and destiny, as regards values, meanings, and factual existence.

The Isle of Paradise — Paradise not otherwise qualified — is the Absolute of the material-gravity control of the First Source and Center. Paradise is motionless, being the only stationary thing in the universe of universes. The Isle of Paradise has a universe location but no position in space. This eternal Isle is the actual source of the physical universes — past, present, and future. The nuclear Isle of Light is a Deity derivative, but it is hardly Deity; neither are the material creations a part of Deity; they are a consequence.

Paradise is not a creator; it is a unique controller of many universe activities, far more of a controller than a reactor. Throughout the material universes Paradise influences the reactions and conduct of all beings having to do with force, energy, and power, but Paradise itself is unique, exclusive, and isolated in the universes. Paradise represents nothing and nothing represents Paradise. It is neither a force nor a presence; it is just *Paradise*.

V. PERSONALITY REALITIES

Personality is a level of deified reality and ranges from the mortal and midwayer level of the higher mind activation of worship and wisdom up through the morontial and spiritual to the attainment of finality of personality status. That is the evolutionary ascent of mortal- and kindred-creature personality, but there are numerous other orders of universe personalities.

Reality is subject to universal expansion, personality to infinite diversification, and both are capable of well-nigh unlimited Deity co-ordination and eternal stabilization. While the metamorphic range of nonpersonal reality is definitely limited, we know of no limitations to the progressive evolution of personality realities.

On attained experiential levels all personality orders or values are associable and even cocreational. Even God and man can coexist in a unified personality, as is so exquisitely demonstrated in the present status of Christ Michael — Son of Man and Son of God.

All subinfinite orders and phases of personality are associative attainables and are potentially cocreational. The prepersonal, the personal, and the superpersonal are all linked together by mutual potential of co-ordinate attainment, progressive achievement, and cocreational capacity. But never does the impersonal directly transmute to the personal. Personality is never spontaneous; it is the gift of the Paradise Father. Personality is superimposed upon energy, and it is associated only with living energy systems; identity can be associated with nonliving energy patterns.

The Universal Father is the secret of the reality of personality, the bestowal of personality, and the destiny of personality. The Eternal Son is the absolute personality, the secret of spiritual energy, morontia spirits, and perfected spirits. The Conjoint Actor is the spirit-mind personality, the source of intelligence, reason, and the universal mind. But the Isle of Paradise is nonpersonal and extraspiritual, being the essence of the universal body, the source and center of physical matter, and the absolute master pattern of universal material reality.

These qualities of universal reality are manifest in Urantian human experience on the following levels:

1. *Body*. The material or physical organism of man. The living electrochemical mechanism of animal nature and origin.

2. *Mind*. The thinking, perceiving, and feeling mechanism of the human organism. The total conscious and unconscious experience. The intelligence associated with the emotional life reaching upward through worship and wisdom to the spirit level.

3. *Spirit*. The divine spirit that indwells the mind of man — the Thought Adjuster. This immortal spirit is prepersonal — not a personality, though destined to become a part of the personality of the surviving mortal creature.

4. *Soul*. The soul of man is an experiential acquirement. As a mortal creature chooses to "do the will of the Father in heaven," so the indwelling spirit becomes the father of a new reality in human experience. The mortal and material mind is the mother of this same emerging reality. The substance of this new reality is neither material nor spiritual — it is morontial. This is

the emerging and immortal soul which is destined to survive mortal death and begin the Paradise ascension.

Personality. The personality of mortal man is neither body, mind, nor spirit; neither is it the soul. Personality is the one changeless reality in an otherwise ever-changing creature experience; and it unifies all other associated factors of individuality. The personality is the unique bestowal which the Universal Father makes upon the living and associated energies of matter, mind, and spirit, and which survives with the survival of the morontial soul.

Morontia is a term designating a vast level intervening between the material and the spiritual. It may designate personal or impersonal realities, living or nonliving energies. The warp of morontia is spiritual; its woof is physical.

VI. ENERGY AND PATTERN

Any and all things responding to the personality circuit of the Father, we call personal. Any and all things responding to the spirit circuit of the Son, we call spirit. Any and all that responds to the mind circuit of the Conjoint Actor, we call mind, mind as an attribute of the Infinite Spirit — mind in all its phases. Any and all that responds to the material-gravity circuit centering in nether Paradise, we call matter — energy-matter in all its metamorphic states.

ENERGY we use as an all-inclusive term applied to spiritual, mindal, and material realms. *Force* is also thus broadly used. *Power* is ordinarily limited to the designation of the electronic level of material or linear-gravity-responsive matter in the grand universe. Power is also employed to designate sovereignty.

Physical energy is a term denoting all phases and forms of phenomenal motion, action, and potential.

In discussing physical-energy manifestations, we generally use the terms cosmic force, emergent energy, and universe power. These are often employed as follows:

1. *Cosmic force* embraces all energies deriving from the Unqualified Absolute but which are as yet unresponsive to Paradise gravity.

2. *Emergent energy* embraces those energies which are responsive to Paradise gravity but are as yet unresponsive to local or linear gravity. This is the pre-electronic level of energy-matter.

3. *Universe power* includes all forms of energy which, while still responding to Paradise gravity, are directly responsive to linear gravity. This is the electronic level of energy-matter and all subsequent evolutions thereof.

Mind is a phenomenon connoting the presence-activity of *living ministry* in addition to varied energy systems; and this is true on all levels of intelligence. In personality, mind ever intervenes between spirit and matter; therefore is the universe illuminated by three kinds of light: material light, intellectual insight, and spirit luminosity.

Light — spirit luminosity — is a word symbol, a figure of speech, which connotes the personality manifestation characteristic of spirit beings of diverse orders. This luminous emanation is in no respect related either to intellectual insight or to physical-light manifestations.

PATTERN can be projected as material, spiritual, or mindal, or any combination of these energies. It can pervade personalities, identities, entities, or nonliving matter. But pattern is pattern and remains pattern; only *copies* are multiplied.

Pattern may configure energy, but it does not control it. Gravity is the sole control of energy-matter. Pattern is not gravity responsive, and there is no relationship between space and pattern; space is neither pattern nor potential pattern. Pattern is a configuration of reality which has already paid all gravity debt; the *reality* of any pattern consists of its energies, its mind, spirit, or material components.

In contrast to the aspect of the *total*, pattern discloses the *individual* aspect of energy and of personality. Personality or identity forms are patterns resultant from energy (physical, spiritual, or mindal) but are not inherent therein. That quality of energy or of personality by virtue of which pattern is caused to appear may be attributed to God — Deity — to Paradise force endowment, to the coexistence of personality and power.

Pattern is a master design from which copies are made. Eternal Paradise is the absolute of patterns; the Eternal Son is the pattern personality; the Universal Father is the direct ancestor-source of both. But Paradise does not bestow pattern, and the Son cannot bestow personality.

VII. THE SUPREME BEING

The Deity mechanism of the master universe is twofold as concerns eternity relationships. God the Father, God the Son, and God the Spirit are eternal — are existential beings — while God the Supreme, God the Ultimate, and God the Absolute are *actualizing* Deity personalities of the post-Havona epochs in the time-space and the time-space-transcended spheres of master universe evolutionary expansion. These actualizing Deity personalities are future eternals from the time when, and as, they power-personalize in the growing universes by the technique of the experiential actualization of the associative-creative potentials of the eternal Paradise Deities.

Deity is, therefore, dual in presence:

1. *Existential* — beings of eternal existence, past, present, and future.
2. *Experiential* — beings actualizing in the post-Havona present but of unending existence throughout all future eternity.

The Father, Son, and Spirit are existential — existential in actuality (though all potentials are supposedly experiential). The Supreme and the Ultimate are wholly experiential. The Deity Absolute is experiential in actualization but existential in potentiality. The essence of Deity is eternal, but only the three original persons of Deity are unqualifiedly eternal. All other Deity personalities have an origin, but they are eternal in destiny.

Having achieved existential Deity expression of himself in the Son and the Spirit, the Father is now achieving experiential expression on hitherto impersonal and unrevealed deity levels as God the Supreme, God the Ultimate, and God the Absolute; but these experiential Deities are not now fully existent; they are in process of actualization.

God the Supreme in Havona is the personal spirit reflection of the triune Paradise Deity. This associative Deity relationship is now creatively expanding outward in God the Sevenfold and is synthesizing in the experiential power of the Almighty Supreme in the grand universe. Paradise Deity, existential as three persons, is thus experientially evolving in two phases of Supremacy, while these dual phases are power-personality unifying as one Lord, the Supreme Being.

The Universal Father achieves freewill liberation from the bonds of infinity and the fetters of eternity by the technique of trinitization, threefold Deity personalization. The Supreme Being is even now evolving as a subeternal personality unification of the sevenfold manifestation of Deity in the time-space segments of the grand universe.

The Supreme Being is not a direct creator, except that he is the father of Majeston, but he is a synthetic co-ordinator of all creature-Creator universe activities. The Supreme Being, now actualizing in the evolutionary universes, is the Deity correlator and synthesizer of time-space divinity, of triune Paradise Deity in experiential association with the Supreme Creators of time and space. When finally actualized, this evolutionary Deity will constitute the eternal fusion of the finite and the infinite — the everlasting and indissoluble union of experiential power and spirit personality.

All time-space finite reality, under the directive urge of the evolving Supreme Being, is engaged in an ever-ascending mobilization and perfecting unification (power-personality synthesis) of all phases and values of finite reality, in association with varied phases of Paradise reality, to the end and for the purpose of subsequently embarking upon the attempt to reach absonite levels of supercreature attainment.

VIII. GOD THE SEVENFOLD

To atone for finity of status and to compensate for creature limitations of concept, the Universal Father has established the evolutionary creature's sevenfold approach to Deity:

1. The Paradise Creator Sons.
2. The Ancients of Days.
3. The Seven Master Spirits.
4. The Supreme Being.
5. God the Spirit.
6. God the Son.
7. God the Father.

This sevenfold Deity personalization in time and space and to the seven superuniverses enables mortal man to attain the presence of God, who is spirit. This sevenfold Deity, to finite time-space creatures sometime power-personalizing in the Supreme Being, is the functional Deity of the mortal evolutionary creatures of the Paradise-ascension career. Such an experiential discovery-career of the realization of God begins with the recognition of the divinity of the Creator Son of the local universe and ascends through the superuniverse Ancients of Days and by way of the person of one of the Seven Master Spirits to the attainment of the discovery and recognition of the divine personality of the Universal Father on Paradise.

The grand universe is the threefold Deity domain of the Trinity of Supremacy, God the Sevenfold, and the Supreme Being. God the Supreme is potential in the Paradise Trinity, from whom he derives his personality and spirit attributes; but he is now actualizing in the Creator Sons, Ancients of Days, and the Master Spirits, from whom he derives his power as Almighty to the superuniverses of time and space. This power manifestation of the immediate God of evolutionary creatures actually time-space evolves concomitantly with them. The Almighty Supreme, evolving on the value-level of nonpersonal activities, and the spirit person of God the Supreme are one reality — the Supreme Being.

The Creator Sons in the Deity association of God the Sevenfold provide the mechanism whereby the mortal becomes immortal and the finite attains the embrace of the infinite. The Supreme Being provides the technique for the power-personality mobilization, the divine synthesis, of all these manifold transactions, thus enabling the finite to attain the absonite and, through other possible future actualizations, to attempt the attainment of the Ultimate. The Creator Sons and their associated Divine Ministers are participants in this supreme mobilization, but the Ancients of Days and the Seven Master Spirits are probably eternally fixed as permanent administrators in the grand universe.

The function of God the Sevenfold dates from the organization of the seven superuniverses, and it will probably expand in connection with the future evolution of the creations of outer space. The organization of these future universes of the primary, secondary, tertiary, and quartan space levels of progressive evolution will undoubtedly witness the inauguration of the transcendent and absonite approach to Deity.

IX. GOD THE ULTIMATE

Just as the Supreme Being progressively evolves from the antecedent divinity endowment of the encompassed grand universe potential of energy and personality, so does God the Ultimate eventuate from the potentials of divinity residing in the transcended time-space domains of the master universe. The actualization of Ultimate Deity signalizes absonite unification of the first experiential Trinity and signifies unifying Deity expansion on the second level of creative self-realization. This constitutes the personality-power equivalent of the universe experiential-Deity actualization of Paradise absonite realities on the eventuating levels of transcended time-space values. The completion of such an experiential unfoldment is designed to afford ultimate service-destiny for all time-space creatures who have attained absonite levels through the completed realization of the Supreme Being and by the ministry of God the Sevenfold.

God the Ultimate is designative of personal Deity functioning on the divinity levels of the absonite and on the universe spheres of supertime and transcended space. The Ultimate is a supersupreme eventuation of Deity. The Supreme is the Trinity unification comprehended by finite beings; the

Ultimate is the unification of the Paradise Trinity comprehended by absonite beings.

The Universal Father, through the mechanism of evolutionary Deity, is actually engaged in the stupendous and amazing act of personality focalization and power mobilization, on their respective universe meaning-levels, of the divine reality values of the finite, the absonite, and even of the absolute.

The first three and past-eternal Deities of Paradise — the Universal Father, the Eternal Son, and the Infinite Spirit — are, in the eternal future, to be personality-complemented by the experiential actualization of associate evolutionary Deities — God the Supreme, God the Ultimate, and possibly God the Absolute.

God the Supreme and God the Ultimate, now evolving in the experiential universes, are not existential — not past eternals, only future eternals, time-space-conditioned and transcendental-conditioned eternals. They are Deities of supreme, ultimate, and possibly supreme-ultimate endowments, but they have experienced historic universe origins. They will never have an end, but they do have personality beginnings. They are indeed actualizations of eternal and infinite Deity potentials, but they themselves are neither unqualifiedly eternal nor infinite.

X. GOD THE ABSOLUTE

There are many features of the eternal reality of the Deity Absolute which cannot be fully explained to the time-space finite mind, but the actualization of *God the Absolute* would be in consequence of the unification of the second experiential Trinity, the Absolute Trinity. This would constitute the experiential realization of absolute divinity, the unification of absolute meanings on absolute levels; but we are not certain regarding the encompassment of all absolute values since we have at no time been informed that the Qualified Absolute is the equivalent of the Infinite. Superultimate destinies are involved in absolute meanings and infinite spirituality, and without both of these unachieved realities we cannot establish absolute values.

God the Absolute is the realization-attainment goal of all superabsonite beings, but the power and personality potential of the Deity Absolute transcends our concept, and we hesitate to discuss those realities which are so far removed from experiential actualization.

XI. THE THREE ABSOLUTES

When the combined thought of the Universal Father and the Eternal Son, functioning in the God of Action, constituted the creation of the divine and central universe, the Father followed the expression of his thought into the word of his Son and the act of their Conjoint Executive by differentiating his Havona presence from the potentials of infinity. And these undisclosed infinity potentials remain space concealed in the Unqualified Absolute and divinely enshrouded in the Deity Absolute, while these two become one in the functioning of the Universal Absolute, the unrevealed infinity-unity of the Paradise Father.

Both potency of cosmic force and potency of spirit force are in process of progressive revelation-realization as the enrichment of all reality is effected by experiential growth and through the correlation of the experiential with the existential by the Universal Absolute. By virtue of the equipoising presence of the Universal Absolute, the First Source and Center realizes extension of experiential power, enjoys identification with his evolutionary creatures, and achieves expansion of experiential Deity on the levels of Supremacy, Ultimacy, and Absoluteness.

When it is not possible fully to distinguish the Deity Absolute from the Unqualified Absolute, their supposedly combined function or co-ordinated presence is designated the action of the Universal Absolute.

1. *The Deity Absolute* seems to be the all-powerful activator, while the Unqualified Absolute appears to be the all-efficient mechanizer of the supremely unified and ultimately co-ordinated universe of universes, even universes upon universes, made, making, and yet to be made.

The Deity Absolute cannot, or at least does not, react to any universe situation in a subabsolute manner. Every response of this Absolute to any given situation appears to be made in terms of the welfare of the whole creation of things and beings, not only in its present state of existence, but also in view of the infinite possibilities of all future eternity.

The Deity Absolute is that potential which was segregated from total, infinite reality by the freewill choice of the Universal Father, and within which all divinity activities — existential and experiential — take place. This is the Qualified Absolute in contradistinction to the Unqualified Absolute; but the Universal Absolute is superadditive to both in the encompassment of all absolute potential.

2. *The Unqualified Absolute* is nonpersonal, extradivine, and undeified. The Unqualified Absolute is therefore devoid of personality, divinity, and all creator prerogatives. Neither fact nor truth, experience nor revelation, philosophy nor absonity are able to penetrate the nature and character of this Absolute without universe qualification.

Let it be made clear that the Unqualified Absolute is a positive reality pervading the grand universe and, apparently, extending with equal space presence on out into the force activities and prematerial evolutions of the staggering stretches of the space regions beyond the seven superuniverses. The Unqualified Absolute is not a mere negativism of philosophic concept predicated on the assumptions of metaphysical sophistries concerning the universality, dominance, and primacy of the unconditioned and the unqualified. The Unqualified Absolute is a positive universe overcontrol in infinity; this overcontrol is space-force unlimited but is definitely conditioned by the presence of life, mind, spirit, and personality, and is further conditioned by the will-reactions and purposeful mandates of the Paradise Trinity.

We are convinced that the Unqualified Absolute is not an undifferentiated and all-pervading influence comparable to the pantheistic concepts of metaphysics. The Unqualified Absolute is force unlimited and Deity conditioned, but we do not fully perceive the relation of this Absolute to the spirit realities of the universes.

3. *The Universal Absolute*, we logically deduce, was inevitable in the Universal Father's absolute freewill act of differentiating universe realities into deified and undeified — personalizable and nonpersonalizable — values. The Universal Absolute is the Deity phenomenon indicative of the resolution of the tension created by the freewill act of thus differentiating universe reality, and functions as the associative co-ordinator of these sum totals of existential potentialities.

The tension-presence of the Universal Absolute signifies the adjustment of differential between deity reality and undeified reality inherent in the separation of the dynamics of freewill divinity from the statics of unqualified infinity.

Always remember: Potential infinity is absolute and inseparable from eternity. Actual infinity in time can never be anything but partial and must therefore be nonabsolute; neither can infinity of actual personality be absolute except in unqualified Deity. And it is the differential of infinity potential in the Unqualified Absolute and the Deity Absolute that eternalizes the Universal Absolute, thereby making it cosmically possible to have material universes in space and spiritually possible to have finite personalities in time.

The finite can coexist in the cosmos along with the Infinite only because the associative presence of the Universal Absolute so perfectly equalizes the tensions between time and eternity, finity and infinity, reality potential and reality actuality, Paradise and space, man and God. Associatively the Universal Absolute constitutes the identification of the zone of progressing evolutional reality existent in the time-space, and in the transcended time-space, universes of subinfinite Deity manifestation.

The Universal Absolute is the potential of the static-dynamic Deity functionally realizable on time-eternity levels as finite-absolute values and as possible of experiential-existential approach. This incomprehensible aspect of Deity may be static, potential, and associative but is not experientially creative or evolutional as concerns the intelligent personalities now functioning in the master universe.

The Absolute. The two Absolutes — qualified and unqualified — while so apparently divergent in function as they may be observed by mind creatures, are perfectly and divinely unified in and by the Universal Absolute. In the last analysis and in the final comprehension all three are one Absolute. On subinfinite levels they are functionally differentiated, but in infinity they are ONE.

We never use the term the Absolute as a negation of aught or as a denial of anything. Neither do we regard the Universal Absolute as self-determinative, a sort of pantheistic and impersonal Deity. The Absolute, in all that pertains to universe personality, is strictly Trinity limited and Deity dominated.

XII. THE TRINITIES

The original and eternal Paradise Trinity is existential and was inevitable. This never-beginning Trinity was inherent in the fact of the differentiation of the personal and the nonpersonal by the Father's unfettered will and factualized when his personal will co-ordinated these dual realities by mind. The post-Havona Trinities are experiential — are inherent in the creation of two subabsolute and evolutional levels of power-personality manifestation in the master universe.

The Paradise Trinity — the eternal Deity union of the Universal Father, the Eternal Son, and the Infinite Spirit — is existential in actuality, but all potentials are experiential. Therefore does this Trinity constitute the only Deity reality embracing infinity, and therefore do there occur the universe phenomena of the actualization of God the Supreme, God the Ultimate, and God the Absolute.

The first and second experiential Trinities, the post-Havona Trinities, cannot be infinite because they embrace *derived Deities*, Deities evolved by the experiential actualization of realities created or eventuated by the existential Paradise Trinity. Infinity of divinity is being ever enriched, if not enlarged, by finity and absonity of creature and Creator experience.

Trinities are truths of relationship and facts of co-ordinate Deity manifestation. Trinity functions encompass Deity realities, and Deity realities always seek realization and manifestation in personalization. God the Supreme, God the Ultimate, and even God the Absolute are therefore divine inevitabilities. These three experiential Deities were potential in the existential Trinity, the Paradise Trinity, but their universe emergence as personalities of power is dependent in part on their own experiential functioning in the universes of power and personality and in part on the experiential achievements of the post-Havona Creators and Trinities.

The two post-Havona Trinities, the Ultimate and the Absolute experiential Trinities, are not now fully manifest; they are in process of universe realization. These Deity associations may be described as follows:

1. *The Ultimate Trinity*, now evolving, will eventually consist of the Supreme Being, the Supreme Creator Personalities, and the absonite Architects of the Master Universe, those unique universe planners who are neither creators nor creatures. God the Ultimate will eventually and inevitably powerize and personalize as the Deity consequence of the unification of this experiential Ultimate Trinity in the expanding arena of the well-nigh limitless master universe.

2. *The Absolute Trinity* — the second experiential Trinity — now in process of actualization, will consist of God the Supreme, God the Ultimate, and the unrevealed Consummator of Universe Destiny. This Trinity functions on both personal and superpersonal levels, even to the borders of the nonpersonal, and its unification in universality would experientialize Absolute Deity.

The Ultimate Trinity is experientially unifying in completion, but we truly doubt the possibility of such full unification of the Absolute Trinity. Our concept, however, of the eternal Paradise Trinity is an ever-present reminder that Deity trinitization may accomplish what is otherwise nonattainable; hence do we postulate the sometime appearance of the *Supreme-Ultimate* and the possible trinitization-factualization of God the Absolute.

The philosophers of the universes postulate a *Trinity of Trinities*, an existential-experiential Trinity Infinite, but they are not able to envisage its personalization; possibly it would equivalate to the person of the Universal Father on the conceptual level of the I AM. But irrespective of all this, the original Paradise Trinity is potentially infinite since the Universal Father actually is infinite.

Acknowledgments

In formulating the succeeding presentations having to do with the portrayal of the character of the Universal Father and the nature of his Paradise associates, together with an attempted description of the perfect central universe and the encircling seven superuniverses, we are to be guided by the mandate of the superuniverse rulers which directs that we shall, in all our efforts to reveal truth and co-ordinate essential knowledge, give preference to the highest existing human concepts pertaining to the subjects to be presented. We may resort to pure revelation only when the concept of presentation has had no adequate previous expression by the human mind.

Successive planetary revelations of divine truth invariably embrace the highest existing concepts of spiritual values as a part of the new and enhanced co-ordination of planetary knowledge. Accordingly, in making these presentations about God and his universe associates, we have selected as the basis of these papers more than one thousand human concepts representing the highest and most advanced planetary knowledge of spiritual values and universe meanings. Wherein these human concepts, assembled from the God-knowing mortals of the past and the present, are inadequate to portray the truth as we are directed to reveal it, we will unhesitatingly supplement them, for this purpose drawing upon our own superior knowledge of the reality and divinity of the Paradise Deities and their transcendent residential universe.

We are fully cognizant of the difficulties of our assignment; we recognize the impossibility of fully translating the language of the concepts of divinity and eternity into the symbols of the language of the finite concepts of the mortal mind. But we know that there dwells within the human mind a fragment of God, and that there sojourns with the human soul the Spirit of Truth; and we further know that these spirit forces conspire to enable material man to grasp the reality of spiritual values and to comprehend the philosophy of universe meanings. But even more certainly we know that these spirits of the Divine Presence are able to assist man in the spiritual appropriation of all truth contributory to the enhancement of the ever-progressing reality of personal religious experience — God-consciousness.

[Indited by an Orvonton Divine Counselor, Chief of the Corps of Superuniverse Personalities assigned to portray on Urantia the truth concerning the Paradise Deities and the universe of universes.]

PART I

The Central and Superuniverses

PAPER 1
THE UNIVERSAL FATHER

THE UNIVERSAL FATHER is the God of all creation, the First Source and Center of all things and beings. First think of God as a creator, then as a controller, and lastly as an infinite upholder. The truth about the Universal Father had begun to dawn upon mankind when the prophet said: "You, God, are alone; there is none beside you. You have created the heaven and the heaven of heavens, with all their hosts; you preserve and control them. By the Sons of God were the universes made. The Creator covers himself with light as with a garment and stretches out the heavens as a curtain." Only the concept of the Universal Father — one God in the place of many gods — enabled mortal man to comprehend the Father as divine creator and infinite controller.

The myriads of planetary systems were all made to be eventually inhabited by many different types of intelligent creatures, beings who could know God, receive the divine affection, and love him in return. The universe of universes is the work of God and the dwelling place of his diverse creatures. "God created the heavens and formed the earth; he established the universe and created this world not in vain; he formed it to be inhabited."

The enlightened worlds all recognize and worship the Universal Father, the eternal maker and infinite upholder of all creation. The will creatures of universe upon universe have embarked upon the long, long Paradise journey, the fascinating struggle of the eternal adventure of attaining God the Father. The transcendent goal of the children of time is to find the eternal God, to comprehend the divine nature, to recognize the Universal Father. God-knowing creatures have only one supreme ambition, just one consuming desire, and that is to become, as they are in their spheres, like him as he is in his Paradise perfection of personality and in his universal sphere of righteous supremacy. From the Universal Father who inhabits eternity there has gone forth the supreme mandate, "Be you perfect, even as I am perfect." In love and mercy the messengers of Paradise have carried this divine exhortation down through the ages and out through the universes, even to such lowly animal-origin creatures as the human races of Urantia.

This magnificent and universal injunction to strive for the attainment of the perfection of divinity is the first duty, and should be the highest ambition, of all the struggling creature creation of the God of perfection. This possibility of the attainment of divine perfection is the final and certain destiny of all man's eternal spiritual progress.

Urantia mortals can hardly hope to be perfect in the infinite sense, but it is entirely possible for human beings, starting out as they do on this planet, to attain the supernal and divine goal which the infinite God has set for mortal man; and when they do achieve this destiny, they will, in all that pertains to self-realization and mind attainment, be just as replete in their sphere of divine perfection as God himself is in his sphere of infinity and eternity. Such perfection may not be universal in the material sense, unlimited in intellectual grasp, or final in spiritual experience, but it is final and complete in all finite aspects of divinity of will, perfection of personality motivation, and God-consciousness.

This is the true meaning of that divine command, "Be you perfect, even as I am perfect," which ever urges mortal man onward and beckons him inward in that long and fascinating struggle for the attainment of higher and higher levels of spiritual values and true universe meanings. This sublime search for the God of universes is the supreme adventure of the inhabitants of all the worlds of time and space.

1. THE FATHER'S NAME

Of all the names by which God the Father is known throughout the universes, those which designate him as the First Source and the Universe Center are most often encountered. The First Father is known by various names in different universes and in different sectors of the same universe. The names which the creature assigns to the Creator are much dependent on the creature's concept of the Creator. The First Source and Universe Center has never revealed himself by name, only by nature. If we believe that we are the children of this Creator, it is only natural that we should eventually call him Father. But this is the name of our own choosing, and it grows out of the recognition of our personal relationship with the First Source and Center.

The Universal Father never imposes any form of arbitrary recognition, formal worship, or slavish service upon the intelligent will creatures of the universes. The evolutionary inhabitants of the worlds of time and space must of themselves — in their own hearts — recognize, love, and voluntarily worship him. The Creator refuses to coerce or compel the submission of the spiritual free wills of his material creatures. The affectionate dedication of the human will to the doing of the Father's will is man's choicest gift to God; in fact, such a consecration of creature will constitutes man's only possible gift of true value to the Paradise Father. In God, man lives, moves, and has his being; there is nothing which man can give to God except this choosing to abide by the Father's will, and such decisions, effected by the intelligent will creatures of the universes, constitute the reality of that true worship which is so satisfying to the love-dominated nature of the Creator Father.

When you have once become truly God-conscious, after you really discover the majestic Creator and begin to experience the realization of the indwelling presence of the divine controller, then, in accordance with your enlightenment and in accordance with the manner and method by which the divine Sons reveal God, you will find a name for the Universal Father which will be adequately expressive of your concept of the First Great Source and Center. And so, on different worlds and in various universes, the Creator becomes known by numerous appellations, in spirit of relationship all meaning the same but, in words and symbols, each name standing for the degree, the depth, of his enthronement in the hearts of his creatures of any given realm.

Near the center of the universe of universes, the Universal Father is generally known by names which may be regarded as meaning the First Source. Farther out in the universes of space, the terms employed to designate the Universal Father more often mean the Universal Center. Still farther out in the starry creation, he is known, as on the headquarters world of your local universe, as the First Creative Source and Divine Center. In one nearby constellation God is called the Father of Universes. In another, the Infinite Upholder, and to the east, the Divine Controller. He has also been designated the Father of Lights, the Gift of Life, and the All-powerful One.

On those worlds where a Paradise Son has lived a bestowal life, God is generally known by some name indicative of personal relationship, tender affection, and fatherly devotion. On your constellation headquarters God is referred to as the Universal Father, and on different planets in your local system of inhabited worlds he is variously known as the Father of Fathers, the Paradise Father, the Havona Father, and the Spirit Father. Those who know God through the revelations of the bestowals of the Paradise Sons, eventually yield to the sentimental appeal of the touching relationship of the creature-Creator association and refer to God as "our Father."

On a planet of sex creatures, in a world where the impulses of parental emotion are inherent in the hearts of its intelligent beings, the term Father becomes a very expressive and appropriate name for the eternal God. He is best known, most universally acknowledged, on your planet, Urantia, by the name *God*. The name he is given is of little importance; the significant thing is that you should know him and aspire to be like him. Your prophets of old truly called him "the everlasting God" and referred to him as the one who "inhabits eternity."

2. THE REALITY OF GOD

God is primal reality in the spirit world; God is the source of truth in the mind spheres; God overshadows all throughout the material realms. To all created intelligences God is a personality, and to the universe of universes he is the First Source and Center of eternal reality. God is neither manlike nor machinelike. The First Father is universal spirit, eternal truth, infinite reality, and father personality.

The eternal God is infinitely more than reality idealized or the universe personalized. God is not simply the supreme desire of man, the mortal quest objectified. Neither is God merely a concept, the power-potential of righteousness. The Universal Father is not a synonym for nature, neither is he natural law personified. God is a transcendent reality, not merely man's traditional concept of supreme values. God is not a psychological focalization of spiritual meanings, neither is he "the noblest work of man." God may be any or all of these concepts in the minds of men, but he is more. He is a saving person and a loving Father to all who enjoy spiritual peace on earth, and who crave to experience personality survival in death.

The actuality of the existence of God is demonstrated in human experience by the indwelling of the divine presence, the spirit Monitor sent from Paradise to live in the mortal mind of man and there to assist in evolving the immortal soul of eternal survival. The presence of this divine Adjuster in the human mind is disclosed by three experiential phenomena:

1. The intellectual capacity for knowing God — God-consciousness.
2. The spiritual urge to find God — God-seeking.
3. The personality craving to be like God — the wholehearted desire to do the Father's will.

The existence of God can never be proved by scientific experiment or by the pure reason of logical deduction. God can be realized only in the realms of human experience; nevertheless, the true concept of the reality of God is reasonable to logic, plausible to philosophy, essential to religion, and indispensable to any hope of personality survival.

Those who know God have experienced the fact of his presence; such God-knowing mortals hold in their personal experience the only positive proof of the existence of the living God which one human being can offer to another. The existence of God is utterly beyond all possibility of demonstration except for the contact between the God-consciousness of the human mind and the God-presence of the Thought Adjuster that indwells the mortal intellect and is bestowed upon man as the free gift of the Universal Father.

In theory you may think of God as the Creator, and he is the personal creator of Paradise and the central universe of perfection, but the universes of time and space are all created and organized by the Paradise corps of the Creator Sons. The Universal Father is not the personal creator of the local universe of Nebadon; the universe in which you live is the creation of his Son Michael. Though the Father does not personally create the evolutionary universes, he does control them in many of their universal relationships and in certain of their manifestations of physical, mindal, and spiritual energies. God the Father is the personal creator of the Paradise universe and, in association with the Eternal Son, the creator of all other personal universe Creators.

As a physical controller in the material universe of universes, the First Source and Center functions in the patterns of the eternal Isle of Paradise, and through this absolute gravity center the eternal God exercises cosmic overcontrol of the physical level equally in the central universe and throughout the universe of universes. As mind, God functions in the Deity of the Infinite Spirit; as spirit, God is manifest in the person of the Eternal Son and in the persons of the divine children of the Eternal Son. This interrelation of the First Source and Center with the co-ordinate Persons and Absolutes of Paradise does not in the least preclude the *direct* personal action of the Universal Father throughout all creation and on all levels thereof. Through the presence of his fragmentized spirit the Creator Father maintains immediate contact with his creature children and his created universes.

3. GOD IS A UNIVERSAL SPIRIT

"God is spirit." He is a universal spiritual presence. The Universal Father is an infinite spiritual reality; he is "the sovereign, eternal, immortal, invisible, and only true God." Even though you are "the offspring of God," you ought not to think that the Father is like yourselves in form and physique because you are said to be created "in his image" — indwelt by Mystery Monitors dispatched from the central abode of his eternal presence. Spirit beings are real, notwithstanding they are invisible to human eyes; even though they have not flesh and blood.

Said the seer of old: "Lo, he goes by me, and I see him not; he passes on also, but I perceive him not." We may constantly observe the works of God, we may be highly conscious of the material evidences of his majestic conduct, but rarely may we gaze upon the visible manifestation of his divinity, not even to behold the presence of his delegated spirit of human indwelling.

The Universal Father is not invisible because he is hiding himself away from the lowly creatures of materialistic handicaps and limited spiritual endowments. The situation rather is: "You cannot see my face, for no mortal can see me and live." No material man could behold the spirit God and preserve his mortal existence. The glory and the spiritual brilliance of the divine personality presence is impossible of approach by the lower groups of spirit beings or by any order of material personalities. The spiritual luminosity of the Father's personal presence is a "light which no mortal man can approach; which no material creature has seen or can see." But it is not necessary to see God with the eyes of the flesh in order to discern him by the faith-vision of the spiritualized mind.

The spirit nature of the Universal Father is shared fully with his coexistent self, the Eternal Son of Paradise. Both the Father and the Son in like manner share the universal and eternal spirit fully and unreservedly with their conjoint personality co-ordinate, the Infinite Spirit. God's spirit is, in and of himself, absolute; in the Son it is unqualified, in the Spirit, universal, and in and by all of them, infinite.

God is a universal spirit; God is the universal person. The supreme personal reality of the finite creation is spirit; the ultimate reality of the personal cosmos is absonite spirit. Only the levels of infinity are absolute, and only on such levels is there finality of oneness between matter, mind, and spirit.

In the universes God the Father is, in potential, the overcontroller of matter, mind, and spirit. Only by means of his far-flung personality circuit does God deal directly with the personalities of his vast creation of will creatures, but he is contactable (outside of Paradise) only in the presences of his fragmented entities, the will of God abroad in the universes. This Paradise spirit that indwells the minds of the mortals of time and there fosters the evolution of the immortal soul of the surviving creature is of the nature and divinity of the Universal Father. But the minds of such evolutionary creatures originate in the local universes and must gain divine perfection by achieving those experiential transformations of spiritual attainment which are the inevitable result of a creature's choosing to do the will of the Father in heaven.

In the inner experience of man, mind is joined to matter. Such material-linked minds cannot survive mortal death. The technique of survival is embraced in those adjustments of the human will and those transformations in the mortal mind whereby such a God-conscious intellect gradually becomes spirit taught and eventually spirit led. This evolution of the human mind from matter association to spirit union results in the transmutation of the potentially spirit phases of the mortal mind into the morontia realities of the immortal soul. Mortal mind subservient to matter is destined to become increasingly material and consequently to suffer eventual personality extinction; mind yielded to spirit is destined to become increasingly spiritual and ultimately to achieve oneness with the surviving and guiding divine spirit and in this way to attain survival and eternity of personality existence.

I come forth from the Eternal, and I have repeatedly returned to the presence of the Universal Father. I know of the actuality and personality of the First Source and Center, the Eternal and Universal Father. I know that, while the great God is absolute, eternal, and infinite, he is also good, divine, and gracious. I know the truth of the great declarations: "God is spirit" and "God is love," and these two attributes are most completely revealed to the universe in the Eternal Son.

4. THE MYSTERY OF GOD

The infinity of the perfection of God is such that it eternally constitutes him mystery. And the greatest of all the unfathomable mysteries of God is the phenomenon of the divine indwelling of mortal minds. The manner in which the Universal Father sojourns with the creatures of time is the most profound of all universe mysteries; the divine presence in the mind of man is the mystery of mysteries.

The physical bodies of mortals are "the temples of God." Notwithstanding that the Sovereign Creator Sons come near the creatures of their inhabited worlds and "draw all men to themselves"; though they "stand at the door" of consciousness "and knock" and delight to come in to all who will "open the doors of their hearts"; although there does exist this intimate personal communion between the Creator Sons and their mortal creatures, nevertheless, mortal men have something from God himself which actually dwells within them; their bodies are the temples thereof.

When you are through down here, when your course has been run in temporary form on earth, when your trial trip in the flesh is finished, when the dust that composes the mortal tabernacle "returns to the earth whence it came"; then, it is revealed, the indwelling "Spirit shall return to God who gave it." There sojourns within each moral being of this planet a fragment of God, a part and parcel of divinity. It is not yet yours by right of possession, but it is designedly intended to be one with you if you survive the mortal existence.

We are constantly confronted with this mystery of God; we are nonplused by the increasing unfolding of the endless panorama of the truth of his infinite goodness, endless mercy, matchless wisdom, and superb character.

The divine mystery consists in the inherent difference which exists between the finite and the infinite, the temporal and the eternal, the time-space creature and the Universal Creator, the material and the spiritual, the imperfection of man and the perfection of Paradise Deity. The God of universal love unfailingly manifests himself to every one of his creatures up to the fullness of that creature's capacity to spiritually grasp the qualities of divine truth, beauty, and goodness.

To every spirit being and to every mortal creature in every sphere and on every world of the universe of universes, the Universal Father reveals all of his gracious and divine self that can be discerned or comprehended by such spirit beings and by such mortal creatures. God is no respecter of persons, either spiritual or material. The divine presence which any child of the universe enjoys at any given moment is limited only by the capacity of such a creature to receive and to discern the spirit actualities of the supermaterial world.

As a reality in human spiritual experience God is not a mystery. But when an attempt is made to make plain the realities of the spirit world to the physical minds of the material order, mystery appears: mysteries so subtle and so profound that only the faith-grasp of the God-knowing mortal can achieve the philosophic miracle of the recognition of the Infinite by the finite, the discernment of the eternal God by the evolving mortals of the material worlds of time and space.

5. PERSONALITY OF THE UNIVERSAL FATHER

Do not permit the magnitude of God, his infinity, either to obscure or eclipse his personality. "He who planned the ear, shall he not hear? He who formed the eye, shall he not see?" The Universal Father is the acme of divine personality; he is the origin and destiny of personality throughout all creation. God is both infinite and personal; he is an infinite personality. The Father is truly a personality, notwithstanding that the infinity of his person places him forever beyond the full comprehension of material and finite beings.

God is much more than a personality as personality is understood by the human mind; he is even far more than any possible concept of a superpersonality. But it is utterly futile to discuss such incomprehensible concepts of divine personality with the minds of material creatures whose maximum concept of the reality of being consists in the idea and ideal of personality. The material creature's highest possible concept of the Universal Creator is embraced within the spiritual ideals of the exalted idea of divine personality.

Therefore, although you may know that God must be much more than the human conception of personality, you equally well know that the Universal Father cannot possibly be anything less than an eternal, infinite, true, good, and beautiful personality.

God is not hiding from any of his creatures. He is unapproachable to so many orders of beings only because he "dwells in a light which no material creature can approach." The immensity and grandeur of the divine personality is beyond the grasp of the unperfected mind of evolutionary mortals. He "measures the waters in the hollow of his hand, measures a universe with the span of his hand. It is he who sits on the circle of the earth, who stretches out the heavens as a curtain and spreads them out as a universe to dwell in." "Lift up your eyes on high and behold who has created all these things, who brings out their worlds by number and calls them all by their names"; and so it is true that "the invisible things of God are partially understood by the things which are made." Today, and as you are, you must discern the invisible Maker through his manifold and diverse creation, as well as through the revelation and ministration of his Sons and their numerous subordinates.

Even though material mortals cannot see the person of God, they should rejoice in the assurance that he is a person; by faith accept the truth which portrays that the Universal Father so loved the world as to provide for the eternal spiritual progression of its lowly inhabitants; that he "delights in his children." God is lacking in none of those superhuman and divine attributes which constitute a perfect, eternal, loving, and infinite Creator personality.

In the local creations (excepting the personnel of the superuniverses) God has no personal or residential manifestation aside from the Paradise Creator Sons who are the fathers of the inhabited worlds and the sovereigns of the local universes. If the faith of the creature were perfect, he would assuredly know that when he had seen a Creator Son he had seen the Universal Father; in seeking for the Father, he would not ask nor expect to see other than the Son. Mortal man simply cannot see God until he achieves completed spirit transformation and actually attains Paradise.

The natures of the Paradise Creator Sons do not encompass all the unqualified potentials of the universal absoluteness of the infinite nature of the First Great Source and Center, but the Universal Father is in every way *divinely* present in the Creator Sons. The Father and his Sons are one. These

Paradise Sons of the order of Michael are perfect personalities, even the pattern for all local universe personality from that of the Bright and Morning Star down to the lowest human creature of progressing animal evolution.

Without God and except for his great and central person, there would be no personality throughout all the vast universe of universes. *God is personality.*

Notwithstanding that God is an eternal power, a majestic presence, a transcendent ideal, and a glorious spirit, though he is all these and infinitely more, nonetheless, he is truly and everlastingly a perfect Creator personality, a person who can "know and be known," who can "love and be loved," and one who can befriend us; while you can be known, as other humans have been known, as the friend of God. He is a real spirit and a spiritual reality.

As we see the Universal Father revealed throughout his universe; as we discern him indwelling his myriads of creatures; as we behold him in the persons of his Sovereign Sons; as we continue to sense his divine presence here and there, near and afar, let us not doubt nor question his personality primacy. Notwithstanding all these far-flung distributions, he remains a true person and everlastingly maintains personal connection with the countless hosts of his creatures scattered throughout the universe of universes.

The idea of the personality of the Universal Father is an enlarged and truer concept of God which has come to mankind chiefly through revelation. Reason, wisdom, and religious experience all infer and imply the personality of God, but they do not altogether validate it. Even the indwelling Thought Adjuster is prepersonal. The truth and maturity of any religion is directly proportional to its concept of the infinite personality of God and to its grasp of the absolute unity of Deity. The idea of a personal Deity becomes, then, the measure of religious maturity after religion has first formulated the concept of the unity of God.

Primitive religion had many personal gods, and they were fashioned in the image of man. Revelation affirms the validity of the personality concept of God which is merely possible in the scientific postulate of a First Cause and is only provisionally suggested in the philosophic idea of Universal

Unity. Only by personality approach can any person begin to comprehend the unity of God.

In the contemplation of Deity, the concept of personality must be divested of the idea of corporeality. A material body is not indispensable to personality in either man or God. The corporeality error is shown in both extremes of human philosophy. In materialism, since man loses his body at death, he ceases to exist as a personality; in pantheism, since God has no body, he is not, therefore, a person. The superhuman type of progressing personality functions in a union of mind and spirit.

Personality is not simply an attribute of God; it rather stands for the totality of the co-ordinated infinite nature and the unified divine will which is exhibited in eternity and universality of perfect expression. Personality, in the supreme sense, is the revelation of God to the universe of universes.

God, being eternal, universal, absolute, and infinite, does not grow in knowledge nor increase in wisdom. God does not acquire experience, as finite man might conjecture or comprehend, but he does, within the realms of his own eternal personality, enjoy those continuous expansions of self-realization which are in certain ways comparable to, and analogous with, the acquirement of new experience by the finite creatures of the evolutionary worlds.

The absolute perfection of the infinite God would cause him to suffer the awful limitations of unqualified finality of perfectness were it not a fact that the Universal Father directly participates in the personality struggle of every imperfect soul in the wide universe who seeks, by divine aid, to ascend to the spiritually perfect worlds on high. This progressive experience of every spirit being and every mortal creature throughout the universe of universes is a part of the Father's ever-expanding Deity-consciousness of the never-ending divine circle of ceaseless self-realization.

It is literally true: "In all your afflictions he is afflicted." "In all your triumphs he triumphs in and with you." His prepersonal divine spirit is a real part of you. The Isle of Paradise responds to all the physical metamorphoses of the universe of universes; the Eternal Son includes all the spirit impulses of all creation; the Conjoint Actor encompasses all the mind expression of the expanding cosmos. The Universal Father realizes in the fullness of the divine consciousness all the individual experience of the progressive struggles of the expanding minds and the ascending spirits of every entity, being, and personality of the whole evolutionary creation of time and space. And all this is literally true, for "in Him we all live and move and have our being."

6. PERSONALITY IN THE UNIVERSE

Human personality is the time-space image-shadow cast by the divine Creator personality. And no actuality can ever be adequately comprehended by an examination of its shadow. Shadows should be interpreted in terms of the true substance.

God is to science a cause, to philosophy an idea, to religion a person, even the loving heavenly Father. God is to the scientist a primal force, to the philosopher a hypothesis of unity, to the religionist a living spiritual experience. Man's inadequate concept of the personality of the Universal Father can be improved only by man's spiritual progress in the universe and will become truly adequate only when the pilgrims of time and space finally attain the divine embrace of the living God on Paradise.

Never lose sight of the antipodal viewpoints of personality as it is conceived by God and man. Man views and comprehends personality, looking from the finite to the infinite; God looks from the infinite to the finite. Man possesses the lowest type of personality; God, the highest, even supreme, ultimate, and absolute. Therefore did the better concepts of the divine personality have patiently to await the appearance of improved ideas of human personality, especially the enhanced revelation of both human and divine personality in the Urantian bestowal life of Michael, the Creator Son.

The prepersonal divine spirit which indwells the mortal mind carries, in its very presence, the valid proof of its actual existence, but the concept of the divine personality can be grasped only by the spiritual insight of genuine personal religious experience. Any person, human or divine, may be known and comprehended quite apart from the external reactions or the material presence of that person.

Some degree of moral affinity and spiritual harmony is essential to friendship between two persons; a loving personality can hardly reveal himself to a loveless person. Even to approach the knowing of a divine personality, all of man's personality endowments must be wholly consecrated to the effort; halfhearted, partial devotion will be unavailing.

The more completely man understands himself and appreciates the personality values of his fellows, the more he will crave to know the Original Personality, and the more earnestly such a God-knowing human will strive to become like the Original Personality. You can argue over opinions about God, but experience with him and in him exists above and beyond all human controversy and mere intellectual logic. The God-knowing man describes his spiritual experiences, not to convince unbelievers, but for the edification and mutual satisfaction of believers.

To assume that the universe can be known, that it is intelligible, is to assume that the universe is mind made and personality managed. Man's mind can only perceive the mind phenomena of other minds, be they human or superhuman. If man's personality can experience the universe, there is a divine mind and an actual personality somewhere concealed in that universe.

God is spirit — spirit personality; man is also a spirit — potential spirit personality. Jesus of Nazareth attained the full realization of this potential of spirit personality in human experience; therefore his life of achieving the Father's will becomes man's most real and ideal revelation of the personality of God. Even though the personality of the Universal Father can be grasped only in actual religious experience, in Jesus' earth life we are inspired by the perfect demonstration of such a realization and revelation of the personality of God in a truly human experience.

7. SPIRITUAL VALUE OF THE PERSONALITY CONCEPT

When Jesus talked about "the living God," he referred to a personal Deity — the Father in heaven. The concept of the personality of Deity facilitates fellowship; it favors intelligent worship; it promotes refreshing trustfulness. Interactions can be had between nonpersonal things, but not fellowship. The fellowship relation of father and son, as between God and man, cannot be enjoyed unless both are persons. Only personalities can commune with each other, albeit this personal communion may be greatly facilitated by the presence of just such an impersonal entity as the Thought Adjuster.

Man does not achieve union with God as a drop of water might find unity with the ocean. Man attains divine union by progressive reciprocal spiritual communion, by personality intercourse with the personal God, by increasingly attaining the divine nature through wholehearted and intelligent conformity to the divine will. Such a sublime relationship can exist only between personalities.

The concept of truth might possibly be entertained apart from personality, the concept of beauty may exist without personality, but the concept of divine goodness is understandable only in relation to personality. Only a person can love and be loved. Even beauty and truth would be divorced from survival hope if they were not attributes of a personal God, a loving Father.

We cannot fully understand how God can be primal, changeless, all-powerful, and perfect, and at the same time be surrounded by an ever-changing and apparently law-limited universe, an evolving universe of relative imperfections. But we can *know* such a truth in our own personal experience since we all maintain identity of personality and unity of will in spite of the constant changing of both ourselves and our environment.

Ultimate universe reality cannot be grasped by mathematics, logic, or philosophy, only by personal experience in progressive conformity to the divine will of a personal God. Neither science, philosophy, nor theology can validate the personality of God. Only the personal experience of the faith sons of the heavenly Father can effect the actual spiritual realization of the personality of God.

The higher concepts of universe personality imply: identity, self-consciousness, self-will, and possibility for self-revelation. And these characteristics further imply fellowship with other and equal personalities, such as exists in the personality associations of the Paradise Deities. And the absolute unity of these associations is so perfect that divinity becomes known by indivisibility, by oneness. "The Lord God is *one*." Indivisibility of personality does not interfere with God's bestowing his spirit to live in the hearts of mortal men. Indivisibility of a human father's personality does not prevent the reproduction of mortal sons and daughters.

This concept of indivisibility in association with the concept of unity implies transcendence of both time and space by the Ultimacy of Deity; therefore neither space nor time can be absolute or infinite. The First Source and Center is that infinity who unqualifiedly transcends all mind, all matter, and all spirit.

The fact of the Paradise Trinity in no manner violates the truth of the divine unity. The three personalities of Paradise Deity are, in all universe reality reactions and in all creature relations, as one. Neither does the existence of these three eternal persons violate the truth of the indivisibility of Deity. I am fully aware that I have at my command no language adequate to make clear to the mortal mind how these universe problems appear to us. But you should not become discouraged; not all of these things are wholly clear to even the high personalities belonging to my group of Paradise beings. Ever bear in mind that these profound truths pertaining to Deity will increasingly clarify as your minds become progressively spiritualized during the successive epochs of the long mortal ascent to Paradise.

[Presented by a Divine Counselor, a member of a group of celestial personalities assigned by the Ancients of Days on Uversa, the headquarters of the seventh superuniverse, to supervise those portions of this forthcoming revelation which have to do with affairs beyond the borders of the local universe of Nebadon. I am commissioned to sponsor those papers portraying the nature and attributes of God because I represent the highest source of information available for such a purpose on any inhabited world. I have served as a Divine Counselor in all seven of the superuniverses and have long resided at the Paradise center of all things. Many times have I enjoyed the supreme pleasure of a sojourn in the immediate personal presence of the Universal Father. I portray the reality and truth of the Father's nature and attributes with unchallengeable authority; I know whereof I speak.]

PAPER 2
THE NATURE OF GOD

INASMUCH as one of man's highest possible concepts of God is embraced within the human idea and ideal of a primal and infinite personality, it is permissible, and may prove helpful, to study certain characteristics of the divine nature which constitute the character of Deity. The nature of God can best be understood by the revelation of the Father which Michael of Nebadon unfolded in his manifold teachings and in his superb mortal life in the flesh. The divine nature can also be better understood by man if he regards himself as a child of God and looks up to the Paradise Creator as a true spiritual Father.

The nature of God can be studied in a revelation of supreme ideas, the divine character can be envisaged as a portrayal of supernal ideals, but the most enlightening and spiritually edifying of all revelations of the divine nature is to be found in the comprehension of the religious life of Jesus of Nazareth, both before and after his attainment of full consciousness of divinity. If the incarnated life of Michael is taken as the background of the revelation of God to man, we may attempt to put in human word symbols certain ideas and ideals concerning the divine nature which may possibly contribute to a further illumination and unification of the human concept of the nature and the character of the personality of the Universal Father.

In all our efforts to enlarge and spiritualize the human concept of God, we are tremendously handicapped by the limited capacity of the mortal mind. We are also seriously handicapped in the execution of our assignment by the limitations of language and by the poverty of material which can be utilized for purposes of illustration or comparison in our efforts to portray divine values and to present spiritual meanings to the finite, mortal mind of man. All our efforts to enlarge the human concept of God would be well-nigh futile except for the fact that the mortal mind is indwelt by the bestowed Adjuster of the Universal Father and is pervaded by the Truth Spirit of the Creator Son. Depending, therefore, on the presence of these divine spirits within the heart of man for assistance in the enlargement of the concept of God, I cheerfully undertake the execution of my mandate to attempt the further portrayal of the nature of God to the mind of man.

1. THE INFINITY OF GOD

"Touching the Infinite, we cannot find him out. The divine footsteps are not known." "His understanding is infinite and his greatness is unsearchable." The blinding light of the Father's presence is such that to his lowly creatures he apparently "dwells in the thick darkness." Not only are his thoughts and plans unsearchable, but "he does great and marvelous things without number." "God is great; we comprehend him not, neither can the number of his years be searched out." "Will God indeed dwell on the earth? Behold, the heaven (universe) and the heaven of heavens (universe of universes) cannot contain him." "How unsearchable are his judgments and his ways past finding out!"

"There is but one God, the infinite Father, who is also a faithful Creator." "The divine Creator is also the Universal Disposer, the source and destiny of souls. He is the Supreme Soul, the Primal Mind, and the Unlimited Spirit of all creation." "The great Controller makes no mistakes. He is resplendent in majesty and glory." "The Creator God is wholly devoid of fear and enmity. He is immortal, eternal, self-existent, divine, and bountiful." "How pure and beautiful, how deep and unfathomable is the supernal Ancestor of all things!" "The Infinite is most excellent in that he imparts himself to men. He is the beginning and the end, the Father of every good and perfect purpose." "With God all things are possible; the eternal Creator is the cause of causes."

Notwithstanding the infinity of the stupendous manifestations of the Father's eternal and universal personality, he is unqualifiedly self-conscious of both his infinity and eternity; likewise he knows fully his perfection and power. He is the only being in the universe, aside from his divine co-ordinates, who experiences a perfect, proper, and complete appraisal of himself.

The Father constantly and unfailingly meets the need of the differential of demand for himself as it changes from time to time in various sections of his master universe. The great God knows and understands himself; he is infinitely self-conscious of all his primal attributes of perfection. God is not a cosmic accident; neither is he a universe experimenter. The Universe Sovereigns may engage in adventure; the Constellation Fathers may experiment; the system heads may practice; but the Universal Father sees the end from the beginning, and his divine plan and eternal purpose actually embrace and comprehend all the experiments and all the adventures of all his subordinates in every world, system, and constellation in every universe of his vast domains.

No thing is new to God, and no cosmic event ever comes as a surprise; he inhabits the circle of eternity. He is without beginning or end of days. To God there is no past, present, or future; all time is present at any given moment. He is the great and only I AM.

The Universal Father is absolutely and without qualification infinite in all his attributes; and this fact, in and of itself, automatically shuts him off from all direct personal communication with finite material beings and other lowly created intelligences.

And all this necessitates such arrangements for contact and communication with his manifold creatures as have been ordained, first, in the personalities of the Paradise Sons of God, who, although perfect in divinity, also often partake of the nature of the very flesh and blood of the planetary races, becoming one of you and one with you; thus, as it were, God becomes man, as occurred in the bestowal of Michael, who was called interchangeably the Son of God and the Son of Man. And second, there are the personalities of the Infinite Spirit, the various orders of the seraphic hosts and other celestial intelligences who draw near to the material beings of lowly origin and in so many ways minister to them and serve them. And third, there are the impersonal Mystery Monitors, Thought Adjusters, the actual gift of the great God himself sent to indwell such as the humans of Urantia, sent without announcement and without explanation. In endless profusion they descend from the heights of glory to grace and indwell the humble minds of those mortals who possess the capacity for God-consciousness or the potential therefor.

In these ways and in many others, in ways unknown to you and utterly beyond finite comprehension, does the Paradise Father lovingly and willingly downstep and otherwise modify, dilute, and attenuate his infinity in order that he may be able to draw nearer the finite minds of his creature children. And so, through a series of personality distributions which are diminishingly absolute, the infinite Father is enabled to enjoy close contact with the diverse intelligences of the many realms of his far-flung universe.

All this he has done and now does, and evermore will continue to do, without in the least detracting from the fact and reality of his infinity, eternity, and primacy. And these things are absolutely true, notwithstanding the difficulty of their comprehension, the mystery in which they are enshrouded, or the impossibility of their being fully understood by creatures such as dwell on Urantia.

Because the First Father is infinite in his plans and eternal in his purposes, it is inherently impossible for any finite being ever to grasp or comprehend these divine plans and purposes in their fullness. Mortal man can glimpse the Father's purposes only now and then, here and there, as they are revealed in relation to the outworking of the plan of creature ascension on its successive levels of universe progression. Though man cannot encompass the significance of infinity, the infinite Father does most certainly fully comprehend and lovingly embrace all the finity of all his children in all universes.

Divinity and eternity the Father shares with large numbers of the higher Paradise beings, but we question whether infinity and consequent universal primacy is fully shared with any save his co-ordinate associates of the Paradise Trinity. Infinity of personality must, perforce, embrace all finitude of personality; hence the truth — literal truth — of the teaching which declares that "In Him we live and move and have our being." That fragment of the pure Deity of the Universal Father which indwells mortal man is a part of the infinity of the First Great Source and Center, the Father of Fathers.

2. THE FATHER'S ETERNAL PERFECTION

Even your olden prophets understood the eternal, never-beginning, never-ending, circular nature of the Universal Father. God is literally and eternally present in his universe of universes. He inhabits the present moment with all his absolute majesty and eternal greatness. "The Father has life in himself, and this life is eternal life." Throughout the eternal ages it has been the Father who "gives to all life." There is infinite perfection in the divine integrity. "I am the Lord; I change not." Our knowledge of the universe of universes discloses not only that he is the Father of lights, but also that in his conduct of interplanetary affairs there "is no variableness neither shadow of changing." He "declares the end from the beginning." He says: "My counsel shall stand; I will do all my pleasures" "according to the eternal purpose which I purposed in my Son." Thus are the plans and purposes of the First Source and Center like himself: eternal, perfect, and forever changeless.

There is finality of completeness and perfection of repleteness in the mandates of the Father. "Whatsoever God does, it shall be forever; nothing can be added to it nor anything taken from it." The Universal Father does not repent of his original purposes of wisdom and perfection. His plans are steadfast, his counsel immutable, while his acts are divine and infallible. "A thousand years in his sight are but as yesterday when it is past and as a watch in the night." The perfection of divinity and the magnitude of eternity are forever beyond the full grasp of the circumscribed mind of mortal man.

The reactions of a changeless God, in the execution of his eternal purpose, may seem to vary in accordance with the changing attitude and the shifting minds of his created intelligences; that is, they may apparently and superficially vary; but underneath the surface and beneath all outward manifestations, there is still present the changeless purpose, the everlasting plan, of the eternal God.

Out in the universes, perfection must necessarily be a relative term, but in the central universe and especially on Paradise, perfection is undiluted; in certain phases it is even absolute. Trinity manifestations vary the exhibition of the divine perfection but do not attenuate it.

God's primal perfection consists not in an assumed righteousness but rather in the inherent perfection of the goodness of his divine nature. He is final, complete, and perfect. There is no thing lacking in the beauty and perfection of his righteous character. And the whole scheme of living existences on the worlds of space is centered in the divine purpose of elevating all will creatures to the high destiny of the experience of sharing the Father's Paradise perfection. God is neither self-centered nor self-contained; he never ceases to bestow himself upon all self-conscious creatures of the vast universe of universes.

God is eternally and infinitely perfect, he cannot personally know imperfection as his own experience, but he does share the consciousness of all the experience of imperfectness of all the struggling creatures of the evolutionary universes of all the Paradise Creator Sons. The personal and liberating touch of the God of perfection overshadows the hearts and encircuits the natures of all those mortal creatures who have ascended to the universe level of moral discernment. In this manner, as well as through the contacts of the divine presence, the Universal Father actually participates in the experience with immaturity and imperfection in the evolving career of every moral being of the entire universe.

Human limitations, potential evil, are not a part of the divine nature, but mortal experience with evil and all man's relations thereto are most certainly a part of God's ever-expanding self-realization in the children of time — creatures of moral responsibility who have been created or evolved by every Creator Son going out from Paradise.

3. JUSTICE AND RIGHTEOUSNESS

God is righteous; therefore is he just. "The Lord is righteous in all his ways." "`I have not done without cause all that I have done,' says the Lord." "The judgments of the Lord are true and righteous altogether." The justice of the Universal Father cannot be influenced by the acts and performances of his creatures, "for there is no iniquity with the Lord our God, no respect of persons, no taking of gifts."

How futile to make puerile appeals to such a God to modify his changeless decrees so that we can avoid the just consequences of the operation of his wise natural laws and righteous spiritual mandates! "Be not deceived; God is not mocked, for whatsoever a man sows that shall he also reap." True, even in the justice of reaping the harvest of wrongdoing, this divine justice is always tempered with mercy. Infinite wisdom is the eternal arbiter which determines the proportions of justice and mercy which shall be meted out in any given circumstance. The greatest punishment (in reality an inevitable consequence) for wrongdoing and deliberate rebellion against the government of God is loss of existence as an individual subject of that government. The final result of wholehearted sin is annihilation. In the last analysis, such sin-identified individuals have destroyed themselves by becoming wholly unreal through their embrace of iniquity. The factual disappearance of such a creature is, however, always delayed until the ordained order of justice current in that universe has been fully complied with.

Cessation of existence is usually decreed at the dispensational or epochal adjudication of the realm or realms. On a world such as Urantia it comes at the end of a planetary dispensation. Cessation of existence can be decreed at such times by co-ordinate action of all tribunals of jurisdiction, extending from the planetary council up through the courts of the Creator Son to the judgment tribunals of the Ancients of Days. The mandate of dissolution originates in the higher courts of the superuniverse following an unbroken confirmation of the indictment originating on the sphere of the wrongdoer's residence; and then, when sentence of extinction has been confirmed on high, the execution is by the direct act of those judges residential on, and operating from, the headquarters of the superuniverse.

When this sentence is finally confirmed, the sin-identified being instantly becomes as though he had not been. There is no resurrection from such a fate; it is everlasting and eternal. The living energy factors of identity are resolved by the transformations of time and the metamorphoses of space into the cosmic potentials whence they once emerged. As for the personality of the iniquitous one, it is deprived of a continuing life vehicle by the creature's failure to make those choices and final decisions which would have assured eternal life. When the continued embrace of sin by the associated mind culminates in complete self-identification with iniquity, then upon the cessation of life, upon cosmic dissolution, such an isolated personality is absorbed into the oversoul of creation, becoming a part of the evolving experience of the Supreme Being. Never again does it appear as a personality; its identity becomes as though it had never been. In the case of an Adjuster-indwelt personality, the experiential spirit values survive in the reality of the continuing Adjuster.

In any universe contest between actual levels of reality, the personality of the higher level will ultimately triumph over the personality of the lower level. This inevitable outcome of universe controversy is inherent in the fact that divinity of quality equals the degree of reality or actuality of any will creature. Undiluted evil, complete error, willful sin, and unmitigated iniquity are inherently and automatically suicidal. Such attitudes of cosmic unreality can survive in the universe only because of transient mercy-tolerance pending the action of the justice-determining and fairness-finding mechanisms of the universe tribunals of righteous adjudication.

The rule of the Creator Sons in the local universes is one of creation and spiritualization. These Sons devote themselves to the effective execution of the Paradise plan of progressive mortal ascension, to the rehabilitation of rebels and wrong thinkers, but when all such loving efforts are finally and forever rejected, the final decree of dissolution is executed by forces acting under the jurisdiction of the Ancients of Days.

4. THE DIVINE MERCY

Mercy is simply justice tempered by that wisdom which grows out of perfection of knowledge and the full recognition of the natural weaknesses and environmental handicaps of finite creatures. "Our God is full of compassion, gracious, long-suffering, and plenteous in mercy." Therefore "whosoever calls upon the Lord shall be saved," "for he will abundantly pardon." "The mercy of the Lord is from everlasting to everlasting"; yes, "his mercy endures forever." "I am the Lord who executes loving-kindness, judgment, and righteousness in the earth, for in these things I delight." "I do not afflict willingly nor grieve the children of men," for I am "the Father of mercies and the God of all comfort."

God is inherently kind, naturally compassionate, and everlastingly merciful. And never is it necessary that any influence be brought to bear upon the Father to call forth his loving-kindness. The creature's need is wholly sufficient to insure the full flow of the Father's tender mercies and his saving grace. Since God knows all about his children, it is easy for him to forgive. The better man understands his neighbor, the easier it will be to forgive him, even to love him.

Only the discernment of infinite wisdom enables a righteous God to minister justice and mercy at the same time and in any given universe situation. The heavenly Father is never torn by conflicting attitudes towards his universe children; God is never a victim of attitudinal antagonisms. God's all-knowingness unfailingly directs his free will in the choosing of that universe conduct which perfectly, simultaneously, and equally satisfies the demands of all his divine attributes and the infinite qualities of his eternal nature.

Mercy is the natural and inevitable offspring of goodness and love. The good nature of a loving Father could not possibly withhold the wise ministry of mercy to each member of every group of his universe children. Eternal justice and divine mercy together constitute what in human experience would be called fairness.

Divine mercy represents a fairness technique of adjustment between the universe levels of perfection and imperfection. Mercy is the justice of Supremacy adapted to the situations of the evolving finite, the righteousness of eternity modified to meet the highest interests and universe welfare of the children of time. Mercy is not a contravention of justice but rather an understanding interpretation of the demands of supreme justice as it is fairly applied to the subordinate spiritual beings and to the material creatures of the evolving universes. Mercy is the justice of the Paradise Trinity wisely and lovingly visited upon the manifold intelligences of the creations of time and space as it is formulated by divine wisdom and determined by the all-knowing mind and the sovereign free will of the Universal Father and all his associated Creators.

5. THE LOVE OF GOD

"God is love"; therefore his only personal attitude towards the affairs of the universe is always a reaction of divine affection. The Father loves us sufficiently to bestow his life upon us. "He makes his sun to rise on the evil and on the good and sends rain on the just and on the unjust."

It is wrong to think of God as being coaxed into loving his children because of the sacrifices of his Sons or the intercession of his subordinate creatures, "for the Father himself loves you." It is in response to this paternal affection that God sends the marvelous Adjusters to indwell the minds of men. God's love is universal; "whosoever will may come." He would "have all men be saved by coming into the knowledge of the truth." He is "not willing that any should perish."

The Creators are the very first to attempt to save man from the disastrous results of his foolish transgression of the divine laws. God's love is by nature a fatherly affection; therefore does he sometimes "chasten us for our own profit, that we may be partakers of his holiness." Even during your fiery trials remember that "in all our afflictions he is afflicted with us."

God is divinely kind to sinners. When rebels return to righteousness, they are mercifully received, "for our God will abundantly pardon." "I am he who blots out your transgressions for my own sake, and I will not remember your sins." "Behold what manner of love the Father has bestowed upon us that we should be called the sons of God."

After all, the greatest evidence of the goodness of God and the supreme reason for loving him is the indwelling gift of the Father — the Adjuster who so patiently awaits the hour when you both shall be eternally made one. Though you cannot find God by searching, if you will submit to the leading of the indwelling spirit, you will be unerringly guided, step by step, life by life, through universe upon universe, and age by age, until you finally stand in the presence of the Paradise personality of the Universal Father.

How unreasonable that you should not worship God because the limitations of human nature and the handicaps of your material creation make it impossible for you to see him. Between you and God there is a tremendous distance (physical space) to be traversed. There likewise exists a great gulf of spiritual differential which must be bridged; but notwithstanding all that physically and spiritually separates you from the Paradise personal presence of God, stop and ponder the solemn fact that God lives within you; he has in his own way already bridged the gulf. He has sent of himself, his spirit, to live in you and to toil with you as you pursue your eternal universe career.

I find it easy and pleasant to worship one who is so great and at the same time so affectionately devoted to the uplifting ministry of his lowly creatures. I naturally love one who is so powerful in creation and in the control thereof, and yet who is so perfect in goodness and so faithful in the loving-kindness which constantly overshadows us. I think I would love God just as much if he were not so great and powerful, as long as he is so good and merciful. We all love the Father more because of his nature than in recognition of his amazing attributes.

When I observe the Creator Sons and their subordinate administrators struggling so valiantly with the manifold difficulties of time inherent in the evolution of the universes of space, I discover that I bear these lesser rulers of the universes a great and profound affection. After all, I think we all, including the mortals of the realms, love the Universal Father and all other beings, divine or human, because we discern that these personalities truly love us. The experience of loving is very much a direct response to the experience of being loved. Knowing that God loves me, I should continue to love him supremely, even though he were divested of all his attributes of supremacy, ultimacy, and absoluteness.

The Father's love follows us now and throughout the endless circle of the eternal ages. As you ponder the loving nature of God, there is only one reasonable and natural personality reaction thereto: You will increasingly love your Maker; you will yield to God an affection analogous to that given by a child to an earthly parent; for, as a father, a real father, a true father, loves his children, so the Universal Father loves and forever seeks the welfare of his created sons and daughters.

But the love of God is an intelligent and farseeing parental affection. The divine love functions in unified association with divine wisdom and all other infinite characteristics of the perfect nature of the Universal Father. God is love, but love is not God. The greatest manifestation of the divine love for mortal beings is observed in the bestowal of the Thought Adjusters, but your greatest revelation of the Father's love is seen in the bestowal life of his Son Michael as he lived on earth the ideal spiritual life. It is the indwelling Adjuster who individualizes the love of God to each human soul.

At times I am almost pained to be compelled to portray the divine affection of the heavenly Father for his universe children by the employment of the human word symbol love. This term, even though it does connote man's highest concept of the mortal relations of respect and devotion, is so frequently designative of so much of human relationship that is wholly ignoble and utterly unfit to be known by any word which is also used to indicate the matchless affection of the living God for his universe creatures! How unfortunate that I cannot make use of some supernal and exclusive term which would convey to the mind of man the true nature and exquisitely beautiful significance of the divine affection of the Paradise Father.

When man loses sight of the love of a personal God, the kingdom of God becomes merely the kingdom of good. Notwithstanding the infinite unity of the divine nature, love is the dominant characteristic of all God's personal dealings with his creatures.

6. THE GOODNESS OF GOD

In the physical universe we may see the divine beauty, in the intellectual world we may discern eternal truth, but the goodness of God is found only in the spiritual world of personal religious experience. In its true essence, religion is a faith-trust in the goodness of God. God could be great and absolute, somehow even intelligent and personal, in philosophy, but in religion God must also be moral; he must be good. Man might fear a great God, but he trusts and loves only a good God. This goodness of God is a part of the personality of God, and its full revelation appears only in the personal religious experience of the believing sons of God.

Religion implies that the superworld of spirit nature is cognizant of, and responsive to, the fundamental needs of the human world. Evolutionary religion may become ethical, but only revealed religion becomes truly and spiritually moral. The olden concept that God is a Deity dominated by kingly morality was upstepped by Jesus to that affectionately touching level of intimate family morality of the parent-child relationship, than which there is none more tender and beautiful in mortal experience.

The "richness of the goodness of God leads erring man to repentance." "Every good gift and every perfect gift comes down from the Father of lights." "God is good; he is the eternal refuge of the souls of men." "The Lord God is merciful and gracious. He is long-suffering and abundant in goodness and truth." "Taste and see that the Lord is good! Blessed is the man who trusts him." "The Lord is gracious and full of compassion. He is the God of salvation." "He heals the brokenhearted and binds up the wounds of the soul. He is man's all-powerful benefactor."

The concept of God as a king-judge, although it fostered a high moral standard and created a law-respecting people as a group, left the individual believer in a sad position of insecurity respecting his status in time and in eternity. The later Hebrew prophets proclaimed God to be a Father to Israel; Jesus revealed God as the Father of each human being. The entire mortal concept of God is transcendently illuminated by the life of Jesus. Selflessness is inherent in parental love. God loves not like a father, but as a father. He is the Paradise Father of every universe personality.

Righteousness implies that God is the source of the moral law of the universe. Truth exhibits God as a revealer, as a teacher. But love gives and craves affection, seeks understanding fellowship such as exists between parent and child. Righteousness may be the divine thought, but love is a father's attitude. The erroneous supposition that the righteousness of God was irreconcilable with the selfless love of the heavenly Father, presupposed absence of unity in the nature of Deity and led directly to the elaboration of the atonement doctrine, which is a philosophic assault upon both the unity and the free-willness of God.

The affectionate heavenly Father, whose spirit indwells his children on earth, is not a divided personality — one of justice and one of mercy — neither does it require a mediator to secure the Father's favor or forgiveness. Divine righteousness is not dominated by strict retributive justice; God as a father transcends God as a judge.

God is never wrathful, vengeful, or angry. It is true that wisdom does often restrain his love, while justice conditions his rejected mercy. His love of righteousness cannot help being exhibited as equal hatred for sin. The Father is not an inconsistent personality; the divine unity is perfect. In the Paradise Trinity there is absolute unity despite the eternal identities of the co-ordinates of God.

God loves the sinner and hates the sin: such a statement is true philosophically, but God is a transcendent personality, and persons can only love and hate other persons. Sin is not a person. God loves the sinner because he is a personality reality (potentially eternal), while towards sin God strikes no personal attitude, for sin is not a spiritual reality; it is not personal; therefore does only the justice of God take cognizance of its existence. The love of God saves the sinner; the law of God destroys the sin. This attitude of the divine nature would apparently change if the sinner finally identified himself wholly with sin just as the same mortal mind may also fully identify itself with the indwelling spirit Adjuster. Such a sin-identified mortal would then become wholly unspiritual in nature (and therefore personally unreal) and would experience eventual extinction of being. Unreality, even incompleteness of creature nature, cannot exist forever in a progressingly real and increasingly spiritual universe.

Facing the world of personality, God is discovered to be a loving person; facing the spiritual world, he is a personal love; in religious experience he is both. Love identifies the volitional will of God. The goodness of God rests at the bottom of the divine free-willness — the universal tendency to love, show mercy, manifest patience, and minister forgiveness.

7. DIVINE TRUTH AND BEAUTY

All finite knowledge and creature understanding are relative. Information and intelligence, gleaned from even high sources, is only relatively complete, locally accurate, and personally true.

Physical facts are fairly uniform, but truth is a living and flexible factor in the philosophy of the universe. Evolving personalities are only partially wise and relatively true in their communications. They can be certain only as far as their personal experience extends. That which apparently may be wholly true in one place may be only relatively true in another segment of creation.

Divine truth, final truth, is uniform and universal, but the story of things spiritual, as it is told by numerous individuals hailing from various spheres, may sometimes vary in details owing to this relativity in the completeness of knowledge and in the repleteness of personal experience as well as in the length and extent of that experience. While the laws and decrees, the thoughts and attitudes, of the First Great Source and Center are eternally, infinitely, and universally true; at the same time, their application to, and adjustment for, every universe, system, world, and created intelligence, are in accordance with the plans and technique of the Creator Sons as they function in their respective universes, as well as in harmony with the local plans and procedures of the Infinite Spirit and of all other associated celestial personalities.

The false science of materialism would sentence mortal man to become an outcast in the universe. Such partial knowledge is potentially evil; it is knowledge composed of both good and evil. Truth is beautiful because it is both replete and symmetrical. When man searches for truth, he pursues the divinely real.

Philosophers commit their gravest error when they are misled into the fallacy of abstraction, the practice of focusing the attention upon one aspect of reality and then of pronouncing such an isolated aspect to be the whole truth. The wise philosopher will always look for the creative design which is behind, and pre-existent to, all universe phenomena. The creator thought invariably precedes creative action.

Intellectual self-consciousness can discover the beauty of truth, its spiritual quality, not only by the philosophic consistency of its concepts, but more certainly and surely by the unerring response of the ever-present Spirit of Truth. Happiness ensues from the recognition of truth because it can be *acted out*; it can be lived. Disappointment and sorrow attend upon error because, not being a reality, it cannot be realized in experience. Divine truth is best known by its *spiritual flavor*.

The eternal quest is for unification, for divine coherence. The far-flung physical universes cohere in the Isle of Paradise; the intellectual universe coheres in the God of mind, the Conjoint Actor; the spiritual universe is coherent in the personality of the Eternal Son. But the isolated mortal of time and space coheres in God the Father through the direct relationship between the indwelling Thought Adjuster and the Universal Father. Man's Adjuster is a fragment of God and everlastingly seeks for divine unification; it coheres with, and in, the Paradise Deity of the First Source and Center.

The discernment of supreme beauty is the discovery and integration of reality: The discernment of the divine goodness in the eternal truth, that is ultimate beauty. Even the charm of human art consists in the harmony of its unity.

The great mistake of most religions has been their failure to associate the goodness of God with the factual truths of science and the appealing beauty of art. As civilization progressed, and since religion continued to pursue the same unwise course of overemphasizing the goodness of God to the relative exclusion of truth and neglect of beauty, there developed an increasing tendency for certain types of men to turn away from the abstract and dissociated concept of isolated goodness. The overstressed and isolated morality of modern religion, which fails to hold the devotion and loyalty of many today, would rehabilitate itself if, in addition to its moral mandates, it would give equal consideration to the truths of science, philosophy, and spiritual experience, and to the beauties of the physical creation, the charm of intellectual art, and the grandeur of genuine character achievement.

The religious challenge of this age is to those farseeing and forward-looking men and women of spiritual insight who will dare to construct a new and appealing philosophy of living out of the enlarged and exquisitely integrated modern concepts of cosmic truth, universe beauty, and divine goodness. Such a new and righteous vision of morality will attract all that is good in the mind of man and challenge that which is best in the human soul. Truth, beauty, and goodness are divine realities, and as man ascends the scale of spiritual living, these supreme qualities of the Eternal become increasingly co-ordinated and unified in God, who is love.

All truth — material, philosophic, or spiritual — is both beautiful and good. All real beauty — material art or spiritual symmetry — is both true and good. All genuine goodness — whether personal morality, social equity, or divine ministry — is equally true and beautiful. Health, sanity, and happiness are integrations of truth, beauty, and goodness as they are blended in human experience. Such levels of efficient living come about through the unification of energy systems, idea systems, and spirit systems.

Truth is coherent, beauty attractive, goodness stabilizing. And when these values of that which is real are co-ordinated in personality experience, the result is a high order of love conditioned by wisdom and qualified by loyalty. The real purpose of all universe education is to effect the better co-ordination of the isolated child of the worlds with the larger realities of his expanding experience. Reality is finite on the human level, infinite and eternal on the higher and divine levels.

[Presented by a Divine Counselor acting by authority of the Ancients of Days on Uversa.]

PAPER 3
THE ATTRIBUTES OF GOD

God is everywhere present; the Universal Father rules the circle of eternity. But he rules in the local universes in the persons of his Paradise Creator Sons, even as he bestows life through these Sons. "God has given us eternal life, and this life is in his Sons." These Creator Sons of God are the personal expression of himself in the sectors of time and to the children of the whirling planets of the evolving universes of space.

The highly personalized Sons of God are clearly discernible by the lower orders of created intelligences, and so do they compensate for the invisibility of the infinite and therefore less discernible Father. The Paradise Creator Sons of the Universal Father are a revelation of an otherwise invisible being, invisible because of the absoluteness and infinity inherent in the circle of eternity and in the personalities of the Paradise Deities.

Creatorship is hardly an attribute of God; it is rather the aggregate of his acting nature. And this universal function of creatorship is eternally manifested as it is conditioned and controlled by all the co-ordinated attributes of the infinite and divine reality of the First Source and Center. We sincerely doubt whether any one characteristic of the divine nature can be regarded as being antecedent to the others, but if such were the case, then the creatorship nature of Deity would take precedence over all other natures, activities, and attributes. And the creatorship of Deity culminates in the universal truth of the Fatherhood of God.

1. GOD'S EVERYWHERENESS

The ability of the Universal Father to be everywhere present, and at the same time, constitutes his omnipresence. God alone can be in two places, in numberless places, at the same time. God is simultaneously present "in heaven above and on the earth beneath"; as the Psalmist exclaimed: "Whither shall I go from your spirit? or whither shall I flee from your presence?"

"`I am a God at hand as well as afar off,' says the Lord. `Do not I fill heaven and earth?'" The Universal Father is all the time present in all parts and in all hearts of his far-flung creation. He is "the fullness of him who fills all and in all," and "who works all in all," and further, the concept of his personality is such that "the heaven (universe) and heaven of heavens (universe of universes) cannot contain him." It is literally true that God is all and in all. But even that is not all of God. The Infinite can be finally revealed only in infinity; the cause can never be fully comprehended by an analysis of effects; the living God is immeasurably greater than the sum total of creation that has come into being as a result of the creative acts of his unfettered free will. God is revealed throughout the cosmos, but the cosmos can never contain or encompass the entirety of the infinity of God.

The Father's presence unceasingly patrols the master universe. "His going forth is from the end of the heaven, and his circuit to the ends of it; and there is nothing hidden from the light thereof."

The creature not only exists in God, but God also lives in the creature. "We know we dwell in him because he lives in us; he has given us his spirit. This gift from the Paradise Father is man's inseparable companion." "He is the ever-present and all-pervading God." "The spirit of the everlasting Father is concealed in the mind of every mortal child." "Man goes forth searching for a friend while that very friend lives within his own heart." "The true God is not afar off; he is a part of us; his spirit speaks from within us." "The

Father lives in the child. God is always with us. He is the guiding spirit of eternal destiny."

Truly of the human race has it been said, "You are of God" because "he who dwells in love dwells in God, and God in him." Even in wrongdoing you torment the indwelling gift of God, for the Thought Adjuster must needs go through the consequences of evil thinking with the human mind of its incarceration.

The omnipresence of God is in reality a part of his infinite nature; space constitutes no barrier to Deity. God is, in perfection and without limitation, discernibly present only on Paradise and in the central universe. He is not thus observably present in the creations encircling Havona, for God has limited his direct and actual presence in recognition of the sovereignty and the divine prerogatives of the co-ordinate creators and rulers of the universes of time and space. Hence must the concept of the divine presence allow for a wide range of both mode and channel of manifestation embracing the presence circuits of the Eternal Son, the Infinite Spirit, and the Isle of Paradise. Nor is it always possible to distinguish between the presence of the Universal Father and the actions of his eternal co-ordinates and agencies, so perfectly do they fulfill all the infinite requirements of his unchanging purpose. But not so with the personality circuit and the Adjusters; here God acts uniquely, directly, and exclusively.

The Universal Controller is potentially present in the gravity circuits of the Isle of Paradise in all parts of the master universe at all times and in the same degree, in accordance with the mass, in response to the physical demands for this presence, and because of the inherent nature of all creation which causes all things to adhere and consist in him. Likewise is the First Source and Center potentially present in the Unqualified Absolute, the repository of the uncreated universes of the eternal future. God thus potentially pervades the physical universes of the past, present, and future. He is the primordial foundation of the coherence of the so-called material creation. This nonspiritual Deity potential becomes actual here and there throughout the level of physical existences by the inexplicable intrusion of some one of his exclusive agencies upon the stage of universe action.

The mind presence of God is correlated with the absolute mind of the

Conjoint Actor, the Infinite Spirit, but in the finite creations it is better discerned in the everywhere functioning of the cosmic mind of the Paradise Master Spirits. Just as the First Source and Center is potentially present in the mind circuits of the Conjoint Actor, so is he potentially present in the tensions of the Universal Absolute. But mind of the human order is a bestowal of the Daughters of the Conjoint Actor, the Divine Ministers of the evolving universes.

The everywhere-present spirit of the Universal Father is co-ordinated with the function of the universal spirit presence of the Eternal Son and the everlasting divine potential of the Deity Absolute. But neither the spiritual activity of the Eternal Son and his Paradise Sons nor the mind bestowals of the Infinite Spirit seem to exclude the direct action of the Thought Adjusters, the indwelling fragments of God, in the hearts of his creature children.

Concerning God's presence in a planet, system, constellation, or a universe, the degree of such presence in any creational unit is a measure of the degree of the evolving presence of the Supreme Being: It is determined by the en masse recognition of God and loyalty to him on the part of the vast universe organization, running down to the systems and planets themselves. Therefore it is sometimes with the hope of conserving and safeguarding these phases of God's precious presence that, when some planets (or even systems) have plunged far into spiritual darkness, they are in a certain sense quarantined, or partially isolated from intercourse with the larger units of creation. And all this, as it operates on Urantia, is a spiritually defensive reaction of the majority of the worlds to save themselves, as far as possible, from suffering the isolating consequences of the alienating acts of a headstrong, wicked, and rebellious minority.

While the Father parentally encircuits all his sons — all personalities — his influence in them is limited by the remoteness of their origin from the Second and the Third Persons of Deity and augmented as their destiny attainment nears such levels. The *fact* of God's presence in creature minds is determined by whether or not they are indwelt by Father fragments, such as the Mystery Monitors, but his *effective* presence is determined by the degree of co-operation accorded these indwelling Adjusters by the minds of their sojourn.

The fluctuations of the Father's presence are not due to the changeableness of God. The Father does not retire in seclusion because he has been slighted; his affections are not alienated because of the creature's wrongdoing. Rather, having been endowed with the power of choice (concerning Himself), his children, in the exercise of that choice, directly determine the degree and limitations of the Father's divine influence in their own hearts and souls. The Father has freely bestowed himself upon us without limit and without favor. He is no respecter of persons, planets, systems, or universes. In the sectors of time he confers differential honor only on the Paradise personalities of God the Sevenfold, the co-ordinate creators of the finite universes.

2. GOD'S INFINITE POWER

All the universes know that "the Lord God omnipotent reigns." The affairs of this world and other worlds are divinely supervised. "He does according to his will in the army of heaven and among the inhabitants of the earth." It is eternally true, "there is no power but of God."

Within the bounds of that which is consistent with the divine nature, it is literally true that "with God all things are possible." The long-drawn-out evolutionary processes of peoples, planets, and universes are under the perfect control of the universe creators and administrators and unfold in accordance with the eternal purpose of the Universal Father, proceeding in harmony and order and in keeping with the all-wise plan of God. There is only one lawgiver. He upholds the worlds in space and swings the universes around the endless circle of the eternal circuit.

Of all the divine attributes, his omnipotence, especially as it prevails in the material universe, is the best understood. Viewed as an unspiritual phenomenon, God is energy. This declaration of physical fact is predicated on the incomprehensible truth that the First Source and Center is the primal cause of the universal physical phenomena of all space. From this divine activity all physical energy and other material manifestations are derived. Light, that is, light without heat, is another of the nonspiritual manifestations of the Deities. And there is still another form of nonspiritual energy which is virtually unknown on Urantia; it is as yet unrecognized.

God controls all power; he has made "a way for the lightning"; he has ordained the circuits of all energy. He has decreed the time and manner of the manifestation of all forms of energy-matter. And all these things are held forever in his everlasting grasp — in the gravitational control centering on nether Paradise. The light and energy of the eternal God thus swing on forever around his majestic circuit, the endless but orderly procession of the universe of universes. All creation circles eternally around the Paradise-Personality center of all things and beings.

The omnipotence of the Father pertains to the everywhere dominance of the absolute level, whereon the three energies, material, mindal, and spiritual, are indistinguishable in close proximity to him — the Source of all things. Creature mind, being neither Paradise monota nor Paradise spirit, is not directly responsive to the Universal Father. God *adjusts* with the mind of imperfection — with Urantia mortals through the Thought Adjusters.

The Universal Father is not a transient force, a shifting power, or a fluctuating energy. The power and wisdom of the Father are wholly adequate to cope with any and all universe exigencies. As the emergencies of human experience arise, he has foreseen them all, and therefore he does not react to the affairs of the universe in a detached way but rather in accordance with the dictates of eternal wisdom and in consonance with the mandates of infinite judgment. Regardless of appearances, the power of God is not functioning in the universe as a blind force.

Situations do arise in which it appears that emergency rulings have been made, that natural laws have been suspended, that misadaptations have been recognized, and that an effort is being made to rectify the situation; but such is not the case. Such concepts of God have their origin in the limited range of your viewpoint, in the finiteness of your comprehension, and in the circumscribed scope of your survey; such misunderstanding of God is due to the profound ignorance you enjoy regarding the existence of the higher laws of the realm, the magnitude of the Father's character, the infinity of his attributes, and the fact of his free-willness.

The planetary creatures of God's spirit indwelling, scattered hither and yon throughout the universes of space, are so nearly infinite in number and order, their intellects are so diverse, their minds are so limited and sometimes so gross, their vision is so curtailed and localized, that it is almost impossible to formulate generalizations of law adequately expressive of the Father's infinite attributes and at the same time to any degree comprehensible to these created intelligences. Therefore, to you the creature, many of the acts of the all-powerful Creator seem to be arbitrary, detached, and not infrequently heartless and cruel. But again I assure you that this is not true. God's doings are all purposeful, intelligent, wise, kind, and eternally considerate of the best good, not always of an individual being, an individual planet, or even an individual universe; but they are for the welfare and best good of all concerned, from the lowest to the highest. In the epochs of time the welfare of the part may sometimes appear to differ from the welfare of the whole; in the circle of eternity such apparent differences are nonexistent.

We are all a part of the family of God, and we must therefore sometimes share in the family discipline. Many of the acts of God which so disturb and confuse us are the result of the decisions and final rulings of all-wisdom, empowering the Conjoint Actor to execute the choosing of the infallible will of the infinite mind, to enforce the decisions of the personality of perfection, whose survey, vision, and solicitude embrace the highest and eternal welfare of all his vast and far-flung creation.

Thus it is that your detached, sectional, finite, gross, and highly materialistic viewpoint and the limitations inherent in the nature of your being constitute such a handicap that you are unable to see, comprehend, or know the wisdom and kindness of many of the divine acts which to you seem fraught with such crushing cruelty, and which seem to be characterized by such utter indifference to the comfort and welfare, to the planetary happiness and personal prosperity, of your fellow creatures. It is because of the limits of human vision, it is because of your circumscribed understanding and finite comprehension, that you misunderstand the motives, and pervert the purposes, of God. But many things occur on the evolutionary worlds which are not the personal doings of the Universal Father.

The divine omnipotence is perfectly co-ordinated with the other attributes of the personality of God. The power of God is, ordinarily, only limited in its universe spiritual manifestation by three conditions or situations:

1. By the nature of God, especially by his infinite love, by truth, beauty, and goodness.
2. By the will of God, by his mercy ministry and fatherly relationship with the personalities of the universe.

3. By the law of God, by the righteousness and justice of the eternal Paradise Trinity.

God is unlimited in power, divine in nature, final in will, infinite in attributes, eternal in wisdom, and absolute in reality. But all these characteristics of the Universal Father are unified in Deity and universally expressed in the Paradise Trinity and in the divine Sons of the Trinity. Otherwise, outside of Paradise and the central universe of Havona, everything pertaining to God is limited by the evolutionary presence of the Supreme, conditioned by the eventuating presence of the Ultimate, and co-ordinated by the three existential Absolutes — Deity, Universal, and Unqualified. And God's presence is thus limited because such is the will of God.

3. GOD'S UNIVERSAL KNOWLEDGE

"God knows all things." The divine mind is conscious of, and conversant with, the thought of all creation. His knowledge of events is universal and perfect. The divine entities going out from him are a part of him; he who "balances the clouds" is also "perfect in knowledge." "The eyes of the Lord are in every place." Said your great teacher of the insignificant sparrow, "One of them shall not fall to the ground without my Father's knowledge," and also, "The very hairs of your head are numbered." "He tells the number of the stars; he calls them all by their names."

The Universal Father is the only personality in all the universe who does actually know the number of the stars and planets of space. All the worlds of every universe are constantly within the consciousness of God. He also says: "I have surely seen the affliction of my people, I have heard their cry, and I know their sorrows." For "the Lord looks from heaven; he beholds all the sons of men; from the place of his habitation he looks upon all the inhabitants of the earth." Every creature child may truly say: "He knows the way I take, and when he has tried me, I shall come forth as gold." "God knows our downsittings and our uprisings; he understands our thoughts afar off and is acquainted with all our ways." "All things are naked and open to the eyes of him with whom we have to do." And it should be a real comfort to every human being to understand that "he knows your frame; he remembers that you are dust." Jesus, speaking of the living God, said, "Your Father knows what you have need of even before you ask him."

God is possessed of unlimited power to know all things; his consciousness is universal. His personal circuit encompasses all personalities, and his knowledge of even the lowly creatures is supplemented indirectly through the descending series of divine Sons and directly through the indwelling Thought Adjusters. And furthermore, the Infinite Spirit is all the time everywhere present.

We are not wholly certain as to whether or not God chooses to foreknow events of sin. But even if God should foreknow the freewill acts of his children, such foreknowledge does not in the least abrogate their freedom. One thing is certain: God is never subjected to surprise.

Omnipotence does not imply the power to do the nondoable, the ungodlike act. Neither does omniscience imply the knowing of the unknowable. But such statements can hardly be made comprehensible to the finite mind. The creature can hardly understand the range and limitations of the will of the Creator.

4. GOD'S LIMITLESSNESS

The successive bestowal of himself upon the universes as they are brought into being in no wise lessens the potential of power or the store of wisdom as they continue to reside and repose in the central personality of Deity. In potential of force, wisdom, and love, the Father has never lessened aught of his possession nor become divested of any attribute of his glorious personality as the result of the unstinted bestowal of himself upon the Paradise Sons, upon his subordinate creations, and upon the manifold creatures thereof.

The creation of every new universe calls for a new adjustment of gravity; but even if creation should continue indefinitely, eternally, even to infinity, so that eventually the material creation would exist without limitations, still the power of control and co-ordination reposing in the Isle of Paradise would be found equal to, and adequate for, the mastery, control, and co-ordination of such an infinite universe. And subsequent to this bestowal of limitless force and power upon a boundless universe, the Infinite would still be surcharged with the same degree of force and energy; the Unqualified Absolute would still be undiminished; God would still possess the same infinite potential, just as if force, energy, and power had never been poured forth for the endowment of universe upon universe.

And so with wisdom: The fact that mind is so freely distributed to the thinking of the realms in no wise impoverishes the central source of divine wisdom. As the universes multiply, and beings of the realms increase in number to the limits of comprehension, if mind continues without end to be bestowed upon these beings of high and low estate, still will God's central personality continue to embrace the same eternal, infinite, and all-wise mind.

The fact that he sends forth spirit messengers from himself to indwell the men and women of your world and other worlds in no wise lessens his ability to function as a divine and all-powerful spirit personality; and there is absolutely no limit to the extent or number of such spirit Monitors which he can and may send out. This giving of himself to his creatures creates a boundless, almost inconceivable future possibility of progressive and successive existences for these divinely endowed mortals. And this prodigal distribution of himself as these ministering spirit entities in no manner diminishes the wisdom and perfection of truth and knowledge which repose in the person of the all-wise, all-knowing, and all-powerful Father.

To the mortals of time there is a future, but God inhabits eternity. Even though I hail from near the very abiding place of Deity, I cannot presume to speak with perfection of understanding concerning the infinity of many of the divine attributes. Infinity of mind alone can fully comprehend infinity of existence and eternity of action.

Mortal man cannot possibly know the infinitude of the heavenly Father. Finite mind cannot think through such an absolute truth or fact. But this same finite human being can actually *feel* — literally experience — the full and undiminished impact of such an infinite Father's LOVE. Such a love can be truly experienced, albeit while quality of experience is unlimited, quantity of such an experience is strictly limited by the human capacity for spiritual receptivity and by the associated capacity to love the Father in return.

Finite appreciation of infinite qualities far transcends the logically limited capacities of the creature because of the fact that mortal man is made in the image of God — there lives within him a fragment of infinity. Therefore man's nearest and dearest approach to God is by and through love, for God is love. And all of such a unique relationship is an actual experience in cosmic sociology, the Creator-creature relationship — the Father-child affection.

5. THE FATHER'S SUPREME RULE

In his contact with the post-Havona creations, the Universal Father does not exercise his infinite power and final authority by direct transmittal but rather through his Sons and their subordinate personalities. And God does all this of his own free will. Any and all powers delegated, if occasion should arise, if it should become the choice of the divine mind, could be exercised direct; but, as a rule, such action only takes place as a result of the failure of the delegated personality to fulfill the divine trust. At such times and in the face of such default and within the limits of the reservation of divine power and potential, the Father does act independently and in accordance with the mandates of his own choice; and that choice is always one of unfailing perfection and infinite wisdom.

The Father rules through his Sons; on down through the universe organization there is an unbroken chain of rulers ending with the Planetary Princes, who direct the destinies of the evolutionary spheres of the Father's vast domains. It is no mere poetic expression that exclaims: "The earth is the Lord's and the fullness thereof." "He removes kings and sets up kings." "The Most Highs rule in the kingdoms of men."

In the affairs of men's hearts the Universal Father may not always have his way; but in the conduct and destiny of a planet the divine plan prevails; the eternal purpose of wisdom and love triumphs.

Said Jesus: "My Father, who gave them to me, is greater than all; and no one is able to pluck them out of my Father's hand." As you glimpse the manifold workings and view the staggering immensity of God's well-nigh limitless creation, you may falter in your concept of his primacy, but you should not fail to accept him as securely and everlastingly enthroned at the Paradise center of all things and as the beneficent Father of all intelligent beings. There is but "one God and Father of all, who is above all and in all," "and he is before all things, and in him all things consist."

The uncertainties of life and the vicissitudes of existence do not in any manner contradict the concept of the universal sovereignty of God. All evolutionary creature life is beset by certain inevitabilities. Consider the following:

1. Is *courage* — strength of character — desirable? Then must man be reared in an environment which necessitates grappling with hardships and reacting to disappointments.

2. Is *altruism* — service of one's fellows — desirable? Then must life experience provide for encountering situations of social inequality.

3. Is *hope* — the grandeur of trust — desirable? Then human existence must constantly be confronted with insecurities and recurrent uncertainties.

4. Is *faith* — the supreme assertion of human thought — desirable? Then must the mind of man find itself in that troublesome predicament where it ever knows less than it can believe.

5. Is *the love of truth* and the willingness to go wherever it leads, desirable? Then must man grow up in a world where error is present and falsehood always possible.

6. Is *idealism* — the approaching concept of the divine — desirable? Then must man struggle in an environment of relative goodness and beauty, surroundings stimulative of the irrepressible reach for better things.

7. Is *loyalty* — devotion to highest duty — desirable? Then must man carry on amid the possibilities of betrayal and desertion. The valor of devotion to duty consists in the implied danger of default.

8. Is *unselfishness* — the spirit of self-forgetfulness — desirable? Then must mortal man live face to face with the incessant clamoring of an

inescapable self for recognition and honor. Man could not dynamically choose the divine life if there were no self-life to forsake. Man could never lay saving hold on righteousness if there were no potential evil to exalt and differentiate the good by contrast.

9. Is *pleasure* — the satisfaction of happiness — desirable? Then must man live in a world where the alternative of pain and the likelihood of suffering are ever-present experiential possibilities.

Throughout the universe, every unit is regarded as a part of the whole. Survival of the part is dependent on co-operation with the plan and purpose of the whole, the wholehearted desire and perfect willingness to do the Father's divine will. The only evolutionary world without error (the possibility of unwise judgment) would be a world without free intelligence. In the Havona universe there are a billion perfect worlds with their perfect inhabitants, but evolving man must be fallible if he is to be free. Free and inexperienced intelligence cannot possibly at first be uniformly wise. The possibility of mistaken judgment (evil) becomes sin only when the human will consciously endorses and knowingly embraces a deliberate immoral judgment.

The full appreciation of truth, beauty, and goodness is inherent in the perfection of the divine universe. The inhabitants of the Havona worlds do not require the potential of relative value levels as a choice stimulus; such perfect beings are able to identify and choose the good in the absence of all contrastive and thought-compelling moral situations. But all such perfect beings are, in moral nature and spiritual status, what they are by virtue of the fact of existence. They have experientially earned advancement only within their inherent status. Mortal man earns even his status as an ascension candidate by his own faith and hope. Everything divine which the human mind grasps and the human soul acquires is an experiential attainment; it is a *reality* of personal experience and is therefore a unique possession in contrast to the inherent goodness and righteousness of the inerrant personalities of Havona.

The creatures of Havona are naturally brave, but they are not courageous in the human sense. They are innately kind and considerate, but hardly altruistic in the human way. They are expectant of a pleasant future, but not hopeful in the exquisite manner of the trusting mortal of the uncertain evolutionary spheres. They have faith in the stability of the universe, but they are utter strangers to that saving faith whereby mortal man climbs from the status of an animal up to the portals of Paradise. They love the truth, but they know nothing of its soul-saving qualities. They are idealists, but they were born that way; they are wholly ignorant of the ecstasy of becoming such by exhilarating choice. They are loyal, but they have never experienced the thrill of wholehearted and intelligent devotion to duty in the face of temptation to default. They are unselfish, but they never gained such levels of experience by the magnificent conquest of a belligerent self. They enjoy pleasure, but they do not comprehend the sweetness of the pleasure escape from the pain potential.

6. THE FATHER'S PRIMACY

With divine selflessness, consummate generosity, the Universal Father relinquishes authority and delegates power, but he is still primal; his hand is on the mighty lever of the circumstances of the universal realms; he has reserved all final decisions and unerringly wields the all-powerful veto scepter of his eternal purpose with unchallengeable authority over the welfare and destiny of the outstretched, whirling, and ever-circling creation.

The sovereignty of God is unlimited; it is the fundamental fact of all creation. The universe was not inevitable. The universe is not an accident, neither is it self-existent. The universe is a work of creation and is therefore wholly subject to the will of the Creator. The will of God is divine truth, living love; therefore are the perfecting creations of the evolutionary universes characterized by goodness — nearness to divinity; by potential evil — remoteness from divinity.

All religious philosophy, sooner or later, arrives at the concept of unified universe rule, of one God. Universe causes cannot be lower than universe effects. The source of the streams of universe life and of the cosmic mind must be above the levels of their manifestation. The human mind cannot be consistently explained in terms of the lower orders of existence. Man's mind can be truly comprehended only by recognizing the reality of higher orders of thought and purposive will. Man as a moral being is inexplicable unless the reality of the Universal Father is acknowledged.

The mechanistic philosopher professes to reject the idea of a universal and sovereign will, the very sovereign will whose activity in the elaboration of universe laws he so deeply reverences. What unintended homage the mechanist pays the law-Creator when he conceives such laws to be self-acting and self-explanatory!

It is a great blunder to humanize God, except in the concept of the indwelling Thought Adjuster, but even that is not such an error as completely to mechanize the idea of the First Great Source and Center.

Does the Paradise Father suffer? I do not know. The Creator Sons most certainly can and sometimes do, even as do mortals. The Eternal Son and the Infinite Spirit suffer in a modified sense. I think the Universal Father does, but I cannot understand *how*; perhaps through the personality circuit or through the individuality of the Thought Adjusters and other bestowals of his eternal nature. He has said of the mortal races, "In all your afflictions I am afflicted." He unquestionably experiences a fatherly and sympathetic understanding; he may truly suffer, but I do not comprehend the nature thereof.

The infinite and eternal Ruler of the universe of universes is power, form, energy, process, pattern, principle, presence, and idealized reality. But he is more; he is personal; he exercises a sovereign will, experiences self-consciousness of divinity, executes the mandates of a creative mind, pursues the satisfaction of the realization of an eternal purpose, and manifests a Father's love and affection for his universe children. And all these more personal traits of the Father can be better understood by observing them as they were revealed in the bestowal life of Michael, your Creator Son, while he was incarnated on Urantia.

God the Father loves men; God the Son serves men; God the Spirit inspires the children of the universe to the ever-ascending adventure of finding God the Father by the ways ordained by God the Sons through the ministry of the grace of God the Spirit.

[Being the Divine Counselor assigned to the presentation of the revelation of the Universal Father, I have continued with this statement of the attributes of Deity.]

PAPER 4
GOD'S RELATION TO THE UNIVERSE

THE UNIVERSAL FATHER has an eternal purpose pertaining to the material, intellectual, and spiritual phenomena of the universe of universes, which he is executing throughout all time. God created the universes of his own free and sovereign will, and he created them in accordance with his all-wise and eternal purpose. It is doubtful whether anyone except the Paradise Deities and their highest associates really knows very much about the eternal purpose of God. Even the exalted citizens of Paradise hold very diverse opinions about the nature of the eternal purpose of the Deities.

It is easy to deduce that the purpose in creating the perfect central universe of Havona was purely the satisfaction of the divine nature. Havona may serve as the pattern creation for all other universes and as the finishing school for the pilgrims of time on their way to Paradise; however, such a supernal creation must exist primarily for the pleasure and satisfaction of the perfect and infinite Creators.

The amazing plan for perfecting evolutionary mortals and, after their attainment of Paradise and the Corps of the Finality, providing further training for some undisclosed future work, does seem to be, at present, one of the chief concerns of the seven superuniverses and their many subdivisions; but this ascension scheme for spiritualizing and training the mortals of time and space is by no means the exclusive occupation of the universe intelligences. There are, indeed, many other fascinating pursuits which occupy the time and enlist the energies of the celestial hosts.

1. THE UNIVERSE ATTITUDE OF THE FATHER

For ages the inhabitants of Urantia have misunderstood the providence of God. There is a providence of divine outworking on your world, but it is not the childish, arbitrary, and material ministry many mortals have conceived it to be. The providence of God consists in the interlocking activities of the celestial beings and the divine spirits who, in accordance with cosmic law, unceasingly labor for the honor of God and for the spiritual advancement of his universe children.

Can you not advance in your concept of God's dealing with man to that level where you recognize that the watchword of the universe is *progress?* Through long ages the human race has struggled to reach its present position. Throughout all these millenniums Providence has been working out the plan of progressive evolution. The two thoughts are not opposed in practice, only in man's mistaken concepts. Divine providence is never arrayed in opposition to true human progress, either temporal or spiritual. Providence is always consistent with the unchanging and perfect nature of the supreme Lawmaker.

"God is faithful" and "all his commandments are just." "His faithfulness is established in the very skies." "Forever, O Lord, your word is settled in heaven. Your faithfulness is to all generations; you have established the earth and it abides." "He is a faithful Creator."

There is no limitation of the forces and personalities which the Father may use to uphold his purpose and sustain his creatures. "The eternal God is our refuge, and underneath are the everlasting arms." "He who dwells in the secret place of the Most High shall abide under the shadow of the Almighty." "Behold, he who keeps us shall neither slumber nor sleep." "We know that all things work together for good to those who love God," "for the eyes of the Lord are over the righteous, and his ears are open to their prayers."

God upholds "all things by the word of his power." And when new worlds are born, he "sends forth his Sons and they are created." God not only creates, but he "preserves them all." God constantly upholds all things material and all beings spiritual. The universes are eternally stable. There is stability in the midst of apparent instability. There is an underlying order and security in the midst of the energy upheavals and the physical cataclysms of the starry realms.

The Universal Father has not withdrawn from the management of the universes; he is not an inactive Deity. If God should retire as the present upholder of all creation, there would immediately occur a universal collapse. Except for God, there would be no such thing as reality. At this very moment, as during the remote ages of the past and in the eternal future, God continues to uphold. The divine reach extends around the circle of eternity. The universe is not wound up like a clock to run just so long and then cease to function; all things are constantly being renewed. The Father unceasingly pours forth energy, light, and life. The work of God is literal as well as spiritual. "He stretches out the north over the empty space and hangs the earth upon nothing."

A being of my order is able to discover ultimate harmony and to detect far-reaching and profound co-ordination in the routine affairs of universe administration. Much that seems disjointed and haphazard to the mortal mind appears orderly and constructive to my understanding. But there is very much going on in the universes that I do not fully comprehend. I have long been a student of, and am more or less conversant with, the recognized forces, energies, minds, morontias, spirits, and personalities of the local universes and the superuniverses. I have a general understanding of how these agencies and personalities operate, and I am intimately familiar with the workings of the accredited spirit intelligences of the grand universe. Notwithstanding my knowledge of the phenomena of the universes, I am constantly confronted with cosmic reactions which I cannot fully fathom. I am continually encountering apparently fortuitous conspiracies of the interassociation of forces, energies, intellects, and spirits, which I cannot satisfactorily explain.

I am entirely competent to trace out and to analyze the working of all phenomena directly resulting from the functioning of the Universal Father, the Eternal Son, the Infinite Spirit, and, to a large extent, the Isle of Paradise. My perplexity is occasioned by encountering what appears to be the performance of their mysterious co-ordinates, the three Absolutes of potentiality. These Absolutes seem to supersede matter, to transcend mind, and to supervene spirit. I am constantly confused and often perplexed by my inability to comprehend these complex transactions which I attribute to the presences and performances of the Unqualified Absolute, the Deity Absolute, and the Universal Absolute.

These Absolutes must be the not-fully-revealed presences abroad in the universe which, in the phenomena of space potency and in the function of other superultimates, render it impossible for physicists, philosophers, or even religionists to predict with certainty as to just how the primordials of force, concept, or spirit will respond to demands made in a complex reality situation involving supreme adjustments and ultimate values.

There is also an organic unity in the universes of time and space which seems to underlie the whole fabric of cosmic events. This living presence of the evolving Supreme Being, this Immanence of the Projected Incomplete, is inexplicably manifested ever and anon by what appears to be an amazingly fortuitous co-ordination of apparently unrelated universe happenings. This must be the function of Providence — the realm of the Supreme Being and the Conjoint Actor.

I am inclined to believe that it is this far-flung and generally unrecognizable control of the co-ordination and interassociation of all phases and forms of universe activity that causes such a variegated and apparently hopelessly confused medley of physical, mental, moral, and spiritual phenomena so unerringly to work out to the glory of God and for the good of men and angels.

But in the larger sense the apparent "accidents" of the cosmos are undoubtedly a part of the finite drama of the time-space adventure of the Infinite in his eternal manipulation of the Absolutes.

2. GOD AND NATURE

Nature is in a limited sense the physical habit of God. The conduct, or action, of God is qualified and provisionally modified by the experimental plans and the evolutionary patterns of a local universe, a galaxy, a constellation, a system, or a planet. God acts in accordance with a well-defined, unchanging, immutable law throughout the wide-spreading master universe; but he modifies the patterns of his action so as to contribute to the co-ordinate and balanced conduct of each universe, galaxy, constellation, system, planet, and personality in accordance with the local objects, aims, and plans of the finite projects of evolutionary unfolding.

Therefore, nature, as mortal man understands it, presents the underlying foundation and fundamental background of a changeless Deity and his immutable laws, modified by, fluctuating because of, and experiencing upheavals through, the working of the local plans, purposes, patterns, and conditions which have been inaugurated and are being carried out by the local universe, galaxy, constellation, system, and planetary forces and personalities. For example: As God's laws have been ordained in Nebadon, they are modified by the plans established by the Creator Son and Creative Spirit of this local universe; and in addition to all this the operation of these laws has been further influenced by the errors, defaults, and insurrections of certain beings resident upon your planet and belonging to your immediate planetary system of Satania.

Nature is a time-space resultant of two cosmic factors: first, the immutability, perfection, and rectitude of Paradise Deity, and second, the experimental plans, executive blunders, insurrectionary errors, incompleteness of development, and imperfection of wisdom of the extra-Paradise creatures, from the highest to the lowest. Nature therefore carries a uniform, unchanging, majestic, and marvelous thread of perfection from the circle of eternity; but in each universe, on each planet, and in each individual life, this nature is modified, qualified, and perchance marred by the acts, the mistakes, and the disloyalties of the creatures of the evolutionary systems and universes; and therefore must nature ever be of a changing mood, whimsical withal, though stable underneath, and varied in accordance with the operating procedures of a local universe.

Nature is the perfection of Paradise divided by the incompletion, evil, and sin of the unfinished universes. This quotient is thus expressive of both the perfect and the partial, of both the eternal and the temporal. Continuing evolution modifies nature by augmenting the content of Paradise perfection and by diminishing the content of the evil, error, and disharmony of relative reality.

God is not personally present in nature or in any of the forces of nature, for the phenomenon of nature is the superimposition of the imperfections of progressive evolution and, sometimes, the consequences of insurrectionary rebellion, upon the Paradise foundations of God's universal law. As it appears on such a world as Urantia, nature can never be the adequate expression, the true representation, the faithful portrayal, of an all-wise and infinite God.

Nature, on your world, is a qualification of the laws of perfection by the evolutionary plans of the local universe. What a travesty to worship nature because it is in a limited, qualified sense pervaded by God; because it is a phase of the universal and, therefore, divine power! Nature also is a manifestation of the unfinished, the incomplete, the imperfect outworkings of the development, growth, and progress of a universe experiment in cosmic evolution.

The apparent defects of the natural world are not indicative of any such corresponding defects in the character of God. Rather are such observed imperfections merely the inevitable stop-moments in the exhibition of the ever-moving reel of infinity picturization. It is these very defect-interruptions of perfection-continuity which make it possible for the finite mind of material man to catch a fleeting glimpse of divine reality in time and space. The material manifestations of divinity appear defective to the evolutionary mind of man only because mortal man persists in viewing the phenomena of nature through natural eyes, human vision unaided by morontia mota or by revelation, its compensatory substitute on the worlds of time.

And nature is marred, her beautiful face is scarred, her features are seared, by the rebellion, the misconduct, the misthinking of the myriads of creatures who are a part of nature, but who have contributed to her disfigurement in time. No, nature is not God. Nature is not an object of worship.

3. GOD'S UNCHANGING CHARACTER

All too long has man thought of God as one like himself. God is not, never was, and never will be jealous of man or any other being in the universe of universes. Knowing that the Creator Son intended man to be the masterpiece of the planetary creation, to be the ruler of all the earth, the sight of his being dominated by his own baser passions, the spectacle of his bowing down before idols of wood, stone, gold, and selfish ambition — these sordid scenes stir God and his Sons to be jealous for man, but never of him.

The eternal God is incapable of wrath and anger in the sense of these human emotions and as man understands such reactions. These sentiments are mean and despicable; they are hardly worthy of being called human, much less divine; and such attitudes are utterly foreign to the perfect nature and gracious character of the Universal Father.

Much, very much, of the difficulty which Urantia mortals have in understanding God is due to the far-reaching consequences of the Lucifer rebellion and the Caligastia betrayal. On worlds not segregated by sin, the evolutionary races are able to formulate far better ideas of the Universal Father; they suffer less from confusion, distortion, and perversion of concept.

God repents of nothing he has ever done, now does, or ever will do. He is all-wise as well as all-powerful. Man's wisdom grows out of the trials and errors of human experience; God's wisdom consists in the unqualified perfection of his infinite universe insight, and this divine foreknowledge effectively directs the creative free will.

The Universal Father never does anything that causes subsequent sorrow or regret, but the will creatures of the planning and making of his Creator personalities in the outlying universes, by their unfortunate choosing, sometimes occasion emotions of divine sorrow in the personalities of their Creator parents. But though the Father neither makes mistakes, harbors regrets, nor experiences sorrows, he is a being with a father's affection, and his heart is undoubtedly grieved when his children fail to attain the spiritual levels they are capable of reaching with the assistance which has been so freely provided by the spiritual-attainment plans and the mortal-ascension policies of the universes.

The infinite goodness of the Father is beyond the comprehension of the finite mind of time; hence must there always be afforded a contrast with comparative evil (not sin) for the effective exhibition of all phases of relative goodness. Perfection of divine goodness can be discerned by mortal imperfection of insight only because it stands in contrastive association with relative imperfection in the relationships of time and matter in the motions of space.

The character of God is infinitely superhuman; therefore must such a nature of divinity be personalized, as in the divine Sons, before it can even be faith-grasped by the finite mind of man.

4. THE REALIZATION OF GOD

God is the only stationary, self-contained, and changeless being in the whole universe of universes, having no outside, no beyond, no past, and no future. God is purposive energy (creative spirit) and absolute will, and these are self-existent and universal.

Since God is self-existent, he is absolutely independent. The very identity of God is inimical to change. "I, the Lord, change not." God is immutable; but not until you achieve Paradise status can you even begin to understand how God can pass from simplicity to complexity, from identity to variation, from quiescence to motion, from infinity to finitude, from the divine to the human, and from unity to duality and triunity. And God can thus modify the manifestations of his absoluteness because divine immutability does not imply immobility; God has will — he *is* will.

God is the being of absolute self-determination; there are no limits to his universe reactions save those which are self-imposed, and his freewill acts are conditioned only by those divine qualities and perfect attributes which inherently characterize his eternal nature. Therefore is God related to the universe as the being of final goodness plus a free will of creative infinity.

The Father-Absolute is the creator of the central and perfect universe and the Father of all other Creators. Personality, goodness, and numerous other characteristics, God shares with man and other beings, but infinity of will is his alone. God is limited in his creative acts only by the sentiments of his eternal nature and by the dictates of his infinite wisdom. God personally chooses only that which is infinitely perfect, hence the supernal perfection of the central universe; and while the Creator Sons fully share his divinity, even phases of his absoluteness, they are not altogether limited by that finality of wisdom which directs the Father's infinity of will. Hence, in the Michael order of sonship, creative free will becomes even more active, wholly divine and well-nigh ultimate, if not absolute. The Father is infinite and eternal, but to deny the possibility of his volitional self-limitation amounts to a denial of this very concept of his volitional absoluteness.

God's absoluteness pervades all seven levels of universe reality. And the whole of this absolute nature is subject to the relationship of the Creator to his universe creature family. Precision may characterize trinitarian justice in the universe of universes, but in all his vast family relationship with the creatures of time the God of universes is governed by *divine sentiment.* First and last — eternally — the infinite God is a *Father.* Of all the possible titles by which he might appropriately be known, I have been instructed to portray the God of all creation as the Universal Father.

In God the Father freewill performances are not ruled by power, nor are they guided by intellect alone; the divine personality is defined as consisting in spirit and manifesting himself to the universes as love. Therefore, in all his personal relations with the creature personalities of the universes, the First Source and Center is always and consistently a loving Father. God is a Father in the highest sense of the term. He is eternally motivated by the perfect idealism of divine love, and that tender nature finds its strongest expression and greatest satisfaction in loving and being loved.

In science, God is the First Cause; in religion, the universal and loving Father; in philosophy, the one being who exists by himself, not dependent on any other being for existence but beneficently conferring reality of existence on all things and upon all other beings. But it requires revelation to show that the First Cause of science and the self-existent Unity of philosophy are the God of religion, full of mercy and goodness and pledged to effect the eternal survival of his children on earth.

We crave the concept of the Infinite, but we worship the experience-idea of God, our anywhere and any-time capacity to grasp the personality and divinity factors of our highest concept of Deity.

The consciousness of a victorious human life on earth is born of that creature faith which dares to challenge each recurring episode of existence when confronted with the awful spectacle of human limitations, by the unfailing declaration: Even if I cannot do this, there lives in me one who can and will do it, a part of the Father-Absolute of the universe of universes. And that is "the victory which overcomes the world, even your faith."

5. ERRONEOUS IDEAS OF GOD

Religious tradition is the imperfectly preserved record of the experiences of the God-knowing men of past ages, but such records are untrustworthy as guides for religious living or as the source of true information about the Universal Father. Such ancient beliefs have been invariably altered by the fact that primitive man was a mythmaker.

One of the greatest sources of confusion on Urantia concerning the nature of God grows out of the failure of your sacred books clearly to distinguish between the personalities of the Paradise Trinity and between Paradise Deity and the local universe creators and administrators. During the past dispensations of partial understanding, your priests and prophets failed clearly to differentiate between Planetary Princes, System Sovereigns, Constellation Fathers, Creator Sons, Superuniverse Rulers, the Supreme Being, and the Universal Father. Many of the messages of subordinate personalities, such as Life Carriers and various orders of angels, have been, in your records, presented as coming from God himself. Urantian religious thought still confuses the associate personalities of Deity with the Universal Father himself, so that all are included under one appellation.

The people of Urantia continue to suffer from the influence of primitive concepts of God. The gods who go on a rampage in the storm; who shake the earth in their wrath and strike down men in their anger; who inflict their judgments of displeasure in times of famine and flood — these are the gods of primitive religion; they are not the Gods who live and rule the universes. Such concepts are a relic of the times when men supposed that the universe was under the guidance and domination of the whims of such imaginary gods. But mortal man is beginning to realize that he lives in a realm of comparative law and order as far as concerns the administrative policies and conduct of the Supreme Creators and the Supreme Controllers.

The barbarous idea of appeasing an angry God, of propitiating an offended Lord, of winning the favor of Deity through sacrifices and penance and even by the shedding of blood, represents a religion wholly puerile and primitive, a philosophy unworthy of an enlightened age of science and truth. Such beliefs are utterly repulsive to the celestial beings and the divine rulers who serve and reign in the universes. It is an affront to God to believe, hold, or teach that innocent blood must be shed in order to win his favor or to divert the fictitious divine wrath.

The ancients believed that "without the shedding of blood there could be no remission of sin." They had not found deliverance from the old and pagan idea that the Gods could not be appeased except by the sight of blood, though Moses did make a distinct advance when he forbade human sacrifices and substituted therefor the ceremonial sacrifice of animals.

The bestowal of a Paradise Son on your world was inherent in the situation of closing a planetary age; it was inescapable, and it was not made necessary for the purpose of winning the favor of God. This bestowal also happened to be the final personal act of a Creator Son in the long adventure of earning the experiential sovereignty of his universe. What a travesty upon the infinite character of God! this teaching that his fatherly heart in all its austere coldness and hardness was so untouched by the misfortunes and sorrows of his creatures that his tender mercies were not forthcoming until he saw his blameless Son bleeding and dying upon the cross of Calvary!

But the inhabitants of Urantia are to find deliverance from these ancient errors and pagan superstitions respecting the nature of the Universal Father. The revelation of the truth about God is appearing, and the human race is destined to know the Universal Father in all that beauty of character and loveliness of attributes so magnificently portrayed by the Creator Son who sojourned on Urantia as the Son of Man and the Son of God.

[Presented by a Divine Counselor of Uversa.]

Urantia 2025: A Revised Urantia Book

PAPER 5
GOD'S RELATION TO THE INDIVIDUAL

If the finite mind of man is unable to comprehend how so great and so majestic a God as the Universal Father can descend from his eternal abode in infinite perfection to fraternize with the individual human creature, then must such a finite intellect rest assurance of divine fellowship upon the truth of the fact that an actual fragment of the living God resides within the intellect of every normal-minded and morally conscious Urantia mortal. The indwelling Thought Adjusters are a part of the eternal Deity of the Paradise Father. Man does not have to go farther than his own inner experience of the soul's contemplation of this spiritual-reality presence to find God and attempt communion with him.

God has distributed the infinity of his eternal nature throughout the existential realities of his six absolute co-ordinates, but he may, at any time, make direct personal contact with any part or phase or kind of creation through the agency of his prepersonal fragments. And the eternal God has also reserved to himself the prerogative of bestowing personality upon the divine Creators and the living creatures of the universe of universes, while he has further reserved the prerogative of maintaining direct and parental contact with all these personal beings through the personality circuit.

1. THE APPROACH TO GOD

The inability of the finite creature to approach the infinite Father is inherent, not in the Father's aloofness, but in the finiteness and material limitations of created beings. The magnitude of the spiritual difference between the highest personality of universe existence and the lower groups of created intelligences is inconceivable. Were it possible for the lower orders of intelligence to be transported instantly into the presence of the Father himself, they would not know they were there. They would there be just as oblivious of the presence of the Universal Father as where they now are. There is a long, long road ahead of mortal man before he can consistently and within the realms of possibility ask for safe conduct into the Paradise presence of the Universal Father. Spiritually, man must be translated many times before he can attain a plane that will yield the spiritual vision which will enable him to see even any one of the Seven Master Spirits.

Our Father is not in hiding; he is not in arbitrary seclusion. He has mobilized the resources of divine wisdom in a never-ending effort to reveal himself to the children of his universal domains. There is an infinite grandeur and an inexpressible generosity connected with the majesty of his love which causes him to yearn for the association of every created being who can comprehend, love, or approach him; and it is, therefore, the limitations inherent in you, inseparable from your finite personality and material existence, that determine the time and place and circumstances in which you may achieve the goal of the journey of mortal ascension and stand in the presence of the Father at the center of all things.

Although the approach to the Paradise presence of the Father must await your attainment of the highest finite levels of spirit progression, you should rejoice in the recognition of the ever-present possibility of immediate communion with the bestowal spirit of the Father so intimately associated with your inner soul and your spiritualizing self.

The mortals of the realms of time and space may differ greatly in innate abilities and intellectual endowment, they may enjoy environments exceptionally favorable to social advancement and moral progress, or they may suffer from the lack of almost every human aid to culture and supposed advancement in the arts of civilization; but the possibilities for spiritual progress in the ascension career are equal to all; increasing levels of spiritual insight and cosmic meanings are attained quite independently of all such sociomoral differentials of the diversified material environments on the evolutionary worlds.

However Urantia mortals may differ in their intellectual, social, economic, and even moral opportunities and endowments, forget not that their spiritual endowment is uniform and unique. They all enjoy the same divine presence of the gift from the Father, and they are all equally privileged to seek intimate personal communion with this indwelling spirit of divine origin, while they may all equally choose to accept the uniform spiritual leading of these Mystery Monitors.

If mortal man is wholeheartedly spiritually motivated, unreservedly consecrated to the doing of the Father's will, then, since he is so certainly and so effectively spiritually endowed by the indwelling and divine Adjuster, there cannot fail to materialize in that individual's experience the sublime consciousness of knowing God and the supernal assurance of surviving for the purpose of finding God by the progressive experience of becoming more and more like him.

Man is spiritually indwelt by a surviving Thought Adjuster. If such a human mind is sincerely and spiritually motivated, if such a human soul desires to know God and become like him, honestly wants to do the Father's will, there exists no negative influence of mortal deprivation nor positive power of possible interference which can prevent such a divinely motivated soul from securely ascending to the portals of Paradise.

The Father desires all his creatures to be in personal communion with him. He has on Paradise a place to receive all those whose survival status and spiritual nature make possible such attainment. Therefore settle in your philosophy now and forever: To each of you and to all of us, God is approachable, the Father is attainable, the way is open; the forces of divine love and the ways and means of divine administration are all interlocked in an effort to facilitate the advancement of every worthy intelligence of every universe to the Paradise presence of the Universal Father.

The fact that vast time is involved in the attainment of God makes the presence and personality of the Infinite none the less real. Your ascension is a part of the circuit of the seven superuniverses, and though you swing around it countless times, you may expect, in spirit and in status, to be ever swinging inward. You can depend upon being translated from sphere to sphere, from the outer circuits ever nearer the inner center, and some day, doubt not, you shall stand in the divine and central presence and see him, figuratively speaking, face to face. It is a question of the attainment of actual and literal spiritual levels; and these spiritual levels are attainable by any being who has been indwelt by a Mystery Monitor, and who has subsequently eternally fused with that Thought Adjuster.

The Father is not in spiritual hiding, but so many of his creatures have hidden themselves away in the mists of their own willful decisions and for the time being have separated themselves from the communion of his spirit and the spirit of his Son by the choosing of their own perverse ways and by the indulgence of the self-assertiveness of their intolerant minds and unspiritual natures.

Mortal man may draw near God and may repeatedly forsake the divine will so long as the power of choice remains. Man's final doom is not sealed until he has lost the power to choose the Father's will. There is never a closure of the Father's heart to the need and the petition of his children. Only do his offspring close their hearts forever to the Father's drawing power when they finally and forever lose the desire to do his divine will — to know him and to be like him. Likewise is man's eternal destiny assured when Adjuster fusion proclaims to the universe that such an ascender has made the final and irrevocable choice to live the Father's will.

The great God makes direct contact with mortal man and gives a part of his infinite and eternal and incomprehensible self to live and dwell within him. God has embarked upon the eternal adventure with man. If you yield to the leadings of the spiritual forces in you and around you, you cannot fail to attain the high destiny established by a loving God as the universe goal of his ascendant creatures from the evolutionary worlds of space.

2. THE PRESENCE OF GOD

The physical presence of the Infinite is the reality of the material universe. The mind presence of Deity must be determined by the depth of individual intellectual experience and by the evolutionary personality level. The spiritual presence of Divinity must of necessity be differential in the universe. It is determined by the spiritual capacity of receptivity and by the degree of the consecration of the creature's will to the doing of the divine will.

God lives in every one of his spirit-born sons. The Paradise Sons always have access to the presence of God, "the right hand of the Father," and all of his creature personalities have access to the "bosom of the Father." This refers to the personality circuit, whenever, wherever, and however contacted, or otherwise entails personal, self-conscious contact and communion with the Universal Father, whether at the central abode or at some other designated place, as on one of the seven sacred spheres of Paradise.

The divine presence cannot, however, be discovered anywhere in nature or even in the lives of God-knowing mortals so fully and so certainly as in your attempted communion with the indwelling Mystery Monitor, the Paradise Thought Adjuster. What a mistake to dream of God far off in the skies when the spirit of the Universal Father lives within your own mind!

It is because of this God fragment that indwells you that you can hope, as you progress in harmonizing with the Adjuster's spiritual leadings, more fully to discern the presence and transforming power of those other spiritual influences that surround you and impinge upon you but do not function as an integral part of you. The fact that you are not intellectually conscious of close and intimate contact with the indwelling Adjuster does not in the least disprove such an exalted experience. The proof of fraternity with the divine Adjuster consists wholly in the nature and extent of the fruits of the spirit which are yielded in the life experience of the individual believer. "By their fruits you shall know them."

It is exceedingly difficult for the meagerly spiritualized, material mind of mortal man to experience marked consciousness of the spirit activities of such divine entities as the Paradise Adjusters. As the soul of joint mind and Adjuster creation becomes increasingly existent, there also evolves a new phase of soul consciousness which is capable of experiencing the presence, and of recognizing the spirit leadings and other supermaterial activities, of the Mystery Monitors.

The entire experience of Adjuster communion is one involving moral status, mental motivation, and spiritual experience. The self-realization of such an achievement is mainly, though not exclusively, limited to the realms of soul consciousness, but the proofs are forthcoming and abundant in the manifestation of the fruits of the spirit in the lives of all such inner-spirit contactors.

3. TRUE WORSHIP

Though the Paradise Deities, from the universe standpoint, are as one, in their spiritual relations with such beings as inhabit Urantia they are also three distinct and separate persons. There is a difference between the Godheads in the matter of personal appeals, communion, and other intimate relations. In the highest sense, we worship the Universal Father and him only. True, we can and do worship the Father as he is manifested in his Creator Sons, but it is the Father, directly or indirectly, who is worshiped and adored.

Supplications of all kinds belong to the realm of the Eternal Son and the Son's spiritual organization. Prayers, all formal communications, everything except adoration and worship of the Universal Father, are matters that concern a local universe; they do not ordinarily proceed out of the realm of the jurisdiction of a Creator Son. But worship is undoubtedly encircuited and dispatched to the person of the Creator by the function of the Father's personality circuit. We further believe that such registry of the homage of an Adjuster-indwelt creature is facilitated by the Father's spirit presence. There exists a tremendous amount of evidence to substantiate such a belief, and I know that all orders of Father fragments are empowered to register the bona fide adoration of their subjects acceptably in the presence of the Universal Father. The Adjusters undoubtedly also utilize direct prepersonal channels of communication with God, and they are likewise able to utilize the spirit-gravity circuits of the Eternal Son.

Worship is for its own sake; prayer embodies a self- or creature-interest element; that is the great difference between worship and prayer. There is absolutely no self-request or other element of personal interest in true worship; we simply worship God for what we comprehend him to be.

Worship asks nothing and expects nothing for the worshiper. We do not worship the Father because of anything we may derive from such veneration; we render such devotion and engage in such worship as a natural and spontaneous reaction to the recognition of the Father's matchless personality and because of his lovable nature and adorable attributes.

The moment the element of self-interest intrudes upon worship, that instant devotion translates from worship to prayer and more appropriately should be directed to the person of the Eternal Son or the Creator Son. But in practical religious experience there exists no reason why prayer should not be addressed to God the Father as a part of true worship.

When you deal with the practical affairs of your daily life, you are in the hands of the spirit personalities having origin in the Third Source and Center; you are co-operating with the agencies of the Conjoint Actor. And so it is: You worship God; pray to, and commune with, the Son; and work out the details of your earthly sojourn in connection with the intelligences of the Infinite Spirit operating on your world and throughout your universe.

The Creator or Sovereign Sons who preside over the destinies of the local universes stand in the place of both the Universal Father and the Eternal Son of Paradise. These Universe Sons receive, in the name of the Father, the adoration of worship and give ear to the pleas of their petitioning subjects throughout their respective creations. To the children of a local universe a Michael Son is, to all practical intents and purposes, God. He is the local universe personification of the Universal Father and the Eternal Son. The Infinite Spirit maintains personal contact with the children of these realms through the Universe Spirits, the administrative and creative associates of the Paradise Creator Sons.

Sincere worship connotes the mobilization of all the powers of the human personality under the dominance of the evolving soul and subject to the divine directionization of the associated Thought Adjuster. The mind of material limitations can never become highly conscious of the real significance of true worship. Man's realization of the reality of the worship experience is chiefly determined by the developmental status of his evolving immortal soul. The spiritual growth of the soul takes place wholly independently of the intellectual self-consciousness.

The worship experience consists in the sublime attempt of the betrothed Adjuster to communicate to the divine Father the inexpressible longings and the unutterable aspirations of the human soul — the conjoint creation of the God-seeking mortal mind and the God-revealing immortal Adjuster. Worship is, therefore, the act of the material mind's assenting to the attempt of its spiritualizing self, under the guidance of the associated spirit, to communicate with God as a faith son of the Universal Father. The mortal mind consents to worship; the immortal soul craves and initiates worship; the divine Adjuster presence conducts such worship in behalf of the mortal mind and the evolving immortal soul. True worship, in the last analysis, becomes an experience realized on four cosmic levels: the intellectual, the morontial, the spiritual, and the personal — the consciousness of mind, soul, and spirit, and their unification in personality.

4. GOD IN RELIGION

The morality of the religions of evolution drives men forward in the God quest by the motive power of fear. The religions of revelation allure men to seek for a God of love because they crave to become like him. But religion is not merely a passive feeling of "absolute dependence" and "surety of survival"; it is a living and dynamic experience of divinity attainment predicated on humanity service.

The great and immediate service of true religion is the establishment of an enduring unity in human experience, a lasting peace and a profound assurance. With primitive man, even polytheism is a relative unification of the evolving concept of Deity; polytheism is monotheism in the making. Sooner or later, God is destined to be comprehended as the reality of values, the substance of meanings, and the life of truth.

God is not only the determiner of destiny; he is man's eternal destination. All nonreligious human activities seek to bend the universe to the distorting service of self; the truly religious individual seeks to identify the self with the universe and then to dedicate the activities of this unified self to the service of the universe family of fellow beings, human and superhuman.

The domains of philosophy and art intervene between the nonreligious and the religious activities of the human self. Through art and philosophy the material-minded man is inveigled into the contemplation of the spiritual realities and universe values of eternal meanings.

All religions teach the worship of Deity and some doctrine of human salvation. The Buddhist religion promises salvation from suffering, unending peace; the Jewish religion promises salvation from difficulties, prosperity predicated on righteousness; the Greek religion promised salvation from disharmony, ugliness, by the realization of beauty; Christianity promises salvation from sin, sanctity; Mohammedanism provides deliverance from the rigorous moral standards of Judaism and Christianity. The religion of Jesus is salvation from self, deliverance from the evils of creature isolation in time and in eternity.

The Hebrews based their religion on goodness; the Greeks on beauty; both religions sought truth. Jesus revealed a God of love, and love is all-embracing of truth, beauty, and goodness.

The Zoroastrians had a religion of morals; the Hindus a religion of metaphysics; the Confucianists a religion of ethics. Jesus lived a religion of service. All these religions are of value in that they are valid approaches to the religion of Jesus. Religion is destined to become the reality of the spiritual unification of all that is good, beautiful, and true in human experience.

The Greek religion had a watchword "Know yourself"; the Hebrews centered their teaching on "Know your God"; the Christians preach a gospel aimed at a "knowledge of the Lord Jesus Christ"; Jesus proclaimed the good news of "knowing God, and yourself as a son of God." These differing concepts of the purpose of religion determine the individual's attitude in various life situations and foreshadow the depth of worship and the nature of his personal habits of prayer. The spiritual status of any religion may be determined by the nature of its prayers.

The concept of a semihuman and jealous God is an inevitable transition between polytheism and sublime monotheism. An exalted anthropomorphism is the highest attainment level of purely evolutionary religion. Christianity has elevated the concept of anthropomorphism from the ideal of the human to the transcendent and divine concept of the person of the glorified

Christ. And this is the highest anthropomorphism that man can ever conceive.

The Christian concept of God is an attempt to combine three separate teachings:

1. *The Hebrew concept* — God as a vindicator of moral values, a righteous God.
2. *The Greek concept* — God as a unifier, a God of wisdom.
3. *Jesus' concept* — God as a living friend, a loving Father, the divine presence.

It must therefore be evident that composite Christian theology encounters great difficulty in attaining consistency. This difficulty is further aggravated by the fact that the doctrines of early Christianity were generally based on the personal religious experience of three different persons: Philo of Alexandria, Jesus of Nazareth, and Paul of Tarsus.

In the study of the religious life of Jesus, view him positively. Think not so much of his sinlessness as of his righteousness, his loving service. Jesus upstepped the passive love disclosed in the Hebrew concept of the heavenly Father to the higher active and creature-loving affection of a God who is the Father of every individual, even of the wrongdoer.

5. THE CONSCIOUSNESS OF GOD

Morality has its origin in the reason of self-consciousness; it is superanimal but wholly evolutionary. Human evolution embraces in its unfolding all endowments antecedent to the bestowal of the Adjusters and to the pouring out of the Spirit of Truth. But the attainment of levels of morality does not deliver man from the real struggles of mortal living. Man's physical environment entails the battle for existence; the social surroundings necessitate ethical adjustments; the moral situations require the making of choices in the highest realms of reason; the spiritual experience (having realized God) demands that man find him and sincerely strive to be like him.

Religion is not grounded in the facts of science, the obligations of society, the assumptions of philosophy, or the implied duties of morality. Religion is an independent realm of human response to life situations and is unfailingly exhibited at all stages of human development which are postmoral. Religion may permeate all four levels of the realization of values and the enjoyment of universe fellowship: the physical or material level of self-preservation; the social or emotional level of fellowship; the moral or duty level of reason; the spiritual level of the consciousness of universe fellowship through divine worship.

The fact-seeking scientist conceives of God as the First Cause, a God of force. The emotional artist sees God as the ideal of beauty, a God of aesthetics. The reasoning philosopher is sometimes inclined to posit a God of universal unity, even a pantheistic Deity. The religionist of faith believes in a God who fosters survival, the Father in heaven, the God of love.

Moral conduct is always an antecedent of evolved religion and a part of even revealed religion, but never the whole of religious experience. Social service is the result of moral thinking and religious living. Morality does not biologically lead to the higher spiritual levels of religious experience. The adoration of the abstract beautiful is not the worship of God; neither is exaltation of nature nor the reverence of unity the worship of God.

Evolutionary religion is the mother of the science, art, and philosophy which elevated man to the level of receptivity to revealed religion, including the bestowal of Adjusters and the coming of the Spirit of Truth. The evolutionary picture of human existence begins and ends with religion, albeit very different qualities of religion, one evolutional and biological, the other revelational and periodical. And so, while religion is normal and natural to man, it is also optional. Man does not have to be religious against his will.

Religious experience, being essentially spiritual, can never be fully understood by the material mind; hence the function of theology, the psychology of religion. The essential doctrine of the human realization of God creates a paradox in finite comprehension. It is well-nigh impossible for human logic and finite reason to harmonize the concept of divine immanence, God within and a part of every individual, with the idea of God's transcendence, the divine domination of the universe of universes. These two essential concepts of Deity must be unified in the faith-grasp of the concept of the transcendence of a personal God and in the realization of the indwelling presence of a fragment of that God in order to justify intelligent worship and validate the hope of personality survival. The difficulties and paradoxes of religion are inherent in the fact that the realities of religion are utterly beyond the mortal capacity for intellectual comprehension.

Mortal man secures three great satisfactions from religious experience, even in the days of his temporal sojourn on earth:

1. *Intellectually* he acquires the satisfactions of a more unified human consciousness.
2. *Philosophically* he enjoys the substantiation of his ideals of moral values.
3. *Spiritually* he thrives in the experience of divine companionship, in the spiritual satisfactions of true worship.

God-consciousness, as it is experienced by an evolving mortal of the realms, must consist of three varying factors, three differential levels of reality realization. There is first the mind consciousness — the comprehension of the *idea* of God. Then follows the soul consciousness — the realization of the *ideal* of God. Last, dawns the spirit consciousness — the realization of the *spirit reality* of God. By the unification of these factors of the divine realization, no matter how incomplete, the mortal personality at all times overspreads all conscious levels with a realization of the *personality* of God. In those mortals who have attained the Corps of the Finality all this will in time lead to the realization of the *supremacy* of God and may subsequently eventuate in the realization of the *ultimacy* of God, some phase of the absonite superconsciousness of the Paradise Father.

The experience of God-consciousness remains the same from generation to generation, but with each advancing epoch in human knowledge the philosophic concept and the theologic definitions of God must change. God-knowingness, religious consciousness, is a universe reality, but no matter how valid (real) religious experience is, it must be willing to subject itself to intelligent criticism and reasonable philosophic interpretation; it must not seek to be a thing apart in the totality of human experience.

Eternal survival of personality is wholly dependent on the choosing of the mortal mind, whose decisions determine the survival potential of the immortal soul. When the mind believes God and the soul knows God, and when, with the fostering Adjuster, they all *desire* God, then is survival assured. Limitations of intellect, curtailment of education, deprivation of culture, impoverishment of social status, even inferiority of the human standards of morality resulting from the unfortunate lack of educational, cultural, and social advantages, cannot invalidate the presence of the divine spirit in such unfortunate and humanly handicapped but believing individuals. The indwelling of the Mystery Monitor constitutes the inception and insures the possibility of the potential of growth and survival of the immortal soul.

The ability of mortal parents to procreate is not predicated on their educational, cultural, social, or economic status. The union of the parental factors under natural conditions is quite sufficient to initiate offspring. A human mind discerning right and wrong and possessing the capacity to worship God, in union with a divine Adjuster, is all that is required in that mortal to initiate and foster the production of his immortal soul of survival qualities if such a spirit-endowed individual seeks God and sincerely desires to become like him, honestly elects to do the will of the Father in heaven.

6. THE GOD OF PERSONALITY

The Universal Father is the God of personalities. The domain of universe personality, from the lowest mortal and material creature of personality status to the highest persons of creator dignity and divine status, has its center and circumference in the Universal Father. God the Father is the bestower and the conservator of every personality. And the Paradise Father is likewise the destiny of all those finite personalities who wholeheartedly choose to do the divine will, those who love God and long to be like him.

Personality is one of the unsolved mysteries of the universes. We are able to form adequate concepts of the factors entering into the make-up of various orders and levels of personality, but we do not fully comprehend the real nature of the personality itself. We clearly perceive the numerous factors which, when put together, constitute the vehicle for human personality, but we do not fully comprehend the nature and significance of such a finite personality.

Personality is potential in all creatures who possess a mind endowment ranging from the minimum of self-consciousness to the maximum of God-consciousness. But mind endowment alone is not personality, neither is spirit nor physical energy. Personality is that quality and value in cosmic reality which is exclusively bestowed by God the Father upon these living systems of the associated and co-ordinated energies of matter, mind, and spirit. Neither is personality a progressive achievement. Personality may be material or spiritual, but there either is personality or there is no personality. The other-than-personal never attains the level of the personal except by the direct act of the Paradise Father.

The bestowal of personality is the exclusive function of the Universal Father, the personalization of the living energy systems which he endows with the attributes of relative creative consciousness and the freewill control thereof. There is no personality apart from God the Father, and no personality exists except for God the Father. The fundamental attributes of human selfhood, as well as the absolute Adjuster nucleus of the human personality, are the bestowals of the Universal Father, acting in his exclusively personal domain of cosmic ministry.

The Adjusters of prepersonal status indwell numerous types of mortal creatures, thus insuring that these same beings may survive mortal death to personalize as morontia creatures with the potential of ultimate spirit attainment. For, when such a creature mind of personality endowment is indwelt by a fragment of the spirit of the eternal God, the prepersonal bestowal of the personal Father, then does this finite personality possess the potential of the divine and the eternal and aspire to a destiny akin to the Ultimate, even reaching out for a realization of the Absolute.

Capacity for divine personality is inherent in the prepersonal Adjuster; capacity for human personality is potential in the cosmic-mind endowment of the human being. But the experiential personality of mortal man is not observable as an active and functional reality until after the material life vehicle of the mortal creature has been touched by the liberating divinity of the Universal Father, being thus launched upon the seas of experience as a self-conscious and a (relatively) self-determinative and self-creative personality. The material self is truly and *unqualifiedly personal.*

The material self has personality and identity, temporal identity; the prepersonal spirit Adjuster also has identity, eternal identity. This material personality and this spirit prepersonality are capable of so uniting their creative attributes as to bring into existence the surviving identity of the immortal soul.

Having thus provided for the growth of the immortal soul and having liberated man's inner self from the fetters of absolute dependence on antecedent causation, the Father stands aside. Now, man having thus been liberated from the fetters of causation response, at least as pertains to eternal destiny, and provision having been made for the growth of the immortal self, the soul, it remains for man himself to will the creation or to inhibit the creation of this surviving and eternal self which is his for the choosing. No other being, force, creator, or agency in all the wide universe of universes can interfere to any degree with the absolute sovereignty of the mortal free will, as it operates within the realms of choice, regarding the eternal destiny of the personality of the choosing mortal. As pertains to eternal survival, God has decreed the sovereignty of the material and mortal will, and that decree is absolute.

The bestowal of creature personality confers relative liberation from slavish response to antecedent causation, and the personalities of all such moral beings, evolutionary or otherwise, are centered in the personality of the Universal Father. They are ever drawn towards his Paradise presence by that kinship of being which constitutes the vast and universal family circle and fraternal circuit of the eternal God. There is a kinship of divine spontaneity in all personality.

The personality circuit of the universe of universes is centered in the person of the Universal Father, and the Paradise Father is personally conscious of, and in personal touch with, all personalities of all levels of self-conscious existence. And this personality consciousness of all creation exists independently of the mission of the Thought Adjusters.

As all gravity is circuited in the Isle of Paradise, as all mind is circuited in the Conjoint Actor and all spirit in the Eternal Son, so is all personality circuited in the personal presence of the Universal Father, and this circuit unerringly transmits the worship of all personalities to the Original and Eternal Personality.

Concerning those personalities who are not Adjuster indwelt: The attribute of choice-liberty is also bestowed by the Universal Father, and such persons are likewise embraced in the great circuit of divine love, the personality circuit of the Universal Father. God provides for the sovereign choice of all true personalities. No personal creature can be coerced into the eternal adventure; the portal of eternity opens only in response to the freewill choice of the freewill sons of the God of free will.

And this represents my efforts to present the relation of the living God to the children of time. And when all is said and done, I can do nothing more helpful than to reiterate that God is your universe Father, and that you are all his planetary children.

[This is the fifth and last of the series presenting the narrative of the Universal Father by a Divine Counselor of Uversa.]

PAPER 6
THE ETERNAL SON

THE ETERNAL SON is the perfect and final expression of the "first" personal and absolute concept of the Universal Father. Accordingly, whenever and however the Father personally and absolutely expresses himself, he does so through his Eternal Son, who ever has been, now is, and ever will be, the living and divine Word. And this Eternal Son is residential at the center of all things, in association with, and immediately enshrouding the personal presence of, the Eternal and Universal Father.

We speak of God's "first" thought and allude to an impossible time origin of the Eternal Son for the purpose of gaining access to the thought channels of the human intellect. Such distortions of language represent our best efforts at contact-compromise with the time-bound minds of mortal creatures. In the sequential sense the Universal Father never could have had a first thought, nor could the Eternal Son ever have had a beginning. But I was instructed to portray the realities of eternity to the time-limited minds of mortals by such symbols of thought and to designate the relationships of eternity by such time concepts of sequentiality.

The Eternal Son is the spiritual personalization of the Paradise Father's universal and infinite concept of divine reality, unqualified spirit, and absolute personality. And thereby does the Son constitute the divine revelation of the creator identity of the Universal Father. The perfect personality of the

Son discloses that the Father is actually the eternal and universal source of all the meanings and values of the spiritual, the volitional, the purposeful, and the personal.

In an effort to enable the finite mind of time to form some sequential concept of the relationships of the eternal and infinite beings of the Paradise Trinity, we utilize such license of conception as to refer to the "Father's first personal, universal, and infinite concept." It is impossible for me to convey to the human mind any adequate idea of the eternal relations of the Deities; therefore do I employ such terms as will afford the finite mind something of an idea of the relationship of these eternal beings in the subsequent eras of time. We believe the Son sprang from the Father; we are taught that both are unqualifiedly eternal. It is apparent, therefore, that no time creature can ever fully comprehend this mystery of a Son who is derived from the Father, and yet who is co-ordinately eternal with the Father himself.

1. IDENTITY OF THE ETERNAL SON

The Eternal Son is the original and only-begotten Son of God. He is God the Son, the Second Person of Deity and the associate creator of all things. As the Father is the First Great Source and Center, so the Eternal Son is the Second Great Source and Center.

The Eternal Son is the spiritual center and the divine administrator of the spiritual government of the universe of universes. The Universal Father is first a creator and then a controller; the Eternal Son is first a cocreator and then a *spiritual administrator*. "God is spirit," and the Son is a personal revelation of that spirit. The First Source and Center is the Volitional Absolute; the Second Source and Center is the Personality Absolute.

The Universal Father never personally functions as a creator except in conjunction with the Son or with the co-ordinate action of the Son. Had the New Testament writer referred to the Eternal Son, he would have uttered the truth when he wrote: "In the beginning was the Word, and the Word was with God, and the Word was God. All things were made by him, and without him was not anything made that was made."

When a Son of the Eternal Son appeared on Urantia, those who fraternized with this divine being in human form alluded to him as "He who was from the beginning, whom we have heard, whom we have seen with our eyes, whom we have looked upon, and our hands have handled, even the Word of life." And this bestowal Son came forth from the Father just as truly as did the Original Son, as is suggested in one of his earthly prayers: "And now, O my Father, glorify me with your own self, with the glory which I had with you before this world was."

The Eternal Son is known by different names in various universes. In the central universe he is known as the Co-ordinate Source, the Cocreator, and the Associate Absolute. On Uversa, the headquarters of the superuniverse, we designate the Son as the Co-ordinate Spirit Center and as the Eternal Spirit Administrator. On Salvington, the headquarters of your local universe, this Son is of record as the Second Eternal Source and Center. The Melchizedeks speak of him as the Son of Sons. On your world, but not in your system of inhabited spheres, this Original Son has been confused with a co-ordinate Creator Son, Michael of Nebadon, who bestowed himself upon the mortal races of Urantia.

Although any of the Paradise Sons may fittingly be called Sons of God, we are in the habit of reserving the designation "the Eternal Son" for this Original Son, the Second Source and Center, cocreator with the Universal Father of the central universe of power and perfection and cocreator of all other divine Sons who spring from the infinite Deities.

2. NATURE OF THE ETERNAL SON

The Eternal Son is just as changeless and infinitely dependable as the Universal Father. He is also just as spiritual as the Father, just as truly an unlimited spirit. To you of lowly origin the Son would appear to be more personal since he is one step nearer you in approachability than is the Universal Father.

The Eternal Son is the eternal Word of God. He is wholly like the Father; in fact, the Eternal Son is God the Father personally manifest to the universe of universes. And thus it was and is and forever will be true of the Eternal Son and of all the co-ordinate Creator Sons: "He who has seen the Son has seen the Father."

In nature the Son is wholly like the spirit Father. When we worship the Universal Father, actually we at the same time worship God the Son and God the Spirit. God the Son is just as divinely real and eternal in nature as God the Father.

The Son not only possesses all the Father's infinite and transcendent righteousness, but the Son is also reflective of all the Father's holiness of character. The Son shares the Father's perfection and jointly shares the responsibility of aiding all creatures of imperfection in their spiritual efforts to attain divine perfection.

The Eternal Son possesses all the Father's character of divinity and attributes of spirituality. The Son is the fullness of God's absoluteness in personality and spirit, and these qualities the Son reveals in his personal management of the spiritual government of the universe of universes.

God is, indeed, a universal spirit; God is spirit; and this spirit nature of the Father is focalized and personalized in the Deity of the Eternal Son. In the Son all spiritual characteristics are apparently greatly enhanced by differentiation from the universality of the First Source and Center. And as the Father shares his spirit nature with the Son, so do they together just as fully and unreservedly share the divine spirit with the Conjoint Actor, the Infinite Spirit.

In the love of truth and in the creation of beauty the Father and the Son are equal except that the Son appears to devote himself more to the realization of the exclusively spiritual beauty of universal values.

In divine goodness I discern no difference between the Father and the Son. The Father loves his universe children as a father; the Eternal Son looks upon all creatures both as father and as brother.

3. MINISTRY OF THE FATHER'S LOVE

The Son shares the justice and righteousness of the Trinity but overshadows these divinity traits by the infinite personalization of the Father's love and mercy; the Son is the revelation of divine love to the universes. As God is love, so the Son is mercy. The Son cannot love more than the Father, but he can show mercy to creatures in one additional way, for he not only is a primal creator like the Father, but he is also the Eternal Son of that same

Father, thereby sharing in the sonship experience of all other sons of the Universal Father.

The Eternal Son is the great mercy minister to all creation. Mercy is the essence of the Son's spiritual character. The mandates of the Eternal Son, as they go forth over the spirit circuits of the Second Source and Center, are keyed in tones of mercy.

To comprehend the love of the Eternal Son, you must first perceive its divine source, the Father, who *is* love, and then behold the unfolding of this infinite affection in the far-flung ministry of the Infinite Spirit and his almost limitless host of ministering personalities.

The ministry of the Eternal Son is devoted to the revelation of the God of love to the universe of universes. This divine Son is not engaged in the ignoble task of trying to persuade his gracious Father to love his lowly creatures and to show mercy to the wrongdoers of time. How wrong to envisage the Eternal Son as appealing to the Universal Father to show mercy to his lowly creatures on the material worlds of space! Such concepts of God are crude and grotesque. Rather should you realize that all the merciful ministrations of the Sons of God are a direct revelation of the Father's heart of universal love and infinite compassion. The Father's love is the real and eternal source of the Son's mercy.

God is love, the Son is mercy. Mercy is applied love, the Father's love in action in the person of his Eternal Son. The love of this universal Son is likewise universal. As love is comprehended on a sex planet, the love of God is more comparable to the love of a father, while the love of the Eternal Son is more like the affection of a mother. Crude, indeed, are such illustrations, but I employ them in the hope of conveying to the human mind the thought that there is a difference, not in divine content but in quality and technique of expression, between the love of the Father and the love of the Son.

4. ATTRIBUTES OF THE ETERNAL SON

The Eternal Son motivates the spirit level of cosmic reality; the spiritual power of the Son is absolute in relation to all universe actualities. He exercises perfect control over the interassociation of all undifferentiated spirit energy and over all actualized spirit reality through his absolute grasp of spirit gravity. All pure unfragmented spirit and all spiritual beings and values are responsive to the infinite drawing power of the primal Son of Paradise. And if the eternal future should witness the appearance of an unlimited universe, the spirit gravity and the spirit power of the Original Son will be found wholly adequate for the spiritual control and effective administration of such a boundless creation.

The Son is omnipotent only in the spiritual realm. In the eternal economy of universe administration, wasteful and needless repetition of function is never encountered; the Deities are not given to useless duplication of universe ministry.

The omnipresence of the Original Son constitutes the spiritual unity of the universe of universes. The spiritual cohesion of all creation rests upon the everywhere active presence of the divine spirit of the Eternal Son. When we conceive of the Father's spiritual presence, we find it difficult to differentiate it in our thinking from the spiritual presence of the Eternal Son. The spirit of the Father is eternally resident in the spirit of the Son.

The Father must be spiritually omnipresent, but such omnipresence appears to be inseparable from the everywhere spirit activities of the Eternal Son. We do, however, believe that in all situations of Father-Son presence of a dual spiritual nature the spirit of the Son is co-ordinate with the spirit of the Father.

In his contact with personality, the Father acts in the personality circuit. In his personal and detectable contact with spiritual creation, he appears in the fragments of the totality of his Deity, and these Father fragments have a solitary, unique, and exclusive function wherever and whenever they appear in the universes. In all such situations the spirit of the Son is co-ordinate with the spiritual function of the fragmented presence of the Universal Father.

Spiritually the Eternal Son is omnipresent. The spirit of the Eternal Son is most certainly with you and around you, but not within you and a part of you like the Mystery Monitor. The indwelling Father fragment adjusts the human mind to progressively divine attitudes, whereupon such an ascending mind becomes increasingly responsive to the spiritual drawing power of the all-powerful spirit-gravity circuit of the Second Source and Center.

The Original Son is universally and spiritually self-conscious. In wisdom the Son is the full equal of the Father. In the realms of knowledge, omniscience, we cannot distinguish between the First and Second Sources; like the Father, the Son knows all; he is never surprised by any universe event; he comprehends the end from the beginning.

The Father and the Son really know the number and whereabouts of all the spirits and spiritualized beings in the universe of universes. Not only does the Son know all things by virtue of his own omnipresent spirit, but the Son, equally with the Father and the Conjoint Actor, is fully cognizant of the vast reflectivity intelligence of the Supreme Being, which intelligence is at all times aware of all things that transpire on all the worlds of the seven superuniverses. And there are other ways in which the Paradise Son is omniscient.

The Eternal Son, as a loving, merciful, and ministering spiritual personality, is wholly and infinitely equal with the Universal Father, while in all those merciful and affectionate personal contacts with the ascendant beings of the lower realms the Eternal Son is just as kind and considerate, just as patient and long-suffering, as are his Paradise Sons in the local universes who so frequently bestow themselves upon the evolutionary worlds of time.

It is needless further to expatiate on the attributes of the Eternal Son. With the exceptions noted, it is only necessary to study the spiritual attributes of God the Father to understand and correctly evaluate the attributes of God the Son.

5. LIMITATIONS OF THE ETERNAL SON

The Eternal Son does not personally function in the physical domains, nor does he function, except through the Conjoint Actor, in the levels of mind ministry to creature beings. But these qualifications do not in any manner otherwise limit the Eternal Son in the full and free exercise of all the divine attributes of *spiritual* omniscience, omnipresence, and omnipotence.

The Eternal Son does not personally pervade the potentials of spirit inherent in the infinity of the Deity Absolute, but as these potentials become actual, they come within the all-powerful grasp of the spirit-gravity circuit of the Son.

Personality is the exclusive gift of the Universal Father. The Eternal Son derives personality from the Father, but he does not, without the Father, bestow personality. The Son gives origin to a vast spirit host, but such derivations are not personalities. When the Son creates personality, he does so in conjunction with the Father or with the Conjoint Creator, who may act for the Father in such relationships. The Eternal Son is thus a cocreator of personalities, but he bestows personality upon no being and of himself, alone, never creates personal beings. This limitation of action does not, however, deprive the Son of the ability to create any or all types of other-than-personal reality.

The Eternal Son is limited in transmittal of creator prerogatives. The Father, in eternalizing the Original Son, bestowed upon him the power and privilege of subsequently joining with the Father in the divine act of producing additional Sons possessing creative attributes, and this they have done and now do. But when these co-ordinate Sons have been produced, the prerogatives of creatorship are apparently not further transmissible. The Eternal Son transmits creatorship powers only to the first or direct personalization. Therefore, when the Father and the Son unite to personalize a Creator Son, they achieve their purpose; but the Creator Son thus brought into existence is never able to transmit or delegate the prerogatives of creatorship to the various orders of Sons which he may subsequently create, notwithstanding that, in the highest local universe Sons, there does appear a very limited reflection of the creative attributes of a Creator Son.

The Eternal Son, as an infinite and exclusively personal being, cannot fragmentize his nature, cannot distribute and bestow individualized portions of his selfhood upon other entities or persons as do the Universal Father and the Infinite Spirit. But the Son can and does bestow himself as an unlimited spirit to bathe all creation and unceasingly draw all spirit personalities and spiritual realities to himself.

Ever remember, the Eternal Son is the personal portrayal of the spirit Father to all creation. The Son is personal and nothing but personal in the Deity sense; such a divine and absolute personality cannot be disintegrated or fragmentized. God the Father and God the Spirit are truly personal, but they are also everything else in addition to being such Deity personalities.

Though the Eternal Son cannot personally participate in the bestowal of the Thought Adjusters, he did sit in council with the Universal Father in the eternal past, approving the plan and pledging endless co-operation, when the Father, in projecting the bestowal of the Thought Adjusters, proposed to the Son, "Let us make mortal man in our own image." And as the spirit fragment of the Father dwells within you, so does the spirit presence of the Son envelop you, while these two forever work as one for your spiritual advancement.

6. THE SPIRIT MIND

The Eternal Son is spirit and has mind, but not a mind or a spirit which mortal mind can comprehend. Mortal man perceives mind on the finite, cosmic, material, and personal levels. Man also observes mind phenomena in living organisms functioning on the subpersonal (animal) level, but it is difficult for him to grasp the nature of mind when associated with supermaterial beings and as a part of exclusive spirit personalities. Mind must, however, be differently defined when it refers to the spirit level of existence, and when it is used to denote spirit functions of intelligence. That kind of mind which is directly allied with spirit is comparable neither to that mind which co-ordinates spirit and matter nor to that mind which is allied only with matter.

Spirit is ever conscious, minded, and possessed of varied phases of identity. Without mind in some phase there would be no spiritual consciousness in the fraternity of spirit beings. The equivalent of mind, the ability to know and be known, is indigenous to Deity. Deity may be personal, prepersonal, superpersonal, or impersonal, but Deity is never mindless, that is, never without the ability at least to communicate with similar entities, beings, or personalities.

The mind of the Eternal Son is like that of the Father but unlike any other mind in the universe, and with the mind of the Father it is ancestor to the diverse and far-flung minds of the Conjoint Creator. The mind of the

Father and the Son, that intellect which is ancestral to the absolute mind of the Third Source and Center, is perhaps best illustrated in the premind of a Thought Adjuster, for, though these Father fragments are entirely outside of the mind circuits of the Conjoint Actor, they have some form of premind; they know as they are known; they enjoy the equivalent of human thinking.

The Eternal Son is wholly spiritual; man is very nearly entirely material; therefore much pertaining to the spirit personality of the Eternal Son, to his seven spiritual spheres encircling Paradise and to the nature of the impersonal creations of the Paradise Son, will have to await your attainment of spirit status following your completion of the morontia ascension of the local universe of Nebadon. And then, as you pass through the superuniverse and on to Havona, many of these spirit-concealed mysteries will clarify as you begin to be endowed with the "mind of the spirit" — spiritual insight.

7. PERSONALITY OF THE ETERNAL SON

The Eternal Son is that infinite personality from whose unqualified personality fetters the Universal Father escaped by the technique of trinitization, and by virtue of which he has ever since continued to bestow himself in endless profusion upon his ever-expanding universe of Creators and creatures. The Son is *absolute personality*; God is *father personality* — the source of personality, the bestower of personality, the cause of personality. Every personal being derives personality from the Universal Father just as the Original Son eternally derives his personality from the Paradise Father.

The personality of the Paradise Son is absolute and purely spiritual, and this absolute personality is also the divine and eternal pattern, first, of the Father's bestowal of personality upon the Conjoint Actor and, subsequently, of his bestowal of personality upon the myriads of his creatures throughout a far-flung universe.

The Eternal Son is truly a merciful minister, a divine spirit, a spiritual power, and a real personality. The Son is the spiritual and personal nature of God made manifest to the universes — the sum and substance of the First Source and Center, divested of all that which is nonpersonal, extradivine, nonspiritual, and pure potential. But it is impossible to convey to the human mind a word picture of the beauty and grandeur of the supernal personality of the Eternal Son. Everything that tends to obscure the Universal Father operates with almost equal influence to prevent the conceptual recognition of the Eternal Son. You must await your attainment of Paradise, and then you will understand why I was unable to portray the character of this absolute personality to the understanding of the finite mind.

8. REALIZATION OF THE ETERNAL SON

Concerning identity, nature, and other attributes of personality, the Eternal Son is the full equal, the perfect complement, and the eternal counterpart of the Universal Father. In the same sense that God is the Universal Father, the Son is the Universal Mother. And all of us, high and low, constitute their universal family.

To appreciate the character of the Son, you should study the revelation of the divine character of the Father; they are forever and inseparably one. As divine personalities they are virtually indistinguishable by the lower orders of intelligence. They are not so difficult of separate recognition by those whose origin is in the creative acts of the Deities themselves. Beings of nativity in the central universe and on Paradise discern the Father and the Son not only as one personal unity of universal control but also as two separate personalities functioning in definite domains of universe administration.

As persons you may conceive of the Universal Father and the Eternal Son as separate individuals, for they indeed are; but in the administration of the universes they are so intertwined and interrelated that it is not always possible to distinguish between them. When, in the affairs of the universes, the Father and the Son are encountered in confusing interassociations, it is not always profitable to attempt to segregate their operations; merely recall that God is the initiating thought and the Son is the expressionful word. In each local universe this inseparability is personalized in the divinity of the Creator Son, who stands for both Father and Son to the creatures of the inhabited worlds.

The Eternal Son is infinite, but he is approachable through the persons of his Paradise Sons and through the patient ministry of the Infinite Spirit.

Without the bestowal service of the Paradise Sons and the loving ministry of the creatures of the Infinite Spirit, beings of material origin could hardly hope to attain the Eternal Son. And it is equally true: With the help and guidance of these celestial agencies the God-conscious mortal will certainly attain Paradise and sometime stand in the personal presence of this majestic Son of Sons.

Even though the Eternal Son is the pattern of mortal personality attainment, you find it easier to grasp the reality of both the Father and the Spirit because the Father is the actual bestower of your human personality and the Infinite Spirit is the absolute source of your mortal mind. But as you ascend in the Paradise path of spiritual progression, the personality of the Eternal Son will become increasingly real to you, and the reality of his infinitely spiritual mind will become more discernible to your progressively spiritualizing mind.

Never can the concept of the Eternal Son shine brightly in your material or subsequent morontial mind; not until you spiritize and commence your spirit ascension will the comprehension of the personality of the Eternal Son begin to equal the vividness of your concept of the personality of the Creator Son of Paradise origin who, in person and as a person, onetime incarnated and lived on Urantia as a man among men.

Throughout your local universe experience the Creator Son, whose personality is comprehensible by man, must compensate for your inability to grasp the full significance of the more exclusively spiritual, but none the less personal, Eternal Son of Paradise. As you progress through Orvonton and Havona, as you leave behind you the vivid picture and deep memories of the Creator Son of your local universe, the passing of this material and morontia experience will be compensated by ever-enlarging concepts and intensifying comprehension of the Eternal Son of Paradise, whose reality and nearness will ever augment as you progress Paradiseward.

The Eternal Son is a grand and glorious personality. Although it is beyond the powers of the mortal and material mind to grasp the actuality of the personality of such an infinite being, doubt not, he is a person. I know whereof I speak. Times almost without number I have stood in the divine presence of this Eternal Son and then journeyed forth in the universe to execute his gracious bidding.

[Indited by a Divine Counselor assigned to formulate this statement depicting the Eternal Son of Paradise.]

PAPER 7
RELATION OF THE ETERNAL SON TO THE UNIVERSE

The Original Son is ever concerned with the execution of the spiritual aspects of the Father's eternal purpose as it progressively unfolds in the phenomena of the evolving universes with their manifold groups of living beings. We do not fully comprehend this eternal plan, but the Paradise Son undoubtedly does.

The Son is like the Father in that he seeks to bestow everything possible of himself upon his co-ordinate Sons and upon their subordinate Sons. And the Son shares the Father's self-distributive nature in the unstinted bestowal of himself upon the Infinite Spirit, their conjoint executive.

As the upholder of spirit realities, the Second Source and Center is the eternal counterpoise of the Isle of Paradise, which so magnificently upholds all things material. Thus is the First Source and Center forever revealed in the material beauty of the exquisite patterns of the central Isle and in the spiritual values of the supernal personality of the Eternal Son.

The Eternal Son is the actual upholder of the vast creation of spirit realities and spiritual beings. The spirit world is the habit, the personal conduct, of the Son, and the impersonal realities of spirit nature are always responsive to the will and purpose of the perfect personality of the Absolute Son.

The Son is not, however, personally responsible for the conduct of all spirit personalities. The will of the personal creature is relatively free and hence determines the actions of such volitional beings. Therefore the freewill spirit world is not always truly representative of the character of the Eternal Son, even as nature on Urantia is not truly revelatory of the perfection and immutability of Paradise and Deity. But no matter what may characterize the freewill action of man or angel, the Son's eternal grasp of the universal gravity control of all spirit realities continues as absolute.

1. THE SPIRIT-GRAVITY CIRCUIT

Everything taught concerning the immanence of God, his omnipresence, omnipotence, and omniscience, is equally true of the Son in the spiritual domains. The pure and universal spirit gravity of all creation, this exclusively spiritual circuit, leads directly back to the person of the Second Source and Center on Paradise. He presides over the control and operation of that ever-present and unerring spiritual grasp of all true spirit values. Thus does the Eternal Son exercise absolute spiritual sovereignty. He literally holds all spirit realities and all spiritualized values, as it were, in the hollow of his hand. The control of universal spiritual gravity is universal spiritual sovereignty.

This gravity control of spiritual things operates independently of time and space; therefore is spirit energy undiminished in transmission. Spirit gravity never suffers time delays, nor does it undergo space diminution. It does not decrease in accordance with the square of the distance of its transmission; the circuits of pure spirit power are not retarded by the mass of the material creation. And this transcendence of time and space by pure spirit energies is inherent in the absoluteness of the Son; it is not due to the interposition of the antigravity forces of the Third Source and Center.

Spirit realities respond to the drawing power of the center of spiritual gravity in accordance with their qualitative value, their actual degree of spirit nature. Spirit substance (quality) is just as responsive to spirit gravity as the organized energy of physical matter (quantity) is responsive to physical gravity. Spiritual values and spirit forces are *real*. From the viewpoint of personality, spirit is the soul of creation; matter is the shadowy physical body.

The reactions and fluctuations of spirit gravity are ever true to the content of spiritual values, the qualitative spiritual status of an individual or a world. This drawing power is instantly responsive to the inter- and intraspirit values of any universe situation or planetary condition. Every time a spiritual reality actualizes in the universes, this change necessitates the immediate and instantaneous readjustment of spirit gravity. Such a new spirit is actually a part of the Second Source and Center; and just as certainly as mortal man becomes a spiritized being, he will attain the spiritual Son, the center and source of spirit gravity.

The Son's spiritual drawing power is inherent to a lesser degree in many Paradise orders of sonship. For there do exist within the absolute spirit-gravity circuit those local systems of spiritual attraction that function in the lesser units of creation. Such subabsolute focalizations of spirit gravity are a part of the divinity of the Creator personalities of time and space and are correlated with the emerging experiential overcontrol of the Supreme Being.

Spirit-gravity pull and response thereto operate not only on the universe as a whole but also even between individuals and groups of individuals. There is a spiritual cohesiveness among the spiritual and spiritized personalities of any world, nation, or believing group of individuals. There is a direct attractiveness of a spirit nature between spiritually minded persons of like tastes and longings. The term *kindred spirits* is not wholly a figure of speech.

Like the material gravity of Paradise, the spiritual gravity of the Eternal Son is absolute. Sin and rebellion may interfere with the operation of local universe circuits, but nothing can suspend the spirit gravity of the Eternal Son. The Lucifer rebellion produced many changes in your system of inhabited worlds and on Urantia, but we do not observe that the resultant spiritual quarantine of your planet in the least affected the presence and function of either the omnipresent spirit of the Eternal Son or the associated spirit-gravity circuit.

All reactions of the spirit-gravity circuit of the grand universe are predictable. We recognize all actions and reactions of the omnipresent spirit of the Eternal Son and find them to be dependable. In accordance with well-known laws, we can and do measure spiritual gravity just as man attempts to compute the workings of finite physical gravity. There is an unvarying response of the Son's spirit to all spirit things, beings, and persons, and this response is always in accordance with the degree of actuality (the qualitative degree of reality) of all such spiritual values.

But alongside this very dependable and predictable function of the spiritual presence of the Eternal Son, there are encountered phenomena which are not so predictable in their reactions. Such phenomena probably indicate the co-ordinate action of the Deity Absolute in the realms of emerging spiritual potentials. We know that the spirit presence of the Eternal Son is the influence of a majestic and infinite personality, but we hardly regard the reactions associated with the conjectured performances of the Deity Absolute as personal.

Viewed from the personality standpoint and by persons, the Eternal Son and the Deity Absolute appear to be related in the following way: The Eternal Son dominates the realm of actual spiritual values, whereas the Deity Absolute seems to pervade the vast domain of potential spirit values. All actual value of spirit nature finds lodgment in the gravity grasp of the Eternal Son but, if potential, then apparently in the presence of the Deity Absolute.

Spirit seems to emerge from the potentials of the Deity Absolute; evolving spirit finds correlation in the experiential and incomplete grasps of the Supreme and the Ultimate; spirit eventually finds final destiny in the absolute grasp of the spiritual gravity of the Eternal Son. This appears to be the cycle of experiential spirit, but existential spirit is inherent in the infinity of the Second Source and Center.

2. THE ADMINISTRATION OF THE ETERNAL SON

On Paradise the presence and personal activity of the Original Son is profound, absolute in the spiritual sense. As we pass outward from Paradise through Havona and into the realms of the seven superuniverses, we detect less and less of the personal activity of the Eternal Son. In the post-Havona universes the presence of the Eternal Son is personalized in the Paradise Sons, conditioned by the experiential realities of the Supreme and the Ultimate, and co-ordinated with the unlimited spirit potential of the Deity Absolute.

In the central universe the personal activity of the Original Son is discernible in the exquisite spiritual harmony of the eternal creation. Havona is so marvelously perfect that the spiritual status and the energy states of this pattern universe are in perfect and perpetual balance.

In the superuniverses the Son is not personally present or resident; in these creations he maintains only a superpersonal representation. These spirit manifestations of the Son are not personal; they are not in the personality circuit of the Universal Father. We know of no better term to use than to designate them *superpersonalities*; and they are finite beings; they are neither absonite nor absolute.

The administration of the Eternal Son in the superuniverses, being exclusively spiritual and superpersonal, is not discernible by creature personalities. Nonetheless, the all-pervading spiritual urge of the Son's personal influence is encountered in every phase of the activities of all sectors of the domains of the Ancients of Days. In the local universes, however, we observe the Eternal Son personally present in the persons of the Paradise Sons. Here the infinite Son spiritually and creatively functions in the persons of the majestic corps of the co-ordinate Creator Sons.

3. RELATION OF THE ETERNAL SON TO THE INDIVIDUAL

In the local universe ascent the mortals of time look to the Creator Son as the personal representative of the Eternal Son. But when they begin the ascent of the superuniverse training regime, the pilgrims of time increasingly detect the supernal presence of the inspiring spirit of the Eternal Son, and they are able to profit by the intake of this ministry of spiritual energization. In Havona the ascenders become still more conscious of the loving embrace of the all-pervading spirit of the Original Son. At no stage of the entire mortal ascension does the spirit of the Eternal Son indwell the mind or soul of the pilgrim of time, but his beneficence is ever near and always concerned with the welfare and spiritual security of the advancing children of time.

The spiritual-gravity pull of the Eternal Son constitutes the inherent secret of the Paradise ascension of surviving human souls. All genuine spirit values and all bona fide spiritualized individuals are held within the unfailing grasp of the spiritual gravity of the Eternal Son. The mortal mind, for example, initiates its career as a material mechanism and is eventually mustered into the Corps of the Finality as a well-nigh perfected spirit existence, becoming progressively less subject to material gravity and correspondingly more responsive to the inward pulling urge of spirit gravity during this entire experience. The spirit-gravity circuit literally pulls the soul of man Paradiseward.

The spirit-gravity circuit is the basic channel for transmitting the genuine prayers of the believing human heart from the level of human consciousness to the actual consciousness of Deity. That which represents true spiritual value in your petitions will be seized by the universal circuit of spirit gravity and will pass immediately and simultaneously to all divine personalities concerned. Each will occupy himself with that which belongs to his personal province. Therefore, in your practical religious experience, it is immaterial whether, in addressing your supplications, you visualize the Creator Son of your local universe or the Eternal Son at the center of all things.

The discriminative operation of the spirit-gravity circuit might possibly be compared to the functions of the neural circuits in the material human body: Sensations travel inward over the neural paths; some are detained and responded to by the lower automatic spinal centers; others pass on to the less automatic but habit-trained centers of the lower brain, while the most important and vital incoming messages flash by these subordinate centers and are immediately registered in the highest levels of human consciousness.

But how much more perfect is the superb technique of the spiritual world! If anything originates in your consciousness that is fraught with supreme spiritual value, when once you give it expression, no power in the universe can prevent its flashing directly to the Absolute Spirit Personality of all creation.

Conversely, if your supplications are purely material and wholly self-centered, there exists no plan whereby such unworthy prayers can find lodgment in the spirit circuit of the Eternal Son. The content of any petition which is not "spirit indited" can find no place in the universal spiritual circuit; such purely selfish and material requests fall dead; they do not ascend in the circuits of true spirit values. Such words are as "sounding brass and a tinkling cymbal."

It is the motivating thought, the spiritual content, that validates the mortal supplication. Words are valueless.

4. THE DIVINE PERFECTION PLANS

The Eternal Son is in everlasting liaison with the Father in the successful prosecution of the divine *plan of progress*: the universal plan for the creation, evolution, ascension, and perfection of will creatures. And, in divine faithfulness, the Son is the eternal equal of the Father.

The Father and his Son are as one in the formulation and prosecution of this gigantic attainment plan for advancing the material beings of time to the perfection of eternity. This project for the spiritual elevation of the ascendant souls of space is a joint creation of the Father and the Son, and they are, with the co-operation of the Infinite Spirit, engaged in associative execution of their divine purpose.

This divine plan of perfection attainment embraces three unique, though marvelously correlated, enterprises of universal adventure:

1. *The Plan of Progressive Attainment.* This is the Universal Father's plan of evolutionary ascension, a program unreservedly accepted by the Eternal Son when he concurred in the Father's proposal, "Let us make mortal creatures in our own image." This provision for upstepping the creatures of time involves the Father's bestowal of the Thought Adjusters and the endowing of material creatures with the prerogatives of personality.

2. *The Bestowal Plan.* The next universal plan is the great Father-revelation enterprise of the Eternal Son and his co-ordinate Sons. This is the proposal of the Eternal Son and consists of his bestowal of the Sons of God

upon the evolutionary creations, there to personalize and factualize, to incarnate and make real, the love of the Father and the mercy of the Son to the creatures of all universes. Inherent in the bestowal plan, and as a provisional feature of this ministration of love, the Paradise Sons act as rehabilitators of that which misguided creature will has placed in spiritual jeopardy. Whenever and wherever there occurs a delay in the functioning of the attainment plan, if rebellion, perchance, should mar or complicate this enterprise, then do the emergency provisions of the bestowal plan become active forthwith. The Paradise Sons stand pledged and ready to function as retrievers, to go into the very realms of rebellion and there restore the spiritual status of the spheres. And such a heroic service a co-ordinate Creator Son did perform on Urantia in connection with his experiential bestowal career of sovereignty acquirement.

3. *The Plan of Mercy Ministry.* When the attainment plan and the bestowal plan had been formulated and proclaimed, alone and of himself, the Infinite Spirit projected and put in operation the tremendous and universal enterprise of mercy ministry. This is the service so essential to the practical and effective operation of both the attainment and the bestowal undertakings, and the spiritual personalities of the Third Source and Center all partake of the spirit of mercy ministry which is so much a part of the nature of the Third Person of Deity. Not only in creation but also in administration, the Infinite Spirit functions truly and literally as the conjoint executive of the Father and the Son.

The Eternal Son is the personal trustee, the divine custodian, of the Father's universal plan of creature ascension. Having promulgated the universal mandate, "Be you perfect, even as I am perfect," the Father intrusted the execution of this tremendous undertaking to the Eternal Son; and the Eternal Son shares the fostering of this supernal enterprise with his divine co-ordinate, the Infinite Spirit. Thus do the Deities effectively cooperate in the work of creation, control, evolution, revelation, and ministration — and if required, in restoration and rehabilitation.

5. THE SPIRIT OF BESTOWAL

The Eternal Son without reservation joined with the Universal Father in broadcasting that tremendous injunction to all creation: "Be you perfect, even as your Father in Havona is perfect." And ever since, that invitation-command has motivated all the survival plans and the bestowal projects of the Eternal Son and his vast family of co-ordinate and associated Sons. And in these very bestowals the Sons of God have become to all evolutionary creatures "the way, the truth, and the life."

The Eternal Son cannot contact directly with human beings as does the Father through the gift of the prepersonal Thought Adjusters, but the Eternal Son does draw near to created personalities by a series of downstepping gradations of divine sonship until he is enabled to stand in man's presence and, at times, as man himself.

The purely personal nature of the Eternal Son is incapable of fragmentation. The Eternal Son ministers as a spiritual influence or as a person, never otherwise. The Son finds it impossible to become a part of creature experience in the sense that the Father-Adjuster participates therein, but the Eternal Son compensates this limitation by the technique of bestowal. What the experience of fragmented entities means to the Universal Father, the incarnation experiences of the Paradise Sons mean to the Eternal Son.

The Eternal Son comes not to mortal man as the divine will, the Thought Adjuster indwelling the human mind, but the Eternal Son did come to mortal man on Urantia when the divine *personality* of his Son, Michael of Nebadon, incarnated in the human nature of Jesus of Nazareth. To share the experience of created personalities, the Paradise Sons of God must assume the very natures of such creatures and incarnate their divine personalities as the actual creatures themselves. Incarnation, the secret of Sonarington, is the technique of the Son's escape from the otherwise all-encompassing fetters of personality absolutism.

Long, long ago the Eternal Son bestowed himself upon each of the circuits of the central creation for the enlightenment and advancement of all the inhabitants and pilgrims of Havona, including the ascending pilgrims of time. On none of these seven bestowals did he function as either an ascender or a Havoner. He existed as himself. His experience was unique; it was not *with* or as a human or other pilgrim but in some way associative in the superpersonal sense.

Neither did he pass through the rest that intervenes between the inner Havona circuit and the shores of Paradise. It is not possible for him, an absolute being, to suspend consciousness of personality, for in him center all lines of spiritual gravity. And during the times of these bestowals the central Paradise lodgment of spiritual luminosity was undimmed, and the Son's grasp of universal spirit gravity was undiminished.

The bestowals of the Eternal Son in Havona are not within the scope of human imagination; they were transcendental. He added to the experience of all Havona then and subsequently, but we do not know whether he added to the supposed experiential capacity of his existential nature. That would fall within the bestowal mystery of the Paradise Sons. We do, however, believe that whatever the Eternal Son acquired on these bestowal missions, he has ever since retained; but we do not know what it is.

Whatever our difficulty in comprehending the bestowals of the Second Person of Deity, we do comprehend the Havona bestowal of a Son of the Eternal Son, who literally passed through the circuits of the central universe and actually shared those experiences which constitute an ascender's preparation for Deity attainment. This was the original Michael, the first-born Creator Son, and he passed through the life experiences of the ascending pilgrims from circuit to circuit, personally journeying a stage of each circle with them in the days of Grandfanda, the first of all mortals to attain Havona.

Whatever else this original Michael revealed, he made the transcendent bestowal of the Original Mother Son real to the creatures of Havona. So real, that forevermore each pilgrim of time who labors in the adventure of making the Havona circuits is cheered and strengthened by the certain knowledge that the Eternal Son of God seven times abdicated the power and glory of Paradise to participate in the experiences of the time-space pilgrims on the seven circuits of progressive Havona attainment.

The Eternal Son is the exemplary inspiration for all the Sons of God in their ministrations of bestowal throughout the universes of time and space. The co-ordinate Creator Sons and the associate Magisterial Sons, together with other unrevealed orders of sonship, all partake of this wonderful willingness to bestow themselves upon the varied orders of creature life and as the creatures themselves. Therefore, in spirit and because of kinship of nature as well as fact of origin, it becomes true that in the bestowal of each Son of God upon the worlds of space, in and through and by these bestowals, the Eternal Son has bestowed himself upon the intelligent will creatures of the universes.

In spirit and nature, if not in all attributes, each Paradise Son is a divinely perfect portraiture of the Original Son. It is literally true, whosoever has seen a Paradise Son has seen the Eternal Son of God.

6. THE PARADISE SONS OF GOD

The lack of a knowledge of the multiple Sons of God is a source of great confusion on Urantia. And this ignorance persists in the face of such statements as the record of a conclave of these divine personalities: "When the Sons of God proclaimed joy, and all of the Morning Stars sang together." Every millennium of sector standard time the various orders of the divine Sons forgather for their periodic conclaves.

The Eternal Son is the personal source of the adorable attributes of mercy and service which so abundantly characterize all orders of the descending Sons of God as they function throughout creation. All the divine nature, if not all the infinity of attributes, the Eternal Son unfailingly transmits to the Paradise Sons who go out from the eternal Isle to reveal his divine character to the universe of universes.

The Original and Eternal Son is the offspring-person of the "first" completed and infinite thought of the Universal Father. Every time the Universal Father and the Eternal Son jointly project a new, original, identical, unique, and absolute personal thought, that very instant this creative idea is perfectly and finally personalized in the being and personality of a new and original Creator Son. In spirit nature, divine wisdom, and co-ordinate creative power, these Creator Sons are potentially equal with God the Father and God the Son.

The Creator Sons go out from Paradise into the universes of time and, with the co-operation of the controlling and creative agencies of the Third Source and Center, complete the organization of the local universes of progressive evolution. These Sons are not attached to, nor are they concerned with, the central and universal controls of matter, mind, and spirit. Hence are they limited in their creative acts by the pre-existence, priority, and primacy of the First Source and Center and his co-ordinate Absolutes. These Sons are able to administer only that which they bring into existence. Absolute administration is inherent in priority of existence and is inseparable from eternity of presence. The Father remains primal in the universes.

Much as the Creator Sons are personalized by the Father and the Son, so are the *Magisterial Sons* personalized by the Son and the Spirit. These are the Sons who, in the experiences of creature incarnation, earn the right to serve as the judges of survival in the creations of time and space.

The Father, Son, and Spirit also unite to personalize the versatile *Trinity Teacher Sons*, who range the grand universe as the supernal teachers of all personalities, human and divine. And there are numerous other orders of Paradise sonship that have not been brought to the attention of Urantia mortals.

Between the Original Mother Son and these hosts of Paradise Sons scattered throughout all creation, there is a direct and exclusive channel of communication, a channel whose function is inherent in the quality of spiritual kinship which unites them in bonds of near-absolute spiritual association. This intersonship circuit is entirely different from the universal circuit of spirit gravity, which also centers in the person of the Second Source and Center. All Sons of God who take origin in the persons of the Paradise Deities are in direct and constant communication with the Eternal Mother Son. And such communication is instantaneous; it is independent of time though sometimes conditioned by space.

The Eternal Son not only has at all times perfect knowledge concerning the status, thoughts, and manifold activities of all orders of Paradise sonship, but he also has perfection of knowledge at all times regarding everything of spiritual value which exists in the hearts of all creatures in the primary central creation of eternity and in the secondary time creations of the co-ordinate Creator Sons.

7. THE SUPREME REVELATION OF THE FATHER

The Eternal Son is a complete, exclusive, universal, and final revelation of the spirit and the personality of the Universal Father. All knowledge of, and information concerning, the Father must come from the Eternal Son and his Paradise Sons. The Eternal Son is from eternity and is wholly and without spiritual qualification one with the Father. In divine personality they are co-ordinate; in spiritual nature they are equal; in divinity they are identical.

The character of God could not possibly be intrinsically improved upon in the person of the Son, for the divine Father is infinitely perfect, but that character and personality are amplified, by divestment of the nonpersonal and nonspiritual, for revelation to creature beings. The First Source and Center is much more than a personality, but all of the spirit qualities of the father personality of the First Source and Center are spiritually present in the absolute personality of the Eternal Son.

The primal Son and his Sons are engaged in making a universal revelation of the spiritual and personal nature of the Father to all creation. In the central universe, the superuniverses, the local universes, or on the inhabited planets, it is a Paradise Son who reveals the Universal Father to men and angels. The Eternal Son and his Sons reveal the avenue of creature approach to the Universal Father. And even we of high origin understand the Father much more fully as we study the revelation of his character and personality in the Eternal Son and in the Sons of the Eternal Son.

The Father comes down to you as a personality only through the divine Sons of the Eternal Son. And you attain the Father by this same living way; you ascend to the Father by the guidance of this group of divine Sons. And this remains true notwithstanding that your very personality is a direct bestowal of the Universal Father.

In all these widespread activities of the far-flung spiritual administration of the Eternal Son, do not forget that the Son is a person just as truly and actually as the Father is a person. Indeed, to beings of the onetime human order the Eternal Son will be more easy to approach than the Universal Father. In the progress of the pilgrims of time through the circuits of Havona, you will be competent to attain the Son long before you are prepared to discern the Father.

More of the character and merciful nature of the Eternal Son of mercy you should comprehend as you meditate on the revelation of these divine attributes which was made in loving service by your own Creator Son, onetime Son of Man on earth, now the exalted sovereign of your local universe — the Son of Man and the Son of God.

[Indited by a Divine Counselor assigned to formulate this statement depicting the Eternal Son of Paradise.]

PAPER 8
THE INFINITE SPIRIT

BACK IN ETERNITY, when the Universal Father's "first" infinite and absolute thought finds in the Eternal Son such a perfect and adequate word for its divine expression, there ensues the supreme desire of both the Thought-God and the Word-God for a universal and infinite agent of mutual expression and combined action.

In the dawn of eternity both the Father and the Son become infinitely cognizant of their mutual interdependence, their eternal and absolute oneness; and therefore do they enter into an infinite and everlasting covenant of divine partnership. This never-ending compact is made for the execution of their united concepts throughout all of the circle of eternity; and ever since this eternity event the Father and the Son continue in this divine union.

We are now face to face with the eternity origin of the Infinite Spirit, the Third Person of Deity. The very instant that God the Father and God the Son conjointly conceive an identical and infinite action — the execution of an absolute thought-plan — that very moment, the Infinite Spirit springs full-fledgedly into existence.

In thus reciting the order of the origin of the Deities, I do so merely to enable you to think of their relationship. In reality they are all three existent from eternity; they are existential. They are without beginning or ending of days; they are co-ordinate, supreme, ultimate, absolute, and infinite. They are and always have been and ever shall be. And they are three distinctly individualized but eternally associated persons, God the Father, God the Son, and God the Spirit.

1. THE GOD OF ACTION

In the eternity of the past, upon the personalization of the Infinite Spirit the divine personality cycle becomes perfect and complete. The God of Action is existent, and the vast stage of space is set for the stupendous drama of creation — the universal adventure — the divine panorama of the eternal ages.

The first act of the Infinite Spirit is the inspection and recognition of his divine parents, the Father-Father and the Mother-Son. He, the Spirit, unqualifiedly identifies both of them. He is fully cognizant of their separate personalities and infinite attributes as well as of their combined nature and united function. Next, voluntarily, with transcendent willingness and inspiring spontaneity, the Third Person of Deity, notwithstanding his equality with the First and Second Persons, pledges eternal loyalty to God the Father and acknowledges everlasting dependence upon God the Son.

Inherent in the nature of this transaction and in mutual recognition of the personality independence of each and the executive union of all three, the cycle of eternity is established. The Paradise Trinity is existent. The stage of universal space is set for the manifold and never-ending panorama of the creative unfolding of the purpose of the Universal Father through the personality of the Eternal Son and by the execution of the God of Action, the executive agency for the reality performances of the Father-Son creator partnership.

The God of Action functions and the dead vaults of space are astir. One billion perfect spheres flash into existence. Prior to this hypothetical eternity moment the space-energies inherent in Paradise are existent and potentially operative, but they have no actuality of being; neither can physical gravity be measured except by the reaction of material realities to its incessant pull. There is no material universe at this (assumed) eternally distant moment, but the very instant that one billion worlds materialize, there is in evidence gravity sufficient and adequate to hold them in the everlasting grasp of Paradise.

There now flashes through the creation of the Gods the second form of energy, and this outflowing spirit is instantly grasped by the spiritual gravity of the Eternal Son. Thus the twofold gravity-embraced universe is touched with the energy of infinity and immersed in the spirit of divinity. In this way is the soil of life prepared for the consciousness of mind made manifest in the associated intelligence circuits of the Infinite Spirit.

Upon these seeds of potential existence, diffused throughout the central creation of the Gods, the Father acts, and creature personality appears. Then does the presence of the Paradise Deities fill all organized space and begin effectively to draw all things and beings Paradiseward.

The Infinite Spirit eternalizes concurrently with the birth of the Havona worlds, this central universe being created by him and with him and in him in obedience to the combined concepts and united wills of the Father and the Son. The Third Person deitizes by this very act of conjoint creation, and he thus forever becomes the Conjoint Creator.

These are the grand and awful times of the creative expansion of the Father and the Son by, and in, the action of their conjoint associate and exclusive executive, the Third Source and Center. There exists no record of these stirring times. We have only the meager disclosures of the Infinite Spirit to substantiate these mighty transactions, and he merely verifies the fact that the central universe and all that pertains thereto eternalized simultaneously with his attainment of personality and conscious existence.

In brief, the Infinite Spirit testifies that, since he is eternal, so also is the central universe eternal. And this is the traditional starting point of the history of the universe of universes. Absolutely nothing is known, and no records are in existence, regarding any event or transaction prior to this stupendous eruption of creative energy and administrative wisdom that crystallized the vast universe which exists, and so exquisitely functions, at the center of all things. Beyond this event lie the unsearchable transactions of eternity and the depths of infinity — absolute mystery.

And we thus portray the sequential origin of the Third Source and Center as an interpretative condescension to the time-bound and space-conditioned mind of mortal creatures. The mind of man must have a starting point for the visualization of universe history, and I have been directed to provide this technique of approach to the historic concept of eternity. In the material mind, consistency demands a First Cause; therefore do we postulate the Universal Father as the First Source and the Absolute Center of all creation, at the same time instructing all creature minds that the Son and the Spirit are coeternal with the Father in all phases of universe history and in all realms of creative activity. And we do this without in any sense being disregardful of the reality and eternity of the Isle of Paradise and of the Unqualified, Universal, and Deity Absolutes.

It is enough of a reach of the material mind of the children of time to conceive of the Father in eternity. We know that any child can best relate himself to reality by first mastering the relationships of the child-parent situation and then by enlarging this concept to embrace the family as a whole. Subsequently the growing mind of the child will be able to adjust to the concept of family relations, to relationships of the community, the world, and then to those of the universe, the superuniverse, even the universe of universes.

2. NATURE OF THE INFINITE SPIRIT

The Conjoint Creator is from eternity and is wholly and without qualification one with the Universal Father and the Eternal Son. The Infinite Spirit reflects in perfection not only the nature of the Paradise Father but also the nature of the Original Son.

The Third Source and Center is known by numerous titles: the Universal Spirit, the Supreme Guide, the Conjoint Creator, the Divine Executive, the Infinite Mind, the Spirit of Spirits, the Paradise Mother Spirit, the Conjoint Actor, the Final Co-ordinator, the Omnipresent Spirit, the Absolute Intelligence, the Divine Action; and on Urantia he is sometimes confused with the cosmic mind.

It is altogether proper to denominate the Third Person of Deity the Infinite Spirit, for God is spirit. But material creatures who tend towards the error of viewing matter as basic reality and mind, together with spirit, as postulates rooted in matter, would better comprehend the Third Source and Center if he were called the Infinite Reality, the Universal Organizer, or the Personality Co-ordinator.

The Infinite Spirit, as a universe revelation of divinity, is unsearchable and utterly beyond human comprehension. To sense the absoluteness of the Spirit, you need only contemplate the infinity of the Universal Father and stand in awe of the eternity of the Original Son.

There is mystery indeed in the person of the Infinite Spirit but not so much as in the Father and the Son. Of all aspects of the Father's nature, the Conjoint Creator most strikingly discloses his infinity. Even if the master universe eventually expands to infinity, the spirit presence, energy control, and mind potential of the Conjoint Actor will be found adequate to meet the demands of such a limitless creation.

Though in every way sharing the perfection, the righteousness, and the love of the Universal Father, the Infinite Spirit inclines towards the mercy attributes of the Eternal Son, thus becoming the mercy minister of the Paradise Deities to the grand universe. Ever and always — universally and eternally — the Spirit is a mercy minister, for, as the divine Sons reveal the love of God, so the divine Spirit depicts the mercy of God.

It is not possible that the Spirit could have more of goodness than the Father since all goodness takes origin in the Father, but in the acts of the Spirit we can the better comprehend such goodness. The Father's faithfulness and the Son's constancy are made very real to the spirit beings and the material creatures of the spheres by the loving ministry and ceaseless service of the personalities of the Infinite Spirit.

The Conjoint Creator inherits all the Father's beauty of thought and character of truth. And these sublime traits of divinity are co-ordinated in the near-supreme levels of the cosmic mind in subordination to the infinite and eternal wisdom of the unconditioned and limitless mind of the Third Source and Center.

3. RELATION OF THE SPIRIT TO THE FATHER AND THE SON

As the Eternal Son is the word expression of the "first" absolute and infinite thought of the Universal Father, so the Conjoint Actor is the perfect execution of the "first" completed creative concept or plan for combined action by the Father-Son personality partnership of absolute thought-word union. The Third Source and Center eternalizes concurrently with the central or fiat creation, and only this central creation is eternal in existence among universes.

Since the personalization of the Third Source, the First Source no more personally participates in universe creation. The Universal Father delegates everything possible to his Eternal Son; likewise does the Eternal Son bestow all possible authority and power upon the Conjoint Creator.

The Eternal Son and the Conjoint Creator have, as partners and through their co-ordinate personalities, planned and fashioned every post-Havona universe which has been brought into existence. The Spirit sustains the same personal relation to the Son in all subsequent creation that the Son sustains to the Father in the first and central creation.

A Creator Son of the Eternal Son and a Creative Spirit of the Infinite Spirit created you and your universe; and while the Father in faithfulness upholds that which they have organized, it devolves upon this Universe Son and this Universe Spirit to foster and sustain their work as well as to minister to the creatures of their own making.

The Infinite Spirit is the effective agent of the all-loving Father and the all-merciful Son for the execution of their conjoint project of drawing to themselves all truth-loving souls on all the worlds of time and space. The very instant the Eternal Son accepted his Father's plan of perfection attainment for the creatures of the universes, the moment the ascension project became a Father-Son plan, that instant the Infinite Spirit became the conjoint administrator of the Father and the Son for the execution of their united and eternal purpose. And in so doing the Infinite Spirit pledged all his resources of divine presence and of spirit personalities to the Father and the Son; he has dedicated *all* to the stupendous plan of exalting surviving will creatures to the divine heights of Paradise perfection.

The Infinite Spirit is a complete, exclusive, and universal revelation of the Universal Father and his Eternal Son. All knowledge of the Father-Son partnership must be had through the Infinite Spirit, the conjoint representative of the divine thought-word union.

The Eternal Son is the only avenue of approach to the Universal Father, and the Infinite Spirit is the only means of attaining the Eternal Son. Only by the patient ministry of the Spirit are the ascendant beings of time able to discover the Son.

At the center of all things the Infinite Spirit is the first of the Paradise Deities to be attained by the ascending pilgrims. The Third Person enshrouds the Second and the First Persons and therefore must always be first recognized by all who are candidates for presentation to the Son and his Father.

And in many other ways does the Spirit equally represent and similarly serve the Father and the Son.

4. THE SPIRIT OF DIVINE MINISTRY

Paralleling the physical universe wherein Paradise gravity holds all things together is the spiritual universe wherein the word of the Son interprets the thought of God and, when "made flesh," demonstrates the loving mercy of the combined nature of the associated Creators. But in and through all this material and spiritual creation there is a vast stage whereon the Infinite Spirit and his spirit offspring show forth the combined mercy, patience, and everlasting affection of the divine parents towards the intelligent children of their co-operative devising and making. Everlasting ministry to mind is the essence of the Spirit's divine character. And all the spirit offspring of the Conjoint Actor partake of this desire to minister, this divine urge to service.

God is love, the Son is mercy, the Spirit is ministry — the ministry of divine love and endless mercy to all intelligent creation. The Spirit is the personification of the Father's love and the Son's mercy; in him are they eternally united for universal service. The Spirit is *love applied* to the creature creation, the combined love of the Father and the Son.

On Urantia the Infinite Spirit is known as an omnipresent influence, a universal presence, but in Havona you shall know him as a personal presence of actual ministry. Here the ministry of the Paradise Spirit is the exemplary and inspiring pattern for each of his co-ordinate Spirits and subordinate personalities ministering to the created beings on the worlds of time and space. In this divine universe the Infinite Spirit fully participated in the seven transcendental appearances of the Eternal Son; likewise did he participate with the original Michael Son in the seven bestowals upon the circuits of Havona, thereby becoming the sympathetic and understanding spirit minister to every pilgrim of time traversing these perfect circles on high.

When a Creator Son of God accepts the creatorship charge of responsibility for a projected local universe, the personalities of the Infinite Spirit pledge themselves as the tireless ministers of this Michael Son when he goes forth on his mission of creative adventure. Especially in the persons of the Creative Daughters, the local universe Mother Spirits, do we find the Infinite Spirit devoted to the task of fostering the ascension of the material creatures to higher and higher levels of spiritual attainment. And all this work of creature ministry is done in perfect harmony with the purposes, and in close association with the personalities, of the Creator Sons of these local universes.

As the Sons of God are engaged in the gigantic task of revealing the Father's personality of love to a universe, so is the Infinite Spirit dedicated to the unending ministry of revealing the combined love of the Father and the Son to the individual minds of all the children of each universe. In these local creations the Spirit does not come down to the material races in the likeness of mortal flesh as do certain of the Sons of God, but the Infinite Spirit and his co-ordinate Spirits do downstep themselves, do joyfully undergo an amazing series of divinity attenuations, until they appear as angels to stand by your side and guide you through the lowly paths of earthly existence.

By this very diminishing series the Infinite Spirit does actually, and as a person, draw very near to every being of the animal-origin spheres. And all this the Spirit does without in the least invalidating his existence as the Third Person of Deity at the center of all things.

The Conjoint Creator is truly and forever the great ministering personality, the universal mercy minister. To comprehend the ministry of the Spirit, ponder the truth that he is the combined portrayal of the Father's unending love and of the Son's eternal mercy. The Spirit's ministry is not, however, restricted solely to the representation of the Eternal Son and the Universal Father. The Infinite Spirit also possesses the power to minister to the creatures of the realm in his own name and right; the Third Person is of divine dignity and also bestows the universal ministry of mercy in his own behalf.

As man learns more of the loving and tireless ministry of the lower orders of the creature family of this Infinite Spirit, he will all the more admire and adore the transcendent nature and matchless character of this combined Action of the Universal Father and the Eternal Son. Indeed is this Spirit "the eyes of the Lord which are ever over the righteous" and "the divine ears which are ever open to their prayers."

5. THE PRESENCE OF GOD

The outstanding attribute of the Infinite Spirit is omnipresence. Throughout all the universe of universes there is everywhere present this all-pervading spirit, which is so akin to the presence of a universal and divine mind. Both the Second Person and the Third Person of Deity are represented on all worlds by their ever-present spirits.

The Father is *infinite* and is therefore limited only by volition. In the bestowal of Adjusters and in the encircuitment of personality, the Father acts alone, but in the contact of spirit forces with intelligent beings, he utilizes the spirits and personalities of the Eternal Son and the Infinite Spirit. He is at will spiritually present equally with the Son or with the Conjoint Actor; he is present *with* the Son and *in* the Spirit. The Father is most certainly everywhere present, and we discern his presence by and through any and all of these diverse but associated forces, influences, and presences.

In your sacred writings the term *Spirit of God* seems to be used interchangeably to designate both the Infinite Spirit on Paradise and the Creative Spirit of your local universe. The Holy Spirit is the spiritual circuit of this Creative Daughter of the Paradise Infinite Spirit. The Holy Spirit is a circuit indigenous to each local universe and is confined to the spiritual realm of that creation; but the Infinite Spirit is omnipresent.

There are many spiritual influences, and they are all as *one*. Even the work of the Thought Adjusters, though independent of all other influences, unvaryingly coincides with the spirit ministry of the combined influences of the Infinite Spirit and a local universe Mother Spirit. As these spiritual presences operate in the lives of Urantians, they cannot be segregated. In your minds and upon your souls they function as one spirit, notwithstanding their diverse origins. And as this united spiritual ministration is experienced, it becomes to you the influence of the Supreme, "who is ever able to keep you from failing and to present you blameless before your Father on high."

Ever remember that the Infinite Spirit is the *Conjoint* Actor; both the Father and the Son are functioning in and through him; he is present not only as himself but also as the Father and as the Son and as the Father-Son. In recognition of this and for many additional reasons the spirit presence of the Infinite Spirit is often referred to as "the spirit of God."

It would also be consistent to refer to the liaison of all spiritual ministry as the spirit of God, for such a liaison is truly the union of the spirits of God the Father, God the Son, God the Spirit, and God the Sevenfold — even the spirit of God the Supreme.

6. PERSONALITY OF THE INFINITE SPIRIT

Do not allow the widespread bestowal and the far-flung distribution of the Third Source and Center to obscure or otherwise detract from the fact of his personality. The Infinite Spirit is a universe presence, an eternal action, a cosmic power, a holy influence, and a universal mind; he is all of these and infinitely more, but he is also a true and divine personality.

The Infinite Spirit is a complete and perfect personality, the divine equal and co-ordinate of the Universal Father and the Eternal Son. The Conjoint Creator is just as real and visible to the higher intelligences of the universes as are the Father and the Son; indeed more so, for it is the Spirit whom all ascenders must attain before they may approach the Father through the Son.

The Infinite Spirit, the Third Person of Deity, is possessed of all the attributes which you associate with personality. The Spirit is endowed with absolute mind: "The Spirit searches all things, even the deep things of God." The Spirit is endowed not only with mind but also with will. In the bestowal of his gifts it is recorded: "But all these works that one and the selfsame Spirit, dividing to every man severally and as he wills."

"The love of the Spirit" is real, as also are his sorrows; therefore "Grieve not the Spirit of God." Whether we observe the Infinite Spirit as Paradise Deity or as a local universe Creative Spirit, we find that the Conjoint Creator is not only the Third Source and Center but also a divine person. This divine personality also reacts to the universe as a person. The Spirit speaks to you, "He who has an ear, let him hear what the Spirit says." "The Spirit himself makes intercession for you." The Spirit exerts a direct and personal influence upon created beings, "For as many as are led by the Spirit of God, they are the sons of God."

Even though we behold the phenomenon of the ministry of the Infinite Spirit to the remote worlds of the universe of universes, even though we envisage this same co-ordinating Deity acting in and through the untold legions of the manifold beings who take origin in the Third Source and Center, even though we recognize the omnipresence of the Spirit, nonetheless, we still affirm that this same Third Source and Center is a person, the Conjoint Creator of all things and all beings and all universes.

In the administration of universes the Father, Son, and Spirit are perfectly and eternally interassociated. Though each is engaged in a personal ministry to all creation, all three are divinely and absolutely interlocked in a service of creation and control which forever makes them *one*.

In the person of the Infinite Spirit the Father and the Son are mutually present, always and in unqualified perfection, for the Spirit is like the Father and like the Son, and also like the Father and the Son as they two are forever one.

[Presented on Urantia by a Divine Counselor of Uversa commissioned by the Ancients of Days to portray the nature and work of the Infinite Spirit.]

PAPER 9
RELATION OF THE INFINITE SPIRIT TO THE UNIVERSE

A STRANGE THING OCCURRED WHEN, in the presence of Paradise, the Universal Father and the Eternal Son unite to personalize themselves. Nothing in this eternity situation foreshadows that the Conjoint Actor would personalize as an unlimited spirituality co-ordinated with absolute mind and endowed with unique prerogatives of energy manipulation. His coming into being completes the Father's liberation from the bonds of centralized perfection and from the fetters of personality absolutism. And this liberation is disclosed in the amazing power of the Conjoint Creator to create beings well adapted to serve as ministering spirits even to the material creatures of the subsequently evolving universes.

The Father is infinite in love and volition, in spiritual thought and purpose; he is the universal upholder. The Son is infinite in wisdom and truth, in spiritual expression and interpretation; he is the universal revealer. Paradise is infinite in potential for force endowment and in capacity for energy dominance; it is the universal stabilizer. The Conjoint Actor possesses unique prerogatives of synthesis, infinite capacity to co-ordinate all existing universe energies, all actual universe spirits, and all real universe intellects; the Third Source and Center is the universal unifier of the manifold energies and diverse creations which have appeared in consequence of the divine plan and the eternal purpose of the Universal Father.

The Infinite Spirit, the Conjoint Creator, is a universal and divine minister. The Spirit unceasingly ministers the Son's mercy and the Father's love, even in harmony with the stable, unvarying, and righteous justice of the Paradise Trinity. His influence and personalities are ever near you; they really know and truly understand you.

Throughout the universes the agencies of the Conjoint Actor ceaselessly manipulate the forces and energies of all space. Like the First Source and Center, the Third is responsive to both the spiritual and the material. The Conjoint Actor is the revelation of the unity of God, in whom all things consist — things, meanings, and values; energies, minds, and spirits.

The Infinite Spirit pervades all space; he indwells the circle of eternity; and the Spirit, like the Father and the Son, is perfect and changeless — absolute.

1. ATTRIBUTES OF THE THIRD SOURCE AND CENTER

The Third Source and Center is known by many names, all designative of relationship and in recognition of function: As God the Spirit, he is the personality co-ordinate and divine equal of God the Son and God the Father. As the Infinite Spirit, he is an omnipresent spiritual influence. As the Universal Manipulator, he is the ancestor of the power-control creatures and the activator of the cosmic forces of space. As the Conjoint Actor, he is the joint representative and partnership executive of the Father-Son. As the Absolute Mind, he is the source of the endowment of intellect throughout the universes. As the God of Action, he is the apparent ancestor of motion, change, and relationship.

Some of the attributes of the Third Source and Center are derived from the Father, some from the Son, while still others are not observed to be actively and personally present in either the Father or the Son — attributes that can hardly be explained except by assuming that the Father-Son partnership which eternalizes the Third Source and Center consistently functions in consonance with, and in recognition of, the eternal fact of the absoluteness of Paradise. The Conjoint Creator embodies the fullness of the combined and infinite concepts of the First and Second Persons of Deity.

While you envisage the Father as an original creator and the Son as a spiritual administrator, you should think of the Third Source and Center as a universal co-ordinator, a minister of unlimited co-operation. The Conjoint Actor is the correlator of all actual reality; he is the Deity repository of the Father's thought and the Son's word and in action is eternally regardful of the material absoluteness of the central Isle. The Paradise Trinity has ordained the universal order of *progress*, and the providence of God is the domain of the Conjoint Creator and the evolving Supreme Being. No actual or actualizing reality can escape eventual relationship with the Third Source and Center.

The Universal Father presides over the realms of pre-energy, prespirit, and personality; the Eternal Son dominates the spheres of spiritual activities; the presence of the Isle of Paradise unifies the domain of physical energy and materializing power; the Conjoint Actor operates not only as an infinite spirit representing the Son but also as a universal manipulator of the forces and energies of Paradise, thus bringing into existence the universal and absolute mind. The Conjoint Actor functions throughout the grand universe as a positive and distinct personality, especially in the higher spheres of spiritual values, physical-energy relationships, and true mind meanings. He functions specifically wherever and whenever energy and spirit associate and interact; he dominates all reactions with mind, wields great power in the spiritual world, and exerts a mighty influence over energy and matter. At all times the Third Source is expressive of the nature of the First Source and Center.

The Third Source and Center perfectly and without qualification shares the omnipresence of the First Source and Center, sometimes being called the Omnipresent Spirit. In a peculiar and very personal manner the God of mind shares the omniscience of the Universal Father and his Eternal Son; the knowledge of the Spirit is profound and complete. The Conjoint Creator manifests certain phases of the omnipotence of the Universal Father but is actually omnipotent only in the domain of mind. The Third Person of Deity is the intellectual center and the universal administrator of the mind realms; herein is he absolute — his sovereignty is unqualified.

The Conjoint Actor seems to be motivated by the Father-Son partnership, but all his actions appear to recognize the Father-Paradise relationship. At times and in certain functions he seems to compensate for the incompleteness of the development of the experiential Deities — God the Supreme and God the Ultimate.

And herein is an infinite mystery: That the Infinite simultaneously revealed his infinity in the Son and as Paradise, and then there springs into existence a being equal to God in divinity, reflective of the Son's spiritual nature, and capable of activating the Paradise pattern, a being provisionally subordinate in sovereignty but in many ways apparently the most versatile in action. And such apparent superiority in action is disclosed in an attribute of the Third Source and Center which is superior even to physical gravity — the universal manifestation of the Isle of Paradise.

In addition to this supercontrol of energy and things physical, the Infinite Spirit is superbly endowed with those attributes of patience, mercy, and love which are so exquisitely revealed in his spiritual ministry. The Spirit is supremely competent to minister love and to overshadow justice with mercy. God the Spirit possesses all the supernal kindness and merciful affection of the Original and Eternal Son. The universe of your origin is being forged out between the anvil of justice and the hammer of suffering; but those who wield the hammer are the children of mercy, the spirit offspring of the Infinite Spirit.

2. THE OMNIPRESENT SPIRIT

God is spirit in a threefold sense: He himself is spirit; in his Son he appears as spirit without qualification; in the Conjoint Actor, as spirit allied with mind. And in addition to these spiritual realities, we think we discern levels of experiential spirit phenomena — the spirits of the Supreme Being, Ultimate Deity, and Deity Absolute.

The Infinite Spirit is just as much a complement of the Eternal Son as the Son is a complement of the Universal Father. The Eternal Son is a spiritualized personalization of the Father; the Infinite Spirit is a personalized spiritualization of the Eternal Son and the Universal Father.

There are many untrammeled lines of spiritual force and sources of supermaterial power linking the people of Urantia directly with the Deities of Paradise. There exist the connection of the Thought Adjusters direct with the Universal Father, the widespread influence of the spiritual-gravity urge of the Eternal Son, and the spiritual presence of the Conjoint Creator. There is a difference in function between the spirit of the Son and the spirit of the Spirit. The Third Person in his spiritual ministry may function as mind plus spirit or as spirit alone.

In addition to these Paradise presences, Urantians benefit by the spiritual influences and activities of the local and the superuniverse, with their almost endless array of loving personalities who ever lead the true of purpose and the honest of heart upward and inward towards the ideals of divinity and the goal of supreme perfection.

The presence of the universal spirit of the Eternal Son we know — we can unmistakably recognize it. The presence of the Infinite Spirit, the Third Person of Deity, even mortal man may know, for material creatures can actually experience the beneficence of this divine influence which functions as the Holy Spirit of local universe bestowal upon the races of mankind. Human beings can also in some degree become conscious of the Adjuster, the impersonal presence of the Universal Father. These divine spirits which work for man's uplifting and spiritualization all act in unison and in perfect co-operation. They are as one in the spiritual operation of the plans of mortal ascension and perfection attainment.

3. THE UNIVERSAL MANIPULATOR

The Isle of Paradise is the source and substance of physical gravity; and that should be sufficient to inform you that gravity is one of the most *real* and eternally dependable things in the whole physical universe of universes. Gravity cannot be modified or annulled except by the forces and energies conjointly sponsored by the Father and the Son, which have been intrusted to, and are functionally associated with, the person of the Third Source and Center.

The Infinite Spirit possesses a unique and amazing power — *antigravity*. This power is not functionally (observably) present in either the Father or the Son. This ability to withstand the pull of material gravity, inherent in the Third Source, is revealed in the personal reactions of the Conjoint Actor to certain phases of universe relationships. And this unique attribute is transmissible to certain of the higher personalities of the Infinite Spirit.

Antigravity can annul gravity within a local frame; it does so by the exercise of equal force presence. It operates only with reference to material gravity, and it is not the action of mind.

Still further does the Conjoint Actor display powers which can transcend force and neutralize energy. Such powers operate by slowing down energy to the point of materialization and by other techniques unknown to you.

The Conjoint Creator is not energy nor the source of energy nor the destiny of energy; he is the *manipulator* of energy. The Conjoint Creator is action — motion, change, modification, co-ordination, stabilization, and equilibrium. The energies subject to the direct or indirect control of Paradise are by nature responsive to the acts of the Third Source and Center and his manifold agencies.

The universe of universes is permeated by the power-control creatures of the Third Source and Center: physical controllers, power directors, power centers, and other representatives of the God of Action who have to do with the regulation and stabilization of physical energies. These unique creatures of physical function all possess varying attributes of power control, such as antigravity, which they utilize in their efforts to establish the physical equilibrium of the matter and energies of the grand universe.

All these material activities of the God of Action appear to relate his function to the Isle of Paradise, and indeed the agencies of power are all regardful of, even dependent on, the absoluteness of the eternal Isle. But the Conjoint Actor does not act for, or in response to, Paradise. He acts, personally, for the Father and the Son. Paradise is not a person. The nonpersonal, impersonal, and otherwise not personal doings of the Third Source and Center are all volitional acts of the Conjoint Actor himself; they are not reflections, derivations, or repercussions of anything or anybody.

Paradise is the pattern of infinity; the God of Action is the activator of that pattern. Paradise is the material fulcrum of infinity; the agencies of the Third Source and Center are the levers of intelligence which motivate the material level and inject spontaneity into the mechanism of the physical creation.

4. THE ABSOLUTE MIND

There is an intellectual nature of the Third Source and Center that is distinct from his physical and spiritual attributes. Such a nature is hardly contactable, but it is associable — intellectually though not personally. It is distinguishable from the physical attributes and the spiritual character of the Third Person on mind levels of function, but to the discernment of personalities this nature never functions independently of physical or spiritual manifestations.

The absolute mind is the mind of the Third Person; it is inseparable from the personality of God the Spirit. Mind, in functioning beings, is not separated from energy or spirit, or both. Mind is not inherent in energy; energy is receptive and responsive to mind; mind can be superimposed upon energy, but consciousness is not inherent in the purely material level. Mind does not have to be added to pure spirit, for spirit is innately conscious and identifying. Spirit is always intelligent, *minded* in some way. It may be this mind or that mind, it may be premind or supermind, even spirit mind, but it does the equivalent of thinking and knowing. The insight of spirit transcends, supervenes, and theoretically antedates the consciousness of mind.

The Conjoint Creator is absolute only in the domain of mind, in the realms of universal intelligence. The mind of the Third Source and Center is infinite; it utterly transcends the active and functioning mind circuits of the universe of universes. The mind endowment of the seven superuniverses is derived from the Seven Master Spirits, the primary personalities of the Conjoint Creator. These Master Spirits distribute mind to the grand universe as the cosmic mind, and your local universe is pervaded by the Nebadon variant of the Orvonton type of cosmic mind.

Infinite mind ignores time, ultimate mind transcends time, cosmic mind is conditioned by time. And so with space: The Infinite Mind is independent of space, but as descent is made from the infinite to the adjutant levels of mind, intellect must increasingly reckon with the fact and limitations of space.

Cosmic force responds to mind even as cosmic mind responds to spirit. Spirit is divine purpose, and spirit mind is divine purpose in action. Energy is thing, mind is meaning, spirit is value. Even in time and space, mind establishes those relative relationships between energy and spirit which are suggestive of mutual kinship in eternity.

Mind transmutes the values of spirit into the meanings of intellect; volition has power to bring the meanings of mind to fruit in both the material and spiritual domains. The Paradise ascent involves a relative and differential growth in spirit, mind, and energy. The personality is the unifier of these components of experiential individuality.

5. THE MINISTRY OF MIND

The Third Source and Center is infinite in mind. If the universe should grow to infinity, still his mind potential would be adequate to endow limitless numbers of creatures with suitable minds and other prerequisites of intellect.

In the domain of *created mind* the Third Person, with his co-ordinate and subordinate associates, rules supreme. The realms of creature mind are of exclusive origin in the Third Source and Center; he is the bestower of mind. Even the Father fragments find it impossible to indwell the minds of men until the way has been properly prepared for them by the mind action and spiritual function of the Infinite Spirit.

The unique feature of mind is that it can be bestowed upon such a wide range of life. Through his creative and creature associates the Third Source and Center ministers to all minds on all spheres. He ministers to human and subhuman intellect through the adjutants of the local universes and, through the agency of the physical controllers, ministers even to the lowest nonexperiencing entities of the most primitive types of living things. And always is the direction of mind a ministry of mind-spirit or mind-energy personalities.

Since the Third Person of Deity is the source of mind, it is quite natural that the evolutionary will creatures find it easier to form comprehensible concepts of the Infinite Spirit than they do of either the Eternal Son or the Universal Father. The reality of the Conjoint Creator is disclosed imperfectly in the very existence of human mind. The Conjoint Creator is the ancestor of the cosmic mind, and the mind of man is an individualized circuit, an impersonal portion, of that cosmic mind as it is bestowed in a local universe by a Creative Daughter of the Third Source and Center.

Because the Third Person is the source of mind, do not presume to reckon that all phenomena of mind are divine. Human intellect is rooted in the material origin of the animal races. Universe intelligence is no more a true revelation of God who is mind than is physical nature a true revelation of the beauty and harmony of Paradise. Perfection is in nature, but nature is not perfect. The Conjoint Creator is the source of mind, but mind is not the Conjoint Creator.

Mind, on Urantia, is a compromise between the essence of thought perfection and the evolving mentality of your immature human nature. The plan for your intellectual evolution is, indeed, one of sublime perfection, but you are far short of that divine goal as you function in the tabernacles of the flesh. Mind is truly of divine origin, and it does have a divine destiny, but your mortal minds are not yet of divine dignity.

Too often, all too often, you mar your minds by insincerity and sear them with unrighteousness; you subject them to animal fear and distort them by useless anxiety. Therefore, though the source of mind is divine, mind as you know it on your world of ascension can hardly become the object of great admiration, much less of adoration or worship. The contemplation of the immature and inactive human intellect should lead only to reactions of humility.

6. THE MIND-GRAVITY CIRCUIT

The Third Source and Center, the universal intelligence, is personally conscious of every *mind*, every intellect, in all creation, and he maintains a personal and perfect contact with all these physical, morontial, and spiritual creatures of mind endowment in the far-flung universes. All these activities of mind are grasped in the absolute mind-gravity circuit which focalizes in the Third Source and Center and is a part of the personal consciousness of the Infinite Spirit.

Much as the Father draws all personality to himself, and as the Son attracts all spiritual reality, so does the Conjoint Actor exercise a drawing power on all minds; he unqualifiedly dominates and controls the universal mind circuit. All true and genuine intellectual values, all divine thoughts and perfect ideas, are unerringly drawn into this absolute circuit of mind.

Mind gravity can operate independently of material and spiritual gravity, but wherever and whenever the latter two impinge, mind gravity always functions. When all three are associated, personality gravity may embrace the material creature — physical or morontial, finite or absonite. But irrespective of this, the endowment of mind even in impersonal beings qualifies them to think and endows them with consciousness despite the total absence of personality.

Selfhood of personality dignity, human or divine, immortal or potentially immortal, does not however originate in either spirit, mind, or matter; it is the bestowal of the Universal Father. Neither is the interaction of spirit, mind, and material gravity a prerequisite to the appearance of personality gravity. The Father's circuit may embrace a mind-material being who is unresponsive to spirit gravity, or it may include a mind-spirit being who is unresponsive to material gravity. The operation of personality gravity is always a volitional act of the Universal Father.

While mind is energy associated in purely material beings and spirit associated in purely spiritual personalities, innumerable orders of personality, including the human, possess minds that are associated with both energy and spirit. The spiritual aspects of creature mind unfailingly respond to the spirit-gravity pull of the Eternal Son; the material features respond to the gravity urge of the material universe.

Cosmic mind, when not associated with either energy or spirit, is subject to the gravity demands of neither material nor spiritual circuits. Pure mind is subject only to the universal gravity grasp of the Conjoint Actor. Pure mind is close of kin to infinite mind, and infinite mind (the theoretical co-ordinate of the absolutes of spirit and energy) is apparently a law in itself.

The greater the spirit-energy divergence, the greater the observable function of mind; the lesser the diversity of energy and spirit, the lesser the observable function of mind. Apparently, the maximum function of the cosmic mind is in the time universes of space. Here mind seems to function in a mid-zone between energy and spirit, but this is not true of the higher levels of mind; on Paradise, energy and spirit are essentially one.

The mind-gravity circuit is dependable; it emanates from the Third Person of Deity on Paradise, but not all the observable function of mind is predictable. Throughout all known creation there parallels this circuit of mind some little-understood presence whose function is not predictable. We believe that this unpredictability is partly attributable to the function of the Universal Absolute. What this function is, we do not know; what actuates it, we can only conjecture; concerning its relation to creatures, we can only speculate.

Certain phases of the unpredictability of finite mind may be due to the incompleteness of the Supreme Being, and there is a vast zone of activities wherein the Conjoint Actor and the Universal Absolute may possibly be tangent. There is much about mind that is unknown, but of this we are sure: The Infinite Spirit is the perfect expression of the mind of the Creator to all creatures; the Supreme Being is the evolving expression of the minds of all creatures to their Creator.

7. UNIVERSE REFLECTIVITY

The Conjoint Actor is able to co-ordinate all levels of universe actuality in such manner as to make possible the simultaneous recognition of the mental, the material, and the spiritual. This is the phenomenon of *universe reflectivity*, that unique and inexplicable power to see, hear, sense, and know all things as they transpire throughout a superuniverse, and to focalize, by reflectivity, all this information and knowledge at any desired point. The action of reflectivity is shown in perfection on each of the headquarters worlds of the seven superuniverses. It is also operative throughout all sectors of the superuniverses and within the boundaries of the local universes. Reflectivity finally focalizes on Paradise.

The phenomenon of reflectivity, as it is disclosed on the superuniverse headquarters worlds in the amazing performances of the reflective personalities there stationed, represents the most complex interassociation of all phases of existence to be found in all creation. Lines of spirit can be traced back to the Son, physical energy to Paradise, and mind to the Third Source; but in the extraordinary phenomenon of universe reflectivity there is a unique and exceptional unification of all three, so associated as to enable the universe rulers to know about remote conditions instantaneously, simultaneously with their occurrence.

Much of the technique of reflectivity we comprehend, but there are many phases which truly baffle us. We know that the Conjoint Actor is the universe center of the mind circuit, that he is the ancestor of the cosmic mind, and that cosmic mind operates under the dominance of the absolute mind gravity of the Third Source and Center. We know further that the circuits of the cosmic mind influence the intellectual levels of all known existence; they contain the universal space reports, and just as certainly they focus in the Seven Master Spirits and converge in the Third Source and Center.

The relationship between the finite cosmic mind and the divine absolute mind appears to be evolving in the experiential mind of the Supreme. We are taught that, in the dawn of time, this experiential mind was bestowed upon the Supreme by the Infinite Spirit, and we conjecture that certain features of the phenomenon of reflectivity can be accounted for only by postulating the activity of the Supreme Mind. If the Supreme is not concerned in reflectivity, we are at a loss to explain the intricate transactions and unerring operations of this consciousness of the cosmos.

Reflectivity appears to be omniscience within the limits of the experiential finite and may represent the emergence of the presence-consciousness of the Supreme Being. If this assumption is true, then the utilization of reflectivity in any of its phases is equivalent to partial contact with the consciousness of the Supreme.

8. PERSONALITIES OF THE INFINITE SPIRIT

The Infinite Spirit possesses full power to transmit many of his powers and prerogatives to his co-ordinate and subordinate personalities and agencies.

The first Deity-creating act of the Infinite Spirit, functioning apart from the Trinity but in some unrevealed association with the Father and the Son, personalized in the existence of the Seven Master Spirits of Paradise, the distributors of the Infinite Spirit to the universes.

There is no direct representative of the Third Source and Center on the headquarters of a superuniverse. Each of these seven creations is dependent on one of the Master Spirits of Paradise, who acts through the seven Reflective Spirits situated at the capital of the superuniverse.

The next and continuing creative act of the Infinite Spirit is disclosed, from time to time, in the production of the Creative Spirits. Every time the Universal Father and the Eternal Son become parent to a Creator Son, the Infinite Spirit becomes ancestor to a local universe Creative Spirit who becomes the close associate of that Creator Son in all subsequent universe experience.

Just as it is necessary to distinguish between the Eternal Son and the Creator Sons, so it is necessary to differentiate between the Infinite Spirit and the Creative Spirits, the local universe co-ordinates of the Creator Sons. What the Infinite Spirit is to the total creation, a Creative Spirit is to a local universe.

The Third Source and Center is represented in the grand universe by a vast array of ministering spirits, messengers, teachers, adjudicators, helpers, and advisers, together with supervisors of certain circuits of physical, morontial, and spiritual nature. Not all of these beings are personalities in the strict meaning of the term. Personality of the finite-creature variety is characterized by:

1. Subjective self-consciousness.
2. Objective response to the Father's personality circuit.

There are creator personalities and creature personalities, and in addition to these two fundamental types there are personalities of the Third Source and Center, beings who are personal to the Infinite Spirit, but who are not unqualifiedly personal to creature beings. These Third Source personalities are not a part of the Father's personality circuit. First Source personality and Third Source personality are mutually contactable; all personality is contactable.

The Father bestows personality by his personal free will. Why he does so we can only conjecture; how he does so we do not know. Neither do we know why the Third Source bestows non-Father personality, but this the Infinite Spirit does in his own behalf, in creative conjunction with the Eternal Son and in numerous ways unknown to you. The Infinite Spirit can also act for the Father in the bestowal of First Source personality.

There are numerous types of Third Source personalities. The Infinite Spirit bestows Third Source personality upon numerous groups who are not included in the Father's personality circuit, such as certain of the power directors. Likewise does the Infinite Spirit treat as personalities numerous groups of beings, such as the Creative Spirits, who are in a class by themselves in their relations to encircuited creatures of the Father.

Both First Source and Third Source personalities are endowed with all and more than man associates with the concept of personality; they have minds embracing memory, reason, judgment, creative imagination, idea association, decision, choice, and numerous additional powers of intellect wholly unknown to mortals. With few exceptions the orders revealed to you possess form and distinct individuality; they are real beings. A majority of them are visible to all orders of spirit existence.

Even you will be able to see your spiritual associates of the lower orders as soon as you are delivered from the limited vision of your present material eyes and have been endowed with a morontia form with its enlarged sensitivity to the reality of spiritual things.

The functional family of the Third Source and Center, as it is revealed in these narratives, falls into three great groups:

I. *The Supreme Spirits.* A group of composite origin that embraces, among others, the following orders:

1. The Seven Master Spirits of Paradise.
2. The Reflective Spirits of the Superuniverses.
3. The Creative Spirits of the Local Universes.

II. *The Power Directors*. A group of control creatures and agencies that function throughout all organized space.

III. *The Personalities of the Infinite Spirit.* This designation does not necessarily imply that these beings are Third Source personalities though some of them are unique as will creatures. They are usually grouped in three major classifications:

1. The Higher Personalities of the Infinite Spirit.
2. The Messenger Hosts of Space.
3. The Ministering Spirits of Time.

These groups serve on Paradise, in the central or residential universe, in the superuniverses, and they embrace orders that function in the local universes, even to the constellations, systems, and planets.

The spirit personalities of the vast family of the Divine and Infinite Spirit are forever dedicated to the service of the ministry of the love of God and the mercy of the Son to all the intelligent creatures of the evolutionary worlds of time and space. These spirit beings constitute the living ladder whereby mortal man climbs from chaos to glory.

[Revealed on Urantia by a Divine Counselor of Uversa commissioned by the Ancients of Days to portray the nature and work of the Infinite Spirit.]

Urantia 2025: A Revised Urantia Book

PAPER 10
THE PARADISE TRINITY

THE PARADISE TRINITY of eternal Deities facilitates the Father's escape from personality absolutism. The Trinity perfectly associates the limitless expression of God's infinite personal will with the absoluteness of Deity. The Eternal Son and the various Sons of divine origin, together with the Conjoint Actor and his universe children, effectively provide for the Father's liberation from the limitations otherwise inherent in primacy, perfection, changelessness, eternity, universality, absoluteness, and infinity.

The Paradise Trinity effectively provides for the full expression and perfect revelation of the eternal nature of Deity. The Stationary Sons of the Trinity likewise afford a full and perfect revelation of divine justice. The Trinity is Deity unity, and this unity rests eternally upon the absolute foundations of the divine oneness of the three original and co-ordinate and coexistent personalities, God the Father, God the Son, and God the Spirit.

From the present situation on the circle of eternity, looking backward into the endless past, we can discover only one inescapable inevitability in universe affairs, and that is the Paradise Trinity. I deem the Trinity to have been inevitable. As I view the past, present, and future of time, I consider nothing else in all the universe of universes to have been inevitable. The present master universe, viewed in retrospect or in prospect, is unthinkable without the Trinity. Given the Paradise Trinity, we can postulate alternate or even multiple ways of doing all things, but without the Trinity of Father, Son, and Spirit we are unable to conceive how the Infinite could achieve threefold and co-ordinate personalization in the face of the absolute oneness of Deity. No other concept of creation measures up to the Trinity standards of the completeness of the absoluteness inherent in Deity unity coupled with the repleteness of volitional liberation inherent in the threefold personalization of Deity.

1. SELF-DISTRIBUTION OF THE FIRST SOURCE AND CENTER

It would seem that the Father, back in eternity, inaugurated a policy of profound self-distribution. There is inherent in the selfless, loving, and lovable nature of the Universal Father something which causes him to reserve to himself the exercise of only those powers and that authority which he apparently finds it impossible to delegate or to bestow.

The Universal Father all along has divested himself of every part of himself that was bestowable on any other Creator or creature. He has delegated to his divine Sons and their associated intelligences every power and all authority that could be delegated. He has actually transferred to his Sovereign Sons, in their respective universes, every prerogative of administrative authority that was transferable. In the affairs of a local universe, he has made each Sovereign Creator Son just as perfect, competent, and authoritative as is the Eternal Son in the original and central universe. He has given away, actually bestowed, with the dignity and sanctity of personality possession, all of himself and all of his attributes, everything he possibly could divest himself of, in every way, in every age, in every place, and to every person, and in every universe except that of his central indwelling.

Divine personality is not self-centered; self-distribution and sharing of personality characterize divine freewill selfhood. Creatures crave association with other personal creatures; Creators are moved to share divinity with their universe children; the personality of the Infinite is disclosed as the Universal

Father, who shares reality of being and equality of self with two co-ordinate personalities, the Eternal Son and the Conjoint Actor.

For knowledge concerning the Father's personality and divine attributes we will always be dependent on the revelations of the Eternal Son, for when the conjoint act of creation was effected, when the Third Person of Deity sprang into personality existence and executed the combined concepts of his divine parents, the Father ceased to exist as the unqualified personality. With the coming into being of the Conjoint Actor and the materialization of the central core of creation, certain eternal changes took place. God gave himself as an absolute personality to his Eternal Son. Thus does the Father bestow the "personality of infinity" upon his only-begotten Son, while they both bestow the "conjoint personality" of their eternal union upon the Infinite Spirit.

For these and other reasons beyond the concept of the finite mind, it is exceedingly difficult for the human creature to comprehend God's infinite father-personality except as it is universally revealed in the Eternal Son and, with the Son, is universally active in the Infinite Spirit.

Since the Paradise Sons of God visit the evolutionary worlds and sometimes even there dwell in the likeness of mortal flesh, and since these bestowals make it possible for mortal man actually to know something of the nature and character of divine personality, therefore must the creatures of the planetary spheres look to the bestowals of these Paradise Sons for reliable and trustworthy information regarding the Father, the Son, and the Spirit.

2. DEITY PERSONALIZATION

By the technique of trinitization the Father divests himself of that unqualified spirit personality which is the Son, but in so doing he constitutes himself the Father of this very Son and thereby possesses himself of unlimited capacity to become the divine Father of all subsequently created, eventuated, or other personalized types of intelligent will creatures. As the *absolute and unqualified personality* the Father can function only as and with the Son, but as a *personal Father* he continues to bestow personality upon the diverse hosts of the differing levels of intelligent will creatures, and he forever maintains personal relations of loving association with this vast family of universe children.

After the Father has bestowed upon the personality of his Son the fullness of himself, and when this act of self-bestowal is complete and perfect, of the infinite power and nature which are thus existent in the Father-Son union, the eternal partners conjointly bestow those qualities and attributes which constitute still another being like themselves; and this conjoint personality, the Infinite Spirit, completes the existential personalization of Deity.

The Son is indispensable to the fatherhood of God. The Spirit is indispensable to the fraternity of the Second and Third Persons. Three persons are a minimum social group, but this is least of all the many reasons for believing in the inevitability of the Conjoint Actor.

The First Source and Center is the infinite *father-personality*, the unlimited source personality. The Eternal Son is the unqualified *personality-absolute*, that divine being who stands throughout all time and eternity as the perfect revelation of the personal nature of God. The Infinite Spirit is the *conjoint personality*, the unique personal consequence of the everlasting Father-Son union.

The personality of the First Source and Center is the personality of infinity minus the absolute personality of the Eternal Son. The personality of the Third Source and Center is the superadditive consequence of the union of the liberated Father-personality and the absolute Son-personality.

The Universal Father, the Eternal Son, and the Infinite Spirit are unique persons; none is a duplicate; each is original; all are united.

The Eternal Son alone experiences the fullness of divine personality relationship, consciousness of both sonship with the Father and paternity to the Spirit and of divine equality with both Father-ancestor and Spirit-associate. The Father knows the experience of having a Son who is his equal, but the Father knows no ancestral antecedents. The Eternal Son has the experience of sonship, recognition of personality ancestry, and at the same time the Son is conscious of being joint parent to the Infinite Spirit. The Infinite Spirit is conscious of twofold personality ancestry but is not parental to a co-ordinate Deity personality. With the Spirit the existential cycle of Deity personalization attains completion; the primary personalities of the Third Source and Center are experiential and are seven in number.

I am of origin in the Paradise Trinity. I know the Trinity as unified Deity; I also know that the Father, Son, and Spirit exist and act in their definite personal capacities. I positively know that they not only act personally and collectively, but that they also co-ordinate their performances in various groupings, so that in the end they function in seven different singular and plural capacities. And since these seven associations exhaust the possibilities for such divinity combination, it is inevitable that the realities of the universe shall appear in seven variations of values, meanings, and personality.

3. THE THREE PERSONS OF DEITY

Notwithstanding there is only one Deity, there are three positive and divine personalizations of Deity. Regarding the endowment of man with the divine Adjusters, the Father said: "Let us make mortal man in our own image." Repeatedly throughout the Urantian writings there occurs this reference to the acts and doings of plural Deity, clearly showing recognition of the existence and working of the three Sources and Centers.

We are taught that the Son and the Spirit sustain the same and equal relations to the Father in the Trinity association. In eternity and as Deities they undoubtedly do, but in time and as personalities they certainly disclose relationships of a very diverse nature. Looking from Paradise out on the universes, these relationships do seem to be very similar, but when viewed from the domains of space, they appear to be quite different.

The divine Sons are indeed the "Word of God," but the children of the Spirit are truly the "Act of God." God speaks through the Son and, with the Son, acts through the Infinite Spirit, while in all universe activities the Son and the Spirit are exquisitely fraternal, working as two equal brothers with admiration and love for an honored and divinely respected common Father.

The Father, Son, and Spirit are certainly equal in nature, co-ordinate in being, but there are unmistakable differences in their universe performances, and when acting alone, each person of Deity is apparently limited in absoluteness.

The Universal Father, prior to his self-willed divestment of the personality, powers, and attributes which constitute the Son and the Spirit, seems to have been (philosophically considered) an unqualified, absolute, and infinite Deity. But such a theoretical First Source and Center without a Son could not in any sense of the word be considered the *Universal Father*; fatherhood is not real without sonship. Furthermore, the Father, to have been absolute in a total sense, must have existed at some eternally distant moment alone. But he never had such a solitary existence; the Son and the Spirit are both coeternal with the Father. The First Source and Center has always been, and will forever be, the eternal Father of the Original Son and, with the Son, the eternal progenitor of the Infinite Spirit.

We observe that the Father has divested himself of all direct manifestations of absoluteness except absolute fatherhood and absolute volition. We do not know whether volition is an inalienable attribute of the Father; we can only observe that he did *not* divest himself of volition. Such infinity of will must have been eternally inherent in the First Source and Center.

In bestowing absoluteness of personality upon the Eternal Son, the Universal Father escapes from the fetters of personality absolutism, but in so doing he takes a step which makes it forever impossible for him to act alone as the personality-absolute. And with the final personalization of coexistent Deity — the Conjoint Actor — there ensues the critical trinitarian interdependence of the three divine personalities with regard to the totality of Deity function in absolute.

God is the Father-Absolute of all personalities in the universe of universes. The Father is personally absolute in liberty of action, but in the universes of time and space, made, in the making, and yet to be made, the Father is not discernibly absolute as total Deity except in the Paradise Trinity.

The First Source and Center functions outside of Havona in the phenomenal universes as follows:

1. As creator, through the Creator Sons, his grandsons.
2. As controller, through the gravity center of Paradise.
3. As spirit, through the Eternal Son.
4. As mind, through the Conjoint Creator.
5. As a Father, he maintains parental contact with all creatures through his personality circuit.
6. As a person, he acts *directly* throughout creation by his exclusive fragments — in mortal man by the Thought Adjusters.
7. As total Deity, he functions only in the Paradise Trinity.

All these relinquishments and delegations of jurisdiction by the Universal Father are wholly voluntary and self-imposed. The all-powerful Father purposefully assumes these limitations of universe authority.

The Eternal Son seems to function as one with the Father in all spiritual respects except in the bestowals of the God fragments and in other prepersonal activities. Neither is the Son closely identified with the intellectual activities of material creatures nor with the energy activities of the material universes. As absolute the Son functions as a person and only in the domain of the spiritual universe.

The Infinite Spirit is amazingly universal and unbelievably versatile in all his operations. He performs in the spheres of mind, matter, and spirit. The Conjoint Actor represents the Father-Son association, but he also functions as himself. He is not directly concerned with physical gravity, with spiritual gravity, or with the personality circuit, but he more or less participates in all other universe activities. While apparently dependent on three existential and absolute gravity controls, the Infinite Spirit appears to exercise three supercontrols. This threefold endowment is employed in many ways to transcend and seemingly to neutralize even the manifestations of primary forces and energies, right up to the superultimate borders of absoluteness. In certain situations these supercontrols absolutely transcend even the primal manifestations of cosmic reality.

4. THE TRINITY UNION OF DEITY

Of all absolute associations, the Paradise Trinity (the first triunity) is unique as an exclusive association of personal Deity. God functions as God only in relation to God and to those who can know God, but as absolute Deity only in the Paradise Trinity and in relation to universe totality.

Eternal Deity is perfectly unified; nevertheless there are three perfectly individualized persons of Deity. The Paradise Trinity makes possible the simultaneous expression of all the diversity of the character traits and infinite powers of the First Source and Center and his eternal co-ordinates and of all the divine unity of the universe functions of undivided Deity.

The Trinity is an association of infinite persons functioning in a nonpersonal capacity but not in contravention of personality. The illustration is crude, but a father, son, and grandson could form a corporate entity which would be nonpersonal but nonetheless subject to their personal wills.

The Paradise Trinity is *real*. It exists as the Deity union of Father, Son, and Spirit; yet the Father, the Son, or the Spirit, or any two of them, can function in relation to this selfsame Paradise Trinity. The Father, Son, and Spirit can collaborate in a non-Trinity manner, but not as three Deities. As persons they can collaborate as they choose, but that is not the Trinity.

Ever remember that what the Infinite Spirit does is the function of the Conjoint Actor. Both the Father and the Son are functioning in and through and as him. But it would be futile to attempt to elucidate the Trinity mystery: three as one and in one, and one as two and acting for two.

The Trinity is so related to total universe affairs that it must be reckoned with in our attempts to explain the totality of any isolated cosmic event or personality relationship. The Trinity functions on all levels of the cosmos, and mortal man is limited to the finite level; therefore must man be content with a finite concept of the Trinity as the Trinity.

As a mortal in the flesh you should view the Trinity in accordance with your individual enlightenment and in harmony with the reactions of your mind and soul. You can know very little of the absoluteness of the Trinity, but as you ascend Paradiseward, you will many times experience astonishment at successive revelations and unexpected discoveries of Trinity supremacy and ultimacy, if not of absoluteness.

5. FUNCTIONS OF THE TRINITY

The personal Deities have attributes, but it is hardly consistent to speak of the Trinity as having attributes. This association of divine beings may more properly be regarded as having *functions*, such as justice administration, totality attitudes, co-ordinate action, and cosmic overcontrol. These functions are actively supreme, ultimate, and (within the limits of Deity) absolute as far as all living realities of personality value are concerned.

The functions of the Paradise Trinity are not simply the sum of the Father's apparent endowment of divinity plus those specialized attributes that are unique in the personal existence of the Son and the Spirit. The Trinity association of the three Paradise Deities results in the evolution, eventuation, and deitization of new meanings, values, powers, and capacities for universal revelation, action, and administration. Living associations, human families, social groups, or the Paradise Trinity are not augmented by mere arithmetical summation. The group potential is always far in excess of the simple sum of the attributes of the component individuals.

The Trinity maintains a unique attitude as the Trinity towards the entire universe of the past, present, and future. And the functions of the Trinity can best be considered in relation to the universe attitudes of the Trinity. Such attitudes are simultaneous and may be multiple concerning any isolated situation or event:

1. *Attitude toward the Finite.* The maximum self-limitation of the Trinity is its attitude toward the finite. The Trinity is not a person, nor is the Supreme Being an exclusive personalization of the Trinity, but the Supreme is the nearest approach to a power-personality focalization of the Trinity which can be comprehended by finite creatures. Hence the Trinity in relation to the finite is sometimes spoken of as the Trinity of Supremacy.

2. *Attitude toward the Absonite.* The Paradise Trinity has regard for those levels of existence which are more than finite but less than absolute, and this relationship is sometimes denominated the Trinity of Ultimacy. Neither the Ultimate nor the Supreme are wholly representative of the Paradise Trinity, but in a qualified sense and to their respective levels, each seems to represent the Trinity during the prepersonal eras of experiential-power development.

3. *The Absolute Attitude* of the Paradise Trinity is in relation to absolute existences and culminates in the action of total Deity.

The Trinity Infinite involves the co-ordinate action of all triunity relationships of the First Source and Center — undeified as well as deified — and hence is very difficult for personalities to grasp. In the contemplation of the Trinity as infinite, do not ignore the seven triunities; thereby certain difficulties of understanding may be avoided, and certain paradoxes may be partially resolved.

But I do not command language which would enable me to convey to the limited human mind the full truth and the eternal significance of the Paradise Trinity and the nature of the never-ending interassociation of the three beings of infinite perfection.

6. THE STATIONARY SONS OF THE TRINITY

All law takes origin in the First Source and Center; he is law. The administration of spiritual law inheres in the Second Source and Center. The revelation of law, the promulgation and interpretation of the divine statutes, is the function of the Third Source and Center. The application of law, justice, falls within the province of the Paradise Trinity and is carried out by certain Sons of the Trinity.

Justice is inherent in the universal sovereignty of the Paradise Trinity, but goodness, mercy, and truth are the universe ministry of the divine personalities, whose Deity union constitutes the Trinity. Justice is not the attitude of the Father, the Son, or the Spirit. Justice is the Trinity attitude of these personalities of love, mercy, and ministry. No one of the Paradise Deities fosters the administration of justice. Justice is never a personal attitude; it is always a plural function.

Evidence, the basis of fairness (justice in harmony with mercy), is supplied by the personalities of the Third Source and Center, the conjoint representative of the Father and the Son to all realms and to the minds of the intelligent beings of all creation.

Judgment, the final application of justice in accordance with the evidence submitted by the personalities of the Infinite Spirit, is the work of the Stationary Sons of the Trinity, beings partaking of the Trinity nature of the united Father, Son, and Spirit.

This group of Trinity Sons embraces the following personalities:

1. Trinitized Secrets of Supremacy.
2. Eternals of Days.
3. Ancients of Days.
4. Unions of Days.
5. Perfections of Days.
6. Recents of Days.
7. Faithfuls of Days.
8. Perfectors of Wisdom.
9. Divine Counselors.
10. Universal Censors.

We are the children of the three Paradise Deities functioning as the Trinity, for I chance to belong to the tenth order of this group, the Universal Censors. These orders are not representative of the attitude of the Trinity in a universal sense; they represent this collective attitude of Deity only in the domains of executive judgment — justice. They were specifically designed by the Trinity for the precise work to which they are assigned, and they represent the Trinity only in those functions for which they were personalized.

The Ancients of Days and their Trinity-origin associates mete out the just judgment of supreme fairness to the seven superuniverses. In the central universe such functions exist in theory only; there fairness is self-evident in perfection, and Havona perfection precludes all possibility of disharmony.

Justice is the collective thought of righteousness; mercy is its personal expression. Mercy is the attitude of love; precision characterizes the operation of law; divine judgment is the soul of fairness, ever conforming to the justice of the Trinity, ever fulfilling the divine love of God. When fully perceived and completely understood, the righteous justice of the Trinity and the merciful love of the Universal Father are coincident. But man has no such full understanding of divine justice. Thus in the Trinity, as man would view it, the personalities of Father, Son, and Spirit are adjusted to co-ordinate ministry of love and law in the experiential universes of time.

7. THE OVERCONTROL OF SUPREMACY

The First, Second, and Third Persons of Deity are equal to each other, and they are one. "The Lord our God is one God." There is perfection of purpose and oneness of execution in the divine Trinity of eternal Deities. The Father, the Son, and the Conjoint Actor are truly and divinely one. Of a truth it is written: "I am the first, and I am the last, and beside me there is no God."

As things appear to the mortal on the finite level, the Paradise Trinity, like the Supreme Being, is concerned only with the total — total planet, total universe, total superuniverse, total grand universe. This totality attitude exists because the Trinity is the total of Deity and for many other reasons.

The Supreme Being is something less and something other than the Trinity functioning in the finite universes; but within certain limits and during the present era of incomplete power-personalization, this evolutionary Deity does appear to reflect the attitude of the Trinity of Supremacy. The Father, Son, and Spirit do not personally function with the Supreme Being, but during the present universe age they collaborate with him as the Trinity. We understand that they sustain a similar relationship to the Ultimate. We often conjecture as to what will be the personal relationship between the Paradise Deities and God the Supreme when he has finally evolved, but we do not really know.

We do not find the overcontrol of Supremacy to be wholly predictable. Furthermore, this unpredictability appears to be characterized by a certain developmental incompleteness, undoubtedly an earmark of the incompleteness of the Supreme and of the incompleteness of finite reaction to the Paradise Trinity.

The mortal mind can immediately think of a thousand and one things — catastrophic physical events, appalling accidents, horrific disasters, painful illnesses, and world-wide scourges — and ask whether such visitations are correlated in the unknown maneuvering of this probable functioning of the Supreme Being. Frankly, we do not know; we are not really sure. But we do observe that, as time passes, all these difficult and more or less mysterious situations always work out for the welfare and progress of the universes. It may be that the circumstances of existence and the inexplicable vicissitudes of living are all interwoven into a meaningful pattern of high value by the function of the Supreme and the overcontrol of the Trinity.

As a son of God you can discern the personal attitude of love in all the acts of God the Father. But you will not always be able to understand how many of the universe acts of the Paradise Trinity redound to the good of the individual mortal on the evolutionary worlds of space. In the progress of eternity the acts of the Trinity will be revealed as altogether meaningful and considerate, but they do not always so appear to the creatures of time.

8. THE TRINITY BEYOND THE FINITE

Many truths and facts pertaining to the Paradise Trinity can only be even partially comprehended by recognizing a function that transcends the finite.

It would be inadvisable to discuss the functions of the Trinity of Ultimacy, but it may be disclosed that God the Ultimate is the Trinity manifestation comprehended by the Transcendentalers. We are inclined to the belief that the unification of the master universe is the eventuating act of the Ultimate and is probably reflective of certain, but not all, phases of the absonite overcontrol of the Paradise Trinity. The Ultimate is a qualified manifestation of the Trinity in relation to the absonite only in the sense that the Supreme thus partially represents the Trinity in relation to the finite.

The Universal Father, the Eternal Son, and the Infinite Spirit are, in a certain sense, the constituent personalities of total Deity. Their union in the Paradise Trinity and the absolute function of the Trinity equivalate to the function of total Deity. And such completion of Deity transcends both the finite and the absonite.

While no single person of the Paradise Deities actually fills all Deity potential, collectively all three do. Three infinite persons seem to be the minimum number of beings required to activate the prepersonal and existential potential of total Deity — the Deity Absolute.

We know the Universal Father, the Eternal Son, and the Infinite Spirit as *persons*, but I do not personally know the Deity Absolute. I love and worship God the Father; I respect and honor the Deity Absolute.

I once sojourned in a universe where a certain group of beings taught that the finaliters, in eternity, were eventually to become the children of the Deity Absolute. But I am unwilling to accept this solution of the mystery which enshrouds the future of the finaliters.

The Corps of the Finality embrace, among others, those mortals of time and space who have attained perfection in all that pertains to the will of God. As creatures and within the limits of creature capacity they fully and truly know God. Having thus found God as the Father of all creatures, these finaliters must sometime begin the quest for the superfinite Father. But this quest involves a grasp of the absonite nature of the ultimate attributes and character of the Paradise Father. Eternity will disclose whether such an attainment is possible, but we are convinced, even if the finaliters do grasp this ultimate of divinity, they will probably be unable to attain the superultimate levels of absolute Deity.

It may be possible that the finaliters will partially attain the Deity Absolute, but even if they should, still in the eternity of eternities the problem of the Universal Absolute will continue to intrigue, mystify, baffle, and challenge the ascending and progressing finaliters, for we perceive that the unfathomability of the cosmic relationships of the Universal Absolute will tend to grow in proportions as the material universes and their spiritual administration continue to expand.

Only infinity can disclose the Father-Infinite.

[Sponsored by a Universal Censor acting by authority from the Ancients of Days resident on Uversa.]

PAPER 11
THE ETERNAL ISLE OF PARADISE

Paradise is the eternal center of the universe of universes and the abiding place of the Universal Father, the Eternal Son, the Infinite Spirit, and their divine co-ordinates and associates. This central Isle is the most gigantic organized body of cosmic reality in all the master universe. Paradise is a material sphere as well as a spiritual abode. All of the intelligent creation of the Universal Father is domiciled on material abodes; hence must the absolute controlling center also be material, literal. And again it should be reiterated that spirit things and spiritual beings are real.

The material beauty of Paradise consists in the magnificence of its physical perfection; the grandeur of the Isle of God is exhibited in the superb intellectual accomplishments and mind development of its inhabitants; the glory of the central Isle is shown forth in the infinite endowment of divine spirit personality — the light of life. But the depths of the spiritual beauty and the wonders of this magnificent ensemble are utterly beyond the comprehension of the finite mind of material creatures. The glory and spiritual splendor of the divine abode are impossible of mortal comprehension. And Paradise is from eternity; there are neither records nor traditions respecting the origin of this nuclear Isle of Light and Life.

1. THE DIVINE RESIDENCE

Paradise serves many purposes in the administration of the universal realms, but to creature beings it exists primarily as the dwelling place of Deity. The personal presence of the Universal Father is resident at the very center of the upper surface of this well-nigh circular, but not spherical, abode of the Deities. This Paradise presence of the Universal Father is immediately surrounded by the personal presence of the Eternal Son, while they are both invested by the unspeakable glory of the Infinite Spirit.

God dwells, has dwelt, and everlastingly will dwell in this same central and eternal abode. We have always found him there and always will. The Universal Father is cosmically focalized, spiritually personalized, and geographically resident at this center of the universe of universes.

We all know the direct course to pursue to find the Universal Father. You are not able to comprehend much about the divine residence because of its remoteness from you. Those who are able to comprehend the central divine creation know God's location and residence just as certainly and literally as you know the location of New York, London, Rome, or Singapore, cities definitely and geographically located on Urantia. If you were an intelligent navigator, equipped with ship, maps, and compass, you could readily find these cities. Likewise, if you had the time and means of passage, were spiritually qualified, and had the necessary guidance, you could be piloted through universe upon universe and from circuit to circuit, ever journeying inward, until at last you would stand before the central shining of the spiritual glory of the Universal Father. Provided with all the necessities for the journey, it is just as possible to find the personal presence of God at the center of all things as to find distant cities on your own planet. That you have not visited these places in no way disproves their reality or actual existence. That so few of the universe creatures have found God on Paradise in no way disproves either the reality of his existence or the actuality of his spiritual person at the center of all things.

The Father is always to be found at this central location. Did he move, universal pandemonium would be precipitated, for there converge in him at this residential center the universal lines of gravity from the ends of creation.

Whether we trace the personality circuit back through the universes or follow the ascending personalities as they journey inward to the Father; whether we trace the lines of material gravity to nether Paradise or follow the insurging cycles of cosmic force; whether we trace the lines of spiritual gravity to the Eternal Son or follow the inward processional of the Paradise Sons of God; whether we trace out the mind circuits or follow the unlimited number of celestial beings who spring from the Infinite Spirit — by any of these observations or by all of them we are led directly back to the Father's presence, to his central abode. Here is God personally, literally, and actually present. And from his infinite being there flow the flood-streams of life, energy, and personality to all universes.

2. NATURE OF THE ETERNAL ISLE

Since you are beginning to glimpse the enormousness of your local material universe, it should become evident to you that such a tremendous material universe must have an adequate and worthy capital. Likewise must each superuniverse. Also, must the master universe have a headquarters commensurate with the dignity and infinitude of the universal Rulers of all this vast and far-flung creation of material realms and living beings.

In form Paradise differs from the inhabited space bodies: it is not spherical. It is definitely ellipsoid, being one-sixth longer in the north-south diameter than in the east-west diameter. The central Isle is essentially flat, and the distance from the upper surface to the nether surface is one tenth that of the east-west diameter.

These differences in dimensions, taken in connection with its stationary status and the greater out-pressure of force-energy at the north end of the Isle, make it possible to establish absolute direction in the master universe.

The central Isle is geographically divided into three domains of activity:

1. Upper Paradise.
2. Peripheral Paradise.
3. Nether Paradise.

We speak of that surface of Paradise which is occupied with personality activities as the upper side, and the opposite surface as the nether side. The periphery of Paradise provides for activities that are not strictly personal or nonpersonal. The Trinity seems to dominate the personal or upper plane, the Unqualified Absolute the nether or impersonal plane. We hardly conceive of the Unqualified Absolute as a person, but we do think of the functional space presence of this Absolute as focalized on nether Paradise.

The eternal Isle is composed of a single form of materialization — stationary systems of reality. This literal substance of Paradise is a homogeneous organization of space potency not to be found elsewhere in all the wide universe of universes. It has received many names in different universes, and the Melchizedeks of Nebadon long since named it absolutum. This Paradise source material is neither dead nor alive; it is the original nonspiritual expression of the First Source and Center; it is Paradise, and Paradise is without duplicate.

It appears to us that the First Source and Center has concentrated all absolute potential for cosmic reality in Paradise as a part of his technique of self-liberation from infinity limitations, as a means of making possible subinfinite, even time-space, creation. But it does not follow that Paradise is time-space limited just because the universe of universes discloses these qualities. Paradise exists without time and has no location in space.

Roughly: space seemingly originates just below nether Paradise; time just above upper Paradise. Time, as you understand it, is not a feature of Paradise existence, though the citizens of the central Isle are fully conscious of nontime sequence of events. Motion is not inherent on Paradise; it is volitional. But the concept of distance, even absolute distance, has very much meaning as it may be applied to relative locations on Paradise. Paradise is nonspatial; hence its areas are absolute and therefore serviceable in many ways beyond the concept of mortal mind.

3. UPPER PARADISE

On upper Paradise there are three grand spheres of activity, the Deity presence, the Most Holy Sphere, and the Holy Area. The vast region immediately surrounding the presence of the Deities is set aside as the Most Holy Sphere and is reserved for the functions of worship, trinitization, and high spiritual attainment. There are no material structures nor purely intellectual creations in this zone; they could not exist there. It is useless for me to undertake to portray to the human mind the divine nature and the beauteous grandeur of the Most Holy Sphere of Paradise. This realm is wholly spiritual, and you are almost wholly material. A purely spiritual reality is, to a purely material being, apparently nonexistent.

While there are no physical materializations in the area of the Most Holy, there are abundant souvenirs of your material days in the Holy Land sectors and still more in the reminiscent historic areas of peripheral Paradise.

The Holy Area, the outlying or residential region, is divided into seven concentric zones. Paradise is sometimes called "the Father's House" since it is his eternal residence, and these seven zones are often designated "the Father's Paradise mansions." The inner or first zone is occupied by Paradise Citizens and the natives of Havona who may chance to be dwelling on Paradise. The next or second zone is the residential area of the natives of the seven superuniverses of time and space. This second zone is in part subdivided into seven immense divisions, the Paradise home of the spirit beings and ascendant creatures who hail from the universes of evolutionary progression. Each of these sectors is exclusively dedicated to the welfare and advancement of the personalities of a single superuniverse, but these facilities are almost infinitely beyond the requirements of the present seven superuniverses.

Each of the seven sectors of Paradise is subdivided into residential units suitable for the lodgment headquarters of all glorified individual working groups now there, or that may arrive, even unto the times of the eternal future.

4. PERIPHERAL PARADISE

The central Isle ends abruptly at the periphery, but its size is so enormous that this terminal angle is relatively indiscernible within any circumscribed area. The peripheral surface of Paradise is occupied, in part, by the landing and dispatching fields for various groups of spirit personalities.

Since the nonpervaded-space zones nearly impinge upon the periphery, all personality transports destined to Paradise land in these regions. Neither upper nor nether Paradise is approachable by transport supernaphim or other types of space traversers.

The Seven Master Spirits have their personal seats of power and authority on the seven spheres of the Spirit, which circle about Paradise in the space between the shining orbs of the Son and the inner circuit of the Havona worlds, but they maintain force-focal headquarters on the Paradise periphery. Here the slowly circulating presences of the Seven Supreme Power Directors indicate the location of the seven flash stations for certain Paradise energies going forth to the seven superuniverses.

Here on peripheral Paradise are the historic and prophetic exhibit areas assigned to the Creator Sons, dedicated to the local universes of time and space. There are currently an enormous number of these historic reservations now set up or in reserve, but these arrangements all together occupy only about four per cent of that portion of the peripheral area thus assigned. We infer that these vast reserves belong to creations sometime to be situated beyond the borders of the present known and inhabited seven superuniverses.

That portion of Paradise which has been designated for the use of the existing universes is occupied only from one to four per cent, while the area assigned to these activities is at least one million times that actually required for such purposes. Paradise is large enough to accommodate the activities of an almost infinite creation.

But a further attempt to visualize to you the glories of Paradise would be futile. You must wait, and ascend while you wait, for truly, "Eye has not seen, nor ear heard, neither has it entered into the mind of mortal man, the things which the Universal Father has prepared for those who survive the life in the flesh on the worlds of time and space."

5. NETHER PARADISE

Concerning nether Paradise, we know only that which is revealed; personalities do not sojourn there. It has nothing whatever to do with the affairs of spirit intelligences, nor does the Deity Absolute there function. We are informed that all physical-energy and cosmic-force circuits have their origin on nether Paradise, and that it is constituted as follows:

1. Directly underneath the location of the Trinity, in the central portion of nether Paradise, is the unknown and unrevealed Zone of Infinity.

2. This Zone is immediately surrounded by an unnamed area.

3. Occupying the outer margins of the under surface is a region having mainly to do with space potency and force-energy. The activities of this vast elliptical force center are not identifiable with the known functions of any triunity, but the primordial force-charge of space appears to be focalized in this area. This center consists of three concentric elliptical zones: The innermost is the focal point of the force-energy activities of Paradise itself; the outermost may possibly be identified with the functions of the Unqualified Absolute, but we are not certain concerning the space functions of the mid-zone.

The *inner zone* of this force center seems to act as a gigantic heart whose pulsations direct currents to the outermost borders of physical space. It directs and modifies force-energies but hardly drives them. The reality pressure-presence of this primal force is definitely greater at the north end of the Paradise center than in the southern regions; this is a uniformly registered difference. The mother force of space seems to flow in at the south and out at the north through the operation of some unknown circulatory system which is concerned with the diffusion of this basic form of force-energy. From time to time there are also noted differences in the east-west pressures. The forces emanating from this zone are not responsive to observable physical gravity but are always obedient to Paradise gravity.

The *mid-zone* of the force center immediately surrounds this area. This mid-zone appears to be static except that it expands and contracts through three cycles of activity. The least of these pulsations is in an east-west direction, the next in a north-south direction, while the greatest fluctuation is in every direction, a generalized expansion and contraction. The function of this mid-area has never been really identified, but it must have something to do with reciprocal adjustment between the inner and the outer zones of the force center. It is believed by many that the mid-zone is the control mechanism of the midspace or quiet zones which separate the successive space levels of the master universe, but no evidence or revelation confirms this. This inference is derived from the knowledge that this mid-area is in some manner related to the functioning of the nonpervaded-space mechanism of the master universe.

The *outer zone* is the largest and most active of the three concentric and elliptical belts of unidentified space potential. This area is the site of unimagined activities, the central circuit point of emanations which proceed spaceward in every direction to the outermost borders of the seven superuniverses and on beyond to overspread the enormous and incomprehensible domains of all outer space. This space presence is entirely impersonal notwithstanding that in some undisclosed manner it seems to be indirectly responsive to the will and mandates of the infinite Deities when acting as the Trinity. This is believed to be the central focalization, the Paradise center, of the space presence of the Unqualified Absolute.

All forms of force and all phases of energy seem to be encircuited; they circulate throughout the universes and return by definite routes. But with the emanations of the activated zone of the Unqualified Absolute there appears to be either an outgoing or an incoming — never both simultaneously. This outer zone pulsates in agelong cycles of gigantic proportions. For a little more than one billion Urantia years the space-force of this center is outgoing; then for a similar length of time it will be incoming. And the space-force manifestations of this center are universal; they extend throughout all pervadable space.

All physical force, energy, and matter are one. All force-energy originally proceeded from nether Paradise and will eventually return thereto following the completion of its space circuit. But the energies and material organizations of the universe of universes did not all come from nether Paradise in their present phenomenal states; space is the womb of several forms of matter and prematter. Though the outer zone of the Paradise force center is the source of space-energies, space does not originate there. Space is not force, energy, or power. Nor do the pulsations of this zone account for the respiration of space, but the incoming and outgoing phases of this zone are synchronized with the two-billion-year expansion-contraction cycles of space.

6. SPACE RESPIRATION

We do not know the actual mechanism of space respiration; we merely observe that all space alternately contracts and expands. This respiration affects both the horizontal extension of pervaded space and the vertical extensions of unpervaded space which exist in the vast space reservoirs above and below Paradise. In attempting to imagine the volume outlines of these space reservoirs, you might think of an hourglass.

As the universes of the horizontal extension of pervaded space expand, the reservoirs of the vertical extension of unpervaded space contract and vice versa. There is a confluence of pervaded and unpervaded space just underneath nether Paradise. Both types of space there flow through the transmuting regulation channels, where changes are wrought making pervadable space nonpervadable and vice versa in the contraction and expansion cycles of the cosmos.

"Unpervaded" space means: unpervaded by those forces, energies, powers, and presences known to exist in pervaded space. We do not know whether vertical (reservoir) space is destined always to function as the equipoise of horizontal (universe) space; we do not know whether there is a creative intent concerning unpervaded space; we really know very little about the space reservoirs, merely that they exist, and that they seem to counterbalance the space-expansion-contraction cycles of the universe of universes.

The cycles of space respiration extend in each phase for a little more than one billion Urantia years. During one phase the universes expand; during the next they contract. Pervaded space is now approaching the mid-point of the expanding phase, while unpervaded space nears the mid-point of the contracting phase, and we are informed that the outermost limits of both space extensions are, theoretically, now approximately equidistant from Paradise. The unpervaded-space reservoirs now extend vertically above upper Paradise and below nether Paradise just as far as the pervaded space of the universe extends horizontally outward from peripheral Paradise to and even beyond the fourth outer space level.

For a billion years of Urantia time the space reservoirs contract while the master universe and the force activities of all horizontal space expand. It thus requires a little over two billion Urantia years to complete the entire expansion-contraction cycle.

7. SPACE FUNCTIONS OF PARADISE

Space does not exist on any of the surfaces of Paradise. If one "looked" directly up from the upper surface of Paradise, one would "see" nothing but unpervaded space going out or coming in, just now coming in. Space does not touch Paradise; only the quiescent *midspace zones* come in contact with the central Isle.

Paradise is the actually motionless nucleus of the relatively quiescent zones existing between pervaded and unpervaded space. Geographically these zones appear to be a relative extension of Paradise, but there probably is some motion in them. We know very little about them, but we observe that these zones of lessened space motion separate pervaded and unpervaded space. Similar zones once existed between the levels of pervaded space, but these are now less quiescent.

The vertical cross section of total space would slightly resemble a Maltese cross, with the horizontal arms representing pervaded (universe) space and the vertical arms representing unpervaded (reservoir) space. The areas between the four arms would separate them somewhat as the midspace zones separate pervaded and unpervaded space. These quiescent midspace zones grow larger and larger at greater and greater distances from Paradise and eventually encompass the borders of all space and completely incapsulate both the space reservoirs and the entire horizontal extension of pervaded space.

Space is neither a subabsolute condition within, nor the presence of, the Unqualified Absolute, neither is it a function of the Ultimate. It is a bestowal of Paradise, and the space of the grand universe and that of all outer regions is believed to be actually pervaded by the ancestral space potency of the Unqualified Absolute. From near approach to peripheral Paradise, this pervaded space extends horizontally outward through the fourth space level and beyond the periphery of the master universe, but how far beyond we do not know.

If you imagine a finite, but inconceivably large, V-shaped plane situated at right angles to both the upper and lower surfaces of Paradise, with its point nearly tangent to peripheral Paradise, and then visualize this plane in elliptical revolution about Paradise, its revolution would roughly outline the volume of pervaded space.

There is an upper and a lower limit to horizontal space with reference to any given location in the universes. If one could move far enough at right angles to the plane of Orvonton, either up or down, eventually the upper or lower limit of pervaded space would be encountered. Within the known dimensions of the master universe these limits draw farther and farther apart at greater and greater distances from Paradise; space thickens, and it thickens somewhat faster than does the plane of creation, the universes.

The relatively quiet zone between the space levels, such as the one separating the seven superuniverses from the first outer space level, are enormous elliptical regions of quiescent space activities. You may visualize the first outer space level, where untold universes are now in process of formation, as a vast space procession swinging around Paradise, bounded above and below by the midspace zones of quiescence and bounded on the inner and outer margins by relatively quiet space zones.

A space level thus functions as an elliptical region of motion surrounded on all sides by relative motionlessness. Such relationships of motion and quiescence constitute a curved space path of lessened resistance to motion which is universally followed by cosmic force and emergent energy as they circle forever around the Isle of Paradise.

This alternate zoning of the master universe, in association with the alternate clockwise and counterclockwise flow, is a factor in the stabilization of physical gravity designed to prevent the accentuation of gravity pressure to the point of disruptive and dispersive activities. Such an arrangement exerts antigravity influence and acts as a brake upon otherwise dangerous velocities.

8. PARADISE GRAVITY

The inescapable pull of gravity effectively grips all the universes of all the superuniverses of the master universe. Gravity is the all-powerful grasp of the physical presence of Paradise. Gravity is the omnipotent strand on which are strung the seven superuniverses and the entire master universe which constitute the universal physical adornment of the eternal God, who is all things, fills all things, and in whom all things consist.

The center and focal point of absolute material gravity is the Isle of Paradise, complemented by the dark gravity bodies encircling Havona and equilibrated by the upper and nether space reservoirs. All known emanations of nether Paradise invariably and unerringly respond to the central gravity pull operating upon the endless circuits of the elliptical space levels of the master universe. Every known form of cosmic reality has the bend of the ages, the trend of the circle, the swing of the great ellipse.

Space is nonresponsive to gravity, but it acts as an equilibrant on gravity. Without the space cushion, explosive action would jerk surrounding space bodies. Pervaded space also exerts an antigravity influence upon physical or linear gravity; space can actually neutralize such gravity action even though it cannot delay it. Absolute gravity is Paradise gravity. Local or linear gravity pertains to the electrical stage of energy or matter; it operates within the central, super-, and outer universes, wherever suitable materialization has taken place.

The numerous forms of cosmic force, physical energy, universe power, and various materializations disclose three general, though not perfectly clear-cut, stages of response to Paradise gravity:

1. *Pregravity Stages (Force)*. This is the first step in the individuation of space potency into the pre-energy forms of cosmic force. This state is analogous to the concept of the primordial force-charge of space, sometimes called pure energy or *segregata*.

2. *Gravity Stages (Energy)*. This modification of the force-charge of space is produced by the action of the Paradise force organizers. It signalizes

the appearance of energy systems responsive to the pull of Paradise gravity. This emergent energy is originally neutral but consequent upon further metamorphosis will exhibit the so-called negative and positive qualities. We designate these stages *ultimata.*

3. *Postgravity Stages (Universe Power).* In this stage, energy-matter discloses response to the control of linear gravity. In the central universe these physical systems are threefold organizations known as *triata.* They are the superpower mother systems of the creations of time and space. The physical systems of the superuniverses are mobilized by the Universe Power Directors and their associates. These material organizations are dual in constitution and are known as *gravita.* The dark gravity bodies encircling Havona are neither triata nor gravita, and their drawing power discloses both forms of physical gravity, linear and absolute.

Space potency is not subject to the interactions of any form of gravitation. This primal endowment of Paradise is not an actual level of reality, but it is ancestral to all relative functional nonspirit realities — all manifestations of force-energy and the organization of power and matter. Space potency is a term difficult to define. It does not mean that which is ancestral to space; its meaning should convey the idea of the potencies and potentials existent within space. It may be roughly conceived to include all those absolute influences and potentials which emanate from Paradise and constitute the space presence of the Unqualified Absolute.

Paradise is the absolute source and the eternal focal point of all energy-matter in the universe of universes. The Unqualified Absolute is the revealer, regulator, and repository of that which has Paradise as its source and origin. The universal presence of the Unqualified Absolute seems to be equivalent to the concept of a potential infinity of gravity extension, an elastic tension of Paradise presence. This concept aids us in grasping the fact that everything is drawn inward towards Paradise. The illustration is crude but nonetheless helpful. It also explains why gravity always acts preferentially in the plane perpendicular to the mass, a phenomenon indicative of the differential dimensions of Paradise and the surrounding creations.

9. THE UNIQUENESS OF PARADISE

Paradise is unique in that it is the realm of primal origin and the final goal of destiny for all spirit personalities. Although it is true that not all of the lower spirit beings of the local universes are immediately destined to Paradise, Paradise still remains the goal of desire for all supermaterial personalities.

Paradise is the geographic center of infinity; it is not a part of universal creation, not even a real part of the eternal Havona universe. We commonly refer to the central Isle as belonging to the divine universe, but it really does not. Paradise is an eternal and exclusive existence.

In the eternity of the past, when the Universal Father gave infinite personality expression of his spirit self in the being of the Eternal Son, simultaneously he revealed the infinity potential of his nonpersonal self as Paradise. Nonpersonal and nonspiritual Paradise appears to have been the inevitable repercussion to the Father's will and act which eternalized the Original Son. Thus did the Father project reality in two actual phases — the personal and the nonpersonal, the spiritual and the nonspiritual. The tension between them, in the face of will to action by the Father and the Son, gave existence to the Conjoint Actor and the central universe of material worlds and spiritual beings.

When reality is differentiated into the personal and the nonpersonal (Eternal Son and Paradise), it is hardly proper to call that which is nonpersonal "Deity" unless somehow qualified. The energy and material repercussions of the acts of Deity could hardly be called Deity. Deity may cause much that is not Deity, and Paradise is not Deity; neither is it conscious as mortal man could ever possibly understand such a term.

Paradise is not ancestral to any being or living entity; it is not a creator. Personality and mind-spirit relationships are transmissible, but pattern is not. Patterns are never reflections; they are duplications — reproductions. Paradise is the absolute of patterns; Havona is an exhibit of these potentials in actuality.

God's residence is central and eternal, glorious and ideal. His home is the beauteous pattern for all universe headquarters worlds; and the central universe of his immediate indwelling is the pattern for all universes in their ideals, organization, and ultimate destiny.

Paradise is the universal headquarters of all personality activities and the source-center of all force-space and energy manifestations. Everything which has been, now is, or is yet to be, has come, now comes, or will come forth from this central abiding place of the eternal Gods. Paradise is the center of all creation, the source of all energies, and the place of primal origin of all personalities.

After all, to mortals the most important thing about eternal Paradise is the fact that this perfect abode of the Universal Father is the real and far-distant destiny of the immortal souls of the mortal and material sons of God, the ascending creatures of the evolutionary worlds of time and space. Every God-knowing mortal who has espoused the career of doing the Father's will has already embarked upon the long, long Paradise trail of divinity pursuit and perfection attainment. And when such an animal-origin being does stand, as countless numbers now do, before the Gods on Paradise, having ascended from the lowly spheres of space, such an achievement represents the reality of a spiritual transformation bordering on the limits of supremacy.

[Presented by a Perfector of Wisdom commissioned thus to function by the Ancients of Days on Uversa.]

PAPER 12
THE UNIVERSE OF UNIVERSES

THE IMMENSITY of the far-flung creation of the Universal Father is utterly beyond the grasp of finite imagination; the enormousness of the master universe staggers the concept of even my order of being. But the mortal mind can be taught much about the plan and arrangement of the universes; you can know something of their physical organization and marvelous administration; you may learn much about the various groups of intelligent beings who inhabit the seven superuniverses of time and the central universe of eternity.

In principle, that is, in eternal potential, we conceive of material creation as being infinite because the Universal Father is actually infinite, but as we study and observe the total material creation, we know that at any given moment in time it is limited, although to your finite minds it is comparatively limitless, virtually boundless.

We are convinced, from the study of physical law and from the observation of the universe of universes, that the infinite Creator is not yet manifest in finality of cosmic expression, that much of the cosmic potential of the Infinite is still self-contained and unrevealed. To created beings the master universe might appear to be almost infinite, but it is far from finished; there are still physical limits to the material creation, and the experiential revelation of the eternal purpose is still in progress.

1. SPACE LEVELS OF THE MASTER UNIVERSE

The universe of universes is not an infinite plane, a boundless cube, nor a limitless circle; it certainly has dimensions. The laws of physical organization and administration prove conclusively that the whole vast aggregation of force-energy and matter-power functions ultimately as a space unit, as an organized and co-ordinated whole. The final proof of both a circular and delimited master universe is afforded by the, to us, well-known fact that all forms of basic energy ever swing around the curved path of the space levels of the master universe in obedience to the incessant and absolute pull of Paradise gravity.

The successive space levels of the master universe constitute the major divisions of pervaded space — total creation, organized and partially inhabited or yet to be organized and inhabited. If the master universe were not a series of elliptical space levels of lessened resistance to motion, alternating with zones of relative quiescence, we conceive that some of the cosmic energies would be observed to shoot off on an infinite range, off on a straight-line path into trackless space; but we never find force, energy, or matter thus behaving; ever they whirl, always swinging onward in the tracks of the great space circuits.

Proceeding outward from Paradise through the horizontal extension of pervaded space, the master universe is existent in six concentric ellipses, the space levels encircling the central Isle:

1. The Central Universe — Havona.
2. The Seven Superuniverses.
3. The First Outer Space Level.
4. The Second Outer Space Level.
5. The Third Outer Space Level.
6. The Fourth and Outermost Space Level.

Havona, the central universe, is not a time creation; it is an eternal existence. This never-beginning, never-ending universe consists of one billion spheres of sublime perfection and is surrounded by the enormous dark gravity bodies. At the center of Havona is the stationary and absolutely stabilized Isle of Paradise, surrounded by its twenty-one satellites. Owing to the enormous encircling masses of the dark gravity bodies about the fringe of the central universe, the mass content of this central creation is far in excess of the total known mass of all seven sectors of the grand universe.

The Paradise-Havona System, the eternal universe encircling the eternal Isle, constitutes the perfect and eternal nucleus of the master universe; all seven of the superuniverses and all regions of outer space revolve in established orbits around the gigantic central aggregation of the Paradise satellites and the Havona spheres.

The Seven Superuniverses exist in an expanded 10 or more dimensional space-time which includes the universes of which they are composed. Each universe is a hypersurface or four dimensional membrane (M-brane). These membrane universes are organized around the headquarters of each superuniverse much like flower petals around a flower. If you had higher dimensional vision their beauty is exquisite. *Nebadon*, your local universe, is one of the newer creations in *Orvonton*, the seventh superuniverse.

The Grand Universe is the present organized and inhabited creation. It consists of the seven superuniverses, each a collection of an enormous number of universes, not to mention the eternal spheres of the central creation. Yet this takes no account of the architectural administrative spheres, neither does it include the outlying groups of unorganized universes. The present ragged edge of the grand universe, its uneven and unfinished periphery, together with the tremendously unsettled condition of the whole astronomical plot, suggests to our students that even the seven superuniverses are, as yet, uncompleted. As we move from within, from the divine center outward in any one direction, we do, eventually, come to the outer limits of the organized and inhabited creation; we come to the outer limits of the grand universe.

The Outer Space Levels. Far out beyond the seven superuniverses, there are assembling vast and unbelievably stupendous circuits of force and materializing energies. Between the energy circuits of the seven superuniverses and this gigantic outer belt of force activity, there is a space zone of comparative quiet. Our students are in doubt as to the exact status of the space-forces existing in this zone of relative quiet which encircles the seven superuniverses. But beyond the periphery of the present grand universe we observe the beginnings of a zone of an unbelievable energy action which increases in volume and intensity. These tremendous forces are situated in the first outer space level, a continuous belt of cosmic activity encircling the whole of the known, organized, and inhabited creation.

Still greater activities are taking place beyond these regions, for the Uversa physicists have detected early evidence of force manifestations beyond the outermost ranges of the phenomena in the first outer space level. These activities undoubtedly presage the organization of the material creations of the second outer space level of the master universe.

The central universe is the creation of eternity; the seven superuniverses are the creations of time; the four outer space levels are undoubtedly destined to eventuate-evolve the ultimacy of creation. And there are those who maintain that the Infinite can never attain full expression short of infinity; and therefore do they postulate an additional and unrevealed creation beyond the fourth and outermost space level, a possible ever-expanding, never-ending universe of infinity. In theory we do not know how to limit either the infinity of the Creator or the potential infinity of creation, but as it exists and is administered, we regard the master universe as having limitations, as being definitely delimited and bounded on its outer margins by open space.

2. THE DOMAINS OF THE UNQUALIFIED ABSOLUTE

When we contemplate the grand universe we should realize that we are entering into the mighty outworking of the unsearchable plans of the Architects of the Master Universe. True, we do possess evidences which are suggestive of the presence of certain Paradise personality influences here and there throughout the vast energy manifestations now characteristic of these outer regions, but from the larger viewpoint the space regions extending beyond the outer borders of the seven superuniverses are generally recognized as constituting the domains of the Unqualified Absolute.

The seven superuniverses are still growing; the periphery of each is gradually expanding; new universes are constantly being stabilized and organized. We are informed that the metamorphosis of cosmic force in these outer space levels is a function of the Paradise force organizers. We also know that these forces are ancestral to those physical energies which at present activate the grand universe.

We know very little of the significance of these tremendous phenomena of outer space. A greater creation of the future is in process of formation. We can observe its immensity, we can discern its extent and sense its majestic dimensions. As far as we know, no material beings on the order of humans, no angels or other spirit creatures, exist in this outer ring. This distant domain is beyond the jurisdiction and administration of the superuniverse governments.

Throughout Orvonton it is believed that a new type of creation is in process, an order of universes destined to become the scene of the future activities of the assembling Corps of the Finality; and if our conjectures are correct, then the endless future may hold for all of you the same enthralling spectacles that the endless past has held for your seniors and predecessors.

3. UNIVERSAL GRAVITY

All forms of force-energy — material, mindal, or spiritual — are alike subject to those grasps, those universal presences, which we call gravity. Personality also is responsive to gravity — to the Father's exclusive circuit; but though this circuit is exclusive to the Father, he is not excluded from the other circuits; the Universal Father is infinite and acts over all four absolute-gravity circuits in the master universe:

1. The Personality Gravity of the Universal Father.
2. The Spirit Gravity of the Eternal Son.
3. The Mind Gravity of the Conjoint Actor.
4. The Cosmic Gravity of the Isle of Paradise.

These four circuits are not related to the nether Paradise force center; they are neither force, energy, nor power circuits. They are absolute presence circuits and like God are independent of time and space.

In this connection it is interesting to record certain observations made on Uversa during recent millenniums by the corps of gravity researchers. This expert group of workers has arrived at the following conclusions regarding the different gravity systems of the master universe:

1. *Physical Gravity.* Having formulated an estimate of the summation of the entire physical-gravity capacity of the grand universe, they have laboriously effected a comparison of this finding with the estimated total of absolute gravity presence now operative. These calculations indicate that the total gravity action on the grand universe is a very small part of the estimated gravity pull of Paradise, computed on the basis of the gravity response of basic physical units of universe matter. These investigators reach the amazing conclusion that the central universe and the surrounding seven superuniverses are at the present time making use of only about five per cent of the active functioning of the Paradise absolute-gravity grasp. In other words: At the present moment about ninety-five per cent of the active cosmic-gravity action of the Isle of Paradise, computed on this totality theory, is engaged in controlling material systems beyond the borders of the present organized universes. These calculations all refer to absolute gravity; linear gravity is an interactive phenomenon which can be computed only by knowing the actual Paradise gravity.

2. *Spiritual Gravity.* By the same technique of comparative estimation and calculation these researchers have explored the present reaction capacity of spirit gravity and, with the co-operation of Solitary Messengers and other spirit personalities, have arrived at the summation of the active spirit gravity of the Second Source and Center. And it is most instructive to note that they find about the same value for the actual and functional presence of spirit gravity in the grand universe that they postulate for the present total of active spirit gravity. In other words: At the present time practically the entire spirit gravity of the Eternal Son, computed on this theory of totality, is observable as functioning in the grand universe. If these findings are dependable, we may conclude that the universes now evolving in outer space are at the present time wholly nonspiritual. And if this is true, it would satisfactorily explain why spirit-endowed beings are in possession of little or no information about these

vast energy manifestations aside from knowing the fact of their physical existence.

3. *Mind Gravity.* By these same principles of comparative computation these experts have attacked the problem of mind-gravity presence and response. The mind unit of estimation was arrived at by averaging three material and three spiritual types of mentality, although the type of mind found in the power directors and their associates proved to be a disturbing factor in the effort to arrive at a basic unit for mind-gravity estimation. There was little to impede the estimation of the present capacity of the Third Source and Center for mind-gravity function in accordance with this theory of totality. Although the findings in this instance are not so conclusive as in the estimates of physical and spirit gravity, they are, comparatively considered, very instructive, even intriguing. These investigators deduce that about eighty-five per cent of the mind-gravity response to the intellectual drawing of the Conjoint Actor takes origin in the existing grand universe. This would suggest the possibility that mind activities are involved in connection with the observable physical activities now in progress throughout the realms of outer space. While this estimate is probably far from accurate, it accords, in principle, with our belief that intelligent force organizers are at present directing universe evolution in the space levels beyond the present outer limits of the grand universe. Whatever the nature of this postulated intelligence, it is apparently not spirit-gravity responsive.

But all these computations are at best estimates based on assumed laws. We think they are fairly reliable. Even if a few spirit beings were located in outer space, their collective presence would not markedly influence calculations involving such enormous measurements.

Personality Gravity is noncomputable. We recognize the circuit, but we cannot measure either qualitative or quantitative realities responsive thereto.

4. SPACE AND MOTION

All units of cosmic energy are in primary revolution, are engaged in the execution of their mission, while swinging around the universal orbit. The superuniverses and their component universes are all moving along the endless circuits of the master universe space levels. Absolutely nothing is stationary in all the master universe except the very center of Havona, the eternal Isle of Paradise, the center of gravity.

The Unqualified Absolute is functionally limited to space, but we are not so sure about the relation of this Absolute to motion. Is motion inherent therein? We do not know. We know that motion is not inherent in space; even the motions of space are not innate. But we are not so sure about the relation of the Unqualified to motion. Who, or what, is really responsible for the gigantic activities of force-energy transmutations now in progress out beyond the borders of the present seven superuniverses? Concerning the origin of motion we have the following opinions:

1. We think the Conjoint Actor initiates motion *in* space.
2. If the Conjoint Actor produces the motions *of* space, we cannot prove it.
3. The Universal Absolute does not originate initial motion but does equalize and control all of the tensions originated by motion.

In outer space the force organizers are apparently responsible for the production of gigantic universe wheels which are now in process of evolution, but their ability so to function must have been made possible by some modification of the space presence of the Unqualified Absolute.

Space is, from the human viewpoint, nothing — negative; it exists only as related to something positive and nonspatial. Space is, however, real. It contains and conditions motion. It even moves. Space motions may be roughly classified as follows:

1. Primary motion — space respiration, the motion of space itself.
2. Secondary motion — the alternate directional swings of the successive space levels.
3. Relative motions — relative in the sense that they are not evaluated with Paradise as a base point. Primary and secondary motions are absolute, motion in relation to unmoving Paradise.

4. Compensatory or correlating movement designed to co-ordinate all other motions.

The entire seven superuniverses participate in the two-billion-year cycles of space respiration along with the outer regions of the master universe. When the superuniverses expand and contract, the universes of which they are composed alternately move against and with the pull of Paradise gravity. The work that is done in moving the material energy mass of creation is space work but not power-energy work.

5. SPACE AND TIME

Space is not infinite, even though it takes origin from Paradise; not absolute, for it is pervaded by the Unqualified Absolute. We do not know the absolute limits of space, but we do know that the absolute of time is eternity.

Time and space are inseparable only in the time-space creations, the seven superuniverses. Nontemporal space (space without time) theoretically exists, but the only truly nontemporal place is Paradise area. Nonspatial time (time without space) exists in mind of the Paradise level of function.

The relatively motionless midspace zones impinging on Paradise and separating pervaded from unpervaded space are the transition zones from time to eternity, hence the necessity of Paradise pilgrims becoming unconscious during this transit when it is to culminate in Paradise citizenship. Time-conscious visitors can go to Paradise without thus sleeping, but they remain creatures of time.

Relationships to time do not exist without motion in space, but consciousness of time does. Sequentiality can consciousize time even in the absence of motion. Man's mind is less time-bound than space-bound because of the inherent nature of mind. Even during the days of the earth life in the flesh, though man's mind is rigidly space-bound, the creative human imagination is comparatively time free. But time itself is not genetically a quality of mind.

There are three different levels of time cognizance:

1. Mind-perceived time — consciousness of sequence, motion, and a sense of duration.
2. Spirit-perceived time — insight into motion Godward and the awareness of the motion of ascent to levels of increasing divinity.
3. Personality *creates* a unique time sense out of insight into Reality plus a consciousness of presence and an awareness of duration.

Unspiritual animals know only the past and live in the present. Spirit-indwelt man has powers of prevision (insight); he may visualize the future. Only forward-looking and progressive attitudes are personally real. Static ethics and traditional morality are just slightly superanimal. Nor is stoicism a high order of self-realization. Ethics and morals become truly human when they are dynamic and progressive, alive with universe reality.

The human personality is not merely a concomitant of time-and-space events; the human personality can also act as the cosmic cause of such events.

6. UNIVERSAL OVERCONTROL

The universe is nonstatic. Stability is not the result of inertia but rather the product of balanced energies, co-operative minds, co-ordinated morontias, spirit overcontrol, and personality unification. Stability is wholly and always proportional to divinity.

In the physical control of the master universe the Universal Father exercises priority and primacy through the Isle of Paradise; God is absolute in the spiritual administration of the cosmos in the person of the Eternal Son. Concerning the domains of mind, the Father and the Son function co-ordinately in the Conjoint Actor.

The Third Source and Center assists in the maintenance of the equilibrium and co-ordination of the combined physical and spiritual energies and organizations by the absoluteness of his grasp of the cosmic mind and by the exercise of his inherent and universal physical- and spiritual-gravity complements. Whenever and wherever there occurs a liaison between the material and the spiritual, such a mind phenomenon is an act of the Infinite Spirit. Mind alone can interassociate the physical forces and energies of the material level with the spiritual powers and beings of the spirit level.

In all your contemplation of universal phenomena, make certain that you take into consideration the interrelation of physical, intellectual, and spiritual energies, and that due allowance is made for the unexpected phenomena attendant upon their unification by personality and for the unpredictable phenomena resulting from the actions and reactions of experiential Deity and the Absolutes.

The universe is highly predictable only in the quantitative or gravity-measurement sense; even the primal physical forces are not responsive to linear gravity, nor are the higher mind meanings and true spirit values of ultimate universe realities. Qualitatively, the universe is not highly predictable as regards new associations of forces, either physical, mindal, or spiritual, although many such combinations of energies or forces become partially predictable when subjected to critical observation. When matter, mind, and spirit are unified by creature personality, we are unable fully to predict the decisions of such a freewill being.

All phases of primordial force, nascent spirit, and other nonpersonal ultimates appear to react in accordance with certain relatively stable but unknown laws and are characterized by a latitude of performance and an elasticity of response which are often disconcerting when encountered in the phenomena of a circumscribed and isolated situation. What is the explanation of this unpredictable freedom of reaction disclosed by these emerging universe actualities? These unknown, unfathomable unpredictables — whether pertaining to the behavior of a primordial unit of force, the reaction of an unidentified level of mind, or the phenomenon of a vast presuperuniverse in the making in the domains of outer space — probably disclose the activities of the Ultimate and the presence-performances of the Absolutes, which antedate the function of all universe Creators.

We do not really know, but we surmise that such amazing versatility and such profound co-ordination signify the presence and performance of the Absolutes, and that such diversity of response in the face of apparently uniform causation discloses the reaction of the Absolutes, not only to the immediate and situational causation, but also to all other related causations throughout the entire master universe.

Individuals have their guardians of destiny; planets, systems, constellations, galaxies, universes, and superuniverses each have their respective rulers who labor for the good of their domains. Havona and even the grand universe are watched over by those intrusted with such high responsibilities. But who fosters and cares for the fundamental needs of the master universe as a whole, from Paradise to the fourth and outermost space level? Existentially such overcare is probably attributable to the Paradise Trinity, but from an experiential viewpoint the appearance of the post-Havona universes is dependent on:

1. The Absolutes in potential.
2. The Ultimate in direction.
3. The Supreme in evolutionary co-ordination.
4. The Architects of the Master Universe in administration prior to the appearance of specific rulers.

The Unqualified Absolute pervades all space. We are not altogether clear as to the exact status of the Deity and Universal Absolutes, but we know the latter functions wherever the Deity and Unqualified Absolutes function. The Deity Absolute may be universally present but hardly space present. The Ultimate is, or sometime will be, space present to the outer margins of the fourth space level. We doubt that the Ultimate will ever have a space presence beyond the periphery of the master universe, but within this limit the Ultimate is progressively integrating the creative organization of the potentials of the three Absolutes.

7. THE PART AND THE WHOLE

There is operative throughout all time and space and with regard to all reality of whatever nature an inexorable and impersonal law which is equivalent to the function of a cosmic providence. Mercy characterizes God's attitude of love for the individual; impartiality motivates God's attitude toward the total. The will of God does not necessarily prevail in the part — the heart of any one personality — but his will does actually rule the whole, the universe of universes.

In all his dealings with all his beings it is true that the laws of God are not inherently arbitrary. To you, with your limited vision and finite viewpoint, the acts of God must often appear to be dictatorial and arbitrary. The laws of God are merely the habits of God, his way of repeatedly doing things; and he ever does all things well. You observe that God does the same thing in the same way, repeatedly, simply because that is the best way to do that particular thing in a given circumstance; and the best way is the right way, and therefore does infinite wisdom always order it done in that precise and perfect manner. You should also remember that nature is not the exclusive act of Deity; other influences are present in those phenomena which man calls nature.

It is repugnant to the divine nature to suffer any sort of deterioration or ever to permit the execution of any purely personal act in an inferior way. It should be made clear, however, that, if, in the divinity of any situation, in the extremity of any circumstance, in any case where the course of supreme wisdom might indicate the demand for different conduct — if the demands of perfection might for any reason dictate another method of reaction, a better one, then and there would the all-wise God function in that better and more suitable way. That would be the expression of a higher law, not the reversal of a lower law.

God is not a habit-bound slave to the chronicity of the repetition of his own voluntary acts. There is no conflict among the laws of the Infinite; they are all perfections of the infallible nature; they are all the unquestioned acts expressive of faultless decisions. Law is the unchanging reaction of an infinite, perfect, and divine mind. The acts of God are all volitional notwithstanding this apparent sameness. In God there "is no variableness neither shadow of changing." But all this which can be truly said of the Universal Father cannot be said with equal certainty of all his subordinate intelligences or of his evolutionary creatures.

Because God is changeless, therefore can you depend, in all ordinary circumstances, on his doing the same thing in the same identical and ordinary way. God is the assurance of stability for all created things and beings. He is God; therefore he changes not.

And all this steadfastness of conduct and uniformity of action is personal, conscious, and highly volitional, for the great God is not a helpless slave to his own perfection and infinity. God is not a self-acting automatic force; he is not a slavish law-bound power. God is neither a mathematical equation nor a chemical formula. He is a freewill and primal personality. He is the Universal Father, a being surcharged with personality and the universal fount of all creature personality.

The will of God does not uniformly prevail in the heart of the God-seeking material mortal, but if the time frame is enlarged beyond the moment to embrace the whole of the first life, then does God's will become increasingly discernible in the spirit fruits which are borne in the lives of the spirit-led children of God. And then, if human life is further enlarged to include the morontia experience, the divine will is observed to shine brighter and brighter in the spiritualizing acts of those creatures of time who have begun to taste the divine delights of experiencing the relationship of the personality of man with the personality of the Universal Father.

The Fatherhood of God and the brotherhood of man present the paradox of the part and the whole on the level of personality. God loves *each* individual as an individual child in the heavenly family. Yet God thus loves every individual; he is no respecter of persons, and the universality of his love brings into being a relationship of the whole, the universal brotherhood.

The love of the Father absolutely individualizes each personality as a unique child of the Universal Father, a child without duplicate in infinity, a will creature irreplaceable in all eternity. The Father's love glorifies each child of God, illuminating each member of the celestial family, sharply silhouetting the unique nature of each personal being against the impersonal levels that lie outside the fraternal circuit of the Father of all. The love of God strikingly portrays the transcendent value of each will creature, unmistakably reveals the high value which the Universal Father has placed upon each and every one of his children from the highest creator personality of Paradise status to the lowest personality of will dignity among the savage tribes of men in the dawn of the human species on some evolutionary world of time and space.

This very love of God for the individual brings into being the divine family of all individuals, the universal brotherhood of the freewill children of the Paradise Father. And this brotherhood, being universal, is a relationship of the whole. Brotherhood, when universal, discloses not the *each* relationship, but the all relationship. Brotherhood is a reality of the total and therefore discloses qualities of the whole in contradistinction to qualities of the part.

Brotherhood constitutes a fact of relationship between every personality in universal existence. No person can escape the benefits or the penalties that may come as a result of relationship to other persons. The part profits or suffers in measure with the whole. The good effort of each man benefits all men; the error or evil of each man augments the tribulation of all men. As moves the part, so moves the whole. As the progress of the whole, so the progress of the part. The relative velocities of part and whole determine whether the part is retarded by the inertia of the whole or is carried forward by the momentum of the cosmic brotherhood.

It is a mystery that God is a highly personal self-conscious being with residential headquarters, and at the same time personally present in such a vast universe and personally in contact with such a well-nigh infinite number of beings. That such a phenomenon is a mystery beyond human comprehension should not in the least lessen your faith. Do not allow the magnitude of the infinity, the immensity of the eternity, and the grandeur and glory of the matchless character of God to overawe, stagger, or discourage you; for the Father is not very far from any one of you; he dwells within you, and in him do we all literally move, actually live, and veritably have our being.

Even though the Paradise Father functions through his divine creators and his creature children, he also enjoys the most intimate inner contact with you, so sublime, so highly personal, that it is even beyond my comprehension — that mysterious communion of the Father fragment with the human soul and with the mortal mind of its actual indwelling. Knowing what you do of these gifts of God, you therefore know that the Father is in intimate touch, not only with his divine associates, but also with his evolutionary mortal children of time. The Father indeed abides on Paradise, but his divine presence also dwells in the minds of men.

Even though the spirit of a Son be poured out upon all flesh, even though a Son once dwelt with you in the likeness of mortal flesh, even though the seraphim personally guard and guide you, how can any of these divine beings of the Second and Third Centers ever hope to come as near to you or to understand you as fully as the Father, who has given a part of himself to be in you, to be your real and divine, even your eternal, self?

8. MATTER, MIND, AND SPIRIT

"God is spirit," but Paradise is not. The material universe is always the arena wherein take place all spiritual activities; spirit beings and spirit ascenders live and work on physical spheres of material reality.

The bestowal of cosmic force, the domain of cosmic gravity, is the function of the Isle of Paradise. All original force-energy proceeds from Paradise, and the matter for the making of untold universes now circulates throughout the master universe in the form of a supergravity presence which constitutes the force-charge of pervaded space.

Whatever the transformations of force in the outlying universes, having gone out from Paradise, it journeys on subject to the never-ending, ever-present, unfailing pull of the eternal Isle, obediently and inherently swinging on forever around the eternal space paths of the master universe. Physical energy is the one reality which is true and steadfast in its obedience to universal law. Only in the realms of creature volition has there been deviation from the divine paths and the original plans. Power and energy are the universal evidences of the stability, constancy, and eternity of the central Isle of Paradise.

The bestowal of spirit and the spiritualization of personalities, the domain of spiritual gravity, is the realm of the Eternal Son. And this spirit gravity of the Son, ever drawing all spiritual realities to himself, is just as real and absolute as is the all-powerful material grasp of the Isle of Paradise. But material-minded man is naturally more familiar with the material manifestations of a physical nature than with the equally real and mighty operations of a spiritual nature which are discerned only by the spiritual insight of the soul.

As the mind of any personality in the universe becomes more spiritual —

Godlike — it becomes less responsive to material gravity. Reality, measured by physical-gravity response, is the antithesis of reality as determined by quality of spirit content. Physical-gravity action is a quantitative determiner of nonspirit energy; spiritual-gravity action is the qualitative measure of the living energy of divinity.

What Paradise is to the physical creation, and what the Eternal Son is to the spiritual universe, the Conjoint Actor is to the realms of mind — the intelligent universe of material, morontial, and spiritual beings and personalities.

The Conjoint Actor reacts to both material and spiritual realities and therefore inherently becomes the universal minister to all intelligent beings, beings who may represent a union of both the material and spiritual phases of creation. The endowment of intelligence, the ministry to the material and the spiritual in the phenomenon of mind, is the exclusive domain of the Conjoint Actor, who thus becomes the partner of the spiritual mind, the essence of the morontia mind, and the substance of the material mind of the evolutionary creatures of time.

Mind is the technique whereby spirit realities become experiential to creature personalities. And in the last analysis the unifying possibilities of even human mind, the ability to co-ordinate things, ideas, and values, is supermaterial.

Though it is hardly possible for the mortal mind to comprehend the seven levels of relative cosmic reality, the human intellect should be able to grasp much of the meaning of three functioning levels of finite reality:

1. *Matter.* Organized energy which is subject to linear gravity except as it is modified by motion and conditioned by mind.
2. *Mind.* Organized consciousness which is not wholly subject to material gravity, and which becomes truly liberated when modified by spirit.
3. *Spirit.* The highest personal reality. True spirit is not subject to physical gravity but eventually becomes the motivating influence of all evolving energy systems of personality dignity.

The goal of existence of all personalities is spirit; material manifestations are relative, and the cosmic mind intervenes between these universal opposites. The bestowal of mind and the ministration of spirit are the work of the associate persons of Deity, the Infinite Spirit and the Eternal Son. Total Deity reality is not mind but spirit-mind — mind-spirit unified by personality. Nevertheless the absolutes of both the spirit and the thing converge in the person of the Universal Father.

On Paradise the three energies, physical, mindal, and spiritual, are coordinate. In the evolutionary cosmos energy-matter is dominant except in personality, where spirit, through the mediation of mind, is striving for the mastery. Spirit is the fundamental reality of the personality experience of all creatures because God is spirit. Spirit is unchanging, and therefore, in all personality relations, it transcends both mind and matter, which are experiential variables of progressive attainment.

In cosmic evolution matter becomes a philosophic shadow cast by mind in the presence of spirit luminosity of divine enlightenment, but this does not invalidate the reality of matter-energy. Mind, matter, and spirit are equally real, but they are not of equal value to personality in the attainment of divinity. Consciousness of divinity is a progressive spiritual experience.

The brighter the shining of the spiritualized personality (the Father in the universe, the fragment of potential spirit personality in the individual creature), the greater the shadow cast by the intervening mind upon its material investment. In time, man's body is just as real as mind or spirit, but in death, both mind (identity) and spirit survive while the body does not. A cosmic reality can be nonexistent in personality experience. And so your Greek figure of speech — the material as the shadow of the more real spirit substance — does have a philosophic significance.

9. PERSONAL REALITIES

Spirit is the basic personal reality in the universes, and personality is basic to all progressing experience with spiritual reality. Every phase of personality experience on every successive level of universe progression swarms with clues to the discovery of alluring personal realities. Man's true destiny consists in the creation of new and spirit goals and then in responding to the cosmic allurements of such supernal goals of nonmaterial value.

Love is the secret of beneficial association between personalities. You cannot really know a person as the result of a single contact. You cannot appreciatingly know music through mathematical deduction, even though music is a form of mathematical rhythm. The number assigned to a telephone subscriber does not in any manner identify the personality of that subscriber or signify anything concerning his character.

Mathematics, material science, is indispensable to the intelligent discussion of the material aspects of the universe, but such knowledge is not necessarily a part of the higher realization of truth or of the personal appreciation of spiritual realities. Not only in the realms of life but even in the world of physical energy, the sum of two or more things is very often something *more* than, or something *different* from, the predictable additive consequences of such unions. The entire science of mathematics, the whole domain of philosophy, the highest physics or chemistry, could not predict or know that the union of two gaseous hydrogen atoms with one gaseous oxygen atom would result in a new and qualitatively superadditive substance — liquid water. The understanding knowledge of this one physiochemical phenomenon should have prevented the development of materialistic philosophy and mechanistic cosmology.

Technical analysis does not reveal what a person or a thing can do. For example: Water is used effectively to extinguish fire. That water will put out fire is a fact of everyday experience, but no analysis of water could ever be made to disclose such a property. Analysis determines that water is composed of hydrogen and oxygen; a further study of these elements discloses that oxygen is the real supporter of combustion and that hydrogen will itself freely burn.

Your religion is becoming real because it is emerging from the slavery of fear and the bondage of superstition. Your philosophy struggles for emancipation from dogma and tradition. Your science is engaged in the agelong contest between truth and error while it fights for deliverance from the bondage of abstraction, the slavery of mathematics, and the relative blindness of mechanistic materialism.

Mortal man has a spirit nucleus. The mind is a personal-energy system existing around a divine spirit nucleus and functioning in a material environment. Such a living relationship of personal mind and spirit constitutes the universe potential of eternal personality. Real trouble, lasting disappointment, serious defeat, or inescapable death can come only after self-concepts presume fully to displace the governing power of the central spirit nucleus, thereby disrupting the cosmic scheme of personality identity.

[Presented by a Perfector of Wisdom acting by authority of the Ancients of Days.]

PAPER 13
THE SACRED SPHERES OF PARADISE

BETWEEN THE CENTRAL Isle of Paradise and the innermost of the Havona planetary circuits there are situated in space three lesser circuits of special spheres. The innermost circuit consists of the seven secret spheres of the Universal Father; the second group is composed of the seven luminous worlds of the Eternal Son; in the outermost are the seven immense spheres of the Infinite Spirit, the executive-headquarters worlds of the Seven Master Spirits.

These three seven-world circuits of the Father, the Son, and the Spirit are spheres of unexcelled grandeur and unimagined glory. Even their material or physical construction is of an order unrevealed to you. Each circuit is diverse in material, and each world of each circuit is different excepting the seven worlds of the Son, which are alike in physical constitution. All twenty-one are enormous spheres, and each group of seven is differently eternalized. As far as we know they have always been; like Paradise they are eternal. There exists neither record nor tradition of their origin.

The seven secret spheres of the Universal Father, circulating about Paradise in close proximity to the eternal Isle, are highly reflective of the spiritual luminosity of the central shining of the eternal Deities, shedding this light of divine glory throughout Paradise and even upon the seven circuits of Havona.

On the seven sacred worlds of the Eternal Son there appear to take origin the impersonal energies of spirit luminosity. No personal being may sojourn on any of these seven shining realms. With spiritual glory they illuminate all Paradise and Havona, and they directionize pure spirit luminosity to the seven superuniverses. These brilliant spheres of the second circuit likewise emit their light (light without heat) to Paradise and to the billion worlds of the seven-circuited central universe.

The seven worlds of the Infinite Spirit are occupied by the Seven Master Spirits, who preside over the destinies of the seven superuniverses, sending forth the spiritual illumination of the Third Person of Deity to these creations of time and space. And all Havona, but not the Isle of Paradise, is bathed in these spiritualizing influences.

Although the worlds of the Father are ultimate status spheres for all Father-endowed personalities, this is not their exclusive function. Many beings and entities other than personal sojourn on these worlds. Each world in the circuit of the Father and the circuit of the Spirit has a distinct type of permanent citizenship, but we think the Son's worlds are inhabited by uniform types of other-than-personal beings. Father fragments are among the natives of Divinington; the other orders of permanent citizenship are unrevealed to you.

The twenty-one Paradise satellites serve many purposes in both central and superuniverses not disclosed in these narratives. You are able to understand so little of the life of these spheres that you cannot hope to gain anything like a consistent view of them, either as to nature or function; thousands of activities are there going on which are unrevealed to you. These twenty-one spheres embrace the potentials of the function of the master universe. These papers afford only a fleeting glimpse of certain circumscribed activities pertaining to the present universe age of the grand universe — rather, one of the seven sectors of the grand universe.

1. THE SEVEN SACRED WORLDS OF THE FATHER

The Father's circuit of sacred life spheres contains the only inherent personality secrets in the universe of universes. These satellites of Paradise, the innermost of the three circuits, are the only forbidden domains concerned with personality in the central universe. Nether Paradise and the worlds of the Son are likewise closed to personalities, but neither of those realms is in any way directly concerned with personality.

The Paradise worlds of the Father are directed by the highest order of the Stationary Sons of the Trinity, the Trinitized Secrets of Supremacy. Of these worlds I can tell little; of their manifold activities I may tell less. Such information concerns only those beings who function thereon and go forth therefrom. And though I am somewhat familiar with six of these special worlds, never have I landed on Divinington; that world is wholly forbidden to me.

One of the reasons for the secrecy of these worlds is because each of these sacred spheres enjoys a specialized representation, or manifestation, of the Deities composing the Paradise Trinity; not a personality, but a unique presence of Divinity which can only be appreciated and comprehended by those particular groups of intelligences resident on, or admissible to, that particular sphere. The Trinitized Secrets of Supremacy are the personal agents of these specialized and impersonal presences of Divinity. And the Secrets of Supremacy are highly personal beings, superbly endowed and marvelously adapted to their exalted and exacting work.

1. DIVININGTON. This world is, in a unique sense, the "bosom of the Father," the personal-communion sphere of the Universal Father, and thereon is a special manifestation of his divinity. Divinington is the Paradise rendezvous of the Thought Adjusters, but it is also the home of numerous other entities, personalities, and other beings taking origin in the Universal Father. Many personalities besides the Eternal Son are of direct origin by the solitary acts of the Universal Father. Only the Father fragments and those personalities and other beings of direct and exclusive origin in the Universal Father fraternize and function on this abode.

The secrets of Divinington include the secret of the bestowal and mission of Thought Adjusters. Their nature, origin, and the technique of their contact with the lowly creatures of the evolutionary worlds is a secret of this Paradise sphere. These amazing transactions do not personally concern the rest of us, and therefore do the Deities deem it proper to withhold certain features of this great and divine ministry from our full understanding. In so far as we come in contact with this phase of divine activity, we are permitted full knowledge of these transactions, but concerning the intimate details of this great bestowal we are not fully informed.

This sphere also holds the secrets of the nature, purpose, and activities of all other forms of Father fragments, of the Gravity Messengers, and of hosts of other beings unrevealed to you. It is highly probable that those truths pertaining to Divinington which are withheld from me, if revealed, would merely confuse and handicap me in my present work, and still again, perhaps they are beyond the conceptual capacity of my order of being.

2. SONARINGTON. This sphere is the "bosom of the Son," the personal receiving world of the Eternal Son. It is the Paradise headquarters of the descending and ascending Sons of God when, and after, they are fully accredited and finally approved. This world is the Paradise home for all Sons of the Eternal Son and of his co-ordinate and associate Sons. There are numerous orders of divine sonship attached to this supernal abode which have not been revealed to mortals since they are not concerned with the plans of the ascension scheme of human spiritual progression through the universes and on to Paradise.

The secrets of Sonarington include the secret of the incarnation of the divine Sons. When a Son of God becomes a Son of Man, is literally born of woman, as occurred on your world over two thousand years ago, it is a universal mystery. It is occurring right along throughout the universes, and it is a Sonarington secret of divine sonship. The Adjusters are a mystery of God the Father. The incarnation of the divine Sons is a mystery of God the Son; it is a secret locked up in the seventh sector of Sonarington, a realm penetrated by none save those who have personally passed through this unique experience. Only those phases of incarnation having to do with your ascension career have been brought to your notice. There are many other phases of the mystery of the incarnation of the Paradise Sons of unrevealed types on missions of universe service which are undisclosed to you. And there are still other Sonarington mysteries.

3. SPIRITINGTON. This world is the "bosom of the Spirit," the Paradise home of the high beings that exclusively represent the Infinite Spirit. Here forgather the Seven Master Spirits and certain of their offspring from all universes. At this celestial abode may also be found numerous unrevealed orders of spirit personalities, beings assigned to the manifold activities of the universe not associated with the plans of upstepping the mortal creatures of time to the Paradise levels of eternity.

The secrets of Spiritington involve the impenetrable mysteries of reflectivity. We tell you of the vast and universal phenomenon of reflectivity, more particularly as it is operative on the headquarters worlds of the seven superuniverses, but we never fully explain this phenomenon, for we do not fully understand it. Much, very much, we do comprehend, but many basic details are still mysterious to us. Reflectivity is a secret of God the Spirit. You have been instructed concerning reflectivity functions in relation to the ascension scheme of mortal survival, and it does so operate, but reflectivity is also an indispensable feature of the normal working of numerous other phases of universe occupation. This endowment of the Infinite Spirit is also utilized in channels other than those of intelligence gathering and information dissemination. And there are other secrets of Spiritington.

4. VICEGERINGTON. This planet is the "bosom of the Father and the Son" and is the secret sphere of certain unrevealed beings who take origin by the acts of the Father and the Son. This is also the Paradise home of many glorified beings of complex ancestry, those whose origin is complicated because of the many diverse techniques operative in the seven superuniverses. Many groups of beings forgather on this world whose identity has not been revealed to Urantia mortals.

The secrets of Vicegerington include the secrets of trinitization, and trinitization constitutes the secret of authority to represent the Trinity, to act as vicegerents of the Gods. Authority to represent the Trinity attaches only to those beings, revealed and unrevealed, who are trinitized, created, eventuated, or eternalized by any two or all three of the Paradise Trinity. Personalities brought into being by the trinitizing acts of certain types of glorified creatures represent no more than the conceptual potential mobilized in that trinitization, albeit such creatures may ascend the path of Deity embrace open to all of their kind.

Nontrinitized beings do not fully understand the technique of trinitization by either two or three Creators or by certain creatures. You will never fully understand such a phenomenon unless, in the far-distant future of your glorified career, you should essay and succeed in such an adventure, because otherwise these secrets of Vicegerington will always be forbidden you. But to me, a high Trinity-origin being, all sectors of Vicegerington are open. I fully understand, and just as fully and sacredly protect, the secret of my origin and destiny.

There are still other forms and phases of trinitization which have not been brought to the notice of the Urantia peoples, and these experiences, in their personal aspects, are duly protected in the secret sector of Vicegerington.

5. SOLITARINGTON. This world is the "bosom of the Father and the Spirit" and is the rendezvous of a magnificent host of unrevealed beings of origin in the conjoint acts of the Universal Father and the Infinite Spirit, beings who partake of the traits of the Father in addition to their Spirit inheritance.

This is also the home of the Solitary Messengers and of other personalities of the superangelic orders. You know of very few of these beings; there are vast numbers of orders unrevealed on Urantia. Because they are domiciled on the fifth world, it does not necessarily follow that the Father had aught to do with the creation of Solitary Messengers or their superangelic associates, but in this universe age he does have to do with their function. During the present universe age this is also the status sphere of the Universe Power Directors.

There are numerous additional orders of spirit personalities, beings unknown to mortal man, who look upon Solitarington as their Paradise home sphere. It should be remembered that all divisions and levels of universe activities are just as fully provided with spirit ministers as is the realm concerned with helping mortal man ascend to his divine Paradise destiny.

The secrets of Solitarington. Besides certain secrets of trinitization, this world holds the secrets of the personal relation of the Infinite Spirit with certain of the higher offspring of the Third Source and Center. On Solitarington are held the mysteries of the intimate association of numerous unrevealed orders with the spirits of the Father, of the Son, and of the Spirit, with the threefold spirit of the Trinity, and with the spirits of the Supreme, the Ultimate, and the Supreme-Ultimate.

6. SERAPHINGTON. This sphere is the "bosom of the Son and the Spirit" and is the home world of the vast hosts of unrevealed beings created by the Son and the Spirit. This is also the destiny sphere of all ministering orders of the angelic hosts, including supernaphim, seconaphim, and seraphim. There also serve in the central and outlying universes many orders of superb spirits who are not "ministering spirits to those who shall be heirs of salvation." All these spirit workers in all levels and realms of universe activities look upon Seraphington as their Paradise home.

The secrets of Seraphington involve a threefold mystery, only one of which I may mention — the mystery of seraphic transport. The ability of various orders of seraphim and allied spirit beings to envelop within their spirit forms all orders of nonmaterial personalities and to carry them away on lengthy interplanetary journeys, is a secret locked up in the sacred sectors of Seraphington. The transport seraphim comprehend this mystery, but they do not communicate it to the rest of us, or perhaps they cannot. The other mysteries of Seraphington pertain to the personal experiences of types of spirit servers as yet not revealed to mortals. And we refrain from discussing the secrets of such closely related beings because you can almost comprehend such near orders of existence, and it would be akin to betrayal of trust to present even our partial knowledge of such phenomena.

7. ASCENDINGTON. This unique world is the "bosom of the Father, Son, and Spirit," the rendezvous of the ascendant creatures of space, the receiving sphere of the pilgrims of time who are passing through the Havona universe on their way to Paradise. Ascendington is the actual Paradise home of the ascendant souls of time and space until they attain Paradise status. You mortals will spend most of your Havona "vacations" on

Ascendington. During your Havona life Ascendington will be to you what the reversion directors were during the local and superuniverse ascension. Here you will engage in thousands of activities which are beyond the grasp of mortal imagination. And as on every previous advance in the Godward ascent, your human self will here enter into new relationships with your divine self.

The secrets of Ascendington include the mystery of the gradual and certain building up in the material and mortal mind of a spiritual and potentially immortal counterpart of character and identity. This phenomenon constitutes one of the most perplexing mysteries of the universes — the evolution of an immortal soul within the mind of a mortal and material creature.

You will never fully understand this mysterious transaction until you reach Ascendington. And that is just why all Ascendington will be open to your wondering gaze. One seventh of Ascendington is forbidden to me — that sector concerned with this very secret which is (or will be) the exclusive experience and possession of your type of being. This experience belongs to your human order of existence. My order of personality is not directly concerned with such transactions. It is therefore forbidden to me and eventually revealed to you. But even after it is revealed to you, for some reason it forever remains your secret. You do not reveal it to us nor to any other order of beings. We know about the eternal fusion of a divine Adjuster and an immortal soul of human origin, but the ascendant finaliters know this very experience as an absolute reality.

2. FATHER-WORLD RELATIONSHIPS

These home worlds of the diverse orders of spiritual beings are tremendous and stupendous spheres, and they are equal to Paradise in their matchless beauty and superb glory. They are rendezvous worlds, reunion spheres, serving as permanent cosmic addresses. As finaliters you will be domiciled on Paradise, but Ascendington will be your home address at all times, even when you enter service in outer space. Through all eternity you will regard Ascendington as your home of sentimental memories and reminiscent recollections. When you become seventh-stage spirit beings, possibly you will give up your residential status on Paradise.

If outer universes are in the making, if they are to be inhabited by time creatures of ascension potential, then we infer that these children of the future will also be destined to look upon Ascendington as their Paradise home world.

Ascendington is the only sacred sphere that will be unreservedly open to your inspection as a Paradise arrival. Vicegerington is the only sacred sphere that is wholly and unreservedly open to my scrutiny. Though its secrets are concerned in my origin, in this universe age I do not regard Vicegerington as my home. Trinity-origin beings and trinitized beings are not the same.

The Trinity-origin beings do not fully share the Father's worlds; they have their sole homes on the Isle of Paradise in close proximity to the Most Holy Sphere. They often appear on Ascendington, the "bosom of the Father-Son-Spirit," where they fraternize with their brethren who have come up from the lowly worlds of space.

You might assume that Creator Sons, being of Father-Son origin, would regard Vicegerington as their home, but such is not the case in this universe age of the function of God the Sevenfold. And there are many similar problems that will perplex you, for you are sure to encounter many difficulties as you attempt to understand these things which are so near Paradise. Nor can you successfully reason out these questions; you know so little. And if you knew more about the Father's worlds, you would simply encounter more difficulties until you knew *all* about them. Status on any of these secret worlds is acquired by service as well as by nature of origin, and the successive universe ages may and do redistribute certain of these personality groupings.

The worlds of the inner circuit are really fraternal or status worlds more than actual residential spheres. Mortals will attain some status on each of the Father's worlds save one. For example: When you mortals attain Havona, you are granted clearance for Ascendington, where you are most welcome, but you are not permitted to visit the other six sacred worlds. Subsequent to your passage through the Paradise regime and after your admission to the Corps of the Finality, you are granted clearance for Sonarington since you are sons of God as well as ascenders — and you are even more. But there will always remain one seventh of Sonarington, the sector of the incarnation secrets of the divine Sons, which will not be open to your scrutiny. Never will those secrets be revealed to the ascendant sons of God.

Eventually you will have full access to Ascendington and relative access to the other spheres of the Father except Divinington. But even when you are granted permission to land on five additional secret spheres, after you have become a finaliter, you will not be allowed to visit all sectors of such worlds. Nor will you be permitted to land on the shores of Divinington, the "bosom of the Father," though you shall surely stand repeatedly at the "right hand of the Father." Never throughout all eternity will there arise any necessity for your presence on the world of the Thought Adjusters.

These rendezvous worlds of spirit life are forbidden ground to the extent that we are asked not to negotiate entrance to those phases of these spheres which are wholly outside our realms of experience. You may become creature perfect even as the Universal Father is deity perfect, but you may not know all the experiential secrets of all other orders of universe personalities. When the Creator has an experiential personality secret with his creature, the Creator preserves that secret in eternal confidence.

All these secrets are supposedly known to the collective body of the Trinitized Secrets of Supremacy. These beings are fully known only by their special world groups; they are little comprehended by other orders. After you attain Paradise, you will know and ardently love the ten Secrets of Supremacy who direct Ascendington. Excepting Divinington, you will also achieve a partial understanding of the Secrets of Supremacy on the other worlds of the Father, though not so perfectly as on Ascendington.

The Trinitized Secrets of Supremacy, as their name might suggest, are related to the Supreme; they are likewise related to the Ultimate and to the future Supreme-Ultimate. These Secrets of Supremacy are the secrets of the Supreme and also the secrets of the Ultimate, even the secrets of the Supreme-Ultimate.

3. THE SACRED WORLDS OF THE ETERNAL SON

The seven luminous spheres of the Eternal Son are the worlds of the seven phases of pure-spirit existence. These shining orbs are the source of the threefold light of Paradise and Havona, their influence being largely, but not wholly, confined to the central universe.

Personality is not present on these Paradise satellites; therefore is there little concerning these pure-spirit abodes which can be presented to the mortal and material personality. We are taught that these worlds teem with the otherwise-than-personal life of the beings of the Eternal Son. We infer that these entities are being assembled for ministry in the projected new universes of outer space. The Paradise philosophers maintain that each Paradise cycle, about two billion years of Urantia time, witnesses the creation of additional reserves of these orders on the secret worlds of the Eternal Son.

As far as I am informed, no personality has ever been on any one of these spheres of the Eternal Son. I have never been assigned to visit one of these worlds in all my long experience in and out of Paradise. Even the personalities cocreated by the Eternal Son do not go to these worlds. We infer that all types of impersonal spirits — regardless of parentage — are admitted to these spirit homes. As I am a person and have a spirit form, no doubt such a world would seem empty and deserted even if I were permitted to pay it a visit. High spirit personalities are not given to the gratification of purposeless curiosity, purely useless adventure. There is at all times altogether too much intriguing and purposeful adventure to permit the development of any great interest in those projects which are either futile or unreal.

4. THE WORLDS OF THE INFINITE SPIRIT

Between the inner circuit of Havona and the shining spheres of the Eternal Son there circle the seven orbs of the Infinite Spirit, worlds inhabited by the offspring of the Infinite Spirit, by the trinitized sons of glorified created personalities, and by other types of unrevealed beings concerned with the effective administration of the many enterprises of the various realms of universe activities.

The Seven Master Spirits are the supreme and ultimate representatives of the Infinite Spirit. They maintain their personal stations, their power focuses, on the periphery of Paradise, but all operations concerned with their management and direction of the grand universe are conducted on and from these seven special executive spheres of the Infinite Spirit. The Seven Master Spirits are, in reality, the mind-spirit balance wheel of the universe of universes, an all-embracing, all-encompassing, and all-co-ordinating power of central location.

From these seven special spheres the Master Spirits operate to equalize and stabilize the cosmic-mind circuits of the grand universe. They also have to do with the differential spiritual attitude and presence of the Deities throughout the grand universe. Physical reactions are uniform, unvarying, and always instantaneous and automatic. But experiential spiritual presence is in accordance with the underlying conditions or states of spiritual receptivity inherent in the individual minds of the realms.

Physical authority, presence, and function are unvarying in all the universes, small or great. The differing factor in spiritual presence, or reaction, is the fluctuating differential in its recognition and reception by will creatures. Whereas the spiritual presence of absolute and existential Deity is in no manner whatever influenced by attitudes of loyalty or disloyalty on the part of created beings, at the same time it is true that the functioning presence of subabsolute and experiential Deity is definitely and directly influenced by the decisions, choices, and will-attitudes of such finite creature beings — by the loyalty and devotion of the individual being, planet, system, constellation, galaxy, or universe. But this spiritual presence of divinity is not whimsical nor arbitrary; its experiential variance is inherent in the freewill endowment of personal creatures.

The determiner of the differential of spiritual presence exists in your own hearts and minds and consists in the manner of your own choosing, in the decisions of your minds, and in the determination of your own wills. This differential is inherent in the freewill reactions of intelligent personal beings, beings whom the Universal Father has ordained shall exercise this liberty of choosing. And the Deities are ever true to the ebb and flow of their spirits in meeting and satisfying the conditions and demands of this differential of creature choice, now bestowing more of their presence in response to a sincere desire for the same and again withdrawing themselves from the scene as their creatures decide adversely in the exercise of their divinely bestowed freedom of choice. And thus does the spirit of divinity become humbly obedient to the choosing of the creatures of the realms.

The executive abodes of the Seven Master Spirits are, in reality, the Paradise headquarters of the seven superuniverses and their correlated segments in outer space. Each Master Spirit presides over one superuniverse, and each of these seven worlds is exclusively assigned to one of the Master Spirits. There is literally no phase of the sub-Paradise administration of the seven superuniverses which is not provided for on these executive worlds. They are not so exclusive as the spheres of the Father or those of the Son, and though residential status is limited to native beings and those who work thereon, these seven administrative planets are always open to all beings who desire to visit them, and who can command the necessary means of transit.

To me, these executive worlds are the most interesting and intriguing spots outside of Paradise. In no other place in the wide universe can one observe such varied activities, involving so many different orders of living beings, having to do with operations on so many diverse levels, occupations at once material, intellectual, and spiritual. When I am accorded a period of release from assignment, if I chance to be on Paradise or in Havona, I usually proceed to one of these busy worlds of the Seven Master Spirits, there to inspire my mind with such spectacles of enterprise, devotion, loyalty, wisdom, and effectiveness. Nowhere else can I observe such an amazing interassociation of personality performances on all seven levels of universe reality. And I am always stimulated by the activities of those who well know how to do their work, and who so thoroughly enjoy doing it.

[Presented by a Perfector of Wisdom commissioned thus to function by the Ancients of Days on Uversa.]

PAPER 14
THE CENTRAL AND DIVINE UNIVERSE

The perfect and divine universe occupies the center of all creation; it is the eternal core around which the vast creations of time and space revolve. Paradise is the gigantic nuclear Isle of absolute stability which rests motionless at the very heart of the magnificent eternal universe. This central planetary family is called Havona and is far-distant from the local universe of Nebadon. It is of enormous dimensions and almost unbelievable mass and consists of one billion spheres of unimagined beauty and superb grandeur, but the true magnitude of this vast creation is really beyond the understanding grasp of the human mind.

This is the one and only settled, perfect, and established aggregation of worlds. This is a wholly created and perfect universe; it is not an evolutionary development. This is the eternal core of perfection, about which swirls that endless procession of universes which constitute the tremendous evolutionary experiment, the audacious adventure of the Creator Sons of God, who aspire to duplicate in time and to reproduce in space the pattern universe, the ideal of divine completeness, supreme finality, ultimate reality, and eternal perfection.

1. THE PARADISE-HAVONA SYSTEM

From the periphery of Paradise to the inner borders of the seven superuniverses there are the following seven space conditions and motions:

1. The quiescent midspace zones impinging on Paradise.
2. The clockwise processional of the three Paradise and the seven Havona circuits.
3. The semiquiet space zone separating the Havona circuits from the dark gravity bodies of the central universe.
4. The inner, counterclockwise-moving belt of the dark gravity bodies.
5. The second unique space zone dividing the two space paths of the dark gravity bodies.
6. The outer belt of dark gravity bodies, revolving clockwise around Paradise.
7. A third space zone — a semiquiet zone — separating the outer belt of dark gravity bodies from the innermost circuits of the seven superuniverses.

The billion worlds of Havona are arranged in seven concentric circuits immediately surrounding the three circuits of Paradise satellites. There are upwards of thirty-five million worlds in the innermost Havona circuit and over two hundred and forty-five million in the outermost, with proportionate numbers intervening. Each circuit differs, but all are perfectly balanced and exquisitely organized, and each is pervaded by a specialized representation of the Infinite Spirit, one of the Seven Spirits of the Circuits. In addition to other functions this impersonal Spirit co-ordinates the conduct of celestial affairs throughout each circuit.

The Havona planetary circuits are not superimposed; their worlds follow each other in an orderly linear procession. The central universe whirls around the stationary Isle of Paradise in one vast plane, consisting of ten concentric stabilized units — the three circuits of Paradise spheres and the seven circuits of Havona worlds. Physically regarded, the Havona and the

Paradise circuits are all one and the same system; their separation is in recognition of functional and administrative segregation.

Time is not reckoned on Paradise; the sequence of successive events is inherent in the concept of those who are indigenous to the central Isle. But time is germane to the Havona circuits and to numerous beings of both celestial and terrestrial origin sojourning thereon. Each Havona world has its own local time, determined by its circuit. All worlds in a given circuit have the same length of year since they uniformly swing around Paradise, and the length of these planetary years decreases from the outermost to the innermost circuit.

Besides Havona-circuit time, there is the Paradise-Havona standard day and other time designations which are determined on, and are sent out from, the seven Paradise satellites of the Infinite Spirit. The Paradise-Havona standard day is based on the length of time required for the planetary abodes of the first or inner Havona circuit to complete one revolution around the Isle of Paradise; and though their velocity is enormous, owing to their situation between the dark gravity bodies and gigantic Paradise, it requires almost one thousand years for these spheres to complete their circuit. You have unwittingly read the truth when your eyes rested on the statement "A day is as a thousand years with God, as but a watch in the night." One Paradise-Havona day is just seven minutes, three and one-eighth seconds less than one thousand years of the present Urantia leap-year calendar.

This Paradise-Havona day is the standard time measurement for the seven superuniverses, although each maintains its own internal time standards.

On the outskirts of this vast central universe, far out beyond the seventh belt of Havona worlds, there swirl an unbelievable number of enormous dark gravity bodies. These multitudinous dark masses are quite unlike other space bodies in many particulars; even in form they are very different. These dark gravity bodies neither reflect nor absorb light; they are nonreactive to physical-energy light.

The great belt of dark gravity bodies is divided into two equal elliptical circuits by a unique space intrusion. The inner belt revolves counterclockwise; the outer revolves clockwise. These alternate directions of motion, coupled with the extraordinary mass of the dark bodies, so effectively equalize the lines of Havona gravity as to render the central universe a physically balanced and perfectly stabilized creation.

The inner procession of dark gravity bodies is tubular in arrangement, consisting of three circular groupings. A cross section of this circuit would exhibit three concentric circles of about equal density. The outer circuit of dark gravity bodies is arranged perpendicularly, being ten thousand times higher than the inner circuit. The up-and-down diameter of the outer circuit is fifty thousand times that of the transverse diameter.

The intervening space which exists between these two circuits of gravity bodies is *unique* in that nothing like it is to be found elsewhere in all the wide universe. This zone is characterized by enormous wave movements of an up-and-down nature and is permeated by tremendous energy activities of an unknown order.

In our opinion, nothing like the dark gravity bodies of the central universe will characterize the future evolution of the outer space levels; we regard these alternate processions of stupendous gravity-balancing bodies as unique in the master universe.

2. CONSTITUTION OF HAVONA

Spirit beings do not dwell in nebulous space; they do not inhabit ethereal worlds; they are domiciled on actual spheres of a material nature, worlds just as real as those on which mortals live. The Havona worlds are actual and literal, albeit their literal substance differs from the material organization of the planets of the seven superuniverses.

The physical realities of Havona represent an order of energy organization radically different from any prevailing in the evolutionary universes of space. Havona energies are threefold; superuniverse units of energy-matter contain a twofold energy charge, although one form of energy exists in negative and positive phases. The creation of the central universe is threefold (Trinity); the creation of a local universe (directly) is twofold, by a Creator Son and a Creative Spirit.

The material of Havona consists of the organization of exactly one thousand basic chemical elements and the balanced function of the seven forms of Havona energy. Each of these basic energies manifests seven phases of excitation, so that the Havona natives respond to forty-nine differing sensation stimuli. In other words, viewed from a purely physical standpoint, the natives of the central universe possess forty-nine specialized forms of sensation. The morontia senses are seventy, and the higher spiritual orders of reaction response vary in different types of beings from seventy to two hundred and ten.

None of the physical beings of the central universe would be visible to Urantians. Neither would any of the physical stimuli of those faraway worlds excite a reaction in your gross sense organs. If a Urantia mortal could be transported to Havona, he would there be deaf, blind, and utterly lacking in all other sense reactions; he could only function as a limited self-conscious being deprived of all environmental stimuli and all reactions thereto.

There are numerous physical phenomena and spiritual reactions transpiring in the central creation which are unknown on worlds such as Urantia. The basic organization of a threefold creation is wholly unlike that of the twofold constitution of the created universes of time and space.

All natural law is co-ordinated on a basis entirely different than in the dual-energy systems of the evolving creations. The entire central universe is organized in accordance with the threefold system of perfect and symmetrical control. Throughout the whole Paradise-Havona system there is maintained a perfect balance between all cosmic realities and all spiritual forces. Paradise, with an absolute grasp of material creation, perfectly regulates and maintains the physical energies of this central universe; the Eternal Son, as a part of his all-embracing spirit grasp, most perfectly sustains the spiritual status of all who indwell Havona. On Paradise nothing is experimental, and the Paradise-Havona system is a unit of creative perfection.

The universal spiritual gravity of the Eternal Son is amazingly active throughout the central universe. All spirit values and spiritual personalities are unceasingly drawn inward towards the abode of the Gods. This Godward urge is intense and inescapable. The ambition to attain God is stronger in the central universe, not because spirit gravity is stronger than in the outlying universes, but because those beings who have attained Havona are more fully spiritualized and hence more responsive to the ever-present action of the universal spirit-gravity pull of the Eternal Son.

Likewise does the Infinite Spirit draw all intellectual values Paradise-ward. Throughout the central universe the mind gravity of the Infinite Spirit functions in liaison with the spirit gravity of the Eternal Son, and these together constitute the combined urge of the ascendant souls to find God, to attain Deity, to achieve Paradise, and to know the Father.

Havona is a spiritually perfect and physically stable universe. The control and balanced stability of the central universe appear to be perfect. Everything physical or spiritual is perfectly predictable, but mind phenomena and personality volition are not. We do infer that sin can be reckoned as impossible of occurrence, but we do this on the ground that the native freewill creatures of Havona have never been guilty of transgressing the will of Deity. Through all eternity these supernal beings have been consistently loyal to the Eternals of Days. Neither has sin appeared in any creature who has entered Havona as a pilgrim. There has never been an instance of misconduct by any creature of any group of personalities ever created in, or admitted to, the central Havona universe. So perfect and so divine are the methods and means of selection in the universes of time that never in the records of Havona has an error occurred; no mistakes have ever been made; no ascendant soul has ever been prematurely admitted to the central universe.

3. THE HAVONA WORLDS

Concerning the government of the central universe, there is none. Havona is so exquisitely perfect that no intellectual system of government is required. There are no regularly constituted courts, neither are there legislative assemblies; Havona requires only administrative direction. Here may be observed the height of the ideals of true self-government.

There is no need of government among such perfect and near-perfect intelligences. They stand in no need of regulation, for they are beings of native perfection interspersed with evolutionary creatures who have long since passed the scrutiny of the supreme tribunals of the superuniverses.

The administration of Havona is not automatic, but it is marvelously perfect and divinely efficient. It is chiefly planetary and is vested in the resident Eternal of Days, each Havona sphere being directed by one of these Trinity-origin personalities. Eternals of Days are not creators, but they are perfect administrators. They teach with supreme skill and direct their planetary children with a perfection of wisdom bordering on absoluteness.

The billion spheres of the central universe constitute the training worlds of the high personalities native to Paradise and Havona and further serve as the final proving grounds for ascending creatures from the evolutionary worlds of time. In the execution of the Universal Father's great plan of creature ascension the pilgrims of time are landed on the receiving worlds of the outer or seventh circuit, and subsequent to increased training and enlarged experience, they are progressively advanced inward, planet by planet and circle by circle, until they finally attain the Deities and achieve residence on Paradise.

At present, although the spheres of the seven circuits are maintained in all their supernal glory, only about one per cent of all planetary capacity is utilized in the work of furthering the Father's universal plan of mortal ascension. About one tenth of one per cent of the area of these enormous worlds is dedicated to the life and activities of the Corps of the Finality, beings eternally settled in light and life who often sojourn and minister on the Havona worlds. These exalted beings have their personal residences on Paradise.

The planetary construction of the Havona spheres is entirely unlike that of the evolutionary worlds and systems of space. Nowhere else in all the grand universe is it convenient to utilize such enormous spheres as inhabited worlds. Triata physical constitution, coupled with the balancing effect of the immense dark gravity bodies, makes it possible so perfectly to equalize the physical forces and so exquisitely to balance the various attractions of this tremendous creation. Antigravity is also employed in the organization of the material functions and the spiritual activities of these enormous worlds.

The architecture, lighting, and heating, as well as the biologic and artistic embellishment, of the Havona spheres, are quite beyond the greatest possible stretch of human imagination. You cannot be told much about Havona; to understand its beauty and grandeur you must see it. But there are real rivers and lakes on these perfect worlds.

Spiritually these worlds are ideally appointed; they are fittingly adapted to their purpose of harboring the numerous orders of differing beings who function in the central universe. Manifold activities take place on these beautiful worlds which are far beyond human comprehension.

4. CREATURES OF THE CENTRAL UNIVERSE

There are seven basic forms of living things and beings on the Havona worlds, and each of these basic forms exists in three distinct phases. Each of these three phases is divided into seventy major divisions, and each major division is composed of one thousand minor divisions, with yet other subdivisions, and so on. These basic life groups might be classified as:

1. Material.
2. Morontial.
3. Spiritual.
4. Absonite.
5. Ultimate.
6. Coabsolute.
7. Absolute.

Decay and death are not a part of the cycle of life on the Havona worlds. In the central universe the lower living things undergo the transmutation of materialization. They do change form and manifestation, but they do not resolve by process of decay and cellular death.

The Havona natives are all the offspring of the Paradise Trinity. They are without creature parents, and they are nonreproducing beings. We cannot portray the creation of these citizens of the central universe, beings who never were created. The entire story of the creation of Havona is an attempt to time-space an eternity fact which has no relation to time or space as mortal man comprehends them. But we must concede human philosophy a point of origin; even personalities far above the human level require a concept of "beginnings." Nevertheless, the Paradise-Havona system is eternal.

The natives of Havona live on the billion spheres of the central universe in the same sense that other orders of permanent citizenship dwell on their respective spheres of nativity. As the material order of sonship carries on the material, intellectual, and spiritual economy of all of the local systems in a superuniverse, so, in a larger sense, do the Havona natives live and function on the billion worlds of the central universe. You might possibly regard these Havoners as material creatures in the sense that the word "material" could be expanded to describe the physical realities of the divine universe.

There is a life that is native to Havona and possesses significance in and of itself. Havoners minister in many ways to Paradise descenders and to superuniverse ascenders, but they also live lives that are unique in the central universe and have relative meaning quite apart from either Paradise or the superuniverses.

As the worship of the faith sons of the evolutionary worlds ministers to the satisfaction of the Universal Father's love, so the exalted adoration of the Havona creatures satiates the perfect ideals of divine beauty and truth. As mortal man strives to do the will of God, these beings of the central universe live to gratify the ideals of the Paradise Trinity. In their very nature they are the will of God. Man rejoices in the goodness of God, Havoners exult in the divine beauty, while you both enjoy the ministry of the liberty of living truth.

Havoners have both optional present and future unrevealed destinies. And there is a progression of native creatures that is peculiar to the central universe, a progression that involves neither ascent to Paradise nor penetration of the superuniverses. This progression to higher Havona status may be suggested as follows:

1. Experiential progress outward from the first to the seventh circuit.
2. Progress inward from the seventh to the first circuit.
3. Intracircuit progress — progression within the worlds of a given circuit.

In addition to the Havona natives, the inhabitants of the central universe embrace numerous classes of pattern beings for various universe groups — advisers, directors, and teachers of their kind and to their kind throughout creation. All beings in all universes are fashioned along the lines of some one order of pattern creature living on some one of the billion worlds of Havona. Even the mortals of time have their goal and ideals of creature existence on the outer circuits of these pattern spheres on high.

Then there are those beings who have attained the Universal Father, and who are entitled to go and come, who are assigned here and there in the universes on missions of special service. And on every Havona world will be found the attainment candidates, those who have physically attained the central universe, but who have not yet achieved that spiritual development which will enable them to claim Paradise residence.

The Infinite Spirit is represented on the Havona worlds by a host of personalities, beings of grace and glory, who administer the details of the intricate intellectual and spiritual affairs of the central universe. On these worlds of divine perfection they perform the work indigenous to the normal conduct of this vast creation and, in addition, carry on the manifold tasks of teaching, training, and ministering to the enormous numbers of ascendant creatures who have climbed to glory from the dark worlds of space.

There are numerous groups of beings native to the Paradise-Havona system that are in no way directly associated with the ascension scheme of creature perfection attainment; therefore are they omitted from the personality classifications presented to the mortal races. Only the major groups of superhuman beings and those orders directly connected with your survival experience are herein presented.

Havona teems with the life of all phases of intelligent beings, who there seek to advance from lower to higher circuits in their efforts to attain higher levels of divinity realization and enlarged appreciation of supreme meanings, ultimate values, and absolute reality.

5. LIFE IN HAVONA

On Urantia you pass through a short and intense test during your initial life of material existence. On the mansion worlds and up through your system, constellation, galaxy, and local universe, you traverse the morontia phases of ascension. On the training worlds of the superuniverse you pass through the true spirit stages of progression and are prepared for eventual transit to Havona. On the seven circuits of Havona your attainment is intellectual, spiritual, and experiential. And there is a definite task to be achieved on each of the worlds of each of these circuits.

Life on the divine worlds of the central universe is so rich and full, so complete and replete, that it wholly transcends the human concept of anything a created being could possibly experience. The social and economic activities of this eternal creation are entirely dissimilar to the occupations of material creatures living on evolutionary worlds like Urantia. Even the technique of Havona thought is unlike the process of thinking on Urantia.

The regulations of the central universe are fittingly and inherently natural; the rules of conduct are not arbitrary. In every requirement of Havona there is disclosed the reason of righteousness and the rule of justice. And these two factors, combined, equal what on Urantia would be denominated fairness. When you arrive in Havona, you will naturally enjoy doing things the way they should be done.

When intelligent beings first attain the central universe, they are received and domiciled on the pilot world of the seventh Havona circuit. As the new arrivals progress spiritually, attain identity comprehension of their superuniverse Master Spirit, they are transferred to the sixth circle. (It is from these arrangements in the central universe that the circles of progress in the human mind have been designated.) After ascenders have attained a realization of Supremacy and are thereby prepared for the Deity adventure, they are taken to the fifth circuit; and after attaining the Infinite Spirit, they are transferred to the fourth. Following the attainment of the Eternal Son, they are removed to the third; and when they have recognized the Universal Father, they go to sojourn on the second circuit of worlds, where they become more familiar with the Paradise hosts. Arrival on the first circuit of Havona signifies the acceptance of the candidates of time into the service of Paradise. Indefinitely, according to the length and nature of the creature ascension, they will tarry on the inner circuit of progressive spiritual attainment. From this inner circuit the ascending pilgrims pass inward to Paradise residence and admission to the Corps of the Finality.

During your sojourn in Havona as a pilgrim of ascent, you will be allowed to visit freely among the worlds of the circuit of your assignment. You will also be permitted to go back to the planets of those circuits you have previously traversed. And all this is possible to those who sojourn on the circles of Havona without the necessity of being ensupernaphimed. The pilgrims of time are able to equip themselves to traverse "achieved" space but must depend on the ordained technique to negotiate "unachieved" space; a pilgrim cannot leave Havona nor go forward beyond his assigned circuit without the aid of a transport supernaphim.

There is a refreshing originality about this vast central creation. Aside from the physical organization of matter and the fundamental constitution of the basic orders of intelligent beings and other living things, there is nothing in common between the worlds of Havona. Every one of these planets is an original, unique, and exclusive creation; each planet is a matchless, superb, and perfect production. And this diversity of individuality extends to all features of the physical, intellectual, and spiritual aspects of planetary existence. Each of these billion perfection spheres has been developed and embellished in accordance with the plans of the resident Eternal of Days. And this is just why no two of them are alike.

Not until you traverse the last of the Havona circuits and visit the last of the Havona worlds, will the tonic of adventure and the stimulus of curiosity disappear from your career. And then will the urge, the forward impulse of eternity, replace its forerunner, the adventure lure of time.

Monotony is indicative of immaturity of the creative imagination and inactivity of intellectual co-ordination with the spiritual endowment. By the time an ascendant mortal begins the exploration of these heavenly worlds, he has already attained emotional, intellectual, and social, if not spiritual, maturity.

Not only will you find undreamed-of changes confronting you as you advance from circuit to circuit in Havona, but your astonishment will be inexpressible as you progress from planet to planet within each circuit. Each of these billion study worlds is a veritable university of surprises. Continuing astonishment, unending wonder, is the experience of those who traverse these circuits and tour these gigantic spheres. Monotony is not a part of the Havona career.

Love of adventure, curiosity, and dread of monotony — these traits inherent in evolving human nature — were not put there just to aggravate and annoy you during your short sojourn on earth, but rather to suggest to you that death is only the beginning of an endless career of adventure, an everlasting life of anticipation, an eternal voyage of discovery.

Curiosity — the spirit of investigation, the urge of discovery, the drive of exploration — is a part of the inborn and divine endowment of evolutionary space creatures. These natural impulses were not given you merely to be frustrated and repressed. True, these ambitious urges must frequently be restrained during your short life on earth, disappointment must be often experienced, but they are to be fully realized and gloriously gratified during the long ages to come.

6. THE PURPOSE OF THE CENTRAL UNIVERSE

The range of the activities of seven-circuited Havona is enormous. In general, they may be described as:

1. Havonal.
2. Paradisiacal.
3. Ascendant-finite — Supreme-Ultimate evolutional.

Many superfinite activities take place in the Havona of the present universe age, involving untold diversities of absonite and other phases of mind and spirit functions. It is possible that the central universe serves many purposes which are not revealed to me, as it functions in numerous ways beyond the comprehension of the created mind. Nevertheless, I will endeavor to depict how this perfect creation ministers to the needs and contributes to the satisfactions of seven orders of universe intelligence.

1. *The Universal Father* — the First Source and Center. God the Father derives supreme parental satisfaction from the perfection of the central creation. He enjoys the experience of love satiety on near-equality levels. The perfect Creator is divinely pleased with the adoration of the perfect creature.

Havona affords the Father supreme achievement gratification. The perfection realization in Havona compensates for the time-space delay of the eternal urge of infinite expansion.

The Father enjoys the Havona reciprocation of the divine beauty. It satisfies the divine mind to afford a perfect pattern of exquisite harmony for all evolving universes.

Our Father beholds the central universe with perfect pleasure because it is a worthy revelation of spirit reality to all personalities of the universe of universes.

The God of universes has favorable regard for Havona and Paradise as the eternal power nucleus for all subsequent universe expansion in time and space.

The eternal Father views with never-ending satisfaction the Havona creation as the worthy and alluring goal for the ascension candidates of time, his mortal grandchildren of space achieving their Creator-Father's eternal home. And God takes pleasure in the Paradise-Havona universe as the eternal home of Deity and the divine family.

2. *The Eternal Son* — the Second Source and Center. To the Eternal Son the superb central creation affords eternal proof of the partnership effectiveness of the divine family — Father, Son, and Spirit. It is the spiritual and material basis for absolute confidence in the Universal Father.

Havona affords the Eternal Son an almost unlimited base for the ever-expanding realization of spirit power. The central universe afforded the Eternal Son the arena wherein he could safely and securely demonstrate the spirit and technique of the bestowal ministry for the instruction of his associate Paradise Sons.

Havona is the reality foundation for the Eternal Son's spirit-gravity control of the universe of universes. This universe affords the Son the gratification of parental craving, spiritual reproduction.

The Havona worlds and their perfect inhabitants are the first and the eternally final demonstration that the Son is the Word of the Father. Thereby is the consciousness of the Son as an infinite complement of the Father perfectly gratified.

And this universe affords the opportunity for the realization of reciprocation of equality fraternity between the Universal Father and the Eternal

Son, and this constitutes the everlasting proof of the infinite personality of each.

3. *The Infinite Spirit* — the Third Source and Center. The Havona universe affords the Infinite Spirit proof of being the Conjoint Actor, the infinite representative of the unified Father-Son. In Havona the Infinite Spirit derives the combined satisfaction of functioning as a creative activity while enjoying the satisfaction of absolute coexistence with this divine achievement.

In Havona the Infinite Spirit found an arena wherein he could demonstrate the ability and willingness to serve as a potential mercy minister. In this perfect creation the Spirit rehearsed for the adventure of ministry in the evolutionary universes.

This perfect creation afforded the Infinite Spirit opportunity to participate in universe administration with both divine parents — to administer a universe as associate-Creator offspring, thereby preparing for the joint administration of the local universes as the Creative Spirit associates of the Creator Sons.

The Havona worlds are the mind laboratory of the creators of the cosmic mind and the ministers to every creature mind in existence. Mind is different on each Havona world and serves as the pattern for all spiritual and material creature intellects.

These perfect worlds are the mind graduate schools for all beings destined for Paradise society. They afforded the Spirit abundant opportunity to test out the technique of mind ministry on safe and advisory personalities.

Havona is a compensation to the Infinite Spirit for his widespread and unselfish work in the universes of space. Havona is the perfect home and retreat for the untiring Mind Minister of time and space.

4. *The Supreme Being* — the evolutionary unification of experiential Deity. The Havona creation is the eternal and perfect proof of the spiritual reality of the Supreme Being. This perfect creation is a revelation of the perfect and symmetrical spirit nature of God the Supreme before the beginnings of the power-personality synthesis of the finite reflections of the Paradise Deities in the experiential universes of time and space.

In Havona the power potentials of the Almighty are unified with the spiritual nature of the Supreme. This central creation is an exemplification of the future-eternal unity of the Supreme.

Havona is a perfect pattern of the universality potential of the Supreme. This universe is a finished portrayal of the future perfection of the Supreme and is suggestive of the potential of the Ultimate.

Havona exhibits finality of spirit values existing as living will creatures of supreme and perfect self-control; mind existing as ultimately equivalent to spirit; reality and unity of intelligence with an unlimited potential.

5. *The Co-ordinate Creator Sons*. Havona is the educational training ground where the Paradise Michaels are prepared for their subsequent adventures in universe creation. This divine and perfect creation is a pattern for every Creator Son. He strives to make his own universe eventually attain to these Paradise-Havona levels of perfection.

A Creator Son uses the creatures of Havona as personality-pattern possibilities for his own mortal children and spirit beings. The Michael and other Paradise Sons view Paradise and Havona as the divine destiny of the children of time.

The Creator Sons know that the central creation is the real source of that indispensable universe overcontrol which stabilizes and unifies their local universes. They know that the personal presence of the ever-present influence of the Supreme and of the Ultimate is in Havona.

Havona and Paradise are the source of a Michael Son's creative power. Here dwell the beings who co-operate with him in universe creation. From Paradise come the Universe Mother Spirits, the cocreators of local universes.

The Paradise Sons regard the central creation as the home of their divine parents — their home. It is the place they enjoy returning to ever and anon.

6. *The Co-ordinate Ministering Daughters*. The Universe Mother Spirits, cocreators of the local universes, secure their prepersonal training on the worlds of Havona in close association with the Spirits of the Circuits. In the central universe the Spirit Daughters of the local universes were duly trained in the methods of co-operation with the Sons of Paradise, all the while subject to the will of the Father.

On the worlds of Havona the Spirit and the Daughters of the Spirit find the mind patterns for all their groups of spiritual and material intelligences, and this central universe is the sometime destiny of those creatures which a Universe Mother Spirit jointly sponsors with an associated Creator Son.

The Universe Mother Creator remembers Paradise and Havona as the place of her origin and the home of the Infinite Mother Spirit, the abode of the personality presence of the Infinite Mind.

From this central universe also came the bestowal of the personal prerogatives of creatorship which a Universe Divine Minister employs as complemental to a Creator Son in the work of creating living will creatures.

And lastly, since these Daughter Spirits of the Infinite Mother Spirit will not likely ever return to their Paradise home, they derive great satisfaction from the universal reflectivity phenomenon associated with the Supreme Being in Havona and personalized in Majeston on Paradise.

7. *The Evolutionary Mortals of the Ascending Career.* Havona is the home of the pattern personality of every mortal type and the home of all superhuman personalities of mortal association who are not native to the creations of time.

These worlds provide the stimulus of all human impulses towards the attainment of true spirit values on the highest conceivable reality levels. Havona is the pre-Paradise training goal of every ascending mortal. Here mortals attain pre-Paradise Deity — the Supreme Being. Havona stands before every will creature as the portal to Paradise and God attainment.

Paradise is the home, and Havona the workshop and playground, of the finaliters. And every God-knowing mortal craves to be a finaliter.

The central universe is not only man's established destiny, but it is also the starting place of the eternal career of the finaliters as they shall sometime be started out on the undisclosed and universal adventure in the experience of exploring the infinity of the Universal Father.

Havona will unquestionably continue to function with absonite significance even in future universe ages which may witness space pilgrims attempting to find God on superfinite levels. Havona has capacity to serve as a training universe for absonite beings. It will probably be the finishing school when the seven superuniverses are functioning as the intermediate school for the graduates of the primary schools of outer space. And we incline to the opinion that the potentials of eternal Havona are really unlimited, that the central universe has eternal capacity to serve as an experiential training universe for all past, present, or future types of created beings.

[Presented by a Perfector of Wisdom commissioned thus to function by the Ancients of Days on Uversa.]

PAPER 15
THE SEVEN SUPERUNIVERSES

As far as the Universal Father is concerned — as a Father — the universes are virtually nonexistent; he deals with personalities; he is the Father of personalities. As far as the Eternal Son and the Infinite Spirit are concerned — as creator partners — the universes are localized and individual under the joint rule of the Creator Sons and the Creative Spirits. As far as the Paradise Trinity is concerned, outside Havona there are just seven inhabited universes, the seven superuniverses which hold jurisdiction over the circle of the first post-Havona space level. The Seven Master Spirits radiate their influence out from the central Isle, thus constituting the vast creation one gigantic wheel, the hub being the eternal Isle of Paradise, the seven spokes the radiations of the Seven Master Spirits, the rim the outer regions of the grand universe.

Early in the materialization of the universal creation the sevenfold scheme of the superuniverse organization and government was formulated. The first post-Havona creation was divided into seven stupendous segments, and the headquarters worlds of these superuniverse governments were designed and constructed. The present scheme of administration has existed from near eternity, and the rulers of these seven superuniverses are rightly called Ancients of Days.

Of the vast body of knowledge concerning the superuniverses, I can hope to tell you little, but there is operative throughout these realms a technique of intelligent control for both physical and spiritual forces, and the universal gravity presences there function in majestic power and perfect harmony. It is important first to gain an adequate idea of the physical constitution and material organization of the superuniverse domains, for then you will be the better prepared to grasp the significance of the marvelous organization provided for the spiritual government and the intellectual advancement of the will creatures who dwell in the myriads of space-time universes of which each of these seven superuniverses is composed.

1. THE SUPERUNIVERSE SPACE LEVEL

We have long since discovered that the seven superuniverses traverse a great ellipse, a gigantic and elongated circle, or hypercircle, in the higher dimensional space-time in which they exist. This cosmic path is well charted and is just as thoroughly known to the superuniverse observers as the orbits of the planets constituting your solar system are known to Urantia astronomers. Urantia is situated in a universe, and a superuniverse, that are not yet fully organized. Your local universe of Nebadon belongs to Orvonton, the seventh superuniverse, which swings on between superuniverses one and six.

2. ORGANIZATION OF THE SUPERUNIVERSES

There are seven superuniverses in the grand universe, with each one being composed of an enormous number of universes. Each universe is a four or more dimensional space-time structure (or hypersurface) existing within the 10 or more dimensional space-time in which the superuniverses exist. Within each universe the spiritual governmental organization, from the lowest level on up, is constituted approximately as follows:

1. *The System.* The lowest basic unit of the supergovernment consists of about one thousand inhabited or inhabitable worlds. Blazing suns, cold worlds, planets too near the hot suns, and other spheres not suitable for creature habitation are not included in this group. These one thousand worlds

adapted to support life are called a system, but in the younger systems only a comparatively small number of these worlds may be inhabited. Each inhabited planet is presided over by a Planetary Prince, and each local system has an architectural sphere as its headquarters and is ruled by a System Sovereign.

2. *The Constellation.* One hundred systems (about 100,000 inhabitable planets) usually make up a constellation. Although this number varies depending on the size of the galaxy and the number of possible constellations. Each constellation has an architectural headquarters sphere and is presided over by threeTertiary Vorondadek Sons, the Most Highs. Each constellation also has a Faithful of Days in observation, as an ambassador of the Paradise Trinity.

3. *The Local Galaxy.* Usually around one hundred constellations (about 10,000,000 inhabitable planets, sometimes less, sometimes orders of magnitude more) constitute a local galaxy. The actual number of constellations varies greatly and thus the number of inhabited planets, depending on the size and type of galaxy. Each galaxy has a magnificent architectural headquarters world and is ruled by three Secondary Vorondadek Sons, with a Recent of Days in observation as a Paradise Trinity ambassador.

4. T*he Minor Sector.* Large groups of galaxies and galactic clusters (and these vary greatly in size and number) constitute a minor sector of the universe government; each has a wonderful headquarters world, wherefrom its rulers, three Primary Vorondadek Sons administer the affairs of the minor sector. There are three Recents of Days ambassadors, Supreme Trinity Personalities, on each minor sector headquarters.

5. *The Major Sector.* At least one hundred minor sectors, sometimes many times this number, make up one major sector. Each major sector is provided with a superb headquarters and is presided over by three Primary Vorondadek Sons with three Perfections of Days functioning as Supreme Trinity Personality ambassadors.

6. *The Local Universe.* Each local universe is made up of enormous

numbers of major sectors; has a magnificent architectural headquarters world and is ruled by one of the co-ordinate Creator Sons of God of the order of Michael. Each universe is blessed by the presence of a Union of Days, a representative of the Paradise Trinity.

7. *The Superuniverse.* An undisclosed number of universes (and this number varies between superuniverses) constitute a superuniverse. Each superuniverse is provided with an enormous and glorious headquarters world and is ruled by three Ancients of Days.

8. *The Grand Universe.* The seven superuniverses, with all of their universes, containing innumerable inhabitable worlds, plus the architectural spheres of each level, along with the one billion inhabited spheres of Havona , make up the present organized grand universe. The superuniverses are ruled and administered indirectly and reflectively from Paradise by the Seven Master Spirits. The billion worlds of Havona are directly administered by the Eternals of Days, one such Supreme Trinity Personality presiding over each of these perfect spheres.

3. THE ANCESTORS OF UNIVERSES

While creation and universe organization remain forever under the control of the infinite Creators and their associates, the whole phenomenon proceeds in accordance with an ordained technique and in conformity to the gravity laws of force, energy, and matter. But there is something of mystery associated with the universal force-charge of space; we quite understand the organization of the material creations from the ultimatonic stage forward, but we do not fully comprehend the cosmic ancestry of the ultimatons. We are confident that these ancestral forces have a Paradise origin because they forever swing through pervaded space in the exact gigantic outlines of Paradise. Though nonresponsive to Paradise gravity, this force-charge of space, the ancestor of all materialization, does always respond to the presence of nether Paradise, being apparently circuited in and out of the nether Paradise center.

The Paradise force organizers transmute space potency into primordial force and evolve this prematerial potential into the primary and secondary energy manifestations of physical reality. When this energy attains gravity-responding levels, the power directors and their associates of the superuniverse regime appear upon the scene and begin their never-ending manipulations designed to establish the manifold power circuits and energy channels of the universes of time and space. Thus does physical matter appear in space, and so is the stage set for the inauguration of universe organization.

This segmentation of energy is a phenomenon which has never been solved by the physicists of Nebadon. Their chief difficulty lies in the relative inaccessibility of the Paradise force organizers, for the living power directors, though they are competent to deal with space-energy, do not have the least conception of the origin of the energies they so skillfully and intelligently manipulate.

Paradise force organizers are universe originators; they are able to initiate about their space presence the tremendous energies which, when once started, can never be stopped or limited until the all-pervading forces are mobilized for the eventual appearance of the ultimatonic units of universe matter *[JFC: ultimatonic units may be strings, or composed of strings, as in the Physics of String Theory].*

4. THE SPHERES OF SPACE

Irrespective of origin, the various spheres of space are classifiable into the following major divisions:

1. The suns — the stars of space.
2. The dark islands of space.
3. Minor space bodies — comets, meteors, and planetesimals.
4. The planets, including the inhabited worlds.
5. Architectural spheres — worlds made to order.

With the exception of the architectural spheres, all space bodies have had an evolutionary origin, evolutionary in the sense that they have not been brought into being by fiat of Deity, evolutionary in the sense that the creative acts of God have unfolded by a time-space technique through the operation of many of the created and eventuated intelligences of Deity.

The laws of physical-energy behavior are basically universal, but local influences have much to do with the physical conditions which prevail on individual planets and in local systems. An almost endless variety of creature life and other living manifestations characterizes the countless worlds of space. There are, however, certain points of similarity in a group of worlds associated in a given system, while there also is a universe pattern of intelligent life. There are physical relationships among those planetary systems which belong to the same physical circuit.

5. THE ARCHITECTURAL SPHERES

While each local universe government level presides near its governing region, yet they exist outside of the space-time dimensions of that universe, and occupy a suitable world made to order and peopled by accredited personalities. These headquarters worlds are architectural spheres, space bodies specifically constructed for their special purpose. These spheres are independently lighted and heated. Each has a sun which gives forth light without heat, like the satellites of Paradise, while each is supplied with heat by the circulation of certain energy currents near the surface of the sphere.

Time is standardized on the headquarters of the superuniverses. The standard day of the superuniverse of Orvonton is equal to almost thirty days of Urantia time, and the Orvonton year equals one hundred standard days. This Uversa year is standard in the seventh superuniverse, and it is twenty-two minutes short of three thousand days of Urantia time, about eight and one fifth of your years.

The headquarters worlds of the seven superuniverses partake of the nature and grandeur of Paradise, their central pattern of perfection. In reality, all headquarters worlds are paradisiacal. They are indeed heavenly abodes, and they increase in material size, morontia beauty, and spirit glory from

Jerusem to the central Isle. And all the satellites of these headquarters worlds are also architectural spheres.

The various headquarters worlds are provided with every phase of material and spiritual creation. All kinds of material, morontial, and spiritual beings are at home on these rendezvous worlds of the universes. As mortal creatures ascend the universe, passing from the material to the spiritual realms, they never lose their appreciation for, and enjoyment of, their former levels of existence.

Jerusem, the headquarters of your local system of Satania, has its seven worlds of transition culture, each of which is encircled by seven satellites, among which are the seven mansion worlds of morontia detention, man's first postmortal residence. As the term heaven has been used on Urantia, it has sometimes meant these seven mansion worlds, the first mansion world being denominated the first heaven, and so on to the seventh.

Edentia, the headquarters of your constellation of Norlatiadek, has its seventy satellites of socializing culture and training, on which ascenders sojourn upon the completion of the Jerusem regime of personality mobilization, unification, and realization.

Zion, the headquarters of your local galaxy (the Milky Way) is surrounded by ten university clusters with seven spheres in each cluster, and broadens your horizons and increases your socialization to include the amazing diversity of all of the physical, morontia, and spiritual cultures of your entire galaxy; while preparing you for the next step in your advancing adventure towards Paradise.

Uminor the third, the headquarters of your minor sector, Ensa, is surrounded by the seven spheres of the higher studies of the ascendant life.

Umajor the fifth, the headquarters of your major sector, Splandon, is surrounded by the seventy spheres of the advancing intellectual training that will be necessary once on Salvington and begins to prepare you for the universities of the superuniverse.

Salvington, the capital of Nebadon, your local universe, is surrounded by ten university clusters of forty-nine spheres each. Hereon is man spiritualized following his galaxy socialization.

Uversa, the headquarters of Orvonton, your superuniverse, is immediately surrounded by the seven higher universities of advanced spiritual training for ascending will creatures. Each of these seven clusters of wonder spheres consists of seventy specialized worlds containing thousands upon thousands of replete institutions and organizations devoted to universe training and spirit culture wherein the pilgrims of time are re-educated and re-examined preparatory to their long flight to Havona. The arriving pilgrims of time are always received on these associated worlds, but the departing graduates are always dispatched for Havona direct from the shores of Uversa.

Uversa is the spiritual and administrative headquarters for all of the inhabited or inhabitable worlds of the superuniverse. The glory, grandeur, and perfection of the Orvonton capital surpass any of the wonders of the time-space creations.

6. ENERGY CONTROL AND REGULATION

The headquarters spheres of the universes and superuniverses are so constructed that they are able to function as efficient power-energy regulators for their various subsectors, serving as focal points for the directionization of energy to their subcomponents. They exert a powerful influence over the balance and control of the physical energies circulating through organized space.

Further regulative functions are performed by the various power centers and physical controllers, living and semiliving intelligent entities constituted for this express purpose. These power centers and controllers are difficult of understanding; the lower orders are not volitional, they do not possess will, they do not choose, their functions are very intelligent but apparently automatic and inherent in their highly specialized organization. The power centers and physical controllers assume direction and partial control of the thirty energy systems which comprise the gravita domain.

The universal plan for the maintenance of equilibrium between matter and energy necessitates the everlasting making and unmaking of the lesser material units. The Universe Power Directors have the ability to condense and detain, or to expand and liberate, varying quantities of energy.

We are able to recognize most of the laws governing universe equilibrium and to predict much pertaining to universe stability. Practically, our forecasts are reliable, but we are always confronted by certain forces which are not wholly amenable to the laws of energy control and matter behavior known to us. The predictability of all physical phenomena becomes increasingly difficult as we proceed outward in the universes from Paradise. As we pass beyond the borders of the personal administration of the Paradise Rulers, we are confronted with increasing inability to reckon in accordance with the standards established and the experience acquired in connection with observations having exclusively to do with physical phenomena. Even in the realms of the seven superuniverses we are living in the midst of force actions and energy reactions which pervade all our domains and extend in unified equilibrium on through all regions of outer space.

The farther out we go, the more certainly we encounter those variational and unpredictable phenomena which are so unerringly characteristic of the unfathomable presence-performances of the Absolutes and the experiential Deities. And these phenomena must be indicative of some universal overcontrol of all things.

The central Havona universe is eternally stabilized. The living power directors and force organizers are the secret of the special control and intelligent direction of the endless metamorphoses of universe making, unmaking, and remaking.

7. CIRCUITS OF THE SUPERUNIVERSES

The universal circuits of Paradise do actually pervade the realms of the seven superuniverses. These presence circuits are: the personality gravity of the Universal Father, the spiritual gravity of the Eternal Son, the mind gravity of the Conjoint Actor, and the material gravity of the eternal Isle.

In addition to the universal Paradise circuits and in addition to the presence-performances of the Absolutes and the experiential Deities, there function within the superuniverse space level only two energy-circuit divisions or power segregations: the superuniverse circuits and the local universe circuits.

The Superuniverse Circuits:

1. The unifying intelligence circuit of one of the Seven Master Spirits of Paradise. Such a cosmic-mind circuit is limited to a single superuniverse.
2. The reflective-service circuit of the seven Reflective Spirits in each superuniverse.
3. The secret circuits of the Mystery Monitors, in some manner interassociated and routed by Divinington to the Universal Father on Paradise.
4. The circuit of the intercommunion of the Eternal Son with his Paradise Sons.
5. The flash presence of the Infinite Spirit.
6. The broadcasts of Paradise, the space reports of Havona.
7. The energy circuits of the power centers and the physical controllers.

The Local Universe Circuits:

1. The bestowal spirit of the Paradise Sons, the Comforter of the bestowal worlds. The Spirit of Truth, the spirit of Michael on Urantia.
2. The circuit of the Divine Ministers, the local universe Mother Spirits, the Holy Spirit of your world.
3. The intelligence-ministry circuit of a local universe, including the diversely functioning presence of the adjutant mind-spirits.

When there develops such a spiritual harmony in a local universe that its individual and combined circuits become indistinguishable from those of the superuniverse, when such identity of function and oneness of ministry actually prevail, then does the local universe immediately swing into the settled circuits of light and life, becoming at once eligible for admission into the spiritual confederation of the perfected union of the supercreation. The requisites for admission to the councils of the Ancients of Days, membership in the superuniverse confederation, are:

1. *Physical Stability*. The stars, planets, and galaxies of a local universe must be in equilibrium; the periods of immediate stellar metamorphosis must be over. The universe must be proceeding on a clear track; its orbit must be safely and finally settled.

2. *Spiritual Loyalty*. There must exist a state of universal recognition of, and loyalty to, the Sovereign Son of God who presides over the affairs of such a local universe. There must have come into being a state of harmonious co-operation between the individual planets, systems, constellations, and galaxies of the entire local universe.

Your local universe is not even reckoned as belonging to the settled physical order of the superuniverse, much less as holding membership in the recognized spiritual family of the supergovernment. Although Nebadon does not yet have representation on Uversa, we of the superuniverse government are dispatched to its worlds on special missions from time to time, even as I have come to Urantia directly from Uversa. We lend every possible assistance to your directors and rulers in the solution of their difficult problems; we are desirous of seeing your universe qualified for full admission into the associated creations of the superuniverse family.

8. RULERS OF THE SUPERUNIVERSES

The headquarters of the superuniverses are the seats of the high spiritual government of the time-space domains. The executive branch of the supergovernment, taking origin in the Councils of the Trinity, is immediately directed by one of the Seven Master Spirits of supreme supervision, beings who sit upon seats of Paradise authority and administer the superuniverses through the Seven Supreme Executives stationed on the seven special worlds of the Infinite Spirit, the outermost satellites of Paradise.

The superuniverse headquarters are the abiding places of the Reflective Spirits and the Reflective Image Aids. From this midway position these marvelous beings conduct their tremendous reflectivity operations, thus ministering to the central universe above and to the local universes below.

Each superuniverse is presided over by three Ancients of Days, the joint chief executives of the supergovernment. In its executive branch the personnel of the superuniverse government consists of seven different groups:

1. Ancients of Days.
2. Perfectors of Wisdom.
3. Divine Counselors.
4. Universal Censors.
5. Mighty Messengers.
6. Those High in Authority.
7. Those without Name and Number.

The three Ancients of Days are immediately assisted by an enormous corps of Perfectors of Wisdom, each of whom has three Divine Counselor associates. One Universal Censor is also attached to each of these superuniverse administration units. These three groups are Co-ordinate Trinity Personalities, taking origin directly and divinely in the Paradise Trinity.

The remaining three orders, Mighty Messengers, Those High in Authority, and Those without Name and Number, are glorified ascendant mortals. The first of these orders came up through the ascendant regime and passed through Havona in the days of Grandfanda. Having attained Paradise, they were mustered into the Corps of the Finality, embraced by the Paradise Trinity, and subsequently assigned to the supernal service of the Ancients of Days. As a class, these three orders are known as Trinitized Sons of Attainment, being of dual origin but now of Trinity service. Thus was the executive branch of the superuniverse government enlarged to include the glorified and perfected children of the evolutionary worlds.

The co-ordinate council of the superuniverse is composed of the seven executive groups previously named and the following sector rulers and other regional overseers:

1. Unions of Days — the Paradise advisers to the rulers of the local universes.
2. Perfections of Days — the Paradise advisors to the rulers of the universe major sectors.
3. Recents of Days — the Paradise advisors to the rulers of the universe minor sectors, and ambassadors to local galaxies.
4. Faithfuls of Days — the Paradise counselors to the Most High rulers of the constellation governments.
5. Trinity Teacher Sons who may chance to be on duty at universe headquarters.
6. Eternals of Days who may happen to be present at universe headquarters.
7. The seven Reflective Image Aids — the spokesmen of the seven Reflective Spirits and through them representatives of the Seven Master Spirits of Paradise.

The Reflective Image Aids also function as the representatives of numerous groups of beings who are influential in the universe and superuniverse governments, but who are not, at present, for various reasons, fully active in their individual capacities. Embraced within this group are: the evolving superuniverse personality manifestation of the Supreme Being, the Unqualified Supervisors of the Supreme, the Qualified Vicegerents of the Ultimate, the unnamed liaison reflectivators of Majeston, and the superpersonal spirit representatives of the Eternal Son.

At almost all times it is possible to find representatives of all groups of created beings on the headquarters worlds of the universe and superuniverses. The routine ministering work is performed by the mighty seconaphim and by other members of the vast family of the Infinite Spirit. In the work of these marvelous centers of administration, control, ministry, and executive judgment, the intelligences of every sphere of universal life are mingled in effective service, wise administration, loving ministry, and just judgment.

The superuniverses do not maintain any sort of ambassadorial representation; they are completely isolated from each other. They know of mutual affairs only through the Paradise clearinghouse maintained by the Seven Master Spirits. Their rulers work in the councils of divine wisdom for the welfare of their own superuniverses regardless of what may be transpiring in other sections of the universal creation. This isolation of the superuniverses will persist until such time as their co-ordination is achieved by the more complete factualization of the personality-sovereignty of the evolving experiential Supreme Being.

9. THE DELIBERATIVE ASSEMBLY

It is on such worlds as Uversa that the beings representative of the autocracy of perfection and the democracy of evolution meet face to face. The executive branch of the supergovernment originates in the realms of perfection; the legislative branch springs from the flowering of the evolutionary universes.

The deliberative assembly of the superuniverse is confined to the headquarters world. This legislative or advisory council consists of seven houses, to each of which every local universe admitted to the superuniverse councils elects a native representative. These representatives are chosen by the high councils of such local universes from among the ascending-pilgrim graduates of Orvonton who are tarrying on Uversa, accredited for transport to Havona. The average term of service is about one hundred years of superuniverse standard time.

Never have I known of a disagreement between the Orvonton executives and the Uversa assembly. Never yet, in the history of our superuniverse, has the deliberative body ever passed a recommendation that the executive division of the supergovernment has even hesitated to carry out. There always has prevailed the most perfect harmony and working agreement, all of which testifies to the fact that evolutionary beings can really attain the heights of perfected wisdom which qualifies them to consort with the personalities of perfect origin and divine nature. The presence of the deliberative assemblies on the superuniverse headquarters reveals the wisdom, and foreshadows the ultimate triumph, of the whole vast evolutionary concept of the Universal Father and his Eternal Son.

10. THE SUPREME TRIBUNALS

When we speak of executive and deliberative branches of the Uversa government, you may, from the analogy of certain forms of Urantian civil government, reason that we must have a third or judicial branch, and we do; but it does not have a separate personnel. Our courts are constituted as follows: There presides, in accordance with the nature and gravity of the case, an Ancient of Days, a Perfector of Wisdom, or a Divine Counselor. The evidence for or against an individual, a planet, system, constellation, galaxy, or universe is presented and interpreted by the Censors. The defense of the children of time and the evolutionary planets is offered by the Mighty Messengers, the official observers of the superuniverse government to the local universes and systems. The attitude of the higher government is portrayed by Those High in Authority. And ordinarily the verdict is formulated by a varying-sized commission consisting equally of Those without Name and Number and a group of understanding personalities chosen from the deliberative assembly.

The courts of the Ancients of Days are the high review tribunals for the spiritual adjudication of all component universes. The Sovereign Sons of the local universes are supreme in their own domains; they are subject to the supergovernment only in so far as they voluntarily submit matters for counsel or adjudication by the Ancients of Days except in matters involving the extinction of will creatures. Mandates of judgment originate in the local universes, but sentences involving the extinction of will creatures are always formulated on, and executed from, the headquarters of the superuniverse. The Sons of the local universes can decree the survival of mortal man, but only the Ancients of Days may sit in executive judgment on the issues of eternal life and death.

In all matters not requiring trial, the submission of evidence, the Ancients of Days or their associates render decisions, and these rulings are always unanimous. We are here dealing with the councils of perfection. There are no disagreements nor minority opinions in the decrees of these supreme and superlative tribunals.

With certain few exceptions the supergovernments exercise jurisdiction over all things and all beings in their respective domains. There is no appeal from the rulings and decisions of the superuniverse authorities since they represent the concurred opinions of the Ancients of Days and that Master Spirit who, from Paradise, presides over the destiny of the superuniverse concerned.

11. PURPOSES OF THE SEVEN SUPERUNIVERSES

There are seven major purposes which are being unfolded in the evolution of the seven superuniverses. Each major purpose in superuniverse evolution will find fullest expression in only one of the seven superuniverses, and therefore does each superuniverse have a special function and a unique nature.

Orvonton, the seventh superuniverse, the one to which your local universe belongs, is known chiefly because of its tremendous and lavish bestowal of merciful ministry to the mortals of the realms. It is renowned for the manner in which justice prevails as tempered by mercy and power rules as conditioned by patience, while the sacrifices of time are freely made to secure the stabilization of eternity. Orvonton is a universe demonstration of love and mercy.

It is, however, very difficult to describe our conception of the true nature of the evolutionary purpose which is unfolding in Orvonton, but it may be suggested by saying that in this supercreation we feel that the six unique purposes of cosmic evolution as manifested in the six associated supercreations are here being interassociated into a meaning-of-the-whole; and it is for this reason that we have sometimes conjectured that the evolved and finished personalization of God the Supreme will in the remote future and from Uversa rule the perfected seven superuniverses in all the experiential majesty of his then attained almighty sovereign power.

As Orvonton is unique in nature and individual in destiny, so also is each of its six associated superuniverses. A great deal that is going on in Orvonton is not, however, revealed to you, and of these unrevealed features of Orvonton life, many are to find most complete expression in some other superuniverse. The seven purposes of superuniverse evolution are operative throughout all seven superuniverses, but each supercreation will give fullest expression to only one of these purposes. To understand more about these superuniverse purposes, much that you do not understand would have to be revealed, and even then you would comprehend but little. This entire narrative presents only a fleeting glimpse of the immense creation of which your world and local system are a part.

Your world is called Urantia, and it is number 606 in the planetary group, or system, of Satania. This system has at present 619 inhabited worlds, and more than two hundred additional planets are evolving favorably toward becoming inhabited worlds at some future time.

Satania has a headquarters world called Jerusem, and it is system number twenty-four in the constellation of Norlatiadek. Your constellation, Norlatiadek, consists of one hundred local systems and has a headquarters world called Edentia. Norlatiadek is number seventy in your Milky Way galaxy.

Your planet is a member of an enormous cosmos; you belong to a well-nigh infinite family of worlds, but your sphere is just as precisely administered and just as lovingly fostered as if it were the only inhabited world in all existence.

[Presented by a Universal Censor hailing from Uversa.]

PAPER 16
THE SEVEN MASTER SPIRITS

The Seven Master Spirits of Paradise are the primary personalities of the Infinite Spirit. In this sevenfold creative act of self-duplication the Infinite Spirit exhausted the associative possibilities mathematically inherent in the factual existence of the three persons of Deity. Had it been possible to produce a larger number of Master Spirits, they would have been created, but there are just seven associative possibilities, and only seven, inherent in three Deities. And this explains why the universe is operated in seven grand divisions, and why the number seven is basically fundamental in its organization and administration.

The Seven Master Spirits thus have their origin in, and derive their individual characteristics from, the following seven likenesses:

1. The Universal Father.
2. The Eternal Son.
3. The Infinite Spirit.
4. The Father and the Son.
5. The Father and the Spirit.
6. The Son and the Spirit.
7. The Father, Son, and Spirit.

We know very little about the action of the Father and the Son in the creation of the Master Spirits. Apparently they were brought into existence by the personal acts of the Infinite Spirit, but we have been definitely instructed that both the Father and the Son participated in their origin.

In spirit character and nature these Seven Spirits of Paradise are as one, but in all other aspects of identity they are very unlike, and the results of their functioning in the superuniverses are such that the individual differences of each are unmistakably discernible. All the afterplans of the seven segments of the grand universe — and even the correlative segments of outer space — have been conditioned by the other-than-spiritual diversity of these Seven Master Spirits of supreme and ultimate supervision.

The Master Spirits have many functions, but at the present time their particular domain is the central supervision of the seven superuniverses. Each Master Spirit maintains an enormous force-focal headquarters, which slowly circulates around the periphery of Paradise, always maintaining a position opposite the superuniverse of immediate supervision and at the Paradise focal point of its specialized power control and segmental energy distribution. The radial boundary lines of any one of the superuniverses do actually converge at the Paradise headquarters of the supervising Master Spirit.

1. RELATION TO TRIUNE DEITY

The Conjoint Creator, the Infinite Spirit, is necessary to the completion of the triune personalization of undivided Deity. This threefold Deity personalization is inherently sevenfold in possibility of individual and associative expression; hence the subsequent plan to create universes inhabited by intelligent and potentially spiritual beings, duly expressive of the Father, Son, and Spirit, made the personalization of the Seven Master Spirits inescapable. We have come to speak of the threefold personalization of Deity as the absolute inevitability, while we have come to look upon the appearance of the Seven Master Spirits as the subabsolute inevitability.

While the Seven Master Spirits are hardly expressive of threefold Deity, they are the eternal portrayal of sevenfold Deity, the active and associative functions of the three ever-existent persons of Deity. By and in and through these Seven Spirits, the Universal Father, the Eternal Son, or the Infinite Spirit, or any dual association, is able to function as such. When the Father, the Son, and the Spirit act together, they can and do function through Master Spirit Number Seven, but not as the Trinity. The Master Spirits singly and collectively represent any and all possible Deity functions, single and several, but not collective, not the Trinity. Master Spirit Number Seven is personally nonfunctional with regard to the Paradise Trinity, and that is just why he can function personally for the Supreme Being.

But when the Seven Master Spirits vacate their individual seats of personal power and superuniverse authority and assemble about the Conjoint Actor in the triune presence of Paradise Deity, then and there are they collectively representative of the functional power, wisdom, and authority of undivided Deity — the Trinity — to and in the evolving universes. Such a Paradise union of the primal sevenfold expression of Deity does actually embrace, literally encompass, all of every attribute and attitude of the three eternal Deities in Supremacy and in Ultimacy. To all practical intents and purposes the Seven Master Spirits do, then and there, encompass the functional domain of the Supreme-Ultimate to and in the master universe.

As far as we can discern, these Seven Spirits are associated with the divine activities of the three eternal persons of Deity; we detect no evidence of direct association with the functioning presences of the three eternal phases of the Absolute. When associated, the Master Spirits represent the Paradise Deities in what may be roughly conceived as the finite domain of action. It might embrace much that is ultimate but not absolute.

2. RELATION TO THE INFINITE SPIRIT

Just as the Eternal and Original Son is revealed through the persons of the constantly increasing number of divine Sons, so is the Infinite and Divine Spirit revealed through the channels of the Seven Master Spirits and their associated spirit groups. At the center of centers the Infinite Spirit is approachable, but not all who attain Paradise are immediately able to discern his personality and differentiated presence; but all who attain the central universe can and do immediately commune with one of the Seven Master

Spirits, the one presiding over the superuniverse from which the newly arrived space pilgrim hails.

To the universe of universes the Paradise Father speaks only through his Son, while he and the Son conjointly act only through the Infinite Spirit. Outside of Paradise and Havona the Infinite Spirit speaks only by the voices of the Seven Master Spirits.

The Infinite Spirit exerts an influence of personal presence within the confines of the Paradise-Havona system; elsewhere his personal spirit presence is exerted by and through one of the Seven Master Spirits. Therefore is the superuniverse spirit presence of the Third Source and Center on any world or in any individual conditioned by the unique nature of the supervisory Master Spirit of that segment of creation. Conversely, the combined lines of spirit force and intelligence pass inward to the Third Person of Deity by way of the Seven Master Spirits.

The Seven Master Spirits are collectively endowed with the supreme-ultimate attributes of the Third Source and Center. While each one individually partakes of this endowment, only collectively do they disclose the attributes of omnipotence, omniscience, and omnipresence. No one of them can so function universally; as individuals and in the exercise of these powers of supremacy and ultimacy each is personally limited to the superuniverse of immediate supervision.

All of everything which has been told you concerning the divinity and personality of the Conjoint Actor applies equally and fully to the Seven Master Spirits, who so effectively distribute the Infinite Spirit to the seven segments of the grand universe in accordance with their divine endowment and in the manner of their differing and individually unique natures. It would therefore be proper to apply to the collective group of seven any or all of the names of the Infinite Spirit. Collectively they are one with the Conjoint Creator on all subabsolute levels.

3. IDENTITY AND DIVERSITY OF THE MASTER SPIRITS

The Seven Master Spirits are indescribable beings, but they are distinctly and definitely personal. They have names, but we elect to introduce them by number. As primary personalizations of the Infinite Spirit, they are akin, but as primary expressions of the seven possible associations of triune Deity, they are essentially diverse in nature, and this diversity of nature determines their differential of superuniverse conduct. These Seven Master Spirits may be described as follows:

Master Spirit Number One. In a special manner this Spirit is the direct representation of the Paradise Father. He is a peculiar and efficient manifestation of the power, love, and wisdom of the Universal Father. He is the close associate and supernal adviser of the chief of Mystery Monitors, that being who presides over the College of Personalized Adjusters on Divinington. In all associations of the Seven Master Spirits, it is always Master Spirit Number One who speaks for the Universal Father.

This Spirit presides over the first superuniverse and, while unfailingly exhibiting the divine nature of a primary personalization of the Infinite Spirit, seems more especially to resemble the Universal Father in character. He is always in personal liaison with the seven Reflective Spirits at the headquarters of the first superuniverse.

Master Spirit Number Two. This Spirit adequately portrays the matchless nature and charming character of the Eternal Son, the first-born of all creation. He is always in close association with all orders of the Sons of God whenever they may happen to be in the residential universe as individuals or in joyous conclave. In all the assemblies of the Seven Master Spirits he always speaks for, and in behalf of, the Eternal Son.

This Spirit directs the destinies of superuniverse number two and rules this vast domain much as would the Eternal Son. He is always in liaison with the seven Reflective Spirits situated at the capital of the second superuniverse.

Master Spirit Number Three. This Spirit personality especially resembles the Infinite Spirit, and he directs the movements and work of many of the high personalities of the Infinite Spirit. He presides over their assemblies and is closely associated with all personalities who take exclusive origin in the Third Source and Center. When the Seven Master Spirits are in council, it is Master Spirit Number Three who always speaks for the Infinite Spirit.

This Spirit is in charge of superuniverse number three, and he administers the affairs of this segment much as would the Infinite Spirit. He is always in liaison with the Reflective Spirits at the headquarters of the third superuniverse.

Master Spirit Number Four. Partaking of the combined natures of the Father and the Son, this Master Spirit is the determining influence regarding Father-Son policies and procedures in the councils of the Seven Master Spirits. This Spirit is the chief director and adviser of those ascendant beings who have attained the Infinite Spirit and thus have become candidates for seeing the Son and the Father. He fosters that enormous group of personalities taking origin in the Father and the Son. When it becomes necessary to represent the Father and the Son in the association of the Seven Master Spirits, it is always Master Spirit Number Four who speaks.

This Spirit fosters the fourth segment of the grand universe in accordance with his peculiar association of the attributes of the Universal Father and the Eternal Son. He is always in personal liaison with the Reflective Spirits of the headquarters of the fourth superuniverse.

Master Spirit Number Five. This divine personality who exquisitely blends the character of the Universal Father and the Infinite Spirit is the adviser of that enormous group of beings known as the power directors, power centers, and physical controllers. This Spirit also fosters all personalities taking origin in the Father and the Conjoint Actor. In the councils of the Seven Master Spirits, when the Father-Spirit attitude is in question, it is always Master Spirit Number Five who speaks.

This Spirit directs the welfare of the fifth superuniverse in such a way as to suggest the combined action of the Universal Father and the Infinite Spirit. He is always in liaison with the Reflective Spirits at the headquarters of the fifth superuniverse.

Master Spirit Number Six. This divine being seems to portray the combined character of the Eternal Son and the Infinite Spirit. Whenever the creatures jointly created by the Son and the Spirit forgather in the central universe, it is this Master Spirit who is their adviser; and whenever, in the councils of the Seven Master Spirits, it becomes necessary to speak conjointly for the Eternal Son and the Infinite Spirit, it is Master Spirit Number Six who responds.

This Spirit directs the affairs of the sixth superuniverse much as would the Eternal Son and the Infinite Spirit. He is always in liaison with the Reflective Spirits at the headquarters of the sixth superuniverse.

Master Spirit Number Seven. The presiding Spirit of the seventh superuniverse is a uniquely equal portrayal of the Universal Father, the Eternal Son, and the Infinite Spirit. The Seventh Spirit, the fostering adviser of all triune-origin beings, is also the adviser and director of all the ascending pilgrims of Havona, those lowly beings who have attained the courts of glory through the combined ministry of the Father, the Son, and the Spirit.

The Seventh Master Spirit is not organically representative of the Paradise Trinity; but it is a known fact that his personal and spiritual nature is the Conjoint Actor's portraiture in equal proportions of the three infinite persons whose Deity union is the Paradise Trinity, and whose function as such is the source of the personal and spiritual nature of God the Supreme. Hence the Seventh Master Spirit discloses a personal and organic relationship to the spirit person of the evolving Supreme. Therefore in the Master Spirit councils on high, when it becomes necessary to cast the ballot for the combined personal attitude of the Father, Son, and Spirit or to depict the spiritual attitude of the Supreme Being, it is Master Spirit Number Seven who functions. He thus inherently becomes the presiding head of the Paradise council of the Seven Master Spirits.

No one of the Seven Spirits is organically representative of the Paradise Trinity, but when they unite as sevenfold Deity, this union in a deity sense — not in a personal sense — equivalates to a functional level associable with Trinity functions. In this sense the "Sevenfold Spirit" is functionally associable with the Paradise Trinity. It is also in this sense that Master Spirit Number Seven sometimes speaks in confirmation of Trinity attitudes or, rather, acts as spokesman for the attitude of the Sevenfold-Spirit-union regarding the attitude of the Threefold-Deity-union, the attitude of the Paradise Trinity.

The multiple functions of the Seventh Master Spirit thus range from a combined portraiture of the personal natures of the Father, Son, and Spirit, through a representation of the personal attitude of God the Supreme, to a disclosure of the deity attitude of the Paradise Trinity. And in certain respects this presiding Spirit is similarly expressive of the attitudes of the Ultimate and of the Supreme-Ultimate.

It is Master Spirit Number Seven who, in his multiple capacities, personally sponsors the progress of the ascension candidates from the worlds of time in their attempts to achieve comprehension of the undivided Deity of Supremacy. Such comprehension involves a grasp of the existential sovereignty of the Trinity of Supremacy so co-ordinated with a concept of the growing experiential sovereignty of the Supreme Being as to constitute the creature grasp of the unity of Supremacy. Creature realization of these three factors equals Havona comprehension of Trinity reality and endows the pilgrims of time with the ability eventually to penetrate the Trinity, to discover the three infinite persons of Deity.

The inability of the Havona pilgrims fully to find God the Supreme is compensated by the Seventh Master Spirit, whose triune nature in such a peculiar manner is revelatory of the spirit person of the Supreme. During the present universe age of the noncontactability of the person of the Supreme, Master Spirit Number Seven functions in the place of the God of ascendant creatures in the matter of personal relationships. He is the one high spirit being that all ascenders are certain to recognize and somewhat comprehend when they reach the centers of glory.

This Master Spirit is always in liaison with the Reflective Spirits of Uversa, the headquarters of the seventh superuniverse, our own segment of creation. His administration of Orvonton discloses the marvelous symmetry of the co-ordinate blending of the divine natures of Father, Son, and Spirit.

4. ATTRIBUTES AND FUNCTIONS OF THE MASTER SPIRITS

The Seven Master Spirits are the full representation of the Infinite Spirit to the evolutionary universes. They represent the Third Source and Center in the relationships of energy, mind, and spirit. While they function as the co-ordinating heads of the universal administrative control of the Conjoint

Actor, do not forget that they have their origin in the creative acts of the Paradise Deities. It is literally true that these Seven Spirits are the personalized physical power, cosmic mind, and spiritual presence of the triune Deity, "the Seven Spirits of God sent forth to all the universe."

The Master Spirits are unique in that they function on all universe levels of reality excepting the absolute. They are, therefore, efficient and perfect supervisors of all phases of administrative affairs on all levels of superuniverse activities. It is difficult for the mortal mind to understand very much about the Master Spirits because their work is so highly specialized yet all-embracing, so exceptionally material and at the same time so exquisitely spiritual. These versatile creators of the cosmic mind are the ancestors of the Universe Power Directors and are, themselves, supreme directors of the vast and far-flung spirit-creature creation.

The Seven Master Spirits are the creators of the Universe Power Directors and their associates, entities who are indispensable to the organization, control, and regulation of the physical energies of the grand universe. And these same Master Spirits very materially assist the Creator Sons in the work of shaping and organizing the local universes.

We are unable to trace any personal connection between the cosmic-energy work of the Master Spirits and the force functions of the Unqualified Absolute. The energy manifestations under the jurisdiction of the Master Spirits are all directed from the periphery of Paradise; they do not appear to be in any direct manner associated with the force phenomena identified with the nether surface of Paradise.

Unquestionably, when we encounter the functional activities of the various Morontia Power Supervisors, we are face to face with certain of the unrevealed activities of the Master Spirits. Who, aside from these ancestors of both physical controllers and spirit ministers, could have contrived so to combine and associate material and spiritual energies as to produce a hitherto nonexistent phase of universe reality — morontia substance and morontia mind?

Much of the reality of the spiritual worlds is of the morontia order, a phase of universe reality wholly unknown on Urantia. The goal of personality existence is spiritual, but the morontia creations always intervene, bridging the gulf between the material realms of mortal origin and the superuniverse spheres of advancing spiritual status. It is in this realm that the Master Spirits make their great contribution to the plan of man's Paradise ascension.

The Seven Master Spirits have personal representatives who function throughout the grand universe; but since a large majority of these subordinate beings are not directly concerned with the ascendant scheme of mortal progression in the path of Paradise perfection, little or nothing has been revealed about them. Much, very much, of the activity of the Seven Master Spirits remains hidden from human understanding because in no way does it directly pertain to your problem of Paradise ascent.

It is highly probable, though we cannot offer definite proof, that the Master Spirit of Orvonton exerts a decided influence in the following spheres of activity:

1. The life-initiation procedures of the local universe Life Carriers.
2. The life activations of the adjutant mind-spirits bestowed upon the worlds by a local universe Creative Spirit.
3. The fluctuations in energy manifestations exhibited by the linear-gravity-responding units of organized matter.
4. The behavior of emergent energy when fully liberated from the grasp of the Unqualified Absolute, thus becoming responsive to the direct influence of linear gravity and to the manipulations of the Universe Power Directors and their associates.
5. The bestowal of the ministry spirit of a local universe Creative Spirit, known on Urantia as the Holy Spirit.
6. The subsequent bestowal of the spirit of the bestowal Sons, on Urantia called the Comforter or the Spirit of Truth.
7. The reflectivity mechanism of the local universes and the superuniverse. Many features connected with this extraordinary phenomenon can hardly be reasonably explained or rationally understood without postulating the activity of the Master Spirits in association with the Conjoint Actor and the Supreme Being.

Notwithstanding our failure adequately to comprehend the manifold workings of the Seven Master Spirits, we are confident there are two realms in the vast range of universe activities with which they have nothing whatever to do: the bestowal and ministry of the Thought Adjusters and the inscrutable functions of the Unqualified Absolute.

5. RELATION TO CREATURES

Each segment of the grand universe, each individual universe and world, enjoys the benefits of the united counsel and wisdom of all Seven Master Spirits but receives the personal touch and tinge of only one. And the personal nature of each Master Spirit entirely pervades and uniquely conditions his superuniverse.

Through this personal influence of the Seven Master Spirits every creature of every order of intelligent beings, outside of Paradise and Havona, must bear the characteristic stamp of individuality indicative of the ancestral nature of some one of these Seven Paradise Spirits. As concerns the seven superuniverses, each native creature, man or angel, will forever bear this badge of natal identification.

The Seven Master Spirits do not directly invade the material minds of the individual creatures on the evolutionary worlds of space. The mortals of Urantia do not experience the personal presence of the mind-spirit influence of the Master Spirit of Orvonton. If this Master Spirit does attain any sort of contact with the individual mortal mind during the earlier evolutionary ages of an inhabited world, it must occur through the ministry of the local universe Creative Spirit, the consort and associate of the Creator Son of God who presides over the destinies of each local creation. But this very Creative Mother Spirit is, in nature and character, quite like the Master Spirit of Orvonton.

The physical stamp of a Master Spirit is a part of man's material origin. The entire morontia career is lived under the continuing influence of this same Master Spirit. It is hardly strange that the subsequent spirit career of such an ascending mortal never fully eradicates the characteristic stamp of this same supervising Spirit. The impress of a Master Spirit is basic to the very existence of every pre-Havona stage of mortal ascension.

The distinctive personality trends exhibited in the life experience of evolutionary mortals, which are characteristic in each superuniverse, and which are directly expressive of the nature of the dominating Master Spirit, are never fully effaced, not even after such ascenders are subjected to the long training and unifying discipline encountered on the one billion educational spheres of Havona. Even the subsequent intense Paradise culture does not suffice to eradicate the earmarks of superuniverse origin. Throughout all eternity an ascendant mortal will exhibit traits indicative of the presiding Spirit of his superuniverse of nativity. Even in the Corps of the Finality, when it is desired to arrive at or to portray a complete Trinity relationship to the evolutionary creation, always a group of seven finaliters is assembled, one from each superuniverse.

6. THE COSMIC MIND

The Master Spirits are the sevenfold source of the cosmic mind, the intellectual potential of the grand universe. This cosmic mind is a subabsolute manifestation of the mind of the Third Source and Center and, in certain ways, is functionally related to the mind of the evolving Supreme Being.

On a world like Urantia we do not encounter the direct influence of the Seven Master Spirits in the affairs of the human races. You live under the immediate influence of the Creative Spirit of Nebadon. Nevertheless these same Master Spirits dominate the basic reactions of all creature mind because they are the actual sources of the intellectual and spiritual potentials which have been specialized in the local universes for function in the lives of those individuals who inhabit the evolutionary worlds of time and space.

The fact of the cosmic mind explains the kinship of various types of human and superhuman minds. Not only are kindred spirits attracted to each other, but kindred minds are also very fraternal and inclined towards cooperation the one with the other. Human minds are sometimes observed to be running in channels of astonishing similarity and inexplicable agreement.

There exists in all personality associations of the cosmic mind a quality which might be denominated the "reality response." It is this universal cosmic endowment of will creatures which saves them from becoming helpless victims of the implied a priori assumptions of science, philosophy, and religion. This reality sensitivity of the cosmic mind responds to certain phases of reality just as energy-material responds to gravity. It would be still more correct to say that these supermaterial realities so respond to the mind of the cosmos.

The cosmic mind unfailingly responds (recognizes response) on three levels of universe reality. These responses are self-evident to clear-reasoning and deep-thinking minds. These levels of reality are:

1. *Causation* — the reality domain of the physical senses, the scientific realms of logical uniformity, the differentiation of the factual and the nonfactual, reflective conclusions based on cosmic response. This is the mathematical form of the cosmic discrimination.
2. *Duty* — the reality domain of morals in the philosophic realm, the arena of reason, the recognition of relative right and wrong. This is the judicial form of the cosmic discrimination.
3. *Worship* — the spiritual domain of the reality of religious experience, the personal realization of divine fellowship, the recognition of spirit values, the assurance of eternal survival, the ascent from the status of servants of God to the joy and liberty of the sons of God. This is the highest insight of the cosmic mind, the reverential and worshipful form of the cosmic discrimination.

These scientific, moral, and spiritual insights, these cosmic responses, are innate in the cosmic mind, which endows all will creatures. The experience of living never fails to develop these three cosmic intuitions; they are constitutive in the self-consciousness of reflective thinking. But it is sad to record that so few persons on Urantia take delight in cultivating these qualities of courageous and independent cosmic thinking.

In the local universe mind bestowals, these three insights of the cosmic mind constitute the a priori assumptions which make it possible for man to function as a rational and self-conscious personality in the realms of science, philosophy, and religion. Stated otherwise, the recognition of the reality of these three manifestations of the Infinite is by a cosmic technique of self-revelation. Matter-energy is recognized by the mathematical logic of the senses; mind-reason intuitively knows its moral duty; spirit-faith (worship) is the religion of the reality of spiritual experience. These three basic factors in reflective thinking may be unified and co-ordinated in personality development, or they may become disproportionate and virtually unrelated in their respective functions. But when they become unified, they produce a strong character consisting in the correlation of a factual science, a moral philosophy, and a genuine religious experience. And it is these three cosmic intuitions that give objective validity, reality, to man's experience in and with things, meanings, and values.

It is the purpose of education to develop and sharpen these innate endowments of the human mind; of civilization to express them; of life experience to realize them; of religion to ennoble them; and of personality to unify them.

7. MORALS, VIRTUE, AND PERSONALITY

Intelligence alone cannot explain the moral nature. Morality, virtue, is indigenous to human personality. Moral intuition, the realization of duty, is a component of human mind endowment and is associated with the other inalienables of human nature: scientific curiosity and spiritual insight. Man's mentality far transcends that of his animal cousins, but it is his moral and religious natures that especially distinguish him from the animal world.

The selective response of an animal is limited to the motor level of behavior. The supposed insight of the higher animals is on a motor level and usually appears only after the experience of motor trial and error. Man is able to exercise scientific, moral, and spiritual insight prior to all exploration or experimentation.

Only a personality can know what it is doing before it does it; only personalities possess insight in advance of experience. A personality can look before it leaps and can therefore learn from looking as well as from leaping. A nonpersonal animal ordinarily learns only by leaping.

As a result of experience an animal becomes able to examine the different ways of attaining a goal and to select an approach based on accumulated experience. But a personality can also examine the goal itself and pass judgment on its worth-whileness, its value. Intelligence alone can discriminate as to the best means of attaining indiscriminate ends, but a moral being possesses an insight which enables him to discriminate between ends as well as between means. And a moral being in choosing virtue is nonetheless intelligent. He knows what he is doing, why he is doing it, where he is going, and how he will get there.

When man fails to discriminate the ends of his mortal striving, he finds himself functioning on the animal level of existence. He has failed to avail himself of the superior advantages of that material acumen, moral discrimination, and spiritual insight which are an integral part of his cosmic-mind endowment as a personal being.

Virtue is righteousness — conformity with the cosmos. To name virtues is not to define them, but to live them is to know them. Virtue is not mere knowledge nor yet wisdom but rather the reality of progressive experience in the attainment of ascending levels of cosmic achievement. In the day-by-day life of mortal man, virtue is realized by the consistent choosing of good rather than evil, and such choosing ability is evidence of the possession of a moral nature.

Man's choosing between good and evil is influenced, not only by the keenness of his moral nature, but also by such influences as ignorance, immaturity, and delusion. A sense of proportion is also concerned in the exercise of virtue because evil may be perpetrated when the lesser is chosen in the place of the greater as a result of distortion or deception. The art of relative estimation or comparative measurement enters into the practice of the virtues of the moral realm.

Man's moral nature would be impotent without the art of measurement, the discrimination embodied in his ability to scrutinize meanings. Likewise would moral choosing be futile without that cosmic insight which yields the consciousness of spiritual values. From the standpoint of intelligence, man ascends to the level of a moral being because he is endowed with personality.

Morality can never be advanced by law or by force. It is a personal and freewill matter and must be disseminated by the contagion of the contact of morally fragrant persons with those who are less morally responsive, but who are also in some measure desirous of doing the Father's will.

Moral acts are those human performances which are characterized by the highest intelligence, directed by selective discrimination in the choice of superior ends as well as in the selection of moral means to attain these ends. Such conduct is virtuous. Supreme virtue, then, is wholeheartedly to choose to do the will of the Father in heaven.

8. URANTIA PERSONALITY

The Universal Father bestows personality upon numerous orders of beings as they function on diverse levels of universe actuality. Urantia human beings are endowed with personality of the finite-mortal type, functioning on the level of the ascending sons of God.

Though we can hardly undertake to define personality, we may attempt to narrate our understanding of the known factors which go to make up the ensemble of material, mental, and spiritual energies whose interassociation constitutes the mechanism wherein and whereon and wherewith the Universal Father causes his bestowed personality to function.

Personality is a unique endowment of original nature whose existence is independent of, and antecedent to, the bestowal of the Thought Adjuster. Nevertheless, the presence of the Adjuster does augment the qualitative manifestation of personality. Thought Adjusters, when they come forth from the Father, are identical in nature, but personality is diverse, original, and exclusive; and the manifestation of personality is further conditioned and qualified by the nature and qualities of the associated energies of a material, mindal, and spiritual nature which constitute the organismal vehicle for personality manifestation.

Personalities may be similar, but they are never the same. Persons of a given series, type, order, or pattern may and do resemble one another, but they are never identical. Personality is that feature of an individual which we know, and which enables us to identify such a being at some future time regardless of the nature and extent of changes in form, mind, or spirit status. Personality is that part of any individual which enables us to recognize and positively identify that person as the one we have previously known, no matter how much he may have changed because of the modification of the vehicle of expression and manifestation of his personality.

Creature personality is distinguished by two self-manifesting and characteristic phenomena of mortal reactive behavior: self-consciousness and associated relative free will.

Self-consciousness consists in intellectual awareness of personality actuality; it includes the ability to recognize the reality of other personalities. It indicates capacity for individualized experience in and with cosmic realities, equivalating to the attainment of identity status in the personality relationships of the universe. Self-consciousness connotes recognition of the actuality of mind ministration and the realization of relative independence of creative and determinative free will.

The relative free will which characterizes the self-consciousness of human personality is involved in:

1. Moral decision, highest wisdom.
2. Spiritual choice, truth discernment.
3. Unselfish love, brotherhood service.
4. Purposeful co-operation, group loyalty.
5. Cosmic insight, the grasp of universe meanings.
6. Personality dedication, wholehearted devotion to doing the Father's will.
7. Worship, the sincere pursuit of divine values and the wholehearted love of the divine Value-Giver.

The Urantia type of human personality may be viewed as functioning in a physical mechanism consisting of the planetary modification of the Nebadon type of organism belonging to the electrochemical order of life activation and endowed with the Nebadon order of the Orvonton series of the cosmic mind of parental reproductive pattern. The bestowal of the divine gift of personality upon such a mind-endowed mortal mechanism confers the dignity of cosmic citizenship and enables such a mortal creature forthwith to become reactive to the constitutive recognition of the three basic mind realities of the cosmos:

1. The mathematical or logical recognition of the uniformity of physical causation.
2. The reasoned recognition of the obligation of moral conduct.
3. The faith-grasp of the fellowship worship of Deity, associated with the loving service of humanity.

The full function of such a personality endowment is the beginning realization of Deity kinship. Such a selfhood, indwelt by a prepersonal fragment of God the Father, is in truth and in fact a spiritual son of God. Such a creature not only discloses capacity for the reception of the gift of the divine presence but also exhibits reactive response to the personality-gravity circuit of the Paradise Father of all personalities.

9. REALITY OF HUMAN CONSCIOUSNESS

The cosmic-mind-endowed, Adjuster-indwelt, personal creature possesses innate recognition-realization of energy reality, mind reality, and spirit reality. The will creature is thus equipped to discern the fact, the law, and the love of God. Aside from these three inalienables of human consciousness, all human experience is really subjective except that intuitive realization of validity attaches to the unification of these three universe reality responses of cosmic recognition.

The God-discerning mortal is able to sense the unification value of these three cosmic qualities in the evolution of the surviving soul, man's supreme undertaking in the physical tabernacle where the moral mind collaborates with the indwelling divine spirit to dualize the immortal soul. From its earliest inception the soul is real; it has cosmic survival qualities.

If mortal man fails to survive natural death, the real spiritual values of his human experience survive as a part of the continuing experience of the Thought Adjuster. The personality values of such a nonsurvivor persist as a factor in the personality of the actualizing Supreme Being. Such persisting qualities of personality are deprived of identity but not of experiential values accumulated during the mortal life in the flesh. The survival of identity is dependent on the survival of the immortal soul of morontia status and increasingly divine value. Personality identity survives in and by the survival of the soul.

Human self-consciousness implies the recognition of the reality of selves other than the conscious self and further implies that such awareness is mutual; that the self is known as it knows. This is shown in a purely human manner in man's social life. But you cannot become so absolutely certain of a fellow being's reality as you can of the reality of the presence of God that lives within you. The social consciousness is not inalienable like the God-consciousness; it is a cultural development and is dependent on knowledge, symbols, and the contributions of the constitutive endowments of man — science, morality, and religion. And these cosmic gifts, socialized, constitute civilization.

Civilizations are unstable because they are not cosmic; they are not innate in the individuals of the races. They must be nurtured by the combined contributions of the constitutive factors of man — science, morality, and religion. Civilizations come and go, but science, morality, and religion always survive the crash.

Jesus not only revealed God to man, but he also made a new revelation of man to himself and to other men. In the life of Jesus you see man at his best. Man thus becomes so beautifully real because Jesus had so much of God in his life, and the realization (recognition) of God is inalienable and constitutive in all men.

Unselfishness, aside from parental instinct, is not altogether natural; other persons are not naturally loved or socially served. It requires the enlightenment of reason, morality, and the urge of religion, God-knowingness, to generate an unselfish and altruistic social order. Man's own personality awareness, self-consciousness, is also directly dependent on this very fact of innate other-awareness, this innate ability to recognize and grasp the reality of other personality, ranging from the human to the divine.

Unselfish social consciousness must be, at bottom, a religious consciousness; that is, if it is objective; otherwise it is a purely subjective philosophic abstraction and therefore devoid of love. Only a God-knowing individual can love another person as he loves himself.

Self-consciousness is in essence a communal consciousness: God and man, Father and son, Creator and creature. In human self-consciousness four universe-reality realizations are latent and inherent:

1. The quest for knowledge, the logic of science.
2. The quest for moral values, the sense of duty.
3. The quest for spiritual values, the religious experience.
4. The quest for personality values, the ability to recognize the reality of God as a personality and the concurrent realization of our fraternal relationship with fellow personalities.

You become conscious of man as your creature brother because you are already conscious of God as your Creator Father. Fatherhood is the relationship out of which we reason ourselves into the recognition of brotherhood. And Fatherhood becomes, or may become, a universe reality to all moral creatures because the Father has himself bestowed personality upon all such beings and has encircuited them within the grasp of the universal personality circuit. We worship God, first, because he is, then, because he is in us, and last, because we are in him.

Is it strange that the cosmic mind should be self-consciously aware of its own source, the infinite mind of the Infinite Spirit, and at the same time conscious of the physical reality of the far-flung universes, the spiritual reality of the Eternal Son, and the personality reality of the Universal Father?

[Sponsored by a Universal Censor from Uversa.]

PAPER 17
THE SEVEN SUPREME SPIRIT GROUPS

THE SEVEN SUPREME Spirit groups are the universal co-ordinating directors of the seven-segmented administration of the grand universe. Although all are classed among the functional family of the Infinite Spirit, the following three groups are usually classified as children of the Paradise Trinity:

1. The Seven Master Spirits.
2. The Seven Supreme Executives.
3. The Reflective Spirits.

The remaining four groups are brought into being by the creative acts of the Infinite Spirit or by his associates of creative status:

4. The Reflective Image Aids.
5. The Seven Spirits of the Circuits.
6. The Local Universe Creative Spirits.
7. The Adjutant Mind-Spirits.

These seven orders are known on Uversa as the seven Supreme Spirit groups. Their functional domain extends from the personal presence of the Seven Master Spirits on the periphery of the eternal Isle, through the seven

Paradise satellites of the Spirit, the Havona circuits, the governments of the superuniverses, and the administration and supervision of the local universes, even to the lowly service of the adjutants bestowed upon the realms of evolutionary mind on the worlds of time and space.

The Seven Master Spirits are the co-ordinating directors of this far-flung administrative realm. In some matters pertaining to the administrative regulation of organized physical power, mind energy, and impersonal spirit ministry, they act personally and directly, and in others they function through their multifarious associates. In all matters of an executive nature — rulings, regulations, adjustments, and administrative decisions — the Master Spirits act in the persons of the Seven Supreme Executives. In the central universe the Master Spirits may function through the Seven Spirits of the Havona Circuits; on the headquarters of the seven superuniverses they reveal themselves through the channel of the Reflective Spirits and act through the persons of the Ancients of Days, with whom they are in personal communication through the Reflective Image Aids.

The Seven Master Spirits do not directly and personally contact universe administration below the courts of the Ancients of Days. Your local universe is administered as a part of our superuniverse by the Master Spirit of Orvonton, but his function in relation to the native beings of Nebadon is immediately discharged and personally directed by the Creative Mother Spirit resident on Salvington, the headquarters of your local universe.

1. THE SEVEN SUPREME EXECUTIVES

The executive headquarters of the Master Spirits occupy the seven Paradise satellites of the Infinite Spirit, which swing around the central Isle between the shining spheres of the Eternal Son and the innermost Havona circuit. These executive spheres are under the direction of the Supreme Executives, a group of seven who were trinitized by the Father, Son, and Spirit in accordance with the specifications of the Seven Master Spirits for beings of a type that could function as their universal representatives.

The Master Spirits maintain contact with the various divisions of the superuniverse governments through these Supreme Executives. It is they who very largely determine the basic constitutive trends of the seven superuniverses. They are uniformly and divinely perfect, but they also possess diversity of personality. They have no presiding head; each time they meet together, they choose one of their number to preside over that joint council. Periodically they journey to Paradise to sit in council with the Seven Master Spirits.

The Seven Supreme Executives function as the administrative co-ordinators of the grand universe; they might be termed the board of managing directors of the post-Havona creation. They are not concerned with the internal affairs of Paradise, and they direct their limited spheres of Havona activity through the Seven Spirits of the Circuits. Otherwise there are few limits to the scope of their supervision; they engage in the direction of things physical, intellectual, and spiritual; they see all, hear all, feel all, even know all, that transpires in the seven superuniverses and in Havona.

These Supreme Executives do not originate policies, nor do they modify universe procedures; they are concerned with the execution of the plans of divinity promulgated by the Seven Master Spirits. Neither do they interfere with the rule of the Ancients of Days in the superuniverses nor with the sovereignty of the Creator Sons in the local universes. They are the co-ordinating executives whose function it is to carry out the combined policies of all duly constituted rulers in the grand universe.

Each of the executives and the facilities of his sphere are devoted to the efficient administration of a single superuniverse. Supreme Executive Number One, functioning on executive sphere number one, is wholly occupied with the affairs of superuniverse number one, and so on to Supreme Executive Number Seven, working from the seventh Paradise satellite of the Spirit and devoting his energies to the management of the seventh superuniverse. The name of this seventh sphere is Orvonton, for the Paradise satellites of the Spirit have the same names as their related superuniverses; in fact, the superuniverses were named after them.

On the executive sphere of the seventh superuniverse the staff engaged in keeping straight the affairs of Orvonton runs into numbers beyond human comprehension and embraces practically every order of celestial intelligence. All superuniverse services of personality dispatch (except Inspired Trinity Spirits and Thought Adjusters) pass through one of these seven executive worlds on their universe journeys to and from Paradise, and here are maintained the central registries for all personalities created by the Third Source and Center who function in the superuniverses. The system of material, morontial, and spiritual records on one of these executive worlds of the Spirit amazes even a being of my order.

The immediate subordinates of the Supreme Executives consist for the greater part of the trinitized sons of Paradise-Havona personalities and of the trinitized offspring of the glorified mortal graduates from the agelong training of the ascendant scheme of time and space. These trinitized sons are designated for service with the Supreme Executives by the chief of the Supreme Council of the Paradise Corps of the Finality.

Each Supreme Executive has two advisory cabinets: The children of the Infinite Spirit on the headquarters of each superuniverse choose representatives from their ranks to serve for one millennium in the primary advisory cabinet of their Supreme Executive. In all matters affecting the ascending mortals of time, there is a secondary cabinet, consisting of mortals of Paradise attainment and of the trinitized sons of glorified mortals; this body is chosen by the perfecting and ascending beings who transiently dwell on the seven superuniverse headquarters. All other chiefs of affairs are appointed by the Supreme Executives.

From time to time, great conclaves take place on these Paradise satellites of the Spirit. Trinitized sons assigned to these worlds, together with the ascenders who have attained Paradise, assemble with the spirit personalities of the Third Source and Center in the reunions of the struggles and triumphs of the ascendant career. The Supreme Executives always preside over such fraternal gatherings.

Once in each Paradise millennium the Seven Supreme Executives vacate their seats of authority and go to Paradise, where they hold their millennial conclave of universal greeting and well-wishing to the intelligent hosts of creation. This eventful occasion takes place in the immediate presence of Majeston, the chief of all reflective spirit groups. And they are thus able to communicate simultaneously with all their associates in the grand universe through the unique functioning of universal reflectivity.

2. MAJESTON — CHIEF OF REFLECTIVITY

The Reflective Spirits are of divine Trinity origin. There are fifty of these unique and somewhat mysterious beings. Seven of these extraordinary personalities were created at a time, and each such creative episode was effected by a liaison of the Paradise Trinity and one of the Seven Master Spirits.

This momentous transaction, occurring in the dawn of time, represents the initial effort of the Supreme Creator Personalities, represented by the Master Spirits, to function as cocreators with the Paradise Trinity. This union of the creative power of the Supreme Creators with the creative potentials of the Trinity is the very source of the actuality of the Supreme Being. Therefore, when the cycle of reflective creation had run its course, when each of the Seven Master Spirits had found perfect creative synchrony with the Paradise Trinity, when the forty-ninth Reflective Spirit had personalized, then a new and far-reaching reaction occurred in the Deity Absolute which imparted new personality prerogatives to the Supreme Being and culminated in the personalization of Majeston, the reflectivity chief and Paradise center of all the work of the forty-nine Reflective Spirits and their associates throughout the universe of universes.

Majeston is a true person, the personal and infallible center of reflectivity phenomena in all seven superuniverses of time and space. He maintains permanent Paradise headquarters near the center of all things at the rendezvous of the Seven Master Spirits. He is concerned solely with the coordination and maintenance of the reflectivity service in the far-flung creation; he is not otherwise involved in the administration of universe affairs.

Majeston is not included in our catalogue of Paradise personalities because he is the only existing personality of divinity created by the Supreme Being in functional liaison with the Deity Absolute. He is a person, but he is exclusively and apparently automatically concerned with this one phase of universe economy; he does not now function in any personal capacity with relation to other (nonreflective) orders of universe personalities.

The creation of Majeston signalized the first supreme creative act of the Supreme Being. This will to action was volitional in the Supreme Being, but the stupendous reaction of the Deity Absolute was not foreknown. Not since the eternity-appearance of Havona had the universe witnessed such a tremendous factualization of such a gigantic and far-flung alignment of power and co-ordination of functional spirit activities. The Deity response to the creative wills of the Supreme Being and his associates was vastly beyond their purposeful intent and greatly in excess of their conceptual forecasts.

We stand in awe of the possibility of what the future ages, wherein the Supreme and the Ultimate may attain new levels of divinity and ascend to new domains of personality function, may witness in the realms of the deitization of still other unexpected and undreamed of beings who will possess unimagined powers of enhanced universe co-ordination. There would seem to be no limit to the Deity Absolute's potential of response to such unification of relationships between experiential Deity and the existential Paradise Trinity.

3. THE REFLECTIVE SPIRITS

The forty-nine Reflective Spirits are of Trinity origin, but each of the seven creative episodes attendant upon their appearance was productive of a type of being in nature resembling the characteristics of the coancestral Master Spirit. Thus they variously reflect the natures and characters of the seven possible combinations of the association of the divinity characteristics of the Universal Father, the Eternal Son, and the Infinite Spirit. For this reason it is necessary to have seven of these Reflective Spirits on the headquarters of each superuniverse. One of each of the seven types is required in order to achieve the perfect reflection of all phases of every possible manifestation of the three Paradise Deities as such phenomena might occur in any part of the seven superuniverses. One of each type was accordingly assigned to service in each of the superuniverses. These groups of seven dissimilar Reflective Spirits maintain headquarters on the capitals of the superuniverses at the reflective focus of each realm, and this is not identical with the point of spiritual polarity.

The Reflective Spirits have names, but these designations are not revealed on the worlds of space. They pertain to the nature and character of these beings and are a part of one of the seven universal mysteries of the secret spheres of Paradise.

The attribute of reflectivity, the phenomenon of the mind levels of the Conjoint Actor, the Supreme Being, and the Master Spirits, is transmissible to all beings concerned in the working of this vast scheme of universal intelligence. And herein is a great mystery: Neither the Master Spirits nor the Paradise Deities, singly or collectively, disclose these powers of co-ordinate universal reflectivity just as they are manifested in these forty-nine liaison personalities of Majeston, and yet they are the creators of all these marvelously endowed beings. Divine heredity does sometimes disclose in the creature certain attributes which are not discernible in the Creator.

The personnel of the reflectivity service, with the exception of Majeston and the Reflective Spirits, are all the creatures of the Infinite Spirit and his immediate associates and subordinates. The Reflective Spirits of each superuniverse are the creators of their Reflective Image Aids, their personal voices to the courts of the Ancients of Days.

The Reflective Spirits are not merely transmitting agents; they are retentive personalities as well. Their offspring, the seconaphim, are also retentive or record personalities. Everything of true spiritual value is registered in duplicate, and one impression is preserved in the personal equipment of some member of one of the numerous orders of secoraphic personalities belonging to the vast staff of the Reflective Spirits.

The formal records of the universes are passed up by and through the angelic recorders, but the true spiritual records are assembled by reflectivity and are preserved in the minds of suitable and appropriate personalities belonging to the family of the Infinite Spirit. These are the live records in contrast with the formal and dead records of the universe, and they are perfectly preserved in the living minds of the recording personalities of the Infinite Spirit.

The reflectivity organization is also the news-gathering and the decree-disseminating mechanism of all creation. It is in constant operation in contrast with the periodic functioning of the various broadcast services.

Everything of import transpiring on a local universe headquarters is inherently reflected to the capital of its superuniverse. And conversely, everything of local universe significance is reflected outward to the local universe capitals from the headquarters of their superuniverse. The reflectivity service from the universes of time up to the superuniverses is apparently automatic or self-operating, but it is not. It is all very personal and intelligent; its precision results from perfection of personality co-operation and therefore can hardly be attributed to the impersonal presence-performances of the Absolutes.

While Thought Adjusters do not participate in the operation of the universal reflectivity system, we have every reason to believe that all Father fragments are fully cognizant of these transactions and are able to avail themselves of their content.

During the present universe age the space range of the extra-Paradise reflectivity service seems to be limited by the periphery of the seven superuniverses. Otherwise, the function of this service seems to be independent of time and space. It appears to be independent of all known subabsolute universe circuits.

On the headquarters of each superuniverse the reflective organization acts as a segregated unit; but on certain special occasions, under the direction of Majeston, all seven may and do act in universal unison, as in the event of the jubilee occasioned by the settling of an entire local universe in light and life and at the times of the millennial greetings of the Seven Supreme Executives.

4. THE REFLECTIVE IMAGE AIDS

The forty-nine Reflective Image Aids were created by the Reflective Spirits, and there are just seven Aids on the headquarters of each superuniverse. The first creative act of the seven Reflective Spirits of Uversa was the production of their seven Image Aids, each Reflective Spirit creating his own Aid. The Image Aids are, in certain attributes and characteristics, perfect reproductions of their Reflective Mother Spirits; they are virtual duplications minus the attribute of reflectivity. They are true images and constantly function as the channel of communication between the Reflective Spirits and the superuniverse authorities. The Image Aids are not merely assistants; they are actual representations of their respective Spirit ancestors; they are images, and they are true to their name.

The Reflective Spirits themselves are true personalities but of such an order as to be incomprehensible to material beings. Even on a superuniverse headquarters sphere they require the assistance of their Image Aids in all personal intercourse with the Ancients of Days and their associates. In contacts between the Image Aids and the Ancients of Days, sometimes one Aid functions acceptably, while on other occasions two, three, four, or even all seven are required for the full and proper presentation of the communication intrusted to their transmission. Likewise, the messages of the Image Aids are variously received by one, two, or all three Ancients of Days, as the content of the communication may require.

The Image Aids serve forever by the sides of their ancestral Spirits, and they have at their disposal an unbelievable host of helper seconaphim. The Image Aids do not directly function in connection with the training worlds of ascending mortals. They are closely associated with the intelligence service of the universal scheme of mortal progression, but you will not personally come in contact with them when you sojourn in the Uversa schools because these seemingly personal beings are devoid of will; they do not exercise the power of choice. They are true images, wholly reflective of the personality and mind of the individual Spirit ancestor. As a class, ascending mortals do not intimately contact with reflectivity. Always some being of the reflective nature will be interposed between you and the actual operation of the service.

5. THE SEVEN SPIRITS OF THE CIRCUITS

The Seven Spirits of the Havona Circuits are the joint impersonal representation of the Infinite Spirit and the Seven Master Spirits to the seven circuits of the central universe. They are the servants of the Master Spirits, whose collective offspring they are. The Master Spirits provide a distinct and diversified administrative individuality in the seven superuniverses. Through these uniform Spirits of the Havona Circuits they are enabled to provide a unified, uniform, and co-ordinated spiritual supervision for the central universe.

The Seven Spirits of the Circuits are each limited to the permeation of a single Havona circuit. They are not directly concerned with the regimes of the Eternals of Days, the rulers of the individual Havona worlds. But they are in liaison with the Seven Supreme Executives, and they synchronize with the central universe presence of the Supreme Being. Their work is wholly confined to Havona.

These Spirits of the Circuits make contact with those who sojourn in Havona through their personal offspring, the tertiary supernaphim. While the Circuit Spirits are coexistent with the Seven Master Spirits, their function in the creation of tertiary supernaphim did not attain major importance until the first pilgrims of time arrived on the outer circuit of Havona in the days of Grandfanda.

As you advance from circuit to circuit in Havona, you will learn of the Spirits of the Circuits, but you will not be able to hold personal communion with them, even though you may personally enjoy, and recognize the impersonal presence of, their spiritual influence.

The Circuit Spirits are related to the native inhabitants of Havona much as the Thought Adjusters are related to the mortal creatures inhabiting the worlds of the evolutionary universes. Like the Thought Adjusters, the Circuit Spirits are impersonal, and they consort with the perfect minds of Havona beings much as the impersonal spirits of the Universal Father indwell the finite minds of mortal men. But the Spirits of the Circuits never become a permanent part of Havona personalities.

6. THE LOCAL UNIVERSE CREATIVE SPIRITS

Much that pertains to the nature and function of the local universe Creative Spirits properly belongs to the narrative of their association with the Creator Sons in the organization and management of the local creations; but there are many features of the prelocal universe experiences of these marvelous beings which may be narrated as a part of this discussion of the seven Supreme Spirit groups.

We are conversant with six phases of the career of a local universe

Mother Spirit, and we speculate much concerning the probability of a seventh stage of activity. These different stages of existence are:

1. *Initial Paradise Differentiation.* When a Creator Son is personalized by the joint action of the Universal Father and the Eternal Son, simultaneously there occurs in the person of the Infinite Spirit what is known as the "supreme reaction of complement." We do not comprehend the nature of this reaction, but we understand that it designates an inherent modification of those personalizable possibilities which are embraced within the creative potential of the Conjoint Creator. The birth of a co-ordinate Creator Son signalizes the birth within the person of the Infinite Spirit of the potential of the future local universe consort of this Paradise Son. We are not cognizant of this new prepersonal identification of entity, but we know that this fact finds place on the Paradise records of the career of such a Creator Son.

2. *Preliminary Creatorship Training.* During the long period of the preliminary training of a Michael Son in the organization and administration of universes, his future consort undergoes further development of entity and becomes group conscious of destiny. We do not know, but we suspect that such a group-conscious entity becomes space cognizant and begins that preliminary training requisite to the acquirement of spirit skill in her future work of collaboration with the complemental Michael in universe creation and administration.

3. *The Stage of Physical Creation.* At the time the creatorship charge is administered to a Michael Son by the Eternal Son, the Master Spirit who directs the superuniverse to which this new Creator Son is destined gives expression to the "prayer of identification" in the presence of the Infinite Spirit; and for the first time, the entity of the subsequent Creative Spirit appears as differentiated from the person of the Infinite Spirit. And proceeding directly to the person of the petitioning Master Spirit, this entity is immediately lost to our recognition, becoming apparently a part of the person of this Master Spirit. The newly identified Creative Spirit remains with the Master Spirit until the moment of the departure of the Creator Son for the adventure of space; whereupon the Master Spirit commits the new Spirit consort to the keeping of the

Creator Son, at the same time administering to the Spirit consort the charge of eternal fidelity and unending loyalty. And then occurs one of the most profoundly touching episodes which ever take place on Paradise. The Universal Father speaks in acknowledgment of the eternal union of the Creator Son and the Creative Spirit and in confirmation of the bestowal of certain joint powers of administration by the Master Spirit of superuniverse jurisdiction.

The Father-united Creator Son and Creative Spirit then go forth on their adventure of universe creation. And they work together in this form of association throughout the long and arduous period of the material organization of their universe.

4. *The Life-Creation Era.* Upon the declaration of intention to create life by the Creator Son, there ensue on Paradise the "personalization ceremonies," participated in by the Seven Master Spirits and personally experienced by the supervising Master Spirit. This is a Paradise Deity contribution to the individuality of the Spirit consort of the Creator Son and becomes manifest to the universe in the phenomenon of "the primary eruption" in the person of the Infinite Spirit. Simultaneously with this phenomenon on Paradise, the heretofore impersonal Spirit consort of the Creator Son becomes, to all practical intents and purposes, a bona fide person. Henceforth and forevermore, this same local universe Mother Spirit will be regarded as a person and will maintain personal relations with all the personality hosts of the ensuing life creation.

5. *The Postbestowal Ages.* Another and great change occurs in the never-ending career of a Creative Spirit when the Creator Son returns to universe headquarters after the completion of his seventh bestowal and subsequent to his acquirement of full universe sovereignty. On that occasion, before the assembled administrators of the universe, the triumphant Creator Son elevates the Universe Mother Spirit to cosovereignty and acknowledges the Spirit consort as his equal.

6. *The Ages of Light and Life.* Upon the establishment of the era of light and life the local universe cosovereign enters upon the sixth phase of a Creative Spirit's career. But we may not portray the nature of this great experience. Such things pertain to a future stage of evolution in Nebadon.

7. *The Unrevealed Career*. We know of these six phases of the career of a local universe Mother Spirit. It is inevitable that we should ask: Is there a seventh career? We are mindful that, when finaliters attain what appears to be their final destiny of mortal ascension, they are of record as entering upon the career of sixth-stage spirits. We conjecture that there awaits the finaliters still another and unrevealed career in universe assignment. It is only to be expected that we would likewise regard the Universe Mother Spirits as having ahead of them some undisclosed career which will constitute their seventh phase of personal experience in universe service and loyal co-operation with the order of the Creator Michaels.

7. THE ADJUTANT MIND-SPIRITS

These adjutant spirits are the sevenfold mind bestowal of a local universe Mother Spirit upon the living creatures of the conjoint creation of a Creator Son and such a Creative Spirit. This bestowal becomes possible at the time of the Spirit's elevation to the status of personality prerogatives. The narration of the nature and functioning of the seven adjutant mind-spirits belongs more appropriately to the story of your local universe of Nebadon.

8. FUNCTIONS OF THE SUPREME SPIRITS

The seven groups of Supreme Spirits constitute the nucleus of the functional family of the Third Source and Center both as the Infinite Spirit and as the Conjoint Actor. The domain of the Supreme Spirits extends from the presence of the Trinity on Paradise to the functioning of mind of the evolutionary-mortal order on the planets of space. Thus do they unify the descending administrative levels and co-ordinate the manifold functions of the personnel thereof. Whether it is a Reflective Spirit group in liaison with the Ancients of Days, a Creative Spirit acting in concert with a Michael Son, or the Seven Master Spirits encircuited around the Paradise Trinity, the activity of the Supreme Spirits is encountered everywhere in the central, super-, and local universes. They function alike with the Trinity personalities of the order of "Days" and with the Paradise personalities of the order of "Sons."

Together with their Infinite Mother Spirit, the Supreme Spirit groups are the immediate creators of the vast creature family of the Third Source and Center. All orders of the ministering spirits spring from this association. Primary supernaphim originate in the Infinite Spirit; secondary beings of this order are created by the Master Spirits; tertiary supernaphim by the Seven Spirits of the Circuits. The Reflective Spirits, collectively, are the mother-makers of a marvelous order of the angelic hosts, the mighty seconaphim of the superuniverse services. A Creative Spirit is the mother of the angelic orders of a local creation; such seraphic ministers are original in each local universe, though they are fashioned after the patterns of the central universe. All these creators of ministering spirits are only indirectly assisted by the central lodgment of the Infinite Spirit, the original and eternal mother of all the angelic ministers.

The seven Supreme Spirit groups are the co-ordinators of the inhabited creation. The association of their directing heads, the Seven Master Spirits, appears to co-ordinate the far-flung activities of God the Sevenfold:

1. Collectively the Master Spirits near-equivalate to the divinity level of the Trinity of Paradise Deities.
2. Individually they exhaust the primary associable possibilities of triune Deity.
3. As diversified representatives of the Conjoint Actor they are the repositories of that spirit-mind-power sovereignty of the Supreme Being which he does not yet personally exercise.
4. Through the Reflective Spirits they synchronize the superuniverse governments of the Ancients of Days with Majeston, the Paradise center of universal reflectivity.
5. In their participation in the individualization of the local universe Divine Ministers, the Master Spirits contribute to the last level of God the Sevenfold, the Creator Son-Creative Spirit union of the local universes.

Functional unity, inherent in the Conjoint Actor, is disclosed to the evolving universes in the Seven Master Spirits, his primary personalities. But in the perfected superuniverses of the future this unity will undoubtedly be inseparable from the experiential sovereignty of the Supreme.

[Presented by a Divine Counselor of Uversa.]

PAPER 18
THE SUPREME TRINITY PERSONALITIES

SUPREME TRINITY PERSONALITIES are all created for specific service. They are designed by the divine Trinity for the fulfillment of certain specific duties, and they are qualified to serve with perfection of technique and finality of devotion. There are seven orders of the Supreme Trinity Personalities:

1. Trinitized Secrets of Supremacy.
2. Eternals of Days.
3. Ancients of Days.
4. Unions of Days.
5. Perfections of Days.
6. Recents of Days.
7. Faithfuls of Days.

Throughout the grand universe these Supreme Trinity Personalities represent the administrative policies of the Paradise Trinity; they represent the justice and are the executive judgment of the Paradise Trinity. They form an interrelated line of administrative perfection extending from the Paradise spheres of the Father to the headquarters worlds of the local universes and down through the major and minor sectors of a universe to the galaxies, and to the capitals of their component constellations.

All Trinity-origin beings are created in Paradise perfection in all their divine attributes. Only in the realms of experience has the passing of time added to their equipment for cosmic service. There is never any danger of default or risk of rebellion with Trinity-origin beings. They are of divinity essence, and they have never been known to depart from the divine and perfect path of personality conduct.

1. THE TRINITIZED SECRETS OF SUPREMACY

There are seven worlds in the innermost circuit of the Paradise satellites, and each of these exalted worlds is presided over by a corps of ten Trinitized Secrets of Supremacy. They are not creators, but they are supreme and ultimate administrators. The conduct of the affairs of these seven fraternal spheres is wholly committed to this corps of seventy supreme directors. Though the offspring of the Trinity supervise these seven sacred spheres nearest Paradise, this group of worlds is universally known as the personal circuit of the Universal Father.

The Trinitized Secrets of Supremacy function in groups of ten as coordinate and joint directors of their respective spheres, but they also function individually in particular fields of responsibility. The work of each of these special worlds is divided into seven major departments, and one of these coordinate rulers presides over each such division of specialized activities. The remaining three act as the personal representatives of triune Deity in relation to the other seven, one representing the Father, one the Son, and one the Spirit.

Although there is a definite class resemblance which typifies the Trinitized Secrets of Supremacy, they also disclose seven distinct group characteristics. The ten supreme directors of Divinington affairs are reflective of the personal character and nature of the Universal Father; and so it is with each of these seven spheres: Each group of ten resembles that Deity or Deity association which is characteristic of their domain. The ten directors who rule Ascendington are reflective of the combined nature of the Father, Son, and Spirit.

I can reveal very little about the work of these high personalities on the seven sacred worlds of the Father, for they are truly the Secrets of Supremacy. There are no arbitrary secrets associated with the approach to the Universal Father, the Eternal Son, or the Infinite Spirit. The Deities are an open book to all who attain divine perfection, but all the Secrets of Supremacy can never be fully attained. Always will we be unable fully to penetrate the realms containing the personality secrets of Deity association with the sevenfold grouping of created beings.

Since the work of these supreme directors has to do with the intimate and personal contact of the Deities with these seven basic groupings of universe beings when domiciled on these seven special worlds or while functioning throughout the grand universe, it is fitting that these very personal relations and extraordinary contacts should be held sacredly secret. The Paradise Creators respect the privacy and sanctity of personality even in their lowly creatures. And this is true both of individuals and of the various separate orders of personalities.

To beings of even high universe attainment these secret worlds ever remain a test of loyalty. It is given us fully and personally to know the eternal Gods, freely to know their characters of divinity and perfection, but it is not granted us fully to penetrate all of the personal relations of the Paradise Rulers with all of their creature beings.

2. THE ETERNALS OF DAYS

Each of the billion worlds of Havona is directed by a Supreme Trinity Personality. These rulers are known as the Eternals of Days, and they number exactly one billion, one for each of the Havona spheres. They are the offspring of the Paradise Trinity, but like the Secrets of Supremacy there are no records of their origin. Forever have these two groups of all-wise fathers ruled their exquisite worlds of the Paradise-Havona system, and they function without rotation or reassignment.

The Eternals of Days are visible to all will creatures dwelling in their domains. They preside over the regular planetary conclaves. Periodically, and by rotation, they visit the headquarters spheres of the seven superuniverses. They are close of kin to, and are the divine equals of, the Ancients of

Days, who preside over the destinies of the seven supergovernments. When an Eternal of Days is absent from his sphere, his world is directed by a Trinity Teacher Son.

Except for the established orders of life, such as the Havona natives and other living creatures of the central universe, the resident Eternals of Days have developed their respective spheres entirely in accordance with their own personal ideas and ideals. They visit each other's planets, but they do not copy or imitate; they are always and wholly original.

The architecture, natural embellishment, morontia structures, and spirit creations are exclusive and unique on each sphere. Every world is a place of everlasting beauty and is wholly unlike any other world in the central universe. And you will each spend a longer or shorter time on each of these unique and thrilling spheres on your way inward through Havona to Paradise. It is natural, on your world, to speak of Paradise as *upward*, but it would be more correct to refer to the divine goal of ascension as *inward*.

3. THE ANCIENTS OF DAYS

When mortals of time graduate from the training worlds surrounding the headquarters of a local universe and are advanced to the educational spheres of their superuniverse, they have progressed in spiritual development to that point where they are able to recognize and communicate with the high spiritual rulers and directors of these advanced realms, including the Ancients of Days.

The Ancients of Days are all basically identical; they disclose the combined character and unified nature of the Trinity. They possess individuality and are in personality diverse, but they do not differ from each other as do the Seven Master Spirits. They provide the uniform directorship of the otherwise differing seven superuniverses, each of which is a distinct, segregated, and unique creation. The Seven Master Spirits are unlike in nature and attributes, but the Ancients of Days, the personal rulers of the superuniverses, are all uniform and superperfect offspring of the Paradise Trinity.

The Seven Master Spirits on high determine the *nature* of their respective superuniverses, but the Ancients of Days dictate the *administration* of these same superuniverses. They superimpose administrative uniformity on creative diversity and insure the harmony of the whole in the face of the underlying creational differences of the seven segmental groupings of the grand universe.

The Ancients of Days were all trinitized at the same time. They represent the beginning of the personality records of the universe of universes, hence their name — Ancients of Days. When you reach Paradise and search the written records of the beginning of things, you will find that the first entry appearing in the personality section is the recital of the trinitization of these twenty-one Ancients of Days.

These high beings always govern in groups of three. There are many phases of activity in which they work as individuals, still others in which any two can function, but in the higher spheres of their administration they must act jointly. They never personally leave their residential worlds, but then they do not have to, for these worlds are the superuniverse focal points of the far-flung reflectivity system.

The personal abodes of each trio of the Ancients of Days are located at the point of spiritual polarity on their headquarters sphere. Such a sphere is divided into seventy administrative sectors and has seventy divisional capitals in which the Ancients of Days reside from time to time.

In power, scope of authority, and extent of jurisdiction the Ancients of Days are the most powerful and mighty of any of the direct rulers of the time-space creations. In all the vast universe of universes they alone are invested with the high powers of final executive judgment concerning the eternal extinction of will creatures. And all three Ancients of Days must participate in the final decrees of the supreme tribunal of a superuniverse.

Aside from the Deities and their Paradise associates, the Ancients of Days are the most perfect, most versatile, and the most divinely endowed rulers in all time-space existence. Apparently they are the supreme rulers of the superuniverses; but they have not experientially earned this right to rule and are therefore destined sometime to be superseded by the Supreme Being, an experiential sovereign, whose vicegerents they will undoubtedly become.

The Supreme Being is achieving the sovereignty of the seven superuniverses by experiential service just as a Creator Son experientially earns the sovereignty of his local universe. But during the present age of the unfinished evolution of the Supreme, the Ancients of Days provide the co-ordinated and perfect administrative overcontrol of the evolving universes of time and space. And the wisdom of originality and the initiative of individuality characterize all the decrees and rulings of the Ancients of Days.

4. THE UNIONS OF DAYS

The Trinity personalities of the order of "Days" do not function in an administrative capacity below the level of the superuniverse governments. In the evolving local universes they act only as counselors and advisers. The Unions of Days are a group of liaison personalities accredited by the Paradise Trinity to the dual rulers of the local universes. Each organized and inhabited local universe has assigned to it one of these Paradise counselors, who acts as the representative of the Trinity, and in some respects, of the Universal Father, to the local creation. The reserve corps of the Unions of Days functions on Paradise as the Supreme Council of Universe Adjustments.

These Trinity observers help to co-ordinate the administrative activities of all branches of the universal government. Since they are Trinity-origin beings, all of the Paradise circuits are available to them for intercommunication, and thus are they always in touch with each other and with all other required personalities up to the supreme councils of Paradise.

A Union of Days is not organically connected with the government of the local universe of his assignment. Aside from his duties as an observer, he acts only at the request of the local authorities. He is an ex officio member of all primary councils and all important conclaves of the local creation, but he does not participate in the technical consideration of administrative problems.

When a local universe is settled in light and life, its glorified beings associate freely with the Union of Days, who then functions in an enlarged capacity in such a realm of evolutionary perfection. But he is still primarily a Trinity ambassador and Paradise counselor.

A local universe is directly ruled by a divine Son of dual Deity origin, but he has constantly by his side a Paradise brother, a Trinity-origin personality. In the event of the temporary absence of a Creator Son from the headquarters of his local universe, the acting rulers are largely guided in their major decisions by the counsel of their Union of Days.

5. THE PERFECTIONS OF DAYS

The Perfections of Days are sent as Paradise ambassadors to the governments of the major sectors of each universe. Three *Perfections of Days* are assigned to each major sector capital.

These advisors of the major sectors are peculiarly perfect in the mastery of administrative details, hence their name — Perfections of Days. In recording the names of these beings of the spiritual world, we are confronted with the problem of translating into your tongue, and very often it is exceedingly difficult to render a satisfactory translation. We dislike to use arbitrary designations which would be meaningless to you; hence we often find it difficult to choose a suitable name, one which will be clear to you and at the same time be somewhat representative of the original.

The Perfections of Days have a moderate-sized corps of Divine Counselors, Perfectors of Wisdom, and Universal Censors attached to them. They have still larger numbers of Mighty Messengers, Those High in Authority, and Those without Name and Number. But much of the routine advisory work of major sector affairs is carried on by the Celestial Guardians and the High Son Assistants. These two groups are drawn from among the trinitized offspring of either Paradise-Havona personalities or glorified mortal finaliters. Certain of these two orders of creature-trinitized beings are retrinitized by the Paradise Deities and then are dispatched to assist the universe governments.

Most of the Celestial Guardians and the High Son Assistants are assigned to the service of the major and the minor sectors, but the Trinitized Custodians (Trinity-embraced seraphim and midwayers) are the officers of the courts of all three divisions, functioning in the tribunals of the Ancients of Days, the Perfections of Days, and the Recents of Days. The Trinitized Ambassadors (Trinity-embraced ascendant mortals of Son- or Spirit-fused nature) may be encountered anywhere in a universe, but the majority are in the service of the minor sectors.

Before the times of the full unfolding of the governmental scheme of the seven superuniverses, practically all administrators of the various divisions of these governments, excepting the Ancients of Days, served apprenticeships of varying duration under the Eternals of Days on the various worlds of the perfect Havona universe. The later trinitized beings likewise passed through a season of training under the Eternals of Days before they were attached to the service of the Ancients of Days, the Perfections of Days, and the Recents of Days. They are all seasoned, tried, and experienced advisors and administrators.

You will early see the Perfections of Days when you advance to the headquarters of Splandon after your sojourn on the worlds of your minor sector, for these exalted advisors are closely associated with the seventy major sector worlds of higher training for the ascendant creatures of time. The Perfections of Days, in person, administer the group pledges to the ascending graduates of the major sector schools.

The work of the pilgrims of time on the worlds surrounding a major sector headquarters is chiefly of an intellectual nature in contrast with the more material and morontial character of the training on the seven educational spheres of a minor sector and with the spiritual undertakings on the four hundred ninety university worlds of a universe headquarters.

6. THE RECENTS OF DAYS

The Recents of Days are among the youngest of the Paradise advisors sent to the universes; in groups of three they act as trinity ambassadors and advisors in the affairs of the minor sectors, but are dispatched singly to serve in the local galaxies. In nature they are co-ordinate with the Perfections of Days. They were all created simultaneously, and together they passed through their Havona training under the Eternals of Days.

The Recents of Days have a corps of associates and assistants similar to that of the Perfections of Days. In addition they have assigned to them enormous numbers of the various subordinate orders of celestial beings. In their role as ambassadors and advisors to the minor sectors they interact with large numbers of the resident ascending mortals, the personnel of the various courtesy colonies, and the various groups originating in the Infinite Spirit.

The governments of the minor sectors are very largely, though not exclusively, concerned with the great physical problems of the universes. The minor sector spheres are the headquarters of the Master Physical Controllers. On these worlds ascending mortals carry on studies and experiments having to do with an examination of the activities of the third order of the Supreme Power Centers and of all seven orders of the Master Physical Controllers.

Since the regime of a minor sector is so extensively concerned with physical problems, its three Recents of Days advisors are seldom together on the capital sphere. Most of the time one is away in conference with the Perfections of Days of the supervising major sector or absent while conferring with the Recents of Days advisor to one of the local galaxies. But at least one of these advisors always remains on duty at the headquarters of a minor sector.

You may get the opportunity to know the three Recents of Days in charge of Ensa, your minor sector, or the one advising on Zion, as you pass through on your way inward to the training worlds of your major sector.

7. THE FAITHFULS OF DAYS

These high Trinity-origin personalities are the Paradise advisers to the rulers of the constellations in each local galaxy. Their Paradise reserve corps is the Advisory Commission of Interuniverse Ethics and Self-government. Faithfuls of Days rotate in service in accordance with the rulings of the supreme council of their reserve corps.

All that a Union of Days is to a Creator Son of a local universe, the Faithfuls of Days are to the Vorondadek Sons who rule the constellations of that local creation. They are supremely devoted and divinely faithful to the welfare of their constellations of assignment, hence the name — *Faithfuls* of Days. They act only as counselors; never do they participate in administrative activities except upon the invitation of the constellation authorities. Neither are they directly concerned in the educational ministry to the pilgrims of ascension on the architectural training spheres surrounding a constellation headquarters. All such undertakings are under the supervision of the Vorondadek Sons.

All Faithfuls of Days functioning in the constellations of a local galaxy are under the jurisdiction of, and report directly to, the Recents of Days of that galaxy. They do not have a far-flung system of intercommunication, being ordinarily self-limited to an interassociation within the limits of a local galaxy. Any Faithful of Days on duty in the Milky Way galaxy can and does communicate with all others of his order on duty in this local galaxy.

Like the Union of Days on a universe headquarters, the Faithfuls of Days maintain their personal residences on the constellation capitals separate from those of the administrative directors of such realms. Their abodes are indeed modest in comparison with the homes of the Vorondadek rulers of the constellations.

The Faithfuls of Days are the last link in the long administrative-advisory chain which reaches from the sacred spheres of the Universal Father near the center of all things to the universes of time and space, and down to the constellations of the local galaxies. The Trinity-origin regime stops with the constellations; no such Paradise advisers are permanently situated on their component systems or on the inhabited worlds. These latter administrative units are wholly under the jurisdiction of beings native to the local universes.

[Presented by a Divine Counselor of Uversa.]

PAPER 19
THE CO-ORDINATE TRINITY-ORIGIN BEINGS

THIS PARADISE GROUP, designated the Co-ordinate Trinity-origin Beings, embraces the Trinity Teacher Sons, also classed among the Paradise Sons of God, three groups of high superuniverse administrators, and the somewhat impersonal category of the Inspired Trinity Spirits. Even the Havona natives may properly be included in this classification of Trinity personalities along with numerous groups of beings resident on Paradise. Those Trinity-origin beings to be considered in this discussion are:

1. Trinity Teacher Sons.
2. Perfectors of Wisdom.
3. Divine Counselors.
4. Universal Censors.
5. Inspired Trinity Spirits.
6. Havona Natives.
7. Paradise Citizens.

Excepting the Trinity Teacher Sons and possibly the Inspired Trinity Spirits, these groups are of definite numbers; their creation is a finished and past event.

1. THE TRINITY TEACHER SONS

Of all the high orders of celestial personalities revealed to you, the Trinity Teacher Sons alone act in a dual capacity. By origin of Trinity nature, in function they are almost wholly devoted to the services of divine sonship. They are the liaison beings who bridge the universe gulf between Trinity- and dual-origin personalities. While the Stationary Sons of the Trinity are of completed numbers, the Teacher Sons are constantly increasing. What the final number of Teacher Sons will be I do not know.

These beings are the only group of the Sons of God revealed to you whose origin is in the Paradise Trinity. They range the central and superuniverses, and an enormous corps is assigned to each local universe. They also serve the individual planets as do the other Paradise Sons of God. Since the scheme of the grand universe is not fully developed, large numbers of Teacher Sons are held in the reserves on Paradise, and they volunteer for emergency duty and unusual service in all divisions of the grand universe, on the lone worlds of space, in the local and superuniverses, and on the worlds of Havona. They also function on Paradise, but it will be more helpful to postpone their detailed consideration until we come to the discussion of the Paradise Sons of God.

In this connection, however, it may be noted that Teacher Sons are the supreme co-ordinating personalities of Trinity origin. In such a far-flung universe of universes there is always great danger of succumbing to the error of the circumscribed viewpoint, to the evil inherent in a segmentalized conception of reality and divinity.

For example: The human mind would ordinarily crave to approach the cosmic philosophy portrayed in these revelations by proceeding from the simple and the finite to the complex and the infinite, from human origins to divine destinies. But that path does not lead to *spiritual wisdom*. Such a procedure is the easiest path to a certain form of *genetic knowledge*, but at best it can only reveal man's origin; it reveals little or nothing about his divine destiny.

Even in the study of man's biologic evolution on Urantia, there are grave objections to the exclusive historic approach to his present-day status and his current problems. The true perspective of any reality problem — human or divine, terrestrial or cosmic — can be had only by the full and unprejudiced study and correlation of three phases of universe reality: origin, history, and destiny. The proper understanding of these three experiential realities affords the basis for a wise estimate of the current status.

When the human mind undertakes to follow the philosophic technique of starting from the lower to approach the higher, whether in biology or theology, it is always in danger of committing four errors of reasoning:

1. It may utterly fail to perceive the final and completed evolutionary goal of either personal attainment or cosmic destiny.
2. It may commit the supreme philosophical blunder by oversimplifying cosmic evolutionary (experiential) reality, thus leading to the distortion of facts, to the perversion of truth, and to the misconception of destinies.
3. The study of causation is the perusal of history. But the knowledge of how a being becomes does not necessarily provide an intelligent understanding of the present status and true character of such a being.
4. History alone fails adequately to reveal future development — destiny. Finite origins are helpful, but only divine causes reveal final effects. Eternal ends are not shown in time beginnings. The present can be truly interpreted only in the light of the correlated past and future.

Therefore, because of these and for still other reasons, do we employ the technique of approaching man and his planetary problems by embarkation on the time-space journey from the infinite, eternal, and divine Paradise Source and Center of all personality reality and all cosmic existence.

2. THE PERFECTORS OF WISDOM

The Perfectors of Wisdom are a specialized creation of the Paradise

Trinity designed to personify the wisdom of divinity in the superuniverses. In common with their co-ordinates, the Divine Counselors and the Universal Censors, the Perfectors of Wisdom passed through the wisdom of Paradise, of Havona, and except for Divinington, of the Father's Paradise spheres. After these experiences the Perfectors of Wisdom were permanently assigned to the service of the Ancients of Days. They serve neither on Paradise nor on the worlds of the Paradise-Havona circuits; they are wholly occupied with the administration of the superuniverse governments.

Wherever and whenever a Perfector of Wisdom functions, there and then divine wisdom functions. There is actuality of presence and perfection of manifestation in the knowledge and wisdom represented in the doings of these mighty and majestic personalities. They do not *reflect* the wisdom of the Paradise Trinity; they *are* that wisdom. They are the sources of wisdom for all teachers in the application of universe knowledge; they are the fountains of discretion and the wellsprings of discrimination to the institutions of learning and discernment in all universes.

Wisdom is twofold in origin, being derived from the perfection of divine insight inherent in perfect beings and from the personal experience acquired by evolutionary creatures. The Perfectors of Wisdom are the divine wisdom of the Paradise perfection of Deity insight. Their administrative associates on Uversa, the Mighty Messengers, Those without Name and Number, and Those High in Authority, when acting together, *are* the universe wisdom of experience. A divine being can have perfection of divine knowledge. An evolutionary mortal can sometime attain perfection of ascendant knowledge, but neither of these beings alone exhausts the potentials of all possible wisdom. Accordingly, whenever in the conduct of the superuniverse it is desired to achieve the maximum of administrative wisdom, these perfectors of the wisdom of divine insight are always associated with those ascendant personalities who have come up to the high responsibilities of superuniverse authority through the experiential tribulations of evolutionary progression.

The Perfectors of Wisdom will always require this complement of experiential wisdom for the completion of their administrative sagacity. But it has been postulated that a high and hitherto unattained level of wisdom may possibly be achieved by the Paradise finaliters *after* they are sometime inducted into the seventh stage of spirit existence. If this inference is correct, then would such perfected beings of evolutionary ascent undoubtedly become the most effective universe administrators ever to be known in all creation. I believe that such is the high destiny of finaliters.

The versatility of the Perfectors of Wisdom enables them to participate in practically all of the celestial services of the ascendant creatures. The Perfectors of Wisdom and my order of personality, the Divine Counselors, together with the Universal Censors, constitute the highest orders of beings who may and do engage in the work of revealing truth to the individual planets and systems, whether in their earlier epochs or when settled in light and life. From time to time we all make contact with the service of the ascending mortals, from an initial-life planet on up through a local universe and the superuniverse, particularly the latter.

3. THE DIVINE COUNSELORS

These Trinity-origin beings are the counsel of Deity to the realms of the seven superuniverses. They are not *reflective* of the divine counsel of the Trinity; they are that counsel. Divine Counselors are the associates and equals of the Universal Censors and the Perfectors of Wisdom, from one to seven Counselors being associated with each of these latter personalities. All three orders participate in the government of the Ancients of Days, in the local universes and down through the major and minor sectors to the individual galaxies and constellations, and even in the councils of the local system sovereigns.

We act as individuals, as I do in inditing this statement, but we also function as a trio whenever the occasion requires. When we act in an executive capacity, always there are associated together a Perfector of Wisdom, a Universal Censor, and from one to seven Divine Counselors.

One Perfector of Wisdom, seven Divine Counselors, and one Universal Censor constitute a tribunal of Trinity divinity, the highest mobile advisory body in the universes of time and space. Such a group of nine is known either as a fact-finding or as a truth-revealing tribunal, and when it sits in judgment upon a problem and renders a decision, it is just as if an Ancient of

Days had adjudicated the matter, for in all the annals of the superuniverses such a verdict has never been reversed by the Ancients of Days.

When the three Ancients of Days function, the Paradise Trinity functions. When the tribunal of nine arrives at a decision following its united deliberations, to all intents and purposes the Ancients of Days have spoken. And it is in this manner that the Paradise Rulers make personal contact, in administrative matters and governmental regulation, with the individual worlds, systems, and universes.

Divine Counselors are the perfection of the divine counsel of the Paradise Trinity. We represent, in fact *are*, the counsel of perfection. When we are supplemented by the experiential counsel of our associates, the perfected and Trinity-embraced beings of evolutionary ascent, our combined conclusions are not only complete but replete. When our united counsel has been associated, adjudicated, confirmed, and promulgated by a Universal Censor, it is very probable that it approaches the threshold of universal totality. Such verdicts represent the nearest possible approach to the absolute attitude of Deity within the time-space limits of the situation involved and the problem concerned.

Seven Divine Counselors in liaison with a trinitized evolutionary trio — a Mighty Messenger, One High in Authority, and One without Name and Number — represent the nearest superuniverse approach to the union of the human viewpoint and the divine attitude on near-paradisiacal levels of spiritual meanings and reality values. Such close approximation of the united cosmic attitudes of the creature and the Creator is only surpassed in the Paradise bestowal Sons, who are, in every phase of personality experience, God and man.

4. THE UNIVERSAL CENSORS

Universal Censors *are* the judgment of Deity. They are not merely reflective of the decisions of perfection; they are the judgment of the Paradise Trinity. Even the Ancients of Days do not sit in judgment except in association with the Universal Censors.

One Censor is commissioned on each of the billion worlds of the central universe, being attached to the planetary administration of the resident Eternal of Days. Neither Perfectors of Wisdom nor Divine Counselors are thus permanently attached to the Havona administrations, nor do we altogether understand why Universal Censors are stationed in the central universe. Their present activities hardly account for their assignment in Havona, and we therefore suspect that they are there in anticipation of the needs of some future universe age in which the Havona population may partially change.

Enormous numbers of Censors are assigned to each of the seven superuniverses. Both in an individual capacity and in association with Perfectors of Wisdom and Divine Counselors, they operate throughout all divisions of the seven superuniverses. Thus the Censors act on all levels of the grand universe, from the perfect worlds of Havona to the councils of the System Sovereigns, and they are an organic part of all dispensational adjudications of the evolutionary worlds.

Whenever and wherever a Universal Censor is present, then and there is the judgment of Deity. And since the Censors always render their verdicts in liaison with Perfectors of Wisdom and Divine Counselors, such decisions embrace the united wisdom, counsel, and judgment of the Paradise Trinity. In this juridical trio the Perfector of Wisdom would be the "I was," the Divine Counselor the "I will be," but the Universal Censor is always "I am."

The Censors are universe totaling personalities. When a thousand witnesses have given testimony — or a million — when the voice of wisdom has spoken and the counsel of divinity has recorded, when the testimony of ascendant perfection has been added, then the Censor functions, and there is immediately revealed an unerring and divine totaling of all that has transpired; and such a disclosure represents the divine conclusion, the sum and substance of a final and perfect decision. Therefore, when a Censor has spoken, no one else may speak, for the Censor has depicted the true and unmistakable total of all that has gone before. When he speaks, there is no appeal.

Most fully do I understand the operation of the mind of a Perfector of Wisdom, but I certainly do not fully comprehend the working of the adjudicating mind of a Universal Censor. It appears to me that the Censors formulate new meanings and originate new values from the association of the facts, truths, and findings presented to them in the course of an investigation of universe affairs. It seems probable that the Universal Censors are able to bring forth original interpretations of the combination of perfect Creator insight and the perfected creature experience. This association of Paradise perfection and universe experience undoubtedly eventuates a new value in ultimates.

But this is not the end of our difficulties regarding the working of the minds of the Universal Censors. Having made due allowances for all that we know or conjecture about the functioning of a Censor in any given universe situation, we find that we are still unable to predict decisions or to forecast verdicts. We very accurately determine the probable result of the association of Creator attitude and creature experience, but such conclusions are not always accurate forecasts of Censor disclosures. It seems likely that the Censors are in some manner in liaison with the Deity Absolute; we are otherwise unable to explain many of their decisions and rulings.

Perfectors of Wisdom, Divine Counselors, and Universal Censors, together with the seven orders of Supreme Trinity Personalities, constitute those ten groups which have been sometimes designated *Stationary Sons of the Trinity*. Together they comprise the grand corps of Trinity administrators, rulers, executives, advisers, counselors, and judges.

It is very difficult to portray the functional limits of the Stationary Sons of the Trinity. It would be incorrect to state that their acts are finite limited, for there are transactions of superuniverse record which indicate otherwise. They act on any level of universe administration or adjudication that may be required by time-space conditions and that pertains to the past, present, and future evolution of the master universe.

5. INSPIRED TRINITY SPIRITS

I will be able to tell you very little concerning the Inspired Trinity Spirits, for they are one of the few wholly secret orders of beings in existence, secret, no doubt, because it is impossible for them fully to reveal themselves even to those of us whose origin is so near the source of their creation. They come into being by the act of the Paradise Trinity and may be utilized by any one or two of the Deities as well as by all three. We do not know whether these Spirits are of completed numbers or are constantly increasing, but we incline to the belief that their number is not fixed.

We fully understand neither the nature nor the conduct of the Inspired Spirits. They may possibly belong to the category of superpersonal spirits. They seem to operate over all known circuits and appear to act well-nigh independently of time and space. But we know little about them except as we deduce their character from the nature of their activities, the results of which we certainly observe here and there in the universes.

Under certain conditions these Inspired Spirits can individualize themselves sufficiently for recognition by beings of Trinity origin. I have seen them; but it would never be possible for the lower orders of celestial beings to recognize one of them. Certain circumstances also arise from time to time in the conduct of the evolving universes in which any being of Trinity origin may directly employ these Spirits in the furtherance of his assignments. We therefore know that they exist, and that under certain conditions we may command and receive their assistance, sometimes recognize their presence. But they are not a part of the manifest and definitely revealed organization intrusted with the conduct of the time-space universes before such material creations are settled in light and life. They have no clearly discernible place in the present economy or administration of the evolving seven superuniverses. They are a secret of the Paradise Trinity.

The Melchizedeks of Nebadon teach that Inspired Trinity Spirits are destined, sometime in the eternal future, to function in the places of the Solitary Messengers, whose ranks are slowly but certainly being depleted by their assignment as associates of certain types of trinitized sons.

The Inspired Spirits are the solitary Spirits of the universe of universes. As Spirits they are very much like the Solitary Messengers except that the latter are distinct personalities. We obtain much of our knowledge of the Inspired Spirits from the Solitary Messengers, who detect their nearness by virtue of an inherent sensitivity to the presence of the Inspired Spirits which functions just as unfailingly as a magnetic needle points to a magnetic pole. When a Solitary Messenger is near an Inspired Trinity Spirit, he is conscious of a qualitative indication of such a divine presence and also of a very definite quantitative registration which enables him actually to know the classification or number of the Spirit presence or presences.

I may relate a further interesting fact: When a Solitary Messenger is on a planet whose inhabitants are indwelt by Thought Adjusters, as on Urantia, he is aware of a qualitative excitation in his detection-sensitivity to spirit presence. In such instances there is no quantitative excitation, only a qualitative agitation. When on a planet to which Adjusters do not come, contact with the natives does not produce any such reaction. This suggests that Thought Adjusters are in some manner related to, or are connected with, the Inspired Spirits of the Paradise Trinity. In some way they may possibly be associated in certain phases of their work; but we do not really know. They both originate near the center and source of all things, but they are not the same order of being. Thought Adjusters spring from the Father alone; Inspired Spirits are the offspring of the Paradise Trinity.

The Inspired Spirits do not apparently belong to the evolutionary scheme of the individual planets or universes, and yet they seem to be almost everywhere. Even as I am engaged in the formulation of this statement, my associated Solitary Messenger's personal sensitivity to the presence of this order of Spirit indicates that there is with us at this very moment, not over twenty-five feet away, a Spirit of the Inspired order and of the third volume of power presence. The third volume of power presence suggests to us the probability that three Inspired Spirits are functioning in liaison.

Of more than twelve orders of beings associated with me at this time, the Solitary Messenger is the only one aware of the presence of these mysterious entities of the Trinity. And further, while we are thus apprised of the nearness of these divine Spirits, we are all equally ignorant of their mission. We really do not know whether they are merely interested observers of our doings, or whether they are, in some manner unknown to us, actually contributing to the success of our undertaking.

We know that the Trinity Teacher Sons are devoted to the *conscious* enlightenment of universe creatures. I have arrived at the settled conclusion that the Inspired Trinity Spirits, by *superconscious* techniques, are also functioning as teachers of the realms. I am persuaded that there is a vast body of essential spiritual knowledge, truth indispensable to high spiritual attainment, which cannot be consciously received; self-consciousness would effectively jeopardize the certainty of reception. If we are right in this concept, and my entire order of being shares it, it may be the mission of these Inspired Spirits to overcome this difficulty, to bridge this gap in the universal scheme of moral enlightenment and spiritual advancement. We think that these two types of Trinity-origin teachers effect some kind of liaison in their activities, but we do not really know.

On the superuniverse training worlds and on the eternal circuits of Havona, I have fraternized with the perfecting mortals — spiritualized and ascendant souls from the evolutionary realms — but never have they been aware of the Inspired Spirits, which ever and anon the powers of detection resident in the Solitary Messengers would indicate were very near us. I have freely conversed with all orders of the Sons of God, high and low, and they likewise are unconscious of the admonitions of the Inspired Trinity Spirits. They can and do look back in their experiences and recount happenings which are difficult to explain if the action of such Spirits is not taken into account. But excepting Solitary Messengers, and sometimes Trinity-origin beings, none of the celestial family have ever been conscious of the nearness of the Inspired Spirits.

I do not believe the Inspired Trinity Spirits are playing hide and seek with me. They are probably trying just as hard to disclose themselves to me as I am to communicate with them; our difficulties and limitations must be mutual and inherent. I am satisfied that there are no arbitrary secrets in the universe; therefore will I never cease in my efforts to solve the mystery of the isolation of these Spirits belonging to my order of creation.

And from all this, you mortals, just now taking your first step on the eternal journey, can well see that you must advance a long way before you will progress by "sight" and "material" assurance. You will long use faith and be dependent on revelation if you hope to progress quickly and safely.

6. HAVONA NATIVES

The Havona natives are the direct creation of the Paradise Trinity, and their number is beyond the concept of your circumscribed minds. Neither is it possible for Urantians to conceive of the inherent endowments of such divinely perfect creatures as these Trinity-origin races of the eternal universe. You can never truly envisage these glorious creatures; you must await your arrival in Havona, when you can greet them as spirit comrades.

During your long sojourn on the billion worlds of Havona culture you will develop an eternal friendship for these superb beings. And how deep is that friendship which grows up between the lowest personal creature from the worlds of space and these high personal beings native to the perfect spheres of the central universe! Ascending mortals, in their long and loving association with the Havona natives, do much to compensate for the spiritual impoverishment of the earlier stages of mortal progression. At the same time, through their contacts with ascending pilgrims, the Havoners gain an experience which to no small extent overcomes the experiential handicap of having always lived a life of divine perfection. The good to both ascending mortal and Havona native is great and mutual.

Havona natives, like all other Trinity-origin personalities, are projected in divine perfection, and as with other Trinity-origin personalities, the passing of time may add to their stores of experiential endowments. But unlike the Stationary Sons of the Trinity, Havoners may evolve in status, may have an unrevealed future eternity-destiny. This is illustrated by those Havoners who service-factualize capacity for fusion with a non-Adjuster Father fragment and so qualify for membership in the Mortal Corps of the Finality. And there are other finaliter corps open to these natives of the central universe.

The status evolution of Havona natives has occasioned much speculation on Uversa. Since they are constantly filtering into the several Paradise Corps of the Finality, and since no more are being created, it is apparent that the number of natives remaining in Havona is constantly diminishing. The ultimate consequences of these transactions have never been revealed to us, but we do not believe that Havona will ever be entirely depleted of its natives. We have entertained the theory that Havoners will possibly cease entering the finaliter corps sometime during the ages of the successive creations of the outer space levels. We have also entertained the thought that in these subsequent universe ages the central universe may be peopled by a mixed group of resident beings, a citizenship consisting only in part of the original Havona natives. We do not know what order or type of creature may be thus destined to residential status in the future Havona, but we have thought of:

1. The univitatia, who are at present the permanent citizens of the local universe constellations.
2. Future types of mortals who may be born on the inhabited spheres of the superuniverses in the flowering of the ages of light and life.
3. The incoming spiritual aristocracy of the successive outer universes.

We know that the Havona of the previous universe age was somewhat different from the Havona of the present age. We deem it no more than reasonable to assume that we are now witnessing those slow changes in the central universe that are anticipatory of the ages to come. One thing is certain: The universe is nonstatic; only God is changeless.

7. PARADISE CITIZENS

There are resident on Paradise numerous groups of superb beings, the Paradise Citizens. They are not directly concerned with the scheme of perfecting ascending will creatures and are not, therefore, fully revealed to Urantia mortals. There are more than three thousand orders of these supernal intelligences, the last group having been personalized simultaneously with the mandate of the Trinity which promulgated the creative plan of the seven superuniverses of time and space.

Paradise Citizens and Havona natives are sometimes designated collectively as *Paradise-Havona personalities*.

This completes the story of those beings who are brought into existence by the Paradise Trinity. None of them have ever gone astray. And yet, in the highest sense, they are all freewill endowed.

Trinity-origin beings possess prerogatives of transit which make them independent of transport personalities, such as seraphim. We all possess the power of moving about freely and quickly in the universe of universes. Excepting the Inspired Trinity Spirits, we cannot attain the almost unbelievable velocity of the Solitary Messengers, but we are able so to utilize the sum total of the transport facilities in space that we can reach any point in a superuniverse, from its headquarters, in less than one year of Urantia time. It required 109 days of your time for me to journey from Uversa to Urantia.

Through these same avenues we are enabled to intercommunicate instantaneously. Our entire order of creation finds itself in touch with every individual embraced within every division of the children of the Paradise Trinity save only the Inspired Spirits.

[Presented by a Divine Counselor of Uversa.]

PAPER 20
THE PARADISE SONS OF GOD

As they function in the superuniverse of Orvonton, the Sons of God are classified under three general heads:

1. The Descending Sons of God.
2. The Ascending Sons of God.
3. The Trinitized Sons of God.

Descending orders of sonship include personalities who are of direct and divine creation. Ascending sons, such as mortal creatures, achieve this status by experiential participation in the creative technique known as evolution. Trinitized Sons are a group of composite origin which includes all beings embraced by the Paradise Trinity even though not of direct Trinity origin.

1. THE DESCENDING SONS OF GOD

All descending Sons of God have high and divine origins. They are dedicated to the descending ministry of service on the worlds and systems of time and space, there to facilitate the progress in the Paradise climb of the lowly creatures of evolutionary origin — the ascending sons of God. Of the numerous orders of descending Sons, seven will be depicted in these narratives. Those Sons who come forth from the Deities on the central Isle of Light and Life are called the *Paradise Sons of God* and embrace the following three orders:

1. Creator Sons — the Michaels.
2. Magisterial Sons — the Avonals.
3. Trinity Teacher Sons — the Daynals.

The remaining four orders of descending sonship are known as the *Local Universe Sons of God:*

4. Melchizedek Sons.
5. Vorondadek Sons.
6. Lanonandek Sons.
7. The Life Carriers.

Melchizedeks are the joint offspring of a local universe Creator Son, Creative Spirit, and Father Melchizedek. Both Vorondadeks and Lanonandeks are brought into being by a Creator Son and his Creative Spirit associate. Vorondadeks are first known as the Most Highs, the Constellation Fathers, but also rule the galaxies and the minor and major sectors of a universe; Lanonandeks are known as System Sovereigns and as Planetary Princes. The threefold order of Life Carriers is brought into being by a Creator Son and Creative Spirit associated with one of the three Ancients of Days of the superuniverse of jurisdiction. But the natures and activities of these Local Universe Sons of God are more properly portrayed in those papers dealing with the affairs of the local creations.

The Paradise Sons of God are of threefold origin: The primary or Creator Sons are brought into being by the Universal Father and the Eternal Son; the secondary or Magisterial Sons are children of the Eternal Son and the Infinite Spirit; the Trinity Teacher Sons are the offspring of the Father, Son, and Spirit. From the standpoint of service, worship, and supplication the Paradise Sons are as one; their spirit is one, and their work is identical in quality and completeness.

As the Paradise orders of Days proved to be divine administrators, so have the orders of Paradise Sons revealed themselves as divine ministers — creators, servers, bestowers, judges, teachers, and truth revealers. They range the universe of universes from the shores of the eternal Isle to the inhabited worlds of time and space, performing manifold services in the central and superuniverses not disclosed in these narratives. They are variously organized, dependent on the nature and whereabouts of their service, but in a local universe both Magisterial and Teacher Sons serve under the direction of the Creator Son who presides over that domain.

The Creator Sons seem to possess a spiritual endowment centering in their persons, which they control and which they can bestow, as did your own Creator Son when he poured out his spirit upon all mortal flesh on Urantia. Each Creator Son is endowed with this spiritual drawing power in his own realm; he is personally conscious of every act and emotion of every descending Son of God serving in his domain. Here is a divine reflection, a local universe duplication, of that absolute spiritual drawing power of the Eternal Son which enables him to reach out to make and maintain contact with all his Paradise Sons, no matter where they may be in all the universe of universes.

The Paradise Creator Sons serve not only as Sons in their descending ministrations of service and bestowal, but when they have completed their bestowal careers, each functions as a universe Father in his own creation, while the other Sons of God continue the service of bestowal and spiritual uplifting designed to win the planets, one by one, to the willing recognition of the loving rule of the Universal Father, culminating in creature consecration to the will of the Paradise Father and in planetary loyalty to the universe sovereignty of his Creator Son.

In a sevenfold Creator Son, Creator and creature are forever blended in understanding, sympathetic, and merciful association. The entire order of Michael, the Creator Sons, is so unique that the consideration of their natures and activities will be reserved to the next paper in this series, while this narrative will be chiefly concerned with the two remaining orders of Paradise sonship: the Magisterial Sons and the Trinity Teacher Sons.

2. THE MAGISTERIAL SONS

Every time an original and absolute concept of being formulated by the Eternal Son unites with a new and divine ideal of loving service conceived by the Infinite Spirit, a new and original Son of God, a Paradise Magisterial Son, is produced. These Sons constitute the order of Avonals in contradistinction to the order of Michael, the Creator Sons. Though not creators in the personal sense, they are closely associated with the Michaels in all their work. The Avonals are planetary ministers and judges, the magistrates of the time-space realms — of all races, to all worlds, and in all universes.

They are a self-governing order, being directed by their supreme council on Paradise, which is made up of experienced Avonals drawn from the services of all universes. But when assigned to, and commissioned in, a local universe, they serve under the direction of the Creator Son of that domain.

Avonals are the Paradise Sons of service and bestowal to the individual planets of the local universes. And since each Avonal Son has an exclusive personality, since no two are alike, their work is individually unique in the realms of their sojourn, where they are often incarnated in the likeness of mortal flesh and sometimes are born of earthly mothers on the evolutionary worlds.

In addition to their services on the higher administrative levels, the Avonals have a threefold function on the inhabited worlds:

1. *Judicial Actions*. They act at the close of the planetary dispensations. In time, scores — hundreds — of such missions may be executed on each individual world, and they may go to the same or to other worlds times without number as dispensation terminators, liberators of the sleeping survivors.

2. *Magisterial Missions*. A planetary visitation of this type usually occurs prior to the arrival of a bestowal Son. On such a mission an Avonal appears as an adult of the realm by a technique of incarnation not involving mortal birth. Subsequent to this first and usual magisterial visit, Avonals may repeatedly serve in a magisterial capacity on the same planet both before and

after the appearance of the bestowal Son. On these additional magisterial missions an Avonal may or may not appear in material and visible form, but on none of them will he be born into the world as a helpless babe.

3. *Bestowal Missions*. The Avonal Sons do all, at least once, bestow themselves upon some mortal race on some evolutionary world. Judicial visits are numerous, magisterial missions may be plural, but on each planet there appears but one bestowal Son. Bestowal Avonals are born of woman as Michael of Nebadon was incarnated on Urantia.

There is no limit to the number of times the Avonal Sons may serve on magisterial and on bestowal missions, but usually, when the experience has been seven times traversed, there is suspension in favor of those who have had less of such service. These Sons of multiple bestowal experience are then assigned to the high personal council of a Creator Son, thus becoming participants in the administration of universe affairs.

In all their work for and on the inhabited worlds, the Magisterial Sons are assisted by two orders of local universe creatures, the Melchizedeks and the archangels, while on bestowal missions they are also accompanied by the Brilliant Evening Stars, likewise of origin in the local creations. In every planetary effort the secondary Paradise Sons, the Avonals, are supported by the full power and authority of a primary Paradise Son, the Creator Son of their local universe of service. To all intents and purposes their work on the inhabited spheres is just as effective and acceptable as would have been the service of a Creator Son upon such worlds of mortal habitation.

3. JUDICIAL ACTIONS

The Avonals are known as Magisterial Sons because they are the high magistrates of the realms, the adjudicators of the successive dispensations of the worlds of time. They preside over the awakening of the sleeping survivors, sit in judgment on the realm, bring to an end a dispensation of suspended justice, execute the mandates of an age of probationary mercy, reassign the space creatures of planetary ministry to the tasks of the new dispensation, and return to the headquarters of their local universe upon the completion of their mission.

When they sit in judgment on the destinies of an age, the Avonals decree the fate of the evolutionary races, but though they may render judgments extinguishing the identity of personal creatures, they do not execute such sentences. Verdicts of this nature are executed by none but the authorities of a superuniverse.

The arrival of a Paradise Avonal on an evolutionary world for the purpose of terminating a dispensation and of inaugurating a new era of planetary progression is not necessarily either a magisterial mission or a bestowal mission. Magisterial missions sometimes, and bestowal missions always, are incarnations; that is, on such assignments the Avonals serve on a planet in material form — literally. Their other visits are "technical," and in this capacity an Avonal is not incarnated for planetary service. If a Magisterial Son comes solely as a dispensational adjudicator, he arrives on a planet as a spiritual being, invisible to the material creatures of the realm. Such technical visits occur repeatedly in the long history of an inhabited world.

Avonal Sons may act as planetary judges prior to both the magisterial and bestowal experiences. On either of these missions, however, the incarnated Son will judge the passing planetary age; likewise does a Creator Son when incarnated on a mission of bestowal in the likeness of mortal flesh. When a Paradise Son visits an evolutionary world and becomes like one of its people, his presence terminates a dispensation and constitutes a judgment of the realm.

4. MAGISTERIAL MISSIONS

Prior to the planetary appearance of a bestowal Son, an inhabited world is usually visited by a Paradise Avonal on a magisterial mission. If it is an initial magisterial visitation, the Avonal is always incarnated as a material being. He appears on the planet of assignment as a full-fledged adult of the mortal races, a being fully visible to, and in physical contact with, the mortal creatures of his day and generation. Throughout a magisterial incarnation the connection of the Avonal Son with the local and the universal spiritual forces is complete and unbroken.

A planet may experience many magisterial visitations both before and after the appearance of a bestowal Son. It may be visited many times by the same or other Avonals, acting as dispensational adjudicators, but such technical missions of judgment are neither bestowal nor magisterial, and the Avonals are never incarnated at such times. Even when a planet is blessed with repeated magisterial missions, the Avonals do not always submit to mortal incarnation; and when they do serve in the likeness of mortal flesh, they always appear as adult beings of the realm; they are not born of woman.

When incarnated on either bestowal or magisterial missions, the Paradise Sons have experienced Adjusters, and these Adjusters are different for each incarnation. The Adjusters that occupy the minds of the incarnated Sons of God can never hope for personality through fusion with the human-divine beings of their indwelling, but they are often personalized by fiat of the Universal Father. Such Adjusters form the supreme Divinington council of direction for the administration, identification, and dispatch of Mystery Monitors to the inhabited realms. They also receive and accredit Adjusters on their return to the "bosom of the Father" upon the mortal dissolution of their earthly tabernacles. In this way the faithful Adjusters of the world judges become the exalted chiefs of their kind.

Urantia has never been host to an Avonal Son on a magisterial mission. Had Urantia followed the general plan of inhabited worlds, it would have been blessed with a magisterial mission sometime between the days of Adam and the bestowal of Christ Michael. But the regular sequence of Paradise Sons on your planet was wholly deranged by the appearance of your Creator Son on his terminal bestowal two thousand years ago.

Urantia may yet be visited by an Avonal commissioned to incarnate on a magisterial mission, but regarding the future appearance of Paradise Sons, not even "the angels in heaven know the time or manner of such visitations," for a Michael-bestowal world becomes the individual and personal ward of a Master Son and, as such, is wholly subject to his own plans and rulings. And with your world, this is further complicated by Michael's promise to return. Regardless of the misunderstandings about the Urantian sojourn of Michael of Nebadon, one thing is certainly authentic — his promise to come back to your world. In view of this prospect, only time can reveal the future order of the visitations of the Paradise Sons of God on Urantia.

5. BESTOWAL OF THE PARADISE SONS OF GOD

The Eternal Son is the eternal Word of God. The Eternal Son is the perfect expression of the "first" absolute and infinite thought of his eternal Father. When a personal duplication or divine extension of this Original Son starts on a bestowal mission of mortal incarnation, it becomes literally true that the divine "Word is made flesh," and that the Word thus dwells among the lowly beings of animal origin.

On Urantia there is a widespread belief that the purpose of a Son's bestowal is, in some manner, to influence the attitude of the Universal Father. But your enlightenment should indicate that this is not true. The bestowals of the Avonal and the Michael Sons are a necessary part of the experiential process designed to make these Sons safe and sympathetic magistrates and rulers of the peoples and planets of time and space. The career of sevenfold bestowal is the supreme goal of all Paradise Creator Sons. And all Magisterial Sons are motivated by this same spirit of service which so abundantly characterizes the primary Creator Sons and the Eternal Son of Paradise.

Some order of Paradise Son must be bestowed upon each mortal-inhabited world in order to make it possible for Thought Adjusters to indwell the minds of all normal human beings on that sphere, for the Adjusters do not come to all bona fide human beings until the Spirit of Truth has been poured out upon all flesh; and the sending of the Spirit of Truth is dependent upon the return to universe headquarters of a Paradise Son who has successfully executed a mission of mortal bestowal upon an evolving world.

During the course of the long history of an inhabited planet, many dispensational adjudications will take place, and more than one magisterial mission may occur, but ordinarily only once will a bestowal Son serve on the sphere. It is only required that each inhabited world have one bestowal Son come to live the full mortal life from birth to death. Sooner or later, regardless of spiritual status, every mortal-inhabited world is destined to become host to a Magisterial Son on a bestowal mission except the one planet in each local universe whereon a Creator Son elects to make his mortal bestowal.

Understanding more about the bestowal Sons, you discern why so much interest attaches to Urantia in the history of Nebadon. Your small and insignificant planet is of local universe concern simply because it is the mortal home world of Jesus of Nazareth. It was the scene of the final and triumphant bestowal of your Creator Son, the arena in which Michael won the supreme personal sovereignty of the universe of Nebadon.

At the headquarters of his local universe a Creator Son, especially after the completion of his own mortal bestowal, spends much of his time in counseling and instructing the college of associate Sons, the Magisterial Sons and others. In love and devotion, with tender mercy and affectionate consideration, these Magisterial Sons bestow themselves upon the worlds of space. And in no way are these planetary services inferior to the mortal bestowals of the Michaels. It is true that your Creator Son selected for the realm of his final adventure in creature experience one which had had unusual misfortunes. But no planet could ever be in such a condition that it would require the bestowal of a Creator Son to effect its spiritual rehabilitation. Any Son of the bestowal group would have equally sufficed, for in all their work on the worlds of a local universe the Magisterial Sons are just as divinely effective and all wise as would have been their Paradise brother, the Creator Son.

Though the possibility of disaster always attends these Paradise Sons during their bestowal incarnations, I have yet to see the record of the failure or default of either a Magisterial or a Creator Son on a mission of bestowal. Both are of origin too close to absolute perfection to fail. They indeed assume the risk, really become like the mortal creatures of flesh and blood and thereby gain the unique creature experience, but within the range of my observation they always succeed. They never fail to achieve the goal of the bestowal mission. The story of their bestowal and planetary service throughout Nebadon constitutes the most noble and fascinating chapter in the history of your local universe.

6. THE MORTAL-BESTOWAL CAREERS

The method whereby a Paradise Son becomes ready for mortal incarnation as a bestowal Son, becomes enmothered on the bestowal planet, is a universal mystery; and any effort to detect the working of this Sonarington technique is doomed to meet with certain failure. Let the sublime knowledge of the mortal life of Jesus of Nazareth sink into your souls, but waste no thought in useless speculation as to how this mysterious incarnation of Michael of Nebadon was effected. Let us all rejoice in the knowledge and assurance that such achievements are possible to the divine nature and waste no time on futile conjectures about the technique employed by divine wisdom to effect such phenomena.

On a mortal-bestowal mission a Paradise Son is always born of woman and grows up as a child of the realm, as Jesus did on Urantia. These Sons of supreme service all pass from infancy through youth to adulthood just as does a human being. In every respect they become like the mortals of the race into which they are born. They make petitions to the Father as do the children of the realms in which they serve. From a material viewpoint, these human-divine Sons live ordinary lives with just one exception: They do not beget offspring on the worlds of their sojourn; that is a universal restriction imposed on all orders of the Paradise bestowal Sons.

As Jesus worked on your world as the carpenter's son, so do other Paradise Sons labor in various capacities on their bestowal planets. You could hardly think of a vocation that has not been followed by some Paradise Son in the course of his bestowal on some one of the evolutionary planets of time.

When a bestowal Son has mastered the experience of living the mortal life, when he has achieved perfection of attunement with his indwelling Adjuster, thereupon he begins that part of his planetary mission designed to illuminate the minds and to inspire the souls of his brethren in the flesh. As teachers, these Sons are exclusively devoted to the spiritual enlightenment of the mortal races on the worlds of their sojourn.

The mortal-bestowal careers of the Michaels and the Avonals, while comparable in most respects, are not identical in all: Never does a Magisterial Son proclaim, "Whosoever has seen the Son has seen the Father," as did your Creator Son when on Urantia and in the flesh. But a bestowed Avonal does declare, "Whosoever has seen me has seen the Eternal Son of God."

The Magisterial Sons are not of immediate descent from the Universal Father, nor do they incarnate subject to the Father's will; always do they bestow themselves as Paradise *Sons* subject to the will of the Eternal Son of Paradise.

When the bestowal Sons, Creator or Magisterial, enter the portals of death, they reappear on the third day. But you should not entertain the idea that they always meet with the tragic end encountered by the Creator Son who sojourned on your world more than two thousand years ago. The extraordinary and unusually cruel experience through which Jesus of Nazareth passed has caused Urantia to become locally known as "the world of the cross." It is not necessary that such inhuman treatment be accorded a Son of God, and the vast majority of planets have afforded them a more considerate reception, allowing them to finish their mortal careers, terminate the age, adjudicate the sleeping survivors, and inaugurate a new dispensation, without imposing a violent death. A bestowal Son must encounter death, must pass through the whole of the actual experience of mortals of the realms, but it is not a requirement of the divine plan that this death be either violent or unusual.

When bestowal Sons are not put to death by violence, they voluntarily relinquish their lives and pass through the portals of death, not to satisfy the demands of "stern justice" or "divine wrath," but rather to complete the bestowal, "to drink the cup" of the career of incarnation and personal experience in all that constitutes a creature's life as it is lived on the planets of mortal existence. Bestowal is a planetary and a universe necessity, and physical death is nothing more than a necessary part of a bestowal mission.

When the mortal incarnation is finished, the Avonal of service proceeds to Paradise, is accepted by the Universal Father, returns to the local universe of assignment, and is acknowledged by the Creator Son. Thereupon the bestowal Avonal and the Creator Son send their conjoint Spirit of Truth to function in the hearts of the mortal races dwelling on the bestowal world. In the presovereignty ages of a local universe, this is the joint spirit of both Sons, implemented by the Creative Spirit. It differs somewhat from the Spirit of Truth which characterizes the local universe ages following a Michael's seventh bestowal.

Upon the completion of a Creator Son's final bestowal the Spirit of Truth previously sent into all Avonal-bestowal worlds of that local universe changes in nature, becoming more literally the spirit of the sovereign Michael. This phenomenon takes place concurrently with the liberation of the Spirit of Truth for service on the Michael-mortal-bestowal planet. Thereafter, each world honored by a Magisterial bestowal will receive the same spirit Comforter from the sevenfold Creator Son, in association with that Magisterial Son, which it would have received had the local universe Sovereign personally incarnated as its bestowal Son.

7. THE TRINITY TEACHER SONS

These highly personal and highly spiritual Paradise Sons are brought into being by the Paradise Trinity. They are known in Havona as the order of Daynals. In Orvonton they are of record as Trinity Teacher Sons, so named because of their parentage. On Salvington they are sometimes denominated the Paradise Spiritual Sons.

The Daynal order of sonship is not an organic part of the local or superuniverse administrations. Its members are neither creators nor retrievers, neither judges nor rulers. They are not so much concerned with universe administration as with moral enlightenment and spiritual development. They are the universal educators, being dedicated to the spiritual awakening and moral guidance of all realms. Their ministry is intimately interrelated with that of the personalities of the Infinite Spirit and is closely associated with the Paradise ascension of creature beings.

These Sons of the Trinity partake of the combined natures of the three Paradise Deities, but in Havona they seem more to reflect the nature of the Universal Father. In the superuniverses they seem to portray the nature of the Eternal Son, while in the local creations they appear to show forth the character of the Infinite Spirit. In all universes they are the embodiment of service and the discretion of wisdom.

Unlike their Paradise brethren, Michaels and Avonals, Trinity Teacher Sons receive no preliminary training in the central universe. They are dispatched directly to the headquarters of the superuniverses and from there are commissioned for service in some local universe. In their ministry to these evolutionary realms they utilize the combined spiritual influence of a

Creator Son and the associated Magisterial Sons, for the Daynals do not possess a spiritual drawing power in and of themselves.

8. LOCAL UNIVERSE MINISTRY OF THE DAYNALS

The Paradise Spiritual Sons are unique Trinity-origin beings and the only Trinity creatures to be so completely associated with the conduct of the dual-origin universes. They are affectionately devoted to the educational ministry to mortal creatures and the lower orders of spiritual beings. They begin their labors in the local systems and, in accordance with experience and achievement, are advanced inward through the constellation service to the highest work of the local creation. Upon certification they may become spiritual ambassadors representing the local universes of their service.

Many of the heads of departments in the Melchizedek schools belong to this order, while the combined staff of the regularly constituted University of Salvington embraces over one hundred thousand including these Sons. Large numbers are stationed on the various morontia-training worlds, but they are not wholly occupied with the spiritual and intellectual advancement of mortal creatures; they are equally concerned with the instruction of seraphic beings and other natives of the local creations. Many of their assistants are drawn from the ranks of the creature-trinitized beings.

The Teacher Sons compose the faculties who administer all examinations and conduct all tests for the qualification and certification of all subordinate phases of universe service, from the duties of outpost sentinels to those of star students. They conduct an agelong course of training, ranging from the planetary courses up to the high College of Wisdom located on Salvington. Recognition indicative of effort and attainment is granted to all, ascending mortal or ambitious cherubim, who complete these adventures in wisdom and truth.

In all universes all the Sons of God are beholden to these ever-faithful and universally efficient Trinity Teacher Sons. They are the exalted teachers of all spirit personalities, even the tried and true teachers of the Sons of God themselves. But of the endless details of the duties and functions of the Teacher Sons I can hardly instruct you. The vast domain of Daynal-sonship activities will be better understood on Urantia when you are more advanced in intelligence, and after the spiritual isolation of your planet has been terminated.

9. PLANETARY SERVICE OF THE DAYNALS

When the progress of events on an evolutionary world indicates that the time is ripe to initiate a spiritual age, the Trinity Teacher Sons always volunteer for this service. You are not familiar with this order of sonship because Urantia has never experienced a spiritual age, a millennium of cosmic enlightenment. But the Teacher Sons even now visit your world for the purpose of formulating plans concerning their projected sojourn on your sphere. They will be due to appear on Urantia after its inhabitants have gained comparative deliverance from the shackles of animalism and from the fetters of materialism.

Trinity Teacher Sons have nothing to do with terminating planetary dispensations. They neither judge the dead nor translate the living, but on each planetary mission they are accompanied by a Magisterial Son who performs these services. Teacher Sons are wholly concerned with the initiation of a spiritual age, with the dawn of the era of spiritual realities on an evolutionary planet. They make real the spiritual counterparts of material knowledge and temporal wisdom.

The Teacher Sons usually remain on their visitation planets for one thousand years of planetary time. One Teacher Son presides over the planetary millennial reign and is assisted by seventy associates of his order. The Daynals do not incarnate or otherwise so materialize themselves as to be visible to mortal beings; therefore is contact with the world of visitation maintained through the activities of the Brilliant Evening Stars, local universe personalities who are associated with the Trinity Teacher Sons.

The Daynals may return many times to an inhabited world, and following their final mission the planet will be ushered into the settled status of a sphere of light and life, the evolutionary goal of all the mortal-inhabited worlds of the present universe age. The Mortal Corps of the Finality has much to do with the spheres settled in light and life, and their planetary activities touch upon those of the Teacher Sons. Indeed, the whole order of

Daynal sonship is intimately connected with all phases of finaliter activities in the evolutionary creations of time and space.

The Trinity Teacher Sons seem to be so completely identified with the regime of mortal progression through the earlier stages of evolutionary ascension that we are often led to speculate regarding their possible association with the finaliters in the undisclosed career of the future universes. We observe that the administrators of the superuniverses are part Trinity-origin personalities and part Trinity-embraced ascendant evolutionary creatures. We firmly believe that the Teacher Sons and the finaliters are now engaged in acquiring the experience of time-association which may be the preliminary training to prepare them for close association in some unrevealed future destiny. On Uversa it is our belief that, when the superuniverses are finally settled in light and life, these Paradise Teacher Sons, who have become so thoroughly familiar with the problems of evolutionary worlds and have been so long associated with the career of evolutionary mortals, will probably be transferred to eternal association with the Paradise Corps of the Finality.

10. UNITED MINISTRY OF THE PARADISE SONS

All the Paradise Sons of God are divine in origin and in nature. The work of each Paradise Son in behalf of each world is just as if the Son of service were the first and only Son of God.

The Paradise Sons are the divine presentation of the acting natures of the three persons of Deity to the domains of time and space. The Creator, Magisterial, and Teacher Sons are the gifts of the eternal Deities to the children of men and to all other universe creatures of ascension potential. These Sons of God are the divine ministers who are unceasingly devoted to the work of helping the creatures of time attain the high spiritual goal of eternity.

In the Creator Sons the love of the Universal Father is blended with the mercy of the Eternal Son and is disclosed to the local universes in the creative power, loving ministry, and understanding sovereignty of the Michaels. In the Magisterial Sons the mercy of the Eternal Son, united with the ministry of the Infinite Spirit, is revealed to the evolutionary domains in the careers of these Avonals of judgment, service, and bestowal. In the Trinity Teacher Sons the love, mercy, and ministry of the three Paradise Deities are co-ordinated on the highest time-space value-levels and are presented to the universes as living truth, divine goodness, and true spiritual beauty.

In the local universes these orders of sonship collaborate to effect the revelation of the Deities of Paradise to the creatures of space: As the Father of a local universe, a Creator Son portrays the infinite character of the Universal Father. As the bestowal Sons of mercy, the Avonals reveal the matchless nature of the Eternal Son of infinite compassion. As the true teachers of ascending personalities, the Trinity Daynal Sons disclose the teacher personality of the Infinite Spirit. In their divinely perfect co-operation, Michaels, Avonals, and Daynals are contributing to the actualization and revelation of the personality and sovereignty of God the Supreme in and to the time-space universes. In the harmony of their triune activities these Paradise Sons of God ever function in the vanguard of the personalities of Deity as they follow the never-ending expansion of the divinity of the First Great Source and Center from the everlasting Isle of Paradise into the unknown depths of space.

[Presented by a Perfector of Wisdom from Uversa.]

PAPER 21
THE PARADISE CREATOR SONS

THE CREATOR SONS are the makers and rulers of the local universes of time and space. These universe creators and sovereigns are of dual origin, embodying the characteristics of God the Father and God the Son. But each Creator Son is different from every other; each is unique in nature as well as in personality; each is the "only-begotten Son" of the perfect deity ideal of his origin.

In the vast work of organizing, evolving, and perfecting a local universe, these high Sons always enjoy the sustaining approval of the Universal Father. The relationship of the Creator Sons with their Paradise Father is touching and superlative. No doubt the profound affection of the Deity parents for their divine progeny is the wellspring of that beautiful and well-nigh divine love which even mortal parents bear their children.

These primary Paradise Sons are personalized as Michaels. As they go forth from Paradise to found their universes, they are known as Creator Michaels. When settled in supreme authority, they are called Master Michaels. Sometimes we refer to the sovereign of your universe of Nebadon as Christ Michael. Always and forever do they reign after the "order of Michael," that being the designation of the first Son of their order and nature.

The original or first-born Michael has never experienced incarnation as a material being, but seven times he passed through the experience of spiritual creature ascent on the seven circuits of Havona, advancing from the outer spheres to the innermost circuit of the central creation. The order of Michael knows the grand universe from one end to the other; there is no essential experience of any of the children of time and space in which the Michaels have not personally participated; they are in fact partakers not only of the divine nature but also of your nature, meaning all natures, from the highest to the lowest.

The original Michael is the presiding head of the primary Paradise Sons when they assemble for conference at the center of all things. Not long since on Uversa we recorded a universal broadcast of a conclave extraordinary on the eternal Isle of one hundred fifty thousand Creator Sons assembled in the parental presence and engaged in deliberations having to do with the progress of the unification and stabilization of the universe of universes. This was a selected group of Sovereign Michaels, sevenfold bestowal Sons.

1. ORIGIN AND NATURE OF CREATOR SONS

When the fullness of absolute spiritual ideation in the Eternal Son encounters the fullness of absolute personality concept in the Universal Father, when such a creative union is finally and fully attained, when such absolute identity of spirit and such infinite oneness of personality concept occur, then, right then and there, without the loss of anything of personality or prerogative by either of the infinite Deities, there flashes into full-fledged being a new and original Creator Son, the only-begotten Son of the perfect ideal and the powerful idea whose union produces this new creator personality of power and perfection.

Each Creator Son is the only-begotten and only-begettable offspring of the perfect union of the original concepts of the two infinite and eternal and perfect minds of the ever-existent Creators of the universe of universes. There never can be another such Son because each Creator Son is the unqualified, finished, and final expression and embodiment of all of every phase of every feature of every possibility of every divine reality that could, throughout all eternity, ever be found in, expressed by, or evolved from, those divine creative potentials which united to bring this Michael Son into existence. Each Creator Son is the absolute of the united deity concepts which constitute his divine origin.

The divine natures of these Creator Sons are, in principle, derived equally from the attributes of both Paradise parents. All partake of the fullness of the divine nature of the Universal Father and of the creative prerogatives of the Eternal Son, but as we observe the practical outworking of the Michael functions in the universes, we discern apparent differences. Some Creator Sons appear to be more like God the Father; others more like God the Son. For example: The trend of administration in the universe of Nebadon suggests that its Creator and ruling Son is one whose nature and character more resemble that of the Eternal Mother Son. It should be further stated that some universes are presided over by Paradise Michaels who appear equally to resemble God the Father and God the Son. And these observations are in no sense implied criticisms; they are simply a recording of fact.

2. THE CREATORS OF LOCAL UNIVERSES

The Paradise Sons of the primary order are the designers, creators, builders, and administrators of their respective domains, the local universes of time and space, the basic creative units of the seven evolutionary superuniverses. A Creator Son is permitted to choose the space site of his future cosmic activity, but before he may begin even the physical organization of his universe, he must spend a long period of observation devoted to the study of the efforts of his older brothers in various creations located in the superuniverse of his projected action. And prior to all this, the Michael Son will have completed his long and unique experience of Paradise observation and Havona training.

When a Creator Son departs from Paradise to embark upon the adventure of universe making, to become the head — virtually the God — of the local universe of his own organization, then, for the first time, he finds himself in intimate contact with, and in many respects dependent upon, the Third Source and Center. The Infinite Spirit, though abiding with the Father and the Son at the center of all things, is destined to function as the actual and effective helper of each Creator Son. Therefore is each Creator Son accompanied by a Creative Daughter of the Infinite Spirit, that being who is destined to become the Divine Minister, the Mother Spirit of the new local universe.

The departure of a Michael Son on this occasion forever liberates his creator prerogatives from the Paradise Sources and Centers, subject only to certain limitations inherent in the pre-existence of these Sources and Centers and to certain other antecedent powers and presences. Among these limitations to the otherwise all-powerful creator prerogatives of a local universe Father are the following:

1. *Energy-matter* is dominated by the Infinite Spirit. Before any new forms of things, great or small, may be created, before any new transformations of energy-matter may be attempted, a Creator Son must secure the consent and working co-operation of the Infinite Spirit.
2. *Creature designs* and types are controlled by the Eternal Son. Before a Creator Son may engage in the creation of any new type of being, any new design of creature, he must secure the consent of the Eternal and Original Mother Son.
3. *Personality* is designed and bestowed by the Universal Father.

The types and patterns of *mind* are determined by the precreature factors of being. After these have been associated to constitute a creature (personal or otherwise), mind is the endowment of the Third Source and Center, the universal source of mind ministry to all beings below the level of Paradise Creators.

The control of *spirit* designs and types depends on the level of their manifestation. In the last analysis, spiritual design is controlled by the Trinity or by the pre-Trinity spirit endowments of the Trinity personalities — Father, Son, and Spirit.

When such a perfect and divine Son has taken possession of the space site of his chosen universe; when the initial problems of universe materialization and of gross equilibrium have been resolved; when he has formed an effective and co-operative working union with the complemental Daughter of the Infinite Spirit — then do this Universe Son and this Universe Spirit initiate that liaison which is designed to give origin to the innumerable hosts of their local universe children. In connection with this event the Creative Spirit focalization of the Paradise Infinite Spirit becomes changed in nature, taking on the personal qualities of the Mother Spirit of a local universe.

Notwithstanding that all Creator Sons are divinely like their Paradise parents, none exactly resembles another; each is unique, diverse, exclusive, and original in *nature* as well as in personality. And since they are the architects and makers of the life plans of their respective realms, this very diversity insures that their domains will also be diverse in every form and phase of Michael-derived living existence which may be created or subsequently evolved therein. Hence the orders of creatures native to the local universes are quite varied. No two are administered or inhabited by dual-origin native beings who are in all respects identical. Within any superuniverse, one half of their inherent attributes are quite alike, being derived from the uniform Creative Spirits; the other half vary, being derived from the diversified Creator Sons. But such diversity does not characterize those creatures of sole origin in the Creative Spirit nor those imported beings who are native to the central or superuniverses.

When a Michael Son is absent from his universe, its government is directed by the first-born native being, the Bright and Morning Star, the local universe chief executive. The advice and counsel of the Union of Days is invaluable at such times. During these absences a Creator Son is able to invest the associated Mother Spirit with the overcontrol of his spiritual presence on the inhabited worlds and in the hearts of his mortal children. And the Mother Spirit of a local universe remains always at its headquarters, extending her fostering care and spiritual ministry to the uttermost parts of such an evolutionary domain.

The personal presence of a Creator Son in his local universe is not necessary to the smooth running of an established material creation. Such Sons may journey to Paradise, and still their universes swing on through space. They may lay down their lines of power to incarnate as the children of time; still their realms whirl on about their respective centers. No material organization is independent of the absolute-gravity grasp of Paradise or of the cosmic overcontrol inherent in the space presence of the Unqualified Absolute.

3. LOCAL UNIVERSE SOVEREIGNTY

A Creator Son is given the range of a universe by the consent of the Paradise Trinity and with the confirmation of the supervising Master Spirit of the superuniverse concerned. Such action constitutes title of physical possession, a cosmic leasehold. But the elevation of a Michael Son from this initial and self-limited stage of rulership to the experiential supremacy of self-earned sovereignty comes as a result of his own personal experiences in the work of universe creation and incarnated bestowal. Until the achievement of bestowal-earned sovereignty, he rules as vicegerent of the Universal Father.

A Creator Son could assert full sovereignty over his personal creation at any time, but he wisely chooses not to. If, prior to passing through the creature bestowals, he assumed an unearned supreme sovereignty, the Paradise personalities resident in his local universe would withdraw. But this has never happened throughout all the creations of time and space.

The fact of creatorship implies the fullness of sovereignty, but the Michaels choose to experientially *earn* it, thereby retaining the full co-operation of all Paradise personalities attached to the local universe administration. We know of no Michael who ever did otherwise; but they all could, they are truly freewill Sons.

The sovereignty of a Creator Son in a local universe passes through six, perhaps seven, stages of experiential manifestation. These appear in the following order:

1. Initial vicegerent sovereignty — the solitary provisional authority exercised by a Creator Son before the acquirement of personal qualities by the associated Creative Spirit.
2. Conjoint vicegerent sovereignty — the joint rule of the Paradise pair subsequent to the personality achievement of the Universe Mother Spirit.
3. Augmenting vicegerent sovereignty — the advancing authority of a Creator Son during the period of his seven creature bestowals.
4. Supreme sovereignty — the settled authority following the completion of the seventh bestowal. In Nebadon, supreme sovereignty dates from the completion of Michael's bestowal on Urantia. It has existed just slightly over two thousand years of your planetary time.
5. Augmenting supreme sovereignty — the advanced relationship growing out of the settling of a majority of the creature domains in light and life. This stage pertains to the unachieved future of your local universe.
6. Trinitarian sovereignty — exercised subsequent to the settling of the entire local universe in light and life.
7. Unrevealed sovereignty — the unknown relationships of a future universe age.

In accepting the initial vicegerent sovereignty of a projected local universe, a Creator Michael takes an oath to the Trinity not to assume supreme sovereignty until the seven creature bestowals have been completed and certified by the superuniverse rulers. But if a Michael Son could not, at will, assert such unearned sovereignty, there would be no meaning in taking an oath not to do so.

Even in the prebestowal ages a Creator Son rules his domain well-nigh supremely when there is no dissent in any of its parts. Limited rulership would hardly be manifest if sovereignty were never challenged. The sovereignty exercised by a prebestowal Creator Son in a universe without rebellion is no greater than in a universe with rebellion; but in the first instance sovereignty limitations are not apparent; in the second, they are.

If ever the authority or administration of a Creator Son is challenged, attacked, or jeopardized, he is eternally pledged to uphold, protect, defend, and if necessary retrieve his personal creation. Such Sons can be troubled or harassed only by the creatures of their own making or by higher beings of their own choosing. It might be inferred that "higher beings," those of origin on levels above a local universe, would be unlikely to trouble a Creator Son, and this is true. But they could if they chose to. Virtue is volitional with personality; righteousness is not automatic in freewill creatures.

Before the completion of the bestowal career a Creator Son rules with certain self-imposed limitations of sovereignty, but subsequent to his finished bestowal service he rules by virtue of his actual experience in the form and likeness of his manifold creatures. When a Creator has seven times sojourned among his creatures, when the bestowal career is finished, then is he supremely settled in universe authority; he has become a Master Son, a sovereign and supreme ruler.

The technique of obtaining supreme sovereignty over a local universe involves the following seven experiential steps:

1. Experientially to penetrate seven creature levels of being through the technique of incarnated bestowal in the very likeness of the creatures on the level concerned.
2. To make an experiential consecration to each phase of the sevenfold will of Paradise Deity as it is personified in the Seven Master Spirits.
3. To traverse each of the seven experiences on the creature levels simultaneously with the execution of one of the seven consecrations to the will of Paradise Deity.
4. On each creature level, experientially to portray the acme of creature life to Paradise Deity and to all universe intelligences.
5. On each creature level, experientially to reveal one phase of the sevenfold will of Deity to the bestowal level and to all the universe.
6. Experientially to unify the sevenfold creature experience with the

sevenfold experience of consecration to the revelation of the nature and will of Deity.

7. To achieve new and higher relationship with the Supreme Being. The repercussion of the totality of this Creator-creature experience augments the superuniverse reality of God the Supreme and the time-space sovereignty of the Almighty Supreme and factualizes the supreme local universe sovereignty of a Paradise Michael.

In settling the question of sovereignty in a local universe, the Creator Son is not only demonstrating his own fitness to rule but is also revealing the nature and portraying the sevenfold attitude of the Paradise Deities. The finite understanding and creature appreciation of the Father's primacy is concerned in the adventure of a Creator Son when he condescends to take upon himself the form and experiences of his creatures. These primary Paradise Sons are the real revealers of the Father's loving nature and beneficent authority, the same Father who, in association with the Son and the Spirit, is the universal head of all power, personality, and government throughout all the universal realms.

4. THE MICHAEL BESTOWALS

There are seven groups of bestowal Creator Sons, and they are so classified in accordance with the number of times they have bestowed themselves upon the creatures of their realms. They range from the initial experience up through five additional spheres of progressive bestowal until they attain the seventh and final episode of creature-Creator experience.

Avonal bestowals are always in the likeness of mortal flesh, but the seven bestowals of a Creator Son involve his appearing on seven creature levels of being and pertain to the revelation of the seven primary expressions of the will and nature of Deity. Without exception, all Creator Sons pass through this seven times giving of themselves to their created children before they assume settled and supreme jurisdiction over the universes of their own creation.

Though these seven bestowals vary in the different universes, they always embrace the mortal-bestowal adventure. In the final bestowal a Creator Son appears as a member of one of the mortal races on some inhabited world. Only once in his sevenfold career as a bestowal Son is a Paradise Michael born of woman as you have the record of the babe of Bethlehem. Only once does he live and die as a member of the lowest order of evolutionary will creatures.

After each of his bestowals a Creator Son proceeds to the "right hand of the Father," there to gain the Father's acceptance of the bestowal and to receive instruction preparatory to the next episode of universe service. Following the seventh and final bestowal a Creator Son receives from the Universal Father supreme authority and jurisdiction over his universe.

It is of record that the divine Son of last appearance on your planet was a Paradise Creator Son who had completed six phases of his bestowal career; consequently, when he gave up the conscious grasp of the incarnated life on Urantia, he could, and did, truly say, "It is finished" — it was literally finished. His death on Urantia completed his bestowal career; it was the last step in fulfilling the sacred oath of a Paradise Creator Son. And when this experience has been acquired, such Sons are supreme universe sovereigns; no longer do they rule as vicegerents of the Father but in their own right and name as "King of Kings and Lord of Lords." With certain stated exceptions these sevenfold bestowal Sons are unqualifiedly supreme in the universes of their abode. Concerning his local universe, "all power in heaven and on earth" was relegated to this triumphant and enthroned Master Son.

Creator Sons, subsequent to the completion of their bestowal careers, are reckoned as a separate order, sevenfold Master Sons. In person the Master Sons are identical with the Creator Sons, but they have undergone such a unique bestowal experience that they are commonly regarded as a different order. When a Creator deigns to effect a bestowal, a real and permanent change is destined to take place. True, the bestowal Son is still and none the less a Creator, but he has added to his nature the experience of a creature, which forever removes him from the divine level of a Creator Son and elevates him to the experiential plane of a Master Son, one who has fully earned the right to rule a universe and administer its worlds. Such beings embody all that can be secured from divine parentage and embrace everything to be derived from perfected-creature experience. Why should man bemoan his lowly origin and enforced evolutionary career when the very Gods must pass through an equivalent experience before they are accounted experientially worthy and competent finally and fully to rule over their universe domains!

5. RELATION OF MASTER SONS TO THE UNIVERSE

The power of a Master Michael is unlimited because derived from experienced association with the Paradise Trinity, is unquestioned because derived from actual experience as the very creatures subject to such authority. The nature of the sovereignty of a sevenfold Creator Son is supreme because it:

1. Embraces the sevenfold viewpoint of Paradise Deity.
2. Embodies a sevenfold attitude of time-space creatures.
3. Perfectly synthesizes Paradise attitude and creature viewpoint.

This experiential sovereignty is thus all-inclusive of the divinity of God the Sevenfold culminating in the Supreme Being. And the personal sovereignty of a sevenfold Son is like the future sovereignty of the sometime-to-be-completed Supreme Being, embracing as it does the fullest possible content of the power and authority of the Paradise Trinity manifestable within the time-space limits concerned.

With the achievement of supreme local universe sovereignty, there passes from a Michael Son the power and opportunity to create entirely new types of creature beings during the present universe age. But a Master Son's loss of power to originate entirely new orders of beings in no way interferes with the work of life elaboration already established and in process of unfoldment; this vast program of universe evolution goes on without interruption or curtailment. The acquirement of supreme sovereignty by a Master Son implies the responsibility of personal devotion to the fostering and the administering of that which has already been designed and created, and of that which will subsequently be produced by those who have been thus designed and created. In time there may develop an almost endless evolution of diverse beings, but no entirely new pattern or type of intelligent creature will henceforth take direct origin from a Master Son. This is the first step, the beginning, of a settled administration in any local universe.

The elevation of a sevenfold bestowal Son to the unquestioned sovereignty of his universe means the beginning of the end of agelong uncertainty and relative confusion. Subsequent to this event, that which cannot be sometime spiritualized will eventually be disorganized; that which cannot be sometime co-ordinated with cosmic reality will eventually be destroyed. When the provisions of endless mercy and nameless patience have been exhausted in an effort to win the loyalty and devotion of the will creatures of the realms, justice and righteousness will prevail. That which mercy cannot rehabilitate justice will eventually annihilate.

The Master Michaels are supreme in their own local universes when once they have been installed as sovereign rulers. The few limitations upon their rule are those inherent in the cosmic pre-existence of certain forces and personalities. Otherwise these Master Sons are supreme in authority, responsibility, and administrative power in their respective universes; they are as Creators and Gods, supreme in virtually all things. There is no penetration beyond their wisdom regarding the functioning of a given universe.

After his elevation to settled sovereignty in a local universe a Paradise Michael is in full control of all other Sons of God functioning in his domain, and he may freely rule in accordance with his concept of the needs of his realms. A Master Son may at will vary the order of the spiritual adjudication and evolutionary adjustment of the inhabited planets. And such Sons do make and carry out the plans of their own choosing in all matters of special planetary needs, in particular regarding the worlds of their creature sojourn and still more concerning the realm of terminal bestowal, the planet of incarnation in the likeness of mortal flesh.

The Master Sons seem to be in perfect communication with their bestowal worlds, not only the worlds of their personal sojourn but all worlds whereon a Magisterial Son has bestowed himself. This contact is maintained by their own spiritual presence, the Spirit of Truth, which they are able to "pour out upon all flesh." These Master Sons also maintain an unbroken connection with the Eternal Mother Son at the center of all things. They possess a sympathetic reach which extends from the Universal Father on high to the lowly races of planetary life in the realms of time.

6. DESTINY OF THE MASTER MICHAELS

No one may with finality of authority presume to discuss either the natures or the destinies of the sevenfold Master Sovereigns of the local universes; nevertheless, we all speculate much regarding these matters. We are taught, and we believe, that each Paradise Michael is the absolute of the dual deity concepts of his origin; thus he embodies actual phases of the infinity of the Universal Father and the Eternal Son. The Michaels must be partial in relation to total infinity, but they are probably absolute in relation to that part of infinity concerned in their origin. But as we observe their work in the present universe age, we detect no action that is more than finite; any conjectured superfinite capacities must be self-contained and as yet unrevealed.

The completion of the creature-bestowal careers and the elevation to supreme universe sovereignty must signify the completed liberation of a Michael's finite-action capacities accompanied by the appearance of capacity for more-than-finite service. For in this connection we note that such Master Sons are then restricted in the production of new types of creature beings, a restriction undoubtedly made necessary by the liberation of their superfinite potentialities.

It is highly probable that these undisclosed creator powers will remain self-contained throughout the present universe age. But sometime in the far-distant future, in the now mobilizing universes of outer space, we believe that the liaison between a sevenfold Master Son and a seventh-stage Creative Spirit may attain to absonite levels of service attended by the appearance of new things, meanings, and values on transcendental levels of ultimate universe significance.

Just as the Deity of the Supreme is actualizing by virtue of experiential service, so are the Creator Sons achieving the personal realization of the Paradise-divinity potentials bound up in their unfathomable natures. When on Urantia, Christ Michael once said, "I am the way, the truth, and the life."

And we believe that in eternity the Michaels are literally destined to be "the way, the truth, and the life," ever blazing the path for all universe personalities as it leads from supreme divinity through ultimate absonity to eternal deity finality.

[Presented by a Perfector of Wisdom from Uversa.]

PAPER 22
THE TRINITIZED SONS OF GOD

THERE ARE three groups of beings who are called Sons of God. In addition to descending and ascending orders of sonship there is a third group known as the Trinitized Sons of God. The trinitized order of sonship is subdivided into three primary divisions in accordance with the origins of its many types of personalities, revealed and unrevealed. These primary divisions are:

1. Deity-trinitized Sons.
2. Trinity-embraced Sons.
3. Creature-trinitized Sons.

Irrespective of origin all Trinitized Sons of God have in common the experience of trinitization, either as a part of their origin or as an experience of Trinity embrace subsequently attained. The Deity-trinitized Sons are unrevealed in these narratives; therefore will this presentation be confined to a portrayal of the remaining two groups, more particularly the Trinity-embraced sons of God.

1. THE TRINITY-EMBRACED SONS

All Trinity-embraced sons are originally of dual or single origin, but subsequent to the Trinity embrace they are forever devoted to Trinity service and assignment. This corps, as revealed and as organized for superuniverse service, embraces seven orders of personalities:

1. Mighty Messengers.
2. Those High in Authority.
3. Those without Name and Number.
4. Trinitized Custodians.
5. Trinitized Ambassadors.
6. Celestial Guardians.
7. High Son Assistants.

These seven groups of personalities are further classified, according to origin, nature, and function, into three major divisions: the Trinitized Sons of Attainment, the Trinitized Sons of Selection, and the Trinitized Sons of Perfection.

The Trinitized Sons of Attainment — the Mighty Messengers, Those High in Authority, and Those without Name and Number — are all Adjuster-fused ascendant mortals who have attained Paradise and the Corps of the Finality. But they are not finaliters; when they have been Trinity embraced, their names are removed from the finaliter roll call. The new sons of this order pass through specific courses of training, for comparatively short periods, on the circuit headquarters planets of the Havona circuits under the direction of the Eternals of Days. Thereafter they are assigned to the services of the Ancients of Days in the seven superuniverses.

The Trinitized Sons of Selection embrace the Trinitized Custodians and the Trinitized Ambassadors. They are recruited from certain of the evolutionary seraphim and translated midway creatures who have traversed Havona and have attained Paradise, as well as from certain of the Spirit-fused and the Son-fused mortals who have likewise ascended to the central Isle of Light and Life. Subsequent to their embrace by the Paradise Trinity and after a brief training in Havona, the Trinitized Sons of Selection are assigned to the courts of the Ancients of Days.

The Trinitized Sons of Perfection. The Celestial Guardians and their co-ordinates, the High Son Assistants, comprise a unique group of twice-trinitized personalities. They are the creature-trinitized sons of Paradise-Havona personalities or of perfected ascendant mortals who have long distinguished themselves in the Corps of the Finality. Some of these creature-trinitized sons, after service with the Supreme Executives of the Seven Master Spirits and after serving under the Trinity Teacher Sons, are retrinitized (embraced) by the Paradise Trinity and then commissioned to the courts of the Ancients of Days as Celestial Guardians and as High Son Assistants. Trinitized Sons of Perfection are assigned directly to the superuniverse service without further training.

Our Trinity-origin associates — Perfectors of Wisdom, Divine Counselors, and Universal Censors — are of stationary numbers, but the Trinity-embraced sons are constantly increasing. All seven orders of Trinity-embraced sons are commissioned as members of one of the seven superuniverse governments, and the number in the service of each superuniverse is exactly the same; not one has ever been lost. Trinity-embraced beings have never gone astray; they may stumble temporarily, but not one has ever been adjudged in contempt of the superuniverse governments. The Sons of Attainment and the Sons of Selection have never faltered in the service of Orvonton, but the Trinitized Sons of Perfection have sometimes erred in judgment and thereby caused transient confusion.

Under the direction of the Ancients of Days all seven orders function very much as self-governing groups. Their scope of service is far-flung; Trinitized Sons of Perfection do not leave the superuniverse of assignment, but their trinitized associates range the grand universe, journeying from the evolutionary worlds of time and space to the eternal Isle of Paradise. They may function in any of the superuniverses, but they do so always as members of the supergovernment of original designation.

Apparently the Trinity-embraced sons have been permanently assigned to the service of the seven superuniverses; certainly this assignment is for the duration of the present universe age, but we have never been informed that it is to be eternal.

2. THE MIGHTY MESSENGERS

Mighty Messengers belong to the ascendant group of the Trinitized Sons. They are a class of perfected mortals who have been rebellion tested or otherwise equally proved as to their personal loyalty; all have passed through some definite test of universe allegiance. At some time in their Paradise ascent they stood firm and loyal in the face of the disloyalty of their superiors, and some did actively and loyally function in the places of such unfaithful leaders.

With such personal records of fidelity and devotion, these ascending mortals pass on through Havona with the stream of the pilgrims of time, attain Paradise, graduate therefrom, and are mustered into the Corps of the Finality. Thereupon they are trinitized in the secret embrace of the Paradise Trinity and subsequently are commissioned to become associated with the Ancients of Days in the administration of the governments of the seven superuniverses.

Every ascendant mortal of insurrectionary experience who functions loyally in the face of rebellion is eventually destined to become a Mighty Messenger of the superuniverse service. Likewise is any ascendant creature who effectively prevents such upheavals of error, evil, or sin; for action designed to prevent rebellion or to effect higher types of loyalty in a universe crisis is regarded as of even greater value than loyalty in the face of actual rebellion.

The senior Mighty Messengers were chosen from those ascendant mortals of time and space who were among the earlier Paradise arrivals, many having traversed Havona in the times of Grandfanda. But the first trinitizing of Mighty Messengers was not effected until the candidate corps contained representatives from each of the seven superuniverses. And the last group of this order to qualify on Paradise embraced ascendant pilgrims from the local universe of Nebadon. Mighty Messengers are embraced by the Paradise Trinity in classes of seven hundred thousand, one hundred thousand for assignment to each superuniverse.

I am a Mighty Messenger, and it may interest Urantians to know that the companion and associate of my mortal experience was also triumphant in the great test, and that, though we were many times and for long periods separated in the agelong inward ascent to Havona, we were embraced in the same seven-hundred-thousand group, and that we spent our time passing through Vicegerington in close and loving association. We were finally commissioned and together assigned to Uversa of Orvonton, and we are often dispatched in company for the execution of assignments requiring the services of two Messengers.

Mighty Messengers, in common with all Trinity-embraced sons, are assigned to all phases of superuniverse activities. They maintain constant connection with their headquarters through the superuniverse reflectivity service. Mighty Messengers serve in all sectors of a superuniverse and frequently execute missions to the local universes and even to the individual worlds, as I do on this occasion.

In the superuniverse courts, Mighty Messengers act as defenders of both individuals and planets when they come up for adjudication; they also assist the Perfections of Days as advisors in the major sectors. As a group, their chief assignment is that of superuniverse observers. They are stationed on the various headquarters worlds and on individual planets of importance as the official observers of the Ancients of Days. When so assigned, they also serve as advisers to the authorities directing the affairs of the spheres of their sojourn. The Messengers take active part in all phases of the ascendant scheme of mortal progression. With their associates of mortal origin they keep the supergovernments in close and personal touch with the status and progression of the plans of the descending Sons of God.

Mighty Messengers are fully conscious of their entire ascendant careers, and that is why they are such useful and sympathetic ministers, understanding messengers, for service on any world of space and to any creature of time. As soon as you are delivered from the flesh, you will communicate freely and understandingly with us since we spring from all the races on all the evolutionary worlds of space, that is, from those mortal races that are indwelt by, and subsequently fused with, Thought Adjusters.

3. THOSE HIGH IN AUTHORITY

Those High in Authority, the second group of the Trinitized Sons of Attainment, are all Adjuster-fused beings of mortal origin. These are the perfected mortals who have exhibited superior administrative ability and have shown extraordinary executive genius throughout their long ascending careers. They are the cream of governing ability derived from the surviving mortals of space.

Seventy thousand of Those High in Authority are trinitized at each Trinity liaison. Though the local universe of Nebadon is a comparatively young creation, it has representatives among a recently trinitized class of this order. Like all separate orders of celestial beings, they maintain their own headquarters on Uversa, and like the other Trinity-embraced sons, their reserves on Uversa act as the central directing body of their order in Orvonton.

Those High in Authority are administrators without limitation. They are the everywhere-present and always-efficient executives of the Ancients of Days. They serve on any sphere, on any inhabited world, and in any phase of activity in any of the seven superuniverses.

Having superb administrative wisdom and unusual executive skill, these brilliant beings assume to present the cause of justice in behalf of the superuniverse tribunals; they foster the execution of justice and the rectification of misadaptations in the evolutionary universes. Therefore, if you should ever be cited for errors of judgment while you are ascending the worlds and spheres of your ordained cosmic progression, it is hardly likely that you would suffer injustice since your prosecutors would be onetime ascendant creatures who are personally familiar with every step of the career you have traversed and are traversing.

4. THOSE WITHOUT NAME AND NUMBER

Those without Name and Number constitute the third and last group of the Trinitized Sons of Attainment; they are the ascendant souls who have developed the ability to worship beyond the skill of all the sons and daughters of the evolutionary races from the worlds of time and space. They have acquired a spiritual concept of the eternal purpose of the Universal Father which comparatively transcends the comprehension of the evolutionary creatures of name or number; therefore are they denominated Those without Name and Number. More strictly translated, their name would be "Those *above* Name and Number." This order of sons is embraced by the Paradise Trinity in groups of seven thousand.

Since Those without Name and Number are the superior spiritual minds of the survival races, they are especially qualified to sit in judgment and to render opinions when a spiritual viewpoint is desirable, and when experience in the ascendant career is essential to an adequate comprehension of the questions involved in the problem to be adjudicated. They are the supreme jurors of Orvonton. A maladministered jury system may be more or less of a travesty of justice on some worlds, but on Uversa and its extension tribunals we employ the highest type of evolved spiritual mentality as juror-judges. Adjudication is the highest function of any government, and those who are intrusted with verdict rendering should be chosen from the highest and most noble types of the most experienced and understanding individuals.

The selection of candidates for the trinitization classes of Mighty Messengers, Those High in Authority, and Those without Name and Number is inherent and automatic. The selective techniques of Paradise are not in any sense arbitrary. Personal experience and spiritual values determine the personnel of the Trinitized Sons of Attainment. Such beings are equal in authority and uniform in administrative status, but they all possess individuality and diverse characters; they are not standardized beings. All are characteristically different, depending on the differentials of their ascendant careers.

In addition to these experiential qualifications, the Trinitized Sons of Attainment have been trinitized in the divine embrace of the Paradise

Deities. Consequently they function as the co-ordinate associates of the Stationary Sons of the Trinity, for the Trinity embrace does seem to precipitate out of the stream of future time many of the unrealized potentials of creature beings. But this is true concerning only that which pertains to the present universe age.

This group of sons is chiefly, but not wholly, concerned with the services of the ascendant career of the time-space mortals. If the viewpoint of a mortal creature is ever in doubt, the question is settled by appeal to an ascendant commission consisting of a Mighty Messenger, One High in Authority, and One without Name and Number.

You mortals who read this message may yourselves ascend to Paradise, attain the Trinity embrace, and in remote future ages be attached to the service of the Ancients of Days in one of the seven superuniverses, and sometime be assigned to enlarge the revelation of truth to some evolving inhabited planet, even as I am now functioning on Urantia.

5. THE TRINITIZED CUSTODIANS

The Trinitized Custodians are Trinitized Sons of Selection. Not only do your races and other mortals of survival value traverse Havona, attain Paradise, and sometimes find themselves destined to superuniverse service with the Stationary Sons of the Trinity, but your faithful seraphic guardians and your equally faithful midway associates may also become candidates for the same Trinity recognition and superb personality destiny.

Trinitized Custodians are ascendant seraphim and translated midway creatures who have passed through Havona and have attained Paradise and the Corps of the Finality. Subsequently they were embraced by the Paradise Trinity and were assigned to the service of the Ancients of Days.

The candidates for the Trinity embrace from among the ascendant seraphim are accorded this recognition because of their valiant co-operation with some ascendant mortal who attained the Corps of the Finality and was subsequently trinitized. My own seraphic guardian of the mortal career went through with me, was later trinitized, and now is attached to the Uversa government as a Trinitized Custodian.

And so with the midway creatures; many are translated and achieve

Paradise and, along with the seraphim and for the same reasons, are Trinity embraced and commissioned as Custodians in the superuniverses.

The Trinitized Custodians are embraced by the Paradise Trinity in groups of seventy thousand, and one seventh of each group is assigned to a superuniverse. They serve on Uversa and on the headquarter worlds of the universes and the major and minor sectors. In their labors they are assisted by a corps of seconaphim and other able superuniverse personalities.

The Trinitized Custodians start out their careers as custodians, and they continue as such in the affairs of the supergovernments. In a way, they are officers of their superuniverse governments, but they do not deal with individuals, as do the Celestial Guardians. The Trinitized Custodians administer group affairs and foster collective projects. They are the custodians of records, plans, and institutions; they act as the trustees of undertakings, personality groups, ascendant projects, morontia plans, universe projections, and innumerable other enterprises.

6. THE TRINITIZED AMBASSADORS

Trinitized Ambassadors are the second order of the Trinitized Sons of Selection and like their associates, the Custodians, are recruited from two types of ascendant creatures. Not all ascending mortals are Adjuster or Father fused; some are Spirit fused, some are Son fused. Certain of these Spirit- and Son-fused mortals reach Havona and attain Paradise. From among these Paradise ascenders, candidates are selected for the Trinity embrace, and from time to time they are trinitized in classes of seven thousand. They are then commissioned in the superuniverses as Trinitized Ambassadors of the Ancients of Days.

Trinitized Ambassadors are selected for the Trinity embrace upon the advices of their Havona teachers. They represent the superior minds of their respective groups and are, therefore, best qualified to assist the superuniverse rulers in understanding and in administering the interests of those worlds from which the Spirit-fused mortals hail. The Son-fused Ambassadors are of great assistance in our dealings with problems involving the Son-fused order of personality.

Trinitized Ambassadors are the emissaries of the Ancients of Days for any and all purposes, to any and all worlds or universes within the superuniverse of their assignment. They render particular and important services on the headquarters of the minor sectors, and they perform the numberless miscellaneous assignments of a superuniverse. They are the emergency or reserve corps of the Trinitized Sons of the supergovernments, and they are therefore available for a great range of duties. They engage in thousands upon thousands of undertakings in superuniverse affairs which it is impossible to portray to human minds since there is nothing transpiring on Urantia that is in any way analogous to these activities.

7. TECHNIQUE OF TRINITIZATION

I cannot fully unfold to the material mind the experience of the supreme creative performance of perfect and perfected spiritual beings — the act of trinitization. The techniques of trinitization are among the secrets of Vicegerington and Solitarington and are revealable to, and understandable by, none save those who have passed through these unique experiences. Therefore is it beyond the possibility of any being successfully to portray to the human mind the nature and purport of this extraordinary transaction.

Aside from the Deities, only Paradise-Havona personalities and certain members of each of the finaliter corps engage in trinitization. Under specialized conditions of Paradise perfection, these superb beings may embark upon the unique adventure of concept-identity, and they are many times successful in the production of a new being, a creature-trinitized son.

The glorified creatures who engage in such adventures of trinitization may participate in only one such experience, whereas with the Paradise Deities there seems to be no limit to the continued enactment of trinitization episodes. Deity seems to be limited in just one respect: There can be only one Original and Infinite Spirit, only one infinite executive of the united will of the Father-Son.

The ascendant Adjuster-fused mortal finaliters who have attained certain levels of Paradise culture and spiritual development are among those who can essay to trinitize a creature being. Mortal-finaliter companies, when stationed on Paradise, are granted a recess every millennium of Havona time. There are seven different ways such finaliters may elect to spend this duty-free period, and one of these is, in association with some fellow finaliter or some Paradise-Havona personality, to attempt the enactment of creature trinitization.

If two mortal finaliters, on going before the Architects of the Master Universe, demonstrate that they have independently chosen an identical concept for trinitization, the Architects are empowered, on their own discretion, to promulgate mandates permitting these glorified mortal ascenders to extend their recess and to remove themselves for a time to the trinitizing sector of the Paradise Citizens. At the end of this assigned retreat, if they report that they have singly and jointly elected to make the paradisiacal effort to spiritualize, idealize, and actualize a selected and original concept which has not theretofore been trinitized, then does Master Spirit Number Seven issue orders authorizing such an extraordinary undertaking.

Unbelievably long periods of time are sometimes consumed in these adventures; an age seems to pass before these faithful and determined onetime mortals — and sometimes Paradise-Havona personalities — finally achieve their goal, really succeed in bringing their chosen concept of universal truth into actual being. And not always do these devoted couples meet with success; many times they fail, and that through no discoverable error on their part. Candidates for trinitization who thus fail are admitted to a special group of finaliters who are designated as beings who have made the supreme effort and sustained the supreme disappointment. When the Paradise Deities unite to trinitize, they always succeed, but not so with a homogeneous pair of creatures, the attempted union of two members of the same order of being.

When a new and original being is trinitized by the Gods, the divine parents are in deity potential unchanged; but when exalted creature beings enact such a creative episode, one of the contracting and participating individuals undergoes a unique personality modification. The two ancestors of a creature-trinitized son become in a certain sense spiritually as one. We believe that this status of bi-unification of certain spiritual phases of personality will probably prevail until such time as the Supreme Being shall have attained full and completed manifestation of personality in the grand universe.

Simultaneously with the appearance of a new creature-trinitized son, there occurs this functional spiritual union of the two ancestors; the two trinitizing parents become one on the ultimate functional level. No created being in the universe can fully explain this amazing phenomenon; it is a near-divine experience. When the Father and the Son united to eternalize the Infinite Spirit, upon the accomplishment of their purpose they immediately became as one and ever since have been one. And while the trinitization union of two creatures is on the order of the infinite scope of the perfect Deity union of the Universal Father and the Eternal Son, the repercussions of creature trinitization are not eternal in nature; they will terminate upon the completed factualization of the experiential Deities.

While these parents of creature-trinitized sons become as one in their universe assignments, they continue to be reckoned as two personalities in the make-up and roll calls of the Corps of the Finality and of the Architects of the Master Universe. During the current universe age, all trinitization-united parents are inseparable in assignment and function; where one goes the other goes, what one does the other does. If parental bi-unification involves a mortal (or other) finaliter and a Paradise-Havona personality, the united parental beings function neither with the Paradisers, Havoners, nor finaliters. Such mixed unions forgather in a special corps made up of similar beings. And in all trinitization unions, mixed or otherwise, the parental beings are conscious of, and can communicate with, each other, and they can perform duties that neither could have previously discharged.

The Seven Master Spirits have authority to sanction the trinitizing union of finaliters and Paradise-Havona personalities, and such mixed liaisons are always successful. The resultant magnificent creature-trinitized sons are representative of concepts unsuited to the comprehension of either the eternal creatures of Paradise or the time creatures of space; hence they become the wards of the Architects of the Master Universe. These trinitized sons of destiny embody ideas, ideals, and experience which apparently pertain to a future universe age and are therefore of no immediate practical value to either the super- or central universe administrations. These unique sons of the children of time and the citizens of eternity are all held in reserve on Vicegerington, where they are engaged in the study of the concepts of time and the realities of eternity in a special sector of the sphere occupied by the secret colleges of the corps of the Creator Sons.

The Supreme Being is the unification of three phases of Deity reality: God the Supreme, the spiritual unification of certain finite aspects of the Paradise Trinity; the Almighty Supreme, the power unification of the grand universe Creators; and the Supreme Mind, the individual contribution of the Third Source and Center and his co-ordinates to the reality of the Supreme Being. In their trinitization adventures the superb creatures of the central universe and Paradise are engaged in a threefold exploration of the Deity of the Supreme which results in the production of three orders of creature-trinitized sons:

1. *Ascender-trinitized Sons.* In their creative efforts the finaliters are attempting to trinitize certain conceptual realities of the Almighty Supreme which they have experientially acquired in their ascension through time and space to Paradise.

2. *Paradise-Havona-trinitized Sons.* The creative efforts of the Paradise Citizens and the Havoners result in the trinitization of certain high spiritual aspects of the Supreme Being which they have experientially acquired on a supersupreme background bordering on the Ultimate and the Eternal.

3. *Trinitized Sons of Destiny.* But when a finaliter and a Paradise-Havoner together trinitize a new creature, this conjoint effort repercusses in certain phases of the Supreme-Ultimate Mind. The resulting creature-trinitized sons are supercreational; they represent actualities of Supreme-Ultimate Deity which have not been otherwise experientially attained, and which, therefore, automatically fall within the province of the Architects of the Master Universe, custodians of those things which transcend the creational limits of the present universe age. The trinitized sons of destiny embody certain aspects of the unrevealed master universe function of the Supreme-Ultimate. We do not know a great deal about these conjoint children of time and eternity, but we know much more than we are permitted to reveal.

8. THE CREATURE-TRINITIZED SONS

In addition to the creature-trinitized sons considered in this narrative, there are numerous unrevealed orders of creature-trinitized beings — the diverse progeny of the multiple liaisons of seven finaliter corps and Paradise-Havona personalities. But all these creature-trinitized beings, revealed and unrevealed, are endowed with personality by the Universal Father.

When new ascender-trinitized and Paradise-Havona-trinitized sons are young and untrained, they are usually dispatched for long periods of service on the seven Paradise spheres of the Infinite Spirit, where they serve under the tutelage of the Seven Supreme Executives. Subsequently they may be adopted for further training in the local universes by the Trinity Teacher Sons.

These adopted sons of high and glorified creature origin are the apprentices, student helpers, of the Teacher Sons, and as regards classification they are often temporarily numbered with these Sons. They may and do execute many noble assignments in self-denial in behalf of their chosen realms of service.

The Teacher Sons in the local universes may nominate their creature-trinitized wards for embrace by the Paradise Trinity. Emerging from this embrace as Trinitized Sons of Perfection, they enter the service of the Ancients of Days in the seven superuniverses, that being the present known destiny of this unique group of twice-trinitized beings.

Not all creature-trinitized sons are Trinity embraced; many become the associates and ambassadors of the Seven Master Spirits of Paradise, of the Reflective Spirits of the superuniverses, and of the Mother Spirits of the local creations. Others may accept special assignments on the eternal Isle. Still others may enter the special services on the secret worlds of the Father and on the Paradise spheres of the Spirit. Eventually many find their way into the conjoint corps of the Trinitized Sons on the inner circuit of Havona.

Excepting the Trinitized Sons of Perfection and those who are forgathering on Vicegerington, the supreme destiny of all creature-trinitized sons appears to be entrance into the Corps of Trinitized Finaliters, one of the seven Paradise Corps of the Finality.

9. THE CELESTIAL GUARDIANS

Creature-trinitized sons are embraced by the Paradise Trinity in classes of seven thousand. These trinitized offspring of perfected humans and of Paradise-Havona personalities are all equally embraced by the Deities, but they are assigned to the superuniverses in accordance with the advice of their former instructors, the Trinity Teacher Sons. Those of more acceptable service are commissioned High Son Assistants; those of less distinguished performance are designated Celestial Guardians.

When these unique beings have been Trinity embraced, they become valuable adjuncts to the superuniverse governments. They are versed in the affairs of the ascendant career, not by personal ascension, but as a result of their service with the Trinity Teacher Sons on the worlds of space. The High Son Assistants are chiefly assigned to aid the Perfections of Days on the headquarters of the major sectors and are ably assisted by a corps of ascendant Son-fused mortals.

The Celestial Guardians are the officers of the courts of the Ancients of Days, functioning as court messengers and as bearers of the summonses and decisions of the various tribunals of the superuniverse governments. They are the apprehending agents of the Ancients of Days; they go forth from Uversa to bring back beings whose presence is required before the superuniverse judges; they execute the mandates for the detention of any personality in the superuniverse. They also accompany Spirit-fused mortals of the local universes when, for any reason, their presence is required on Uversa.

The Celestial Guardians and their associates, the High Son Assistants, have never been indwelt by Adjusters. Neither are they Spirit nor Son fused. The embrace of the Paradise Trinity does, however, compensate for the nonfused status of the Trinitized Sons of Perfection. The Trinity embrace may act solely upon the idea which is personified in a creature-trinitized son, leaving the embraced son otherwise unchanged, but such a limitation occurs only when so planned.

These twice-trinitized sons are marvelous beings, but they are neither as versatile nor dependable as their ascendant associates; they lack that tremendous and profound personal experience which the rest of the sons belonging to this group have acquired by actually climbing up to glory from the dark domains of space. We of the ascendant career love them and do all in our power to compensate their deficiencies, but they make us ever grateful for our lowly origin and our capacity for experience. Their willingness to recognize and acknowledge their deficiencies in the experiencible realities of universe ascension is transcendently beautiful and sometimes most touchingly pathetic.

Trinitized Sons of Perfection are limited in contrast to other Trinity-embraced sons because their experiential capacity is time-space inhibited. They are experience-deficient, despite long training with the Supreme Executives and the Teacher Sons, and if this were not the case, experiential saturation would preclude their being left in reserve for acquiring experience in a future universe age. There is simply nothing in all universal existence which can take the place of actual personal experience, and these creature-trinitized sons are held in reserve for experiential function in some future universe epoch.

On the mansion worlds I have often seen these dignified officers of the high courts of the superuniverse look so longingly and appealingly at even the recent arrivals from the evolutionary worlds of space that one could not help realizing that these possessors of nonexperiential trinitization really envied their supposedly less fortunate brethren who ascend the universal path by steps of bona fide experience and actual living. Notwithstanding their handicaps and limitations they are a wonderfully useful and ever-willing corps of workers when it comes to the execution of the complex administrative plans of the superuniverse governments.

10. HIGH SON ASSISTANTS

The High Son Assistants are the superior group of the retrinitized trinitized sons of glorified ascendant beings of the Mortal Corps of the Finality and of their eternal associates, the Paradise-Havona personalities. They are assigned to the superuniverse service and function as personal aids to the high sons of the governments of the Ancients of Days. They might fittingly be denominated private secretaries. They act, from time to time, as clerks for special commissions and other group associations of the high sons. They serve Perfectors of Wisdom, Divine Counselors, Universal Censors, Mighty Messengers, Those High in Authority, and Those without Name and Number.

If, in discussing the Celestial Guardians, I have seemed to call attention to the limitations and handicaps of these twice-trinitized sons, let me now, in all fairness, call attention to their one point of great strength, the attribute which makes them almost invaluable to us. These beings owe their very existence to the fact that they are the personification of a single and supreme concept. They are the personality embodiment of some divine idea, some universal ideal, as it has never before been conceived, expressed, or trinitized. And they have subsequently been Trinity embraced; thus they show forth and actually embody the very wisdom of the divine Trinity as concerns the idea-ideal of their personality existence. As far as that particular concept is revealable to the universes, these personalities embody all of everything that any creature or Creator intelligence could possibly conceive, express, or exemplify. *They are that idea personified.*

Can you not see that such living concentrations of a single supreme concept of universe reality would be of untold service to those who are intrusted with the administration of the superuniverses?

Not long since I was directed to head a commission of six — one of each of the high sons — assigned to the study of three problems pertaining to a group of new universes in the south parts of Orvonton. I was made acutely aware of the value of the High Son Assistants when I made requisition on the chief of their order on Uversa for temporary assignment of such secretaries to my commission. The first of our ideas was represented by a High Son Assistant on Uversa, who was forthwith attached to our group. Our second problem was embodied in a High Son Assistant assigned to superuniverse number three. We secured much help from this source through the central universe clearinghouse for the co-ordination and dissemination of essential knowledge, but nothing comparable to the assistance afforded by the actual presence of a personality who is a concept creature-trinitized in supremacy and Deity-trinitized in finality. Concerning our third problem, the records of Paradise disclosed that such an idea had never been creature trinitized.

High Son Assistants are unique and original personalizations of tremendous concepts and stupendous ideals. And as such they are able to impart inexpressible illumination to our deliberations from time to time. When I am acting on some remote assignment out in the universes of space, think what it means, by way of assistance, if I am so fortunate as to have attached to my mission a High Son Assistant who is the fullness of divine concept regarding the very problem I have been sent to attack and solve; and I have repeatedly had this very experience. The only difficulty with this plan is that no superuniverse can have a complete edition of these trinitized ideas; we only get one seventh of these beings; so it is only about one time in seven that we enjoy the personal association of these beings even when the records indicate that the idea has been trinitized.

We could use to great advantage much larger numbers of these beings on Uversa. Because of their value to the superuniverse administrations, we, in every way possible, encourage the pilgrims of space and also the residents of Paradise to attempt trinitization after they have contributed to one another those experiential realities which are essential to the enactment of such creative adventures.

The High Son Assistants serve on universe headquarter worlds and in both the major and minor sectors, even as they function on Uversa. They very often accompany us on our assignments to the remote universes. High Son Assistants are not permanently assigned to any Son or to any commission. They are in constant circulation, serving where the idea or ideal which they *are* can best further the eternal purposes of the Paradise Trinity, whose sons they have become.

They are touchingly affectionate, superbly loyal, exquisitely intelligent, supremely wise — regarding a single idea — and transcendently humble. While they can impart to you the lore of the universe concerning their one idea or ideal, they are also eager to learn and can be observed seeking knowledge and information on hosts of other subjects, even from the ascending mortals.

And this is the narrative of the origin, nature, and functioning of certain of those who are called the Trinitized Sons of God, more particularly of those who have passed through the divine embrace of the Paradise Trinity, and who have then been assigned to the services of the superuniverses, there to give wise and understanding co-operation with the administrators of the Ancients of Days in their untiring efforts to facilitate the inward progress of the ascending mortals of time toward their immediate Havona destination and their eventual Paradise goal.

[Narrated by a Mighty Messenger of the revelatory corps of Orvonton.]

PAPER 23
THE SOLITARY MESSENGERS

Solitary Messengers are the personal and universal corps of the Conjoint Creator; they are the first and senior order of the Higher Personalities of the Infinite Spirit. They represent the initial creative action of the Infinite Spirit in solitary function for the purpose of bringing into existence solitary personality spirits. Neither the Father nor the Son directly participated in this stupendous spiritualization.

These spirit messengers were personalized in a single creative episode, and their number is stationary. Although I have one of these extraordinary beings associated with me on this present mission, I do not know how many such personalities exist in the universe of universes.

1. NATURE AND ORIGIN OF SOLITARY MESSENGERS

Immediately following the creation of the Seven Spirits of the Havona Circuits the Infinite Spirit brought into being the vast corps of Solitary Messengers. There is no part of the universal creation which is pre-existent to the Solitary Messengers except Paradise and the Havona circuits; they have functioned throughout the grand universe from near eternity. They are fundamental to the divine technique of the Infinite Spirit for self-revelation to, and personal contact with, the far-flung creations of time and space.

Notwithstanding that these messengers are existent from the near times of eternity, they are all aware of a beginning of selfhood. They are conscious of time, being the first of the creation of the Infinite Spirit to possess such a time consciousness. They are the first-born creatures of the Infinite Spirit to be personalized in time and spiritualized in space.

These solitary spirits came forth in the dawn of time as full-fledged and perfectly endowed spirit beings. They are all equal, and there are no classes or subdivisions founded on personal variation. Their classifications are based wholly on the type of work to which they are assigned from time to time.

Mortals start out as well-nigh material beings on the worlds of space and ascend inward towards the Great Centers; these solitary spirits start out at the center of all things and crave assignment to the remote creations, even to the individual worlds of the outermost local universes and even on beyond.

Though denominated Solitary Messengers, they are not lonesome spirits, for they truly like to work alone. They are the only beings in all creation who can and do enjoy a solitary existence, albeit they equally enjoy association with the very few orders of universe intelligence with whom they can fraternize.

Solitary Messengers are not isolated in their service; they are constantly in touch with the wealth of the intellect of all creation as they are capable of "listening in" on all the broadcasts of the realms of their sojourn. They can also intercommunicate with members of their own immediate corps, those beings doing the same kind of work in the same superuniverse. They could communicate with others of their number, but they have been directed by the council of the Seven Master Spirits not to do so, and they are a loyal group; they do not disobey or default. There is no record that a Solitary Messenger ever stumbled into darkness.

The Solitary Messengers, like the Universe Power Directors, are among the very few types of beings operating throughout the realms who are exempt from apprehension or detention by the tribunals of time and space. They could be cited to appear before no one except the Seven Master Spirits, but not in all the annals of the master universe has this Paradise council ever been called upon to adjudicate the case of a Solitary Messenger.

These messengers of solitary assignment are a dependable, self-reliant, versatile, thoroughly spiritual, and broadly sympathetic group of created beings derived from the Third Source and Center; they operate by the authority of the Infinite Spirit resident on the central Isle of Paradise and as personalized on the headquarters spheres of the local universes. They are constant partakers of the direct circuit emanating from the Infinite Spirit, even when they function in the local creations under the immediate influence of the local universe Mother Spirits.

There is a technical reason why these Solitary Messengers must travel and work alone. For short periods and when stationary, they can collaborate in a group, but when thus ensembled, they are altogether cut off from the sustenance and direction of their Paradise circuit; they are wholly isolated. When in transit, or when operating in the circuits of space and the currents of time, if two or more of this order are in close proximity, both or all are thrown out of liaison with the higher circulating forces. They are "short circuited" as you might describe it in illustrative symbols. Therefore they have inherent within them a power of automatic alarm, a warning signal, which unerringly operates to apprise them of approaching conflicts and unfailingly keeps them sufficiently separated as not to interfere with their proper and effective functioning. They also possess inherent and automatic powers which detect and indicate the proximity of both the Inspired Trinity Spirits and the divine Thought Adjusters.

These messengers possess no power of personality extension or reproduction, but there is practically no work of the universes in which they cannot engage, and to which they cannot contribute something essential and helpful. Especially are they the great timesavers for those who are concerned in the administration of universe affairs; and they assist us all, from the highest to the lowest.

2. ASSIGNMENTS OF SOLITARY MESSENGERS

Solitary Messengers are not permanently attached to any individual or group of celestial personalities. They are on duty, always by assignment, and during such service they work under the immediate supervision of those who direct the realms of their attachment. Among themselves they have neither organization nor government of any kind; they are Solitary Messengers.

Solitary Messengers are assigned by the Infinite Spirit to the following seven divisions of service:

1. Messengers of the Paradise Trinity.
2. Messengers of the Havona Circuits.
3. Messengers of the Superuniverses.
4. Messengers of the Local Universes.
5. Explorers of Undirected Assignment.
6. Ambassadors and Emissaries of Special Assignment.
7. Revelators of Truth.

These spirit messengers are in every sense interchangeable from one type of service to another; such transfers are constantly taking place. There are no separate orders of Solitary Messengers; they are spiritually alike and in every sense equal. While they are generally designated by number, they are known to the Infinite Spirit by personal names. They are known to the rest of us by the name or number designative of their current assignment.

1. *Messengers of the Paradise Trinity.* I am not permitted to reveal much of the work of the group of messengers assigned to the Trinity. They are the trusted and secret servants of the Deities, and when intrusted with special messages which involve the unrevealed policies and future conduct of the Gods, they have never been known to divulge a secret or betray the confidence reposed in their order. And all this is related in this connection, not to appear boastful of their perfection, but rather to point out that the Deities can and do create *perfect* beings.

The confusion and turmoil of Urantia do not signify that the Paradise

Rulers lack either interest or ability to manage affairs differently. The Creators are possessed of full power to make Urantia a veritable paradise, but such an Eden would not contribute to the development of those strong, noble, and experienced characters which the Gods are so surely forging out on your world between the anvils of necessity and the hammers of anguish. Your anxieties and sorrows, your trials and disappointments, are just as much a part of the divine plan on your sphere as are the exquisite perfection and infinite adaptation of all things to their supreme purpose on the worlds of the central and perfect universe.

2. *Messengers of the Havona Circuits.* Throughout the ascendant career you will be vaguely, but increasingly, able to detect the presence of the Solitary Messengers, but not until you reach Havona will you recognize them unmistakably. The first of the messengers you will see face to face will be those of the Havona circuits.

Solitary Messengers enjoy special relations with the natives of the Havona worlds. These messengers, who are so functionally handicapped when associating with one another, can and do have a very close and personal communion with the Havona natives. But it is quite impossible to convey to human minds the supreme satisfactions consequent upon the contact of the minds of these divinely perfect beings with the spirits of such near-transcendent personalities.

3. *Messengers of the Superuniverses.* The Ancients of Days, those personalities of Trinity origin who preside over the destinies of the seven superuniverses, those trios of divine power and administrative wisdom, are bountifully supplied with Solitary Messengers. It is only through this order of messengers that the triune rulers of one superuniverse can directly and personally communicate with the rulers of another. Solitary Messengers are the only available type of spirit intelligence — aside, possibly, from the Inspired Trinity Spirits — that can be dispatched from the headquarters of one superuniverse directly to the headquarters of another. All other personalities must make such excursions by way of Havona and the executive worlds of the Master Spirits.

There are some kinds of information which cannot be obtained either by Gravity Messengers, reflectivity, or broadcast. And when the Ancients of

Days would certainly know these things, they must dispatch a Solitary Messenger to the source of knowledge. Long before the presence of life on Urantia the messenger now associated with me was assigned on a mission out of Uversa to the central universe — was absent from the roll calls of Orvonton for almost a million years but returned in due time with the desired information.

There is no limitation upon the service of Solitary Messengers in the superuniverses; they may function as executioners of the high tribunals or as intelligence gatherers for the good of the realm. Of all the supercreations they most delight to serve in Orvonton because here the need is greatest and the opportunities for heroic effort are greatly multiplied. In the more needy realms we all enjoy the satisfaction of a more replete function.

4. *Messengers of the Local Universes.* In the services of a local universe there is no limit upon the functioning of the Solitary Messengers. They are the faithful revealers of the motives and intent of the local universe Mother Spirit, although they are under the full jurisdiction of the reigning Master Son. And this is true of all messengers operating in a local universe, whether they are traveling out directly from universe headquarters, or whether they are acting temporarily in liaison with Constellation Fathers, System Sovereigns, or Planetary Princes. Before the concentration of all power in the hands of a Creator Son at the time of his elevation as sovereign ruler of his universe, these messengers of the local universes function under the general direction of the Ancients of Days and are immediately responsible to their resident representative, the Union of Days.

5. *Explorers of Undirected Assignment.* When the reserve corps of the Solitary Messengers is overrecruited, there issues from one of the Seven Supreme Power Directors a call for exploration volunteers; and there is never a lack of volunteers, for they delight to be dispatched as free and untrammeled explorers, to experience the thrill of finding the organizing nucleuses of new worlds and universes.

They go forth to investigate the clues furnished by the space contemplators of the realms. Undoubtedly the Paradise Deities know of the existence of these undiscovered energy systems of space, but they never divulge such information. If the Solitary Messengers did not explore and chart these newly organizing energy centers, such phenomena would long remain unnoticed even by the intelligences of adjacent realms.

These messenger-explorers of undirected assignment patrol the master universe. They are constantly out on exploring expeditions to the uncharted regions of all outer space. Very much of the information which we possess of transactions in the realms of outer space, we owe to the explorations of the Solitary Messengers as they often work and study with the celestial astronomers.

6. *Ambassadors and Emissaries of Special Assignment.* Local universes situated within the same superuniverse customarily exchange ambassadors selected from their native orders of sonship. But to avoid delay, Solitary Messengers are frequently asked to go as ambassadors from one local creation to another, to represent and interpret one realm to another.

When it develops that it will require too much time for a native ambassador to reach a far-distant local universe, a Solitary Messenger is often asked to proceed there immediately to act as ambassador ad interim. Solitary Messengers can go in very short order, not independently of time and space as do the Gravity Messengers, but nearly so. They also serve in other circumstances as emissaries of special assignment.

7. *Revelators of Truth.* The Solitary Messengers regard the assignment to reveal truth as the highest trust of their order. And they function ever and anon in this capacity, from the superuniverses to the individual planets of space. They are frequently attached to commissions which are sent to enlarge the revelation of truth to the worlds and systems.

3. TIME AND SPACE SERVICES OF SOLITARY MESSENGERS

The Solitary Messengers are the highest type of perfect and confidential personality available in all realms for the quick transmission of important and urgent messages when it is inexpedient to utilize either the broadcast service or the reflectivity mechanism. They serve in an endless variety of assignments, helping out the spiritual and material beings of the realms, particularly where the element of time is involved. Of all orders assigned to the services of the superuniverse domains, they are the highest and most versatile personalized beings who can come so near to defying time and space.

The universe is well supplied with spirits who utilize gravity for purposes of transit; they can go anywhere any time — instanter — but they are not persons. Certain other gravity traversers are personal beings, such as Gravity Messengers and Transcendental Recorders, but they are not available to the super- and the local universe administrators. The worlds teem with angels and men and other highly personal beings, but they are handicapped by time and space: The limit of velocity for most nonenseraphimed beings is 186,280 miles of your world per second of your time; the midway creatures and certain others can, often do, attain double velocity — 372,560 miles per second — while the seraphim and others can traverse space at triple velocity, about 558,840 miles per second. There are, however, no transit or messenger personalities who function between the instantaneous velocities of the gravity traversers and the comparatively slow speeds of the seraphim, except the Solitary Messengers.

Solitary Messengers are, therefore, generally used for dispatch and service in those situations where personality is essential to the achievement of the assignment, and where it is desired to avoid the loss of time which would be occasioned by the sending of any other readily available type of personal messenger. They are the only definitely personalized beings who can synchronize with the combined universal currents of the grand universe. Their velocity in traversing space is variable, depending on a great variety of interfering influences, but the record shows that on the journey to fulfill this mission my associate messenger proceeded at the rate of 841,621,642,000 of your miles per second of your time.

It is wholly beyond my ability to explain to the material type of mind how a spirit can be a real person and at the same time traverse space at such tremendous velocities. But these very Solitary Messengers actually come to, and go from, Urantia at these incomprehensible speeds; indeed, the whole economy of universal administration would be largely deprived of its personal element were this not a fact.

The Solitary Messengers are able to function as emergency lines of communication throughout remote space regions, realms not embraced within the established circuits of the grand universe. It develops that one messenger, when so functioning, can transmit a message or send an impulse through space to a fellow messenger about one hundred light-years away as Urantia astronomers estimate stellar distances.

Of the myriads of beings who co-operate with us in the conduct of the affairs of the superuniverse, none are more important in practical helpfulness and timesaving assistance. In the universes of space we must reckon with the handicaps of time; hence the great service of the Solitary Messengers, who, by means of their personal prerogatives of communication, are somewhat independent of space and, by virtue of their tremendous transit velocities, are so nearly independent of time.

I am at a loss to explain to Urantia mortals how the Solitary Messengers can be without form and yet possess real and definite personalities. Although they are without that form which would naturally be associated with personality, they do possess a spirit presence which is discernible by all higher types of spirit beings. The Solitary Messengers are the only class of beings who seem to be possessed of well-nigh all the advantages of a formless spirit coupled with all the prerogatives of a full-fledged personality. They are true persons, yet endowed with nearly all of the attributes of impersonal spirit manifestation.

In the seven superuniverses, ordinarily — but not always — everything which tends to increase any creature's liberation from the handicaps of time and space proportionately diminishes personality prerogatives. Solitary Messengers are an exception to this general law. They are in their activities all but unrestricted in the utilization of any and all of the limitless avenues of spiritual expression, divine service, personal ministry, and cosmic communication. If you could view these extraordinary beings in the light of my experience in universe administration, you would comprehend how difficult it would be to co-ordinate superuniverse affairs were it not for their versatile co-operation.

No matter how much the universe may enlarge, no more Solitary Messengers will probably ever be created. As the universes grow, the expanded work of administration must be increasingly borne by other types of spirit ministers and by those beings who take origin in these new creations, such as the creatures of the Sovereign Sons and the local universe Mother Spirits.

4. SPECIAL MINISTRY OF SOLITARY MESSENGERS

The Solitary Messengers seem to be personality co-ordinators for all types of spirit beings. Their ministry helps to make all the personalities of the far-flung spiritual world akin. They contribute much to the development, in all spirit beings, of a consciousness of group identity. Every type of spirit being is served by special groups of Solitary Messengers who foster the ability of such beings to understand and fraternize with all other types and orders, however dissimilar.

The Solitary Messengers demonstrate such an amazing ability to co-ordinate all types and orders of finite personality — even to make contact with the absonite regime of the master universe overcontrollers — that some of us postulate that the creation of these messengers by the Infinite Spirit is in some manner related to the Conjoint Actor's bestowal of Supreme-Ultimate Mind.

When a finaliter and a Paradise Citizen co-operate in the trinitization of a "child of time and eternity" — a transaction involving the unrevealed mind potentials of the Supreme-Ultimate — and when such an unclassified personality is dispatched to Vicegerington, a Solitary Messenger (a conjectured personality repercussion of the bestowal of such deity mind) is always assigned as guardian-companion to such a creature-trinitized son. This messenger accompanies the new son of destiny to the world of his assignment and nevermore leaves Vicegerington. When thus attached to the destinies of a child of time and eternity, a Solitary Messenger is forever transferred to the sole supervision of the Architects of the Master Universe. What the future of such an extraordinary association may be, we do not know. For ages these partnerships of unique personalities have continued to forgather on Vicegerington, but not even a single pair has ever gone forth therefrom.

Solitary Messengers are of stationary numbers, but the trinitization of the sons of destiny is apparently an unlimited technique. Since each trinitized son of destiny has assigned to him a Solitary Messenger, it appears to us that at some time in the remote future the supply of messengers will become exhausted. Who will take up their work in the grand universe? Will their service be assumed by some new development among the Inspired Trinity Spirits? Is the grand universe at some remote period going to be more nearly administered by Trinity-origin beings while the single- and dual-origin creatures move on into the realms of outer space? If the messengers return to their former service, will these sons of destiny accompany them? Will the trinitizations between finaliters and Paradise-Havoners cease when the supply of Solitary Messengers has been absorbed as guardian-companions of these sons of destiny? Are all our efficient Solitary Messengers going to be concentrated on Vicegerington? Are these extraordinary spirit personalities going to be eternally associated with these trinitized sons of unrevealed destiny? What significance should we attach to the fact that these couples forgathering on Vicegerington are under the exclusive direction of those mighty mystery beings, the Architects of the Master Universe? These and many similar questions we ask ourselves, and ask numerous other orders of celestial beings, but we do not know the answers.

This transaction, together with many similar occurrences in universe administration, unmistakably indicates that the personnel of the grand universe, even that of Havona and Paradise, is undergoing a definite and certain reorganization in co-ordination with, and with reference to, the vast energy evolutions now taking place throughout the realms of outer space.

We incline to the belief that the eternal future will witness phenomena of universe evolution which will far transcend all that the eternal past has experienced. And we anticipate such tremendous adventures, even as you should, with keen relish and ever-heightening expectation.

[Presented by a Divine Counselor from Uversa.]

PAPER 24
HIGHER PERSONALITIES OF THE INFINITE SPIRIT

ON UVERSA we divide all personalities and entities of the Conjoint Creator into three grand divisions: the Higher Personalities of the Infinite Spirit, the Messenger Hosts of Space, and the Ministering Spirits of Time, those spirit beings who are concerned with teaching and ministering to the will creatures of the ascendant scheme of mortal progression.

Those Higher Personalities of the Infinite Spirit that find mention in these narratives function throughout the grand universe in seven divisions:

1. Solitary Messengers.
2. Universe Circuit Supervisors.
3. Census Directors.
4. Personal Aids of the Infinite Spirit.
5. Associate Inspectors.
6. Assigned Sentinels.
7. Graduate Guides.

Solitary Messengers, Circuit Supervisors, Census Directors, and the Personal Aids are characterized by the possession of tremendous endowments of antigravity. The Solitary Messengers are without known general headquarters; they roam the universe of universes. The Universe Circuit Supervisors and the Census Directors maintain headquarters on the capitals of the superuniverses. The Personal Aids of the Infinite Spirit are stationed on the central Isle of Light. The Associate Inspectors and the Assigned Sentinels are respectively stationed on the capitals of the local universes and on the capitals of their component subunits. The Graduate Guides are resident in the Havona universe and function on all its billion worlds. Most of these higher personalities have stations in the local universes, but they are not organically attached to the administrations of the evolutionary realms.

Of the seven classes composing this group, only the Solitary Messengers and perhaps the Personal Aids range the universe of universes. Solitary Messengers are encountered from Paradise outward: through the Havona circuits to the superuniverse capitals and thence out to the local universes, and even to the inhabited worlds. Although Solitary Messengers belong to the Higher Personalities of the Infinite Spirit, their origin, nature, and service have been discussed in the preceding paper.

1. THE UNIVERSE CIRCUIT SUPERVISORS

The vast power currents of space and the circuits of spirit energy may seem to operate automatically; they may appear to function without let or hindrance, but such is not the case. All these stupendous systems of energy are under control; they are subject to intelligent supervision. Universe Circuit Supervisors are concerned, not with the realms of purely physical or material energy — the domain of the Universe Power Directors — but with the circuits of relative spiritual energy and with those modified circuits which are essential to the maintenance of both the highly developed spiritual beings and the morontia or transition type of intelligent creatures. The supervisors do not give origin to circuits of energy and superessence of divinity, but in general they have to do with all higher spirit circuits of time and eternity and with all relative spirit circuits concerned in the administration of the component parts of the grand universe. They direct and manipulate all such spirit-energy circuits outside the Isle of Paradise.

Universe Circuit Supervisors are the exclusive creation of the Infinite

Spirit, and they function solely as the agents of the Conjoint Actor. They are personalized for service in the following four orders:

1. Supreme Circuit Supervisors.
2. Associate Circuit Supervisors.
3. Secondary Circuit Supervisors.
4. Tertiary Circuit Supervisors.

The supreme supervisors of Havona and the associate supervisors of the seven superuniverses are of completed numbers; no more of these orders are being created. The supreme supervisors are seven in number and are stationed on the pilot worlds of the seven Havona circuits. The circuits of the seven superuniverses are in the charge of a marvelous group of seven associate supervisors, who maintain headquarters on the seven Paradise spheres of the Infinite Spirit, the worlds of the Seven Supreme Executives. From here they supervise and direct the circuits of the superuniverses of space.

On these Paradise spheres of the Spirit the seven associate circuit supervisors and the first order of the Supreme Power Centers effect a liaison which, under the direction of the Supreme Executives, results in the sub-Paradise co-ordination of all material and spiritual circuits passing out to the seven superuniverses.

On the headquarters worlds of each superuniverse are stationed the secondary supervisors for the local universes of time and space. Secondary supervisors are being created right along; from time to time they appear in groups of seventy on the worlds of the Supreme Executives. We obtain them on requisition as we arrange for the establishment of separate circuits of spirit energy and liaison power to the newly evolving universes of our jurisdiction.

A tertiary circuit supervisor functions on the headquarters world of every local universe. This order, like the secondary supervisors, is of continuous creation, being created in groups of seven hundred. They are assigned to the local universes by the Ancients of Days.

Circuit supervisors are created for their specific tasks, and they eternally serve in the groups of their original assignment. They are not rotated in service and hence make an agelong study of the problems found in the realms of their original assignment. For example: Tertiary circuit supervisor No. 572,842 has functioned on Salvington since the early concept of your local universe, and he is a member of the personal staff of Michael of Nebadon.

Whether acting in the local or higher universes, circuit supervisors direct all concerned as to the proper circuits to employ for the transmission of all spirit messages and for the transit of all personalities. In their work of circuit supervision these efficient beings utilize all agencies, forces, and personalities in the universe of universes. They employ the unrevealed "high spirit personalities of circuit control" and are ably assisted by numerous staffs composed of personalities of the Infinite Spirit. It is they who would isolate an evolutionary world if its Planetary Prince should rebel against the Universal Father and his vicegerent Son. They are able to throw any world out of certain universe circuits of the higher spiritual order, but they cannot annul the material currents of the power directors.

The Universe Circuit Supervisors have something of the same relationship to spirit circuits that the Universe Power Directors have to material circuits. The two orders are complemental, together having the oversight of all spirit and all material circuits that are controllable and manipulatable by creatures.

The circuit supervisors exercise certain oversight of those mind circuits which are spirit associated much as the power directors have certain jurisdiction over those phases of mind which are physical-energy associated — mechanical mind. In general the functions of each order are expanded by liaison with the other, but the circuits of pure mind are subject to the supervision of neither. Neither are the two orders co-ordinate; in all their manifold labors the Universe Circuit Supervisors are subject to the Seven Supreme Power Directors and their subordinates.

While the circuit supervisors are entirely alike within their respective orders, they are all distinct individuals. They are truly personal beings, but they possess a type of other-than-Father-endowed personality not encountered in any other type of creature in all universal existence.

Although you will recognize and know them as you journey inward towards Paradise, you will have no personal relations with them. They are circuit supervisors, and they attend strictly and efficiently to their business. They deal solely with those personalities and entities having the oversight of those activities which are concerned with the circuits subject to their supervision.

2. THE CENSUS DIRECTORS

Notwithstanding that the cosmic mind of the Universal Intelligence is cognizant of the presence and whereabouts of all *thinking* creatures, there is operative in the universe of universes an independent method of keeping count of all will creatures.

The Census Directors are a special and completed creation of the Infinite Spirit, and they exist in numbers unknown to us. They are so created as to be able to maintain perfect synchrony with the reflectivity technique of the superuniverses, while at the same time they are personally sensitive and responsive to intelligent will. These directors, by a not-fully-understood technique, are made immediately aware of the birth of will in any part of the grand universe. They are, therefore, always competent to give us the number, nature, and whereabouts of all will creatures in any part of the central creation and the seven superuniverses. But they do not function on Paradise; there is no need for them there. On Paradise knowledge is inherent; the Deities know all things.

Seven Census Directors operate in Havona, one being stationed on the pilot world of each Havona circuit. Excepting these seven and the reserves of the order on the Paradise worlds of the Spirit, all Census Directors function under the jurisdiction of the Ancients of Days.

One Census Director presides at the headquarters of each superuniverse, while subject to such a chief director are an enormous number of other directors, one on the capital of every local universe. All personalities of this order are equal excepting those on the Havona pilot worlds and the seven superuniverse chiefs.

In the seventh superuniverse the chief of all Orvonton directors is Usatia. Like the other superuniverse chiefs, he is not directly attuned to the registration of intelligent will. He is solely attuned to his subordinates stationed in the Orvonton universes; thus he acts as a magnificent totaling personality for their reports coming in from the capitals of the local creations.

From time to time the official recorders of Uversa place on their records the status of the superuniverse as it is indicated by the registrations in and upon the personality of Usatia. Such census data is indigenous to the superuniverses; these reports are transmitted neither to Havona nor to Paradise.

The Census Directors are concerned with human beings — as with other will creatures — only to the extent of recording the fact of will function. They are not concerned with the records of your life and its doings; they are not in any sense recording personalities. The Census Director of Nebadon, now stationed on Salvington, is at this very moment personally conscious and aware of your living presence here on Urantia; and he will afford the records confirmation of your death the moment you cease to function as a will creature.

Census Directors register the existence of a new will creature when the first act of will is performed; they indicate the death of a will creature when the last act of will takes place. The partial emergence of will observed in the reactions of certain of the higher animals does not belong to the domain of the Census Directors. They keep count of nothing but bona fide will creatures, and they are responsive to nothing but *will function.* Exactly how they register the function of will, we do not know.

These beings always have been, and always will be, Census Directors. They would be comparatively useless in any other division of universe labor. But they are infallible in function; they never default, neither do they falsify. And notwithstanding their marvelous powers and unbelievable prerogatives, they are persons; they have recognizable spirit presence and form.

3. PERSONAL AIDS OF THE INFINITE SPIRIT

We have no authentic knowledge as to the time or manner of the creation of the Personal Aids. Their number must be legion, but it is not of record on Uversa. We hold the opinion that the Infinite Spirit is not limited as to numbers in the creation of these Personal Aids.

The Personal Aids of the Infinite Spirit exist for the exclusive assistance of the Paradise presence of the Third Person of Deity. Although attached directly to the Infinite Spirit and located on Paradise, they flash to and fro to the uttermost parts of creation. Wherever the circuits of the Conjoint Creator extend, there these Personal Aids may appear for the purpose of executing the bidding of the Infinite Spirit. They traverse space much as do the Solitary Messengers but are not persons in the sense that the messengers are.

The Personal Aids are all equal and identical; they disclose no differentiation of individuality. Though the Conjoint Actor looks upon them as true personalities, it is difficult for others to regard them as real persons; they do not manifest a spirit presence to other spirit beings. Paradise-origin beings are always aware of the proximity of these Aids; but we do not recognize a personality presence. The lack of such a presence-form undoubtedly renders them all the more serviceable to the Third Person of Deity.

Of all the revealed orders of spirit beings taking origin in the Infinite Spirit, the Personal Aids are about the only ones you will not encounter on your inward ascent to Paradise.

4. THE ASSOCIATE INSPECTORS

The Seven Supreme Executives, on the seven Paradise spheres of the Infinite Spirit, collectively function as the administrative board of supermanagers for the seven superuniverses. The Associate Inspectors are the personal embodiment of the authority of the Supreme Executives to the local universes of time and space. These high observers of the affairs of the local creations are the joint offspring of the Infinite Spirit and the Seven Master Spirits of Paradise.

Associate Inspectors work under the direct supervision of the Seven Supreme Executives, being their personal and powerful representatives to the local universes of time and space. An inspector is stationed on the headquarters sphere of each local creation and is a close associate of the resident Union of Days.

The Associate Inspectors receive reports and recommendations only from their subordinates, the Assigned Sentinels, stationed on the capitals of the local systems of inhabited worlds, while they make reports only to their immediate superior, the Supreme Executive of the superuniverse concerned.

5. THE ASSIGNED SENTINELS

The Assigned Sentinels are co-ordinating personalities and liaison representatives of the Seven Supreme Executives. They were personalized on Paradise by the Infinite Spirit and were created for the specific purposes of their assignment.

Much as an Associate Inspector represents the Seven Supreme Executives to a whole local universe, so in each of the systems of that local creation there is an Assigned Sentinel, who acts as the direct representative of the far-distant and supreme board of supercontrol for the affairs of all seven superuniverses. The sentinels on duty in the local system governments of Orvonton are acting under the direct authority of Supreme Executive Number Seven, the co-ordinator of the seventh superuniverse. But in their administrative organization all sentinels commissioned in a local universe are subordinate to the Associate Inspector stationed at universe headquarters.

Within a local creation the Assigned Sentinels serve in rotation, being transferred from system to system. They are usually changed every millennium of local universe time. They are among the highest ranking personalities stationed on a system capital, but they never participate in deliberations concerned with system affairs. In the local systems they serve as the ex officio heads of the four and twenty administrators hailing from the evolutionary worlds, but otherwise, ascending mortals have little contact with them. The sentinels are almost exclusively concerned in keeping the Associate Inspector of their universe fully informed on all matters relating to the welfare and state of the systems of their assignment.

Assigned Sentinels and Associate Inspectors do not report to the Supreme Executives through a superuniverse headquarters. They are responsible solely to the Supreme Executive of the superuniverse concerned; their activities are distinct from the administration of the Ancients of Days.

The Supreme Executives, Associate Inspectors, and Assigned Sentinels, together with the omniaphim and a host of unrevealed personalities, constitute an efficient, direct, centralized, but far-flung system of advisory and administrative co-ordination of all the grand universe of things and beings.

6. THE GRADUATE GUIDES

The Graduate Guides, as a group, sponsor and conduct the high university of technical instruction and spiritual training which is so essential to mortal attainment of the goal of the ages: God, rest, and then eternity of perfected service. These highly personal beings take their name from the nature and purpose of their work. They are exclusively devoted to the tasks of guiding the mortal graduates from the superuniverses of time through the Havona course of instruction and training which serves to prepare the ascending pilgrims for admission to Paradise and the Corps of the Finality.

I am not forbidden to undertake to tell you of the work of these Graduate Guides, but it is so ultraspiritual that I despair of being able to adequately portray to the material mind a concept of their manifold activities. On the mansion worlds, after your vision range is extended and you are freed from the fetters of material comparisons, you can begin to comprehend the meaning of those realities which "eye cannot see nor ear hear, and which have never entered the concept of human minds," even those things which "God has prepared for those who love such eternal verities." You are not always to be so limited in the range of your vision and spiritual comprehension.

The Graduate Guides are engaged in piloting the pilgrims of time through the seven circuits of Havona worlds. The guide who greets you upon your arrival on the receiving world of the outer Havona circuit will remain with you throughout your entire career on the heavenly circuits. Though you will associate with countless other personalities during your sojourn on a billion worlds, your Graduate Guide will follow you to the end of your Havona progression and will witness your entrance into the terminal slumber of time, the sleep of eternity transit to the Paradise goal, where, upon awakening, you will be greeted by the Paradise Companion assigned to welcome you and perhaps to remain with you until you are initiated as a member of the Mortal Corps of the Finality.

The number of Graduate Guides is beyond the power of human minds to grasp, and they continue to appear. Their origin is something of a mystery. They have not existed from eternity; they mysteriously appear as they are needed. There is no record of a Graduate Guide in all the realms of the central universe until that far-distant day when the first mortal pilgrim of all time made his way to the outer belt of the central creation. The instant he arrived on the pilot world of the outer circuit, he was met with friendly greetings by Malvorian, the first of the Graduate Guides and now the chief of their supreme council and the director of their vast educational organization.

On the Paradise records of Havona, in the section denominated "Graduate Guides," there appears this initial entry:

"And Malvorian, the first of this order, did greet and instruct the pilgrim discoverer of Havona and did conduct him from the outer circuits of initial experience, step by step and circuit by circuit, until he stood in the very presence of the Source and Destiny of all personality, subsequently crossing the threshold of eternity to Paradise."

At that far-distant time I was attached to the service of the Ancients of Days on Uversa, and we all rejoiced in the assurance that, eventually, pilgrims from our superuniverse would reach Havona. For ages we had been taught that the evolutionary creatures of space would attain Paradise, and the thrill of all time swept through the heavenly courts when the first pilgrim actually arrived.

The name of this pilgrim discoverer of Havona is *Grandfanda*, and he hailed from planet 341 of system 84 in constellation 62 from the first large stabilized galaxy of local universe 1,131 situated in superuniverse number one. His arrival was the signal for the establishment of the broadcast service of the universe of universes. Theretofore only the broadcasts of the superuniverses and the local universes had been in operation, but the announcement of the arrival of Grandfanda at the portals of Havona signalized the inauguration of the "space reports of glory," so named because the initial universe broadcast reported the Havona arrival of the first of the evolutionary beings to attain entrance upon the goal of ascendant existence.

Graduate Guides never leave the Havona worlds; they are dedicated to the service of the graduate pilgrims of time and space. And you will sometime meet these noble beings face to face if you do not reject the certain and all-perfected plan designed to effect your survival and ascension.

7. ORIGIN OF THE GRADUATE GUIDES

Though evolution is not the order of the central universe, we believe that the Graduate Guides are the perfected or more experienced members of another order of central universe creatures, the Havona Servitals. Graduate Guides show such a breadth of sympathy and such a capacity for understanding the ascendant creatures that we are convinced they have gained this culture by actual service in the superuniverse realms as the Havona Servitals of universal ministry. If this view is not correct, how then can we account for the continuous disappearance of the senior or more experienced servitals?

A servital will be long absent from Havona on superuniverse assignment, having been on many such missions previously, will return home, be granted the privilege of "personal contact" with the Paradise Central Shining, will be embraced by the Luminous Persons, and disappear from the recognition of his spirit fellows, never more to reappear among those of his kind.

On returning from superuniverse service, a Havona Servital may enjoy numerous divine embraces and emerge therefrom merely an exalted servital. Experiencing the luminous embrace does not necessarily signify that the servital must translate into a Graduate Guide, but almost one quarter of those who achieve the divine embrace never return to the service of the realms.

There appears on the high records a succession of such entries as this:

"And servital number 842,842,682,846,782 of Havona, named Sudna, came over from the superuniverse service, was received on Paradise, knew the Father, entered the divine embrace, and is not."

When such an entry appears on the records, the career of such a servital is closed. But in just three moments (a little less than three days of your time) a newborn Graduate Guide "spontaneously" appears on the outer circuit of the Havona universe. And the number of Graduate Guides, allowing for a slight difference, due no doubt to those in transition, exactly equals the number of vanished servitals.

There is an additional reason for supposing the Graduate Guides to be evolved Havona Servitals, and that is the unfailing tendency of these guides and their associated servitals to form such extraordinary attachments. The manner in which these supposedly separate orders of beings understand and sympathize with one another is wholly inexplicable. It is refreshing and inspiring to witness their mutual devotion.

The Seven Master Spirits and the associated Seven Supreme Power Directors, respectively, are the personal repositories of the mind potential and of the power potential of the Supreme Being which he does not, as yet, operate personally. And when these Paradise associates collaborate to create the Havona Servitals, the latter are inherently involved in certain phases of Supremacy. Havona Servitals are thus, in actuality, a reflection in the perfect central universe of certain evolutionary potentialities of the time-space domains, all of which is disclosed when a servital undergoes transformation and re-creation. We believe that this transformation takes place in response to the will of the Infinite Spirit, undoubtedly acting in behalf of the Supreme. Graduate Guides are not created by the Supreme Being, but we all conjecture that experiential Deity is in some way concerned in those transactions which bring these beings into existence.

The Havona now traversed by ascending mortals differs in many respects from the central universe as it was before the times of Grandfanda. The arrival of mortal ascenders on the Havona circuits inaugurated sweeping modifications in the organization of the central and divine creation, modifications undoubtedly initiated by the Supreme Being — the God of evolutionary creatures — in response to the arrival of the first of his experiential children from the seven superuniverses. The appearance of the Graduate Guides, together with the creation of the tertiary supernaphim, is indicative of these performances of God the Supreme.

[Presented by a Divine Counselor of Uversa.]

PAPER 25
THE MESSENGER HOSTS OF SPACE

RANKING INTERMEDIATELY in the family of the Infinite Spirit are the Messenger Hosts of Space. These versatile beings function as the connecting links between the higher personalities and the ministering spirits. The messenger hosts include the following orders of celestial beings:

1. Havona Servitals.
2. Universal Conciliators.
3. Technical Advisers.
4. Custodians of Records on Paradise.
5. Celestial Recorders.
6. Morontia Companions.
7. Paradise Companions.

Of the seven groups enumerated, only three — servitals, conciliators, and Morontia Companions — are created as such; the remaining four represent attainment levels of the angelic orders. In accordance with inherent nature and attained status, the messenger hosts variously serve in the universe of universes but always subject to the direction of those who rule the realms of their assignment.

1. THE HAVONA SERVITALS

Though denominated servitals, these "midway creatures" of the central universe are not servants in any menial sense of the word. In the spiritual world there is no such thing as menial work; all service is sacred and exhilarating; neither do the higher orders of beings look down upon the lower orders of existence.

The Havona Servitals are the joint creative work of the Seven Master Spirits and their associates, the Seven Supreme Power Directors. This creative collaboration comes the nearest to being the pattern for the long list of reproductions of the dual order in the evolutionary universes, extending from the creation of a Bright and Morning Star by a Creator Son-Creative Spirit liaison down to sex procreation on worlds like Urantia.

The number of servitals is prodigious, and more are being created all the time. They appear in groups of one thousand on the third moment following the assembly of the Master Spirits and the Supreme Power Directors at their joint area in the far northerly sector of Paradise. Every fourth servital is more physical in type than the others; that is, out of each thousand, seven hundred and fifty are apparently true to spirit type, but two hundred and fifty are semiphysical in nature. These *fourth creatures* are somewhat on the order of material beings (material in the Havona sense), resembling the physical power directors more than the Master Spirits.

In personality relationships the spiritual is dominant over the material, even though it does not now so appear on Urantia; and in the production of Havona Servitals the law of spirit dominance prevails; the established ratio yields three spiritual beings to one semiphysical.

The newly created servitals, together with newly appearing Graduate Guides, all pass through the courses of training which the senior guides continuously conduct on each of the seven Havona circuits. Servitals are then assigned to the activities for which they are best adapted, and since they are of two types — spiritual and semiphysical — there are few limits to the range of work these versatile beings can do. The higher or spirit groups are assigned selectively to the services of the Father, the Son, and the Spirit, and to the work of the Seven Master Spirits. In large numbers they are dispatched, from time to time, to serve on the study worlds encircling the headquarters spheres of the seven superuniverses, the worlds devoted to the final training and spiritual culture of the ascending souls of time who are preparing for advancement to the circuits of Havona. Both spirit servitals and their more physical fellows are also designated assistants and associates of the Graduate Guides in helping and instructing the various orders of ascending creatures who have attained Havona, and who seek to attain Paradise.

The Havona Servitals and the Graduate Guides manifest a transcendent devotion to their work and a touching affection for one another, an affection which, while spiritual, you could only understand by comparison with the phenomenon of human love. There is divine pathos in the separation of the servitals from the guides, as so often occurs when the servitals are dispatched on missions beyond the limits of the central universe; but they go with joy and not with sorrow. The satisfying joy of high duty is the eclipsing emotion of spiritual beings. Sorrow cannot exist in the face of the consciousness of divine duty faithfully performed. And when man's ascending soul stands before the Supreme Judge, the decision of eternal import will not be determined by material successes or quantitative achievements; the verdict reverberating through the high courts declares: "Well done, good and faithful servant; you have been faithful over a few essentials; you shall be made ruler over universe realities."

On superuniverse service the Havona Servitals are always assigned to that domain presided over by the Master Spirit whom they most resemble in general and special spirit prerogatives. They serve only on the educational worlds surrounding the capitals of the seven superuniverses. They engage in an endless variety of activities in connection with the work of these educational worlds comprising the superuniversities of the superuniverse of Orvonton. Here they are your companions; they have come down from your next career to study you and to inspire you with the reality and certainty of your eventual graduation from the universes of time to the realms of eternity. And in these contacts the servitals gain that preliminary experience of ministering to the ascending creatures of time which is so helpful in their subsequent work on the Havona circuits as associates of the

Graduate Guides or — as translated servitals — as Graduate Guides themselves.

2. THE UNIVERSAL CONCILIATORS

For every Havona Servital created, seven Universal Conciliators are brought into being, one in each superuniverse. This creative enactment involves a definite superuniverse technique of reflective response to transactions taking place on Paradise.

On the headquarters worlds of the seven superuniverses there function the seven reflections of the Seven Master Spirits. It is difficult to undertake to portray the natures of these Reflective Spirits to material minds. They are true personalities; still each member of a superuniverse group is perfectly reflective of just one of the Seven Master Spirits. And every time the Master Spirits associate themselves with the power directors for the purpose of creating a group of Havona Servitals, there is a simultaneous focalization upon one of the Reflective Spirits in each of the superuniverse groups, and forthwith and full-fledgedly an equal number of Universal Conciliators appear on the headquarters worlds of the supercreations. If, in the creation of servitals, Master Spirit Number Seven should take the initiative, none but the Reflective Spirits of the seventh order would become pregnant with conciliators; and concurrently with the creation of one thousand Orvontonlike servitals, one thousand of the seventh-order conciliators would appear on each superuniverse capital. Out of these episodes, reflecting the sevenfold nature of the Master Spirits, arise the seven created orders of conciliators serving in each superuniverse.

Conciliators of pre-Paradise status do not serve interchangeably between superuniverses, being restricted to their native segments of creation. Every superuniverse corps, embracing one seventh of each created order, therefore spends a very long time under the influence of one of the Master Spirits to the exclusion of the others, for, while all seven are *reflected* on the superuniverse capitals, only one is *dominant* in each supercreation.

Each of the seven supercreations is actually pervaded by that one of the Master Spirits who presides over its destinies. Each superuniverse thus becomes like a gigantic mirror reflecting the nature and character of the supervising Master Spirit, and all of this is further continued in every subsidiary local universe by the presence and function of the Creative Mother Spirits. The effect of such an environment upon evolutionary growth is so profound that in their postsuperuniverse careers the conciliators collectively manifest forty-nine experiential viewpoints, or insights, each angular — hence incomplete — but all mutually compensatory and together tending to encompass the circle of Supremacy.

In each superuniverse the Universal Conciliators find themselves strangely and innately segregated into groups of four, associations in which they continue to serve. In each group, three are spirit personalities, and one, like the fourth creatures of the servitals, is a semimaterial being. This quartet constitutes a conciliating commission and is made up as follows:

1. *The Judge-Arbiter.* The one unanimously designated by the other three as the most competent and best qualified to act as judicial head of the group.

2. *The Spirit-Advocate.* The one appointed by the judge-arbiter to present evidence and to safeguard the rights of all personalities involved in any matter assigned to the adjudication of the conciliating commission.

3. *The Divine Executioner.* The conciliator qualified by inherent nature to make contact with the material beings of the realms and to execute the decisions of the commission. Divine executioners, being fourth creatures — quasi-material beings — are almost, but not quite, visible to the short-range vision of the mortal races.

4. *The Recorder.* The remaining member of the commission automatically becomes the recorder, the clerk of the tribunal. He makes certain that all records are properly prepared for the archives of the superuniverse and for the records of the local universe. If the commission is serving on an evolutionary world, a third report, with the assistance of the executioner, is prepared for the physical records of the system government of jurisdiction.

When in session a commission functions as a group of three since the advocate is detached during adjudication and participates in the formulation of the verdict only at the conclusion of the hearing. Hence these commissions are sometimes called referee trios.

The conciliators are of great value in keeping the universe of universes running smoothly. Traversing space at the seraphic rate of triple velocity, they serve as the traveling courts of the worlds, commissions devoted to the quick adjudication of minor difficulties. Were it not for these mobile and eminently fair commissions, the tribunals of the spheres would be hopelessly overspread with the minor misunderstandings of the realms.

These referee trios do not pass upon matters of eternal import; the soul, the eternal prospects of a creature of time, is never placed in jeopardy by their acts. Conciliators do not deal with questions extending beyond the temporal existence and the cosmic welfare of the creatures of time. But when a commission has once accepted jurisdiction of a problem, its rulings are final and always unanimous; there is no appeal from the decision of the judge-arbiter.

3. THE FAR-REACHING SERVICE OF CONCILIATORS

Conciliators maintain group headquarters on the capital of their superuniverse, where their primary reserve corps is held. Their secondary reserves are stationed on the capitals of the local universes. The younger and less experienced commissioners begin their service on the lower worlds, worlds like Urantia, and are advanced to the adjudication of greater problems after they have acquired riper experience.

The order of conciliators is wholly dependable; not one has ever gone astray. Though not infallible in wisdom and judgment, they are of unquestioned reliability and unerring in faithfulness. They take origin on the headquarters of a superuniverse and eventually return thereto, advancing through the following levels of universe service:

1. *Conciliators to the Worlds.* Whenever the supervising personalities of the individual worlds become greatly perplexed or actually deadlocked concerning the proper procedure under existing circumstances, and if the matter is not of sufficient importance to be brought before the regularly

constituted tribunals of the realm, then, upon the receipt of a petition of two personalities, one from each contention, a conciliating commission will begin to function forthwith.

When these administrative and jurisdictional difficulties have been placed in the hands of the conciliators for study and adjudication, they are supreme in authority. But they will not formulate a decision until all the evidence has been heard, and there is absolutely no limit to their authority to call witnesses from anywhere and everywhere. And while their decisions may not be appealed, sometimes matters so develop that the commission closes its records at a given point, concludes its opinions, and transfers the whole question to the higher tribunals of the realm.

The commissioners' decisions are placed on the planetary records and, if necessary, are put into effect by the divine executioner. His power is very great, and the range of his activities on an inhabited world is very wide. Divine executioners are masterful manipulators of that which is in the interests of that which ought to be. Their work is sometimes carried out for the apparent welfare of the realm, and sometimes their acts on the worlds of time and space are difficult of explanation. Though executing decrees in defiance of neither natural law nor the ordained usages of the realm, they do ofttimes effect their strange doings and enforce the mandates of the conciliators in accordance with the higher laws of the system administration.

2. *Conciliators to the System Headquarters.* From service on the evolutionary worlds these commissions of four are advanced to duty on a system headquarters. Here they have much work to do, and they prove to be the understanding friends of men, angels, and other spirit beings. The referee trios are not so much concerned with personal differences as with group contentions and with misunderstandings arising between different orders of creatures; and on a system headquarters there live both spiritual and material beings, as well as the combined types, such as the Material Sons.

The moment the Creators bring into existence evolving individuals with the power of choice, that moment a departure is made from the smooth working of divine perfection; misunderstandings are certain to arise, and provision for the fair adjustment of these honest differences of viewpoint must be made. We should all remember that the all-wise and all-powerful Creators could have made the local universes just as perfect as Havona. No conciliating commissions need function in the central universe. But the Creators did not choose in their all-wisdom to do this. And while they have produced universes which abound in differences and teem with difficulties, they have likewise provided the mechanisms and the means for composing all these differences and for harmonizing all this seeming confusion.

3. *The Constellation Conciliators.* From service in the systems the conciliators are promoted to the adjudication of the problems of a constellation, taking up the minor difficulties arising between its systems of inhabited worlds. Not many problems developing on the constellation headquarters fall under their jurisdiction, but they are kept busy going from system to system gathering evidence and preparing preliminary statements. If the contention is honest, if the difficulties arise out of sincere differences of opinion and honest diversity of viewpoints, no matter how few persons may be involved, no matter how apparently trivial the misunderstanding, a conciliating commission can always be had to pass upon the merits of the controversy.

4. *Conciliators to the Local Galaxies.* From the constellations the conciliators are advanced to service in the local galaxy. They are of great assistance to the various constellation rulers and the hosts of personalities concerned with the co-ordination and administration of the various constellations as they interact in the affairs of the galaxy.

5. *Conciliators to the universe Minor Sectors.* From the problems of local galaxies the commissioners are advanced to the study of questions arising in the minor sectors of their universe. The farther they ascend inward from the individual planets, the fewer are the material duties of the divine executioner; gradually he assumes a new role of mercy-justice interpreter, at the same time — being quasi-material — keeping the commission as a whole in sympathetic touch with the material aspects of its investigations.

6. *Conciliators to the universe Major Sectors.* The character of the work of the commissioners continues to change as they advance. There is less and less of misunderstanding to adjudicate and more and more of mysterious phenomena to explain and interpret. From stage to stage they are evolving

from arbiters of differences to *explainers of mysteries* — judges evolving into interpretative teachers. Arbiters of those who through ignorance permit difficulties and misunderstandings to arise, they once were; but they are now becoming instructors of those who are sufficiently intelligent and tolerant to avoid clashes of mind and wars of opinions. The higher a creature's education, the more respect he has for the knowledge, experience, and opinions of others.

7. *Conciliators to the Local Universes.* In this larger work of a universe the commissioners are of great assistance to both the Melchizedeks and the Magisterial Sons and to the rulers and the hosts of personalities concerned with the co-ordination and administration of the entire local universe. The different orders of seraphim and other residents of the headquarters spheres of a local universe also avail themselves of the help and decisions of the referee trios.

It is almost impossible to explain the nature of those differences which may arise in the detailed affairs of a system, a constellation, a galaxy, a minor or major sector, or a universe. Difficulties do develop, but they are very unlike the petty trials and travails of material existence as it is lived on the evolutionary worlds.

8. *Conciliators to the Superuniverse.* Here the conciliators become co-ordinate — four mutually understood and perfectly functioning arbiter-teachers. The divine executioner is divested of retributive power and becomes the physical voice of the spirit trio. By this time these counselors and teachers have become expertly familiar with most of the actual problems and difficulties encountered in the conduct of superuniverse affairs. Thus they become wonderful advisers and wise teachers of the ascending pilgrims who are in residence on the educational spheres surrounding the headquarters worlds of the superuniverses.

All conciliators serve under the general supervision of the Ancients of Days and under the immediate direction of the Image Aids until such time as they are advanced to Paradise. During the Paradise sojourn they report to the Master Spirit who presides over the superuniverse of their origin.

From time to time, as the numbers of the superuniverse conciliators increase, they are translated to the council of perfection on Paradise, from which they subsequently emerge as the co-ordinating corps evolved by the Infinite Spirit for the universe of universes, a marvelous group of beings which is constantly increasing in numbers and efficiency. By experiential ascent and Paradise training they have acquired a unique grasp of the emerging reality of the Supreme Being, and they roam the universe of universes on special assignment.

The members of a conciliating commission are never separated. A group of four forever serve together just as they were originally associated. Even in their glorified service they continue to function as quartets of accumulated cosmic experience and perfected experiential wisdom. They are eternally associated as the embodiment of the supreme justice of time and space.

4. TECHNICAL ADVISERS

These legal and technical minds of the spirit world were not created as such. From the early supernaphim and omniaphim, large numbers of the most orderly minds were chosen by the Infinite Spirit as the nucleus of this vast and versatile group. And ever since that far-distant time, actual experience in the application of the laws of perfection to the plans of evolutionary creation has been required of all who aspire to become Technical Advisers.

The Technical Advisers are recruited from the ranks of the following personality orders:

1. The Supernaphim.
2. The Seconaphim.
3. The Tertiaphim.
4. The Omniaphim.
5. The Seraphim.
6. Certain Types of Ascending Mortals.
7. Certain Types of Ascending Midwayers.

Technical Advisers frequently function as individuals but are organized for service and maintain common headquarters on the spheres of assignment in groups of seven. In each group at least five must be of permanent status, while two may be of temporary association. Ascending mortals and ascending midway creatures serve on these advisory commissions while pursuing the Paradise ascent, but they do not enter the regular courses of training for Technical Advisers, nor do they ever become permanent members of the order.

Those mortals and midwayers who serve transiently with the advisers are chosen for such work because of their expertness in the concept of universal law and supreme justice. As you journey toward your Paradise goal, constantly acquiring added knowledge and enhanced skill, you are continuously afforded the opportunity to give out to others the wisdom and experience you have already accumulated; all the way in to Havona you enact the role of a pupil-teacher. You will work your way through the ascending levels of this vast experiential university by imparting to those just below you the new-found knowledge of your advancing career. In the universal regime you are not reckoned as having possessed yourself of knowledge and truth until you have demonstrated your ability and your willingness to impart this knowledge and truth to others.

After long training and actual experience, any of the ministering spirits above the status of cherubim are permitted to receive permanent appointment as Technical Advisers. All candidates voluntarily enter this order of service; but having once assumed such responsibilities, they may not relinquish them. Only the Ancients of Days can transfer these advisers to other activities.

The training of Technical Advisers, begun in the Melchizedek colleges of the local universes, continues to the courts of the Ancients of Days. From this superuniverse training they proceed to the "schools of the seven circles" located on the pilot worlds of the Havona circuits. And from the pilot worlds they are received into the "college of the ethics of law and the technique of Supremacy," the Paradise training school for the perfecting of Technical Advisers.

These advisers are more than legal experts; they are students and teachers of *applied* law, the laws of the universe applied to the lives and destinies of all who inhabit the vast domains of the far-flung creation. As time passes, they become the living law libraries of time and space, preventing endless trouble and needless delays by instructing the personalities of time regarding the forms and modes of procedure most acceptable to the rulers of eternity. They are able so to counsel the workers of space as to enable them to function in harmony with the requirements of Paradise; they are the teachers of all creatures concerning the technique of the Creators.

Such a living library of applied law could not be created; such beings must be evolved by actual experience. The infinite Deities are existential, hence are compensated for lack of experience; they know all even before they experience all, but they do not impart this nonexperiential knowledge to their subordinate creatures.

Technical Advisers are dedicated to the work of preventing delay, facilitating progress, and counseling achievement. There is always a *best* and *right* way to do things; there is always the technique of perfection, a divine method, and these advisers know how to direct us all in the finding of this better way.

These exceedingly wise and practical beings are always closely associated with the service and work of the Universal Censors. The Melchizedeks are provided with an able corps. The rulers of the systems, constellations, galaxies, minor and major sectors, universes, and superuniverses are all bountifully supplied with these technical or legal reference minds of the spiritual world. A special group act as law counselors to the Life Carriers, advising these Sons concerning the extent of permissible departure from the established order of life propagation and otherwise instructing them respecting their prerogatives and latitudes of function. They are the advisers of all classes of beings regarding the proper usages and techniques of all spirit-world transactions. But they do not directly and personally deal with the material creatures of the realms.

Besides counseling regarding legal usages, Technical Advisers are equally devoted to the efficient interpretation of all laws concerning creature beings — physical, mindal, and spiritual. They are available to the Universal Conciliators and to all others who desire to know the truth of law; in other words, to know how the Supremacy of Deity may be depended upon to react in a given situation having factors of an established physical, mindal, and spiritual order. They even essay to elucidate the technique of the Ultimate.

Technical Advisers are selected and tested beings; I have never known one of them to go astray. We have no records on Uversa of their ever having been adjudged in contempt of the divine laws they so effectively interpret and so eloquently expound. There is no known limit to the domain of their service, neither has any been placed upon their progress. They continue as advisers even to the portals of Paradise; the whole universe of law and experience is open to them.

5. THE CUSTODIANS OF RECORDS ON PARADISE

From among the tertiary supernaphim in Havona, certain of the senior chief recorders are chosen as Custodians of Records, as keepers of the formal archives of the Isle of Light, those archives which stand in contrast to the living records of registry in the minds of the custodians of knowledge, sometimes designated the "living library of Paradise."

The recording angels of the inhabited planets are the source of all individual records. Throughout the universes other recorders function regarding both formal records and living records. From Urantia to Paradise, both recordings are encountered: in a local universe, more of the written records and less of the living; on Paradise, more of the living and less of the formal; on Uversa, both are equally available.

Every occurrence of significance in the organized and inhabited creation is a matter of record. While events of no more than local importance find only a local recording, those of wider significance are dealt with accordingly. From the planets, systems, constellations, and galaxies of Nebadon, everything of universe import is posted on Salvington; and from such universe capitals those episodes are advanced to higher recording which pertain to the affairs of the supergovernments. Paradise also has a relevant summary of superuniverse and Havona data; and this historic and cumulative story of the universe of universes is in the custody of these exalted tertiary supernaphim.

While certain of these beings have been dispatched to the superuniverses to serve as Chiefs of Records directing the activities of the Celestial Recorders, not one has ever been transferred from the permanent roll call of their order.

6. THE CELESTIAL RECORDERS

These are the recorders who execute all records in duplicate, making an original spirit recording and a semimaterial counterpart. This they can do because of their peculiar ability simultaneously to manipulate both spiritual and material energy. Celestial Recorders are not created as such; they are ascendant seraphim from the local universes. They are received, classified, and assigned to their spheres of work by the councils of the Chiefs of Records on the headquarters of the seven superuniverses. There also are located the schools for training Celestial Recorders. The school on Uversa is conducted by the Perfectors of Wisdom and the Divine Counselors.

As the recorders advance in universe service, they continue their system of dual recording, thus making their records always available to all classes of beings, from those of the material order to the high spirits of light. In your transition experience, as you ascend from this material world, you will always be able to consult the records of, and to be otherwise conversant with, the history and traditions of your status sphere.

The recorders are a tested and tried corps. Never have I known of the defection of a Celestial Recorder, and never has there been discovered a falsification in their records. They are subjected to a dual inspection, their records being scrutinized by their exalted fellows from Uversa and by the Mighty Messengers, who certify to the correctness of the quasi-physical duplicates of the original spirit records.

The senior or graduate recorders are the superuniverse custodians and forwarders of the sponsored records of time and space. Their permanent headquarters are in the circular abodes surrounding the area of records on Uversa. They never leave the custody of these records to others; as individuals they may be absent, but never in large numbers.

Like those supernaphim who have become Custodians of Records, the corps of Celestial Recorders is of permanent assignment. Once seraphim and supernaphim are mustered into these services, they will respectively remain Celestial Recorders and Custodians of Records until the day of the new and modified administration of the full personalization of God the Supreme.

On Uversa these senior Celestial Recorders can show the records of everything of cosmic import in all Orvonton since the far-distant times of the arrival of the Ancients of Days, while on the eternal Isle the Custodians of Records guard the archives of that realm which testify to the transactions of Paradise since the times of the personification of the Infinite Spirit.

7. THE MORONTIA COMPANIONS

These children of the local universe Mother Spirits are the friends and associates of all who live the ascending morontia life. They are not indispensable to an ascender's real work of creature progression, neither do they in any sense displace the work of the seraphic guardians who often accompany their mortal associates on the Paradise journey. The Morontia Companions are simply gracious hosts to those who are just beginning the long inward ascent. They are also skillful play sponsors and are ably assisted in this work by the reversion directors.

Though you will have earnest and progressively difficult tasks to perform on the morontia training worlds of Nebadon, you will always be provided with regular seasons of rest and reversion. Throughout the journey to Paradise there will always be time for rest and spirit play; and in the career of light and life there is always time for worship and new achievement.

These Morontia Companions are such friendly associates that, when you finally leave the last phase of the morontia experience, as you prepare to embark upon the superuniverse spirit adventure, you will truly regret that these companionable creatures cannot accompany you, but they serve exclusively in the local universes. At every stage of the ascending career all contactable personalities will be friendly and companionable, but not until you meet the Paradise Companions will you find another group so devoted to friendship and companionship.

The work of the Morontia Companions is more fully depicted in those narratives dealing with the affairs of your local universe.

8. THE PARADISE COMPANIONS

The Paradise Companions are a composite or assembled group recruited from the ranks of the seraphim, seconaphim, supernaphim, and omniaphim. Though serving for what you would regard as an extraordinary length of time, they are not of permanent status. When this ministry has been completed, as a rule (but not invariably) they return to those duties they performed when summoned to Paradise service.

Members of the angelic hosts are nominated for this service by the local universe Mother Spirits, by the superuniverse Reflective Spirits, and by Majeston of Paradise. They are summoned to the central Isle and are commissioned as Paradise Companions by one of the Seven Master Spirits. Aside from permanent status on Paradise, this temporary service of Paradise companionship is the highest honor ever conferred upon the ministering spirits.

These selected angels are dedicated to the service of companionship and are assigned as associates to all classes of beings who may chance to be alone on Paradise, chiefly to the ascendant mortals but also to all others who are alone on the central Isle. Paradise Companions have nothing especial to accomplish in behalf of those with whom they fraternize; they are simply companions. Almost every other being you mortals will encounter during your Paradise sojourn — aside from your fellow pilgrims — will have something definite to do with you or for you; but these companions are assigned only to be with you and to commune with you as personality associates. They are often assisted in their ministry by the gracious and brilliant Paradise Citizens.

Mortals come from races that are very social. The Creators well know that it is "not good for man to be alone," and provision is accordingly made for companionship, even on Paradise.

If you, as an ascendant mortal, should reach Paradise in the company of the companion or close associate of your earthly career, or if your seraphic guardian of destiny should chance to arrive with you or were waiting for you, then no permanent companion would be assigned you. But if you arrive alone, a companion will certainly welcome you as you awaken on the Isle of Light from the terminal sleep of time. Even if it is known that you will be accompanied by someone of ascendant association, temporary companions will be designated to welcome you to the eternal shores and to escort you to the reservation made ready for the reception of you and your associates. You may be certain of being warmly welcomed when you experience the resurrection into eternity on the everlasting shores of Paradise.

Reception companions are assigned during the terminal days of the ascenders' sojourn on the last circuit of Havona, and they carefully examine the records of mortal origin and eventful ascent through the worlds of space and the circles of Havona. When they greet the mortals of time, they are already well versed in the careers of these arriving pilgrims and immediately prove to be sympathetic and intriguing companions.

During your prefinaliter sojourn on Paradise, if for any reason you should be temporarily separated from your associate of the ascending career — mortal or seraphic — a Paradise Companion would be forthwith assigned for counsel and companionship. When once assigned to an ascendant mortal of solitary residence on Paradise, the companion remains with this person until he either is rejoined by his ascendant associates or is duly mustered into the Corps of the Finality.

Paradise Companions are assigned in order of waiting except that an ascender is never placed in the charge of a companion whose nature is unlike his superuniverse type. If a Urantia mortal were arriving on Paradise today, there would be assigned to him the first waiting companion either of origin in Orvonton or otherwise of the nature of the Seventh Master Spirit. Hence the omniaphim serve not with the ascendant creatures from the seven superuniverses.

Many additional services are performed by the Paradise Companions: If an ascending mortal should reach the central universe alone and, while traversing Havona, should fail in some phase of the Deity adventure, in due course he would be remanded to the universes of time, and forthwith a call would be made to the reserves of the Paradise Companions. One of this order would be assigned to follow the defeated pilgrim, to be with him and to comfort and cheer him, and to remain with him until he returned to the central universe to resume the Paradise ascent.

If an ascending pilgrim met defeat in the Deity adventure while traversing Havona in the company of an ascending seraphim, the guardian angel of the mortal career, she would elect to accompany her mortal associate. These seraphim always volunteer and are permitted to accompany their long-time mortal comrades back to the service of time and space.

But not so with two closely associated mortal ascenders: If one attains God while the other temporarily fails, the successful individual invariably chooses to go back to the evolutionary creations with the disappointed personality, but this is not permitted. Instead, a call is made to the reserves of the Paradise Companions, and one of the volunteers is selected to accompany the disappointed pilgrim. A volunteer Paradise Citizen then becomes associated with the successful mortal, who tarries on the central Isle awaiting the Havona return of the defeated comrade and in the meantime teaches in certain Paradise schools, presenting the adventurous story of the evolutionary ascent.

[Sponsored by One High in Authority from Uversa.]

PAPER 26
MINISTERING SPIRITS OF THE CENTRAL UNIVERSE

Supernaphim are the ministering spirits of Paradise and the central universe; they are the highest order of the lowest group of the children of the Infinite Spirit — the angelic hosts. Such ministering spirits are to be encountered from the Isle of Paradise to the worlds of time and space. No major part of the organized and inhabited creation is without their services.

1. THE MINISTERING SPIRITS

Angels are the ministering-spirit associates of the evolutionary and ascending will creatures of all space; they are also the colleagues and working associates of the higher hosts of the divine personalities of the spheres. The angels of all orders are distinct personalities and are highly individualized. They all have a large capacity for appreciation of the ministrations of the reversion directors. Together with the Messenger Hosts of Space, the ministering spirits enjoy seasons of rest and change; they possess very social natures and have an associative capacity far transcending that of human beings.

The ministering spirits of the grand universe are classified as follows:

1. Supernaphim.
2. Seconaphim.
3. Tertiaphim.
4. Omniaphim.
5. Seraphim.
6. Cherubim and Sanobim.
7. Midway Creatures.

The individual members of the angelic orders are not altogether stationary as to personal status in the universe. Angels of certain orders may become Paradise Companions for a season; some become Celestial Recorders; others ascend to the ranks of the Technical Advisers. Certain of the cherubim may aspire to seraphic status and destiny, while evolutionary seraphim can achieve the spiritual levels of the ascending Sons of God.

The seven orders of ministering spirits, as revealed, are grouped for presentation in accordance with their functions of greatest importance to ascending creatures:

1. *The Ministering Spirits of the Central Universe.* The three orders of *supernaphim* serve in the Paradise-Havona system. Primary or Paradise supernaphim are created by the Infinite Spirit. The secondary and tertiary orders, serving in Havona, are respectively the offspring of the Master Spirits and of the Spirits of the Circuits.

2. *The Ministering Spirits of the Superuniverses* — the seconaphim, the tertiaphim, and the omniaphim. *Seconaphim*, the children of the Reflective Spirits, variously serve in the seven superuniverses. *Tertiaphim*, of origin in the Infinite Spirit, are eventually dedicated to the liaison service of the Creator Sons and the Ancients of Days. *Omniaphim* are created concertedly by the Infinite Spirit and the Seven Supreme Executives, and they are the exclusive servants of the latter. The discussion of these three orders forms the subject of a succeeding narrative in this series.

3. *The Ministering Spirits of the Local Universes* embrace the *seraphim* and their assistants, the *cherubim*. With these offspring of a Universe Mother Spirit mortal ascenders have initial contact. The *midway creatures*, of nativity on the inhabited worlds, are not really of the angelic orders proper, though often functionally grouped with the ministering spirits. Their story, with an account of the seraphim and cherubim, is presented in those papers dealing with the affairs of your local universe.

All orders of the angelic hosts are devoted to the various universe services, and they minister in one way or another to the higher orders of celestial beings; but it is the supernaphim, seconaphim, and seraphim who, in large numbers, are employed in the furtherance of the ascending scheme of progressive perfection for the children of time. Functioning in the central, super-, and local universes, they form that unbroken chain of spirit ministers which has been provided by the Infinite Spirit for the help and guidance of all who seek to attain the Universal Father through the Eternal Son.

Supernaphim are limited in "spirit polarity" regarding only one phase of action, that with the Universal Father. They can work singly except when directly employing the exclusive circuits of the Father. When they are in power reception on the Father's direct ministry, supernaphim must voluntarily associate in pairs to be able to function. Seconaphim are likewise limited and in addition must work in pairs in order to synchronize with the circuits of the Eternal Son. Seraphim can work singly as discrete and localized personalities, but they are able to encircuit only when polarized as liaison pairs. When such spirit beings are associated as pairs, the one is spoken of as complemental to the other. Complemental relationships may be transient; they are not necessarily of a permanent nature.

These brilliant creatures of light are sustained directly by the intake of the spiritual energy of the primary circuits of the universe. Urantia mortals must obtain light-energy through the vegetative incarnation, but the angelic hosts are encircuited; they "have food that you know not." They also partake of the circulating teachings of the marvelous Trinity Teacher Sons; they have a reception of knowledge and an intake of wisdom much resembling their technique of assimilating the life energies.

2. THE MIGHTY SUPERNAPHIM

The supernaphim are the skilled ministers to all types of beings who sojourn on Paradise and in the central universe. These high angels are created in three major orders: primary, secondary, and tertiary.

Primary supernaphim are the exclusive offspring of the Conjoint Creator. They divide their ministry about equally between certain groups of the Paradise Citizens and the ever-enlarging corps of ascendant pilgrims. These angels of the eternal Isle are highly efficacious in furthering the essential training of both groups of Paradise dwellers. They contribute much that is helpful to the mutual understanding of these two unique orders of universe creatures — the one being the highest type of divine and perfect will creature, and the other, the perfected evolution of the lowest type of will creature in all the universe of universes.

The work of the primary supernaphim is so unique and distinctive that it will be separately considered in the succeeding narrative.

Secondary supernaphim are the directors of the affairs of ascending beings on the seven circuits of Havona. They are equally concerned in ministering to the educational training of numerous orders of Paradise Citizens who sojourn for long periods on the world circuits of the central creation, but we may not discuss this phase of their service.

There are seven types of these high angels, each of origin in one of the Seven Master Spirits and in nature patterned accordingly. Collectively, the Seven Master Spirits create many different groups of unique beings and entities, and the individual members of each order are comparatively uniform in nature. But when these same Seven Spirits create individually, the resulting orders are always sevenfold in nature; the children of each Master Spirit partake of the nature of their creator and are accordingly diverse from the others. Such is the origin of the secondary supernaphim, and the angels of all seven created types function in all channels of activity open to their entire order, chiefly on the seven circuits of the central and divine universe.

Each of the seven planetary circuits of Havona is under the direct supervision of one of the Seven Spirits of the Circuits, themselves the collective — hence uniform — creation of the Seven Master Spirits. Though partaking of the nature of the Third Source and Center, these seven subsidiary Spirits of Havona were not a part of the original pattern universe. They were in function after the original (eternal) creation but long before the times of Grandfanda. They undoubtedly appeared as a creative response of the Master Spirits to the emerging purpose of the Supreme Being, and they were discovered in function upon the organization of the grand universe. The Infinite Spirit and all his creative associates, as universal co-ordinators, seem abundantly endowed with the ability to make suitable creative responses to the simultaneous developments in the experiential Deities and in the evolving universes.

Tertiary supernaphim take origin in these Seven Spirits of the Circuits. Each one of them, on the separate Havona circles, is empowered by the Infinite Spirit to create a sufficient number of high superaphic ministers of the tertiary order to meet the needs of the central universe. While the Circuit Spirits produced comparatively few of these angelic ministers prior to the arrival in Havona of the pilgrims of time, the Seven Master Spirits did not even begin the creation of secondary supernaphim until the landing of Grandfanda. As the older of the two orders, the tertiary supernaphim will therefore receive first consideration.

3. THE TERTIARY SUPERNAPHIM

These servants of the Seven Master Spirits are the angelic specialists of the various circuits of Havona, and their ministry extends to both the ascending pilgrims of time and the descending pilgrims of eternity. On the billion study worlds of the perfect central creation, your superaphic associates of all orders will be fully visible to you. There you will all be, in the highest sense, fraternal and understanding beings of mutual contact and sympathy. You will also fully recognize and exquisitely fraternize with the descending pilgrims, the Paradise Citizens, who traverse these circuits from within outward, entering Havona through the pilot world of the first circuit and proceeding outward to the seventh.

The ascending pilgrims from the seven superuniverses pass through Havona in the opposite direction, entering by way of the pilot world of the seventh circuit and proceeding inward. There is no time limit set on the progress of the ascending creatures from world to world and from circuit to circuit, just as no fixed span of time is arbitrarily assigned to residence on the morontia worlds. But, whereas adequately developed individuals may be exempted from sojourn on one or more of the local universe training worlds, no pilgrim may avoid passing through all seven of the Havona circuits of progressive spiritualization.

That corps of tertiary supernaphim which is chiefly assigned to the service of the pilgrims of time is classified as follows:

1. *The Harmony Supervisors*. It must be apparent that some sort of co-ordinating influence would be required, even in perfect Havona, to maintain the system and to insure harmony in all the work of preparing the pilgrims of time for their subsequent Paradise achievements. Such is the real mission of the harmony supervisors — to keep everything moving along smoothly and expeditiously. Originating on the first circuit, they serve throughout Havona, and their presence on the circuits means that nothing can possibly go amiss. A great ability to co-ordinate a diversity of activities involving personalities of differing orders — even multiple levels — enables these supernaphim to give assistance wherever and whenever required. They contribute enormously to the mutual understanding of the pilgrims of time and the pilgrims of eternity.

2. *The Chief Recorders*. These angels are created on the second circuit but operate everywhere in the central universe. They record in triplicate, executing records for the literal files of Havona, for the spiritual files of their order, and for the formal records of Paradise. In addition they automatically transmit the transactions of true-knowledge import to the living libraries of Paradise, the custodians of knowledge of the primary order of supernaphim.

3. *The Broadcasters*. The children of the third Circuit Spirit function

throughout Havona, although their official station is located on planet number seventy in the outermost circle. These master technicians are the broadcast receivers and senders of the central creation and the directors of the space reports of all Deity phenomena on Paradise. They can operate all of the basic circuits of space.

4. *The Messengers* take origin on circuit number four. They range the Paradise-Havona system as bearers of all messages requiring personal transmission. They serve their fellows, the celestial personalities, the Paradise pilgrims, and even the ascendant souls of time.

5. *The Intelligence Co-ordinators*. These tertiary supernaphim, the children of the fifth Circuit Spirit, are always the wise and sympathetic promoters of fraternal association between the ascending and the descending pilgrims. They minister to all the inhabitants of Havona, and especially to the ascenders, by keeping them currently informed regarding the affairs of the universe of universes. By virtue of personal contacts with the broadcasters and the reflectors, these "living newspapers" of Havona are instantly conversant with all information passing over the vast news circuits of the central universe. They secure intelligence by the Havona graph method, which enables them automatically to assimilate as much information in one hour of Urantia time as would require a thousand years for your most rapid communication technique to record.

6. *The Transport Personalities*. These beings, of origin on circuit number six, usually operate from planet number forty in the outermost circuit. It is they who take away the disappointed candidates who transiently fail in the Deity adventure. They stand ready to serve all who must come and go in the service of Havona, and who are not space traversers.

7. *The Reserve Corps*. The fluctuations in the work with the ascendant beings, the Paradise pilgrims, and other orders of beings sojourning in Havona, make it necessary to maintain these reserves of supernaphim on the pilot world of the seventh circle, where they take origin. They are created without special design and are competent to take up service in the less

exacting phases of any of the duties of their superaphic associates of the tertiary order.

4. THE SECONDARY SUPERNAPHIM

The secondary supernaphim are ministers to the seven planetary circuits of the central universe. Part are devoted to the service of the pilgrims of time, and one half of the entire order is assigned to the training of the Paradise pilgrims of eternity. These Paradise Citizens, in their pilgrimage through the Havona circuits, are also attended by volunteers from the Mortal Finality Corps, an arrangement that has prevailed since the completion of the first finaliter group.

According to their periodic assignment to the ministry of the ascending pilgrims, secondary supernaphim work in the following seven groups:

1. Pilgrim Helpers.
2. Supremacy Guides.
3. Trinity Guides.
4. Son Finders.
5. Father Guides.
6. Counselors and Advisers.
7. Complements of Rest.

Each of these working groups contains angels of all seven created types, and a pilgrim of space is always tutored by secondary supernaphim of origin in the Master Spirit who presides over that pilgrim's superuniverse of nativity. When you mortals of Urantia attain Havona, you will certainly be piloted by supernaphim whose created natures — like your own evolved natures — are derived from the Master Spirit of Orvonton. And since your tutors spring from the Master Spirit of your own superuniverse, they are especially qualified to understand, comfort, and assist you in all your efforts to attain Paradise perfection.

The pilgrims of time are transported past the dark gravity bodies of Havona to the outer planetary circuit by the transport personalities of the primary order of seconaphim, operating from the headquarters of the seven superuniverses. A majority, but not all, of the seraphim of planetary and local universe service who have been accredited for the Paradise ascent will part with their mortal associates before the long flight to Havona and will at once begin a long and intense training for supernal assignment, expecting to achieve, as seraphim, perfection of existence and supremacy of service. And this they do, hoping to rejoin the pilgrims of time, to be reckoned among those who forever follow the course of such mortals as have attained the Universal Father and have received assignment to the undisclosed service of the Corps of the Finality.

The pilgrim lands on the receiving planet of Havona, the pilot world of the seventh circuit, with only one endowment of perfection, perfection of purpose. The Universal Father has decreed: "Be you perfect, even as I am perfect." That is the astounding invitation-command broadcast to the finite children of the worlds of space. The promulgation of that injunction has set all creation astir in the co-operative effort of the celestial beings to assist in bringing about the fulfillment and realization of that tremendous command of the First Great Source and Center.

When, through and by the ministry of all the helper hosts of the universal scheme of survival, you are finally deposited on the receiving world of Havona, you arrive with only one sort of perfection — *perfection of purpose*. Your purpose has been thoroughly proved; your faith has been tested. You are known to be disappointment proof. Not even the failure to discern the Universal Father can shake the faith or seriously disturb the trust of an ascendant mortal who has passed through the experience that all must traverse in order to attain the perfect spheres of Havona. By the time you reach Havona, your sincerity has become sublime. Perfection of purpose and divinity of desire, with steadfastness of faith, have secured your entrance to the settled abodes of eternity; your deliverance from the uncertainties of time is full and complete; and now must you come face to face with the problems of Havona and the immensities of Paradise, to meet which you have so long been in training in the experiential epochs of time on the world schools of space.

Faith has won for the ascendant pilgrim a perfection of purpose which admits the children of time to the portals of eternity. Now must the pilgrim helpers begin the work of developing that perfection of understanding and that technique of comprehension which are so indispensable to Paradise perfection of personality.

Ability to comprehend is the mortal passport to Paradise. Willingness to believe is the key to Havona. The acceptance of sonship, co-operation with the indwelling Adjuster, is the price of evolutionary survival.

5. THE PILGRIM HELPERS

The first of the seven groups of secondary supernaphim to be encountered are the pilgrim helpers, those beings of quick understanding and broad sympathy who welcome the much-traveled ascenders of space to the stabilized worlds and settled economy of the central universe. Simultaneously these high ministers begin their work for the Paradise pilgrims of eternity, the first of whom arrived on the pilot world of the inner Havona circuit concomitantly with the landing of Grandfanda on the pilot world of the outer circuit. Back in those far-distant days the pilgrims from Paradise and the pilgrims of time first met on the receiving world of circuit number four.

These pilgrim helpers, functioning on the seventh circle of Havona worlds, conduct their work for the ascending mortals in three major divisions: first, the supreme understanding of the Paradise Trinity; second, the spiritual comprehension of the Father-Son partnership; and third, the intellectual recognition of the Infinite Spirit. Each of these phases of instruction is divided into seven branches of twelve minor divisions of seventy subsidiary groups; and each of these seventy subsidiary groupings of instruction is presented in one thousand classifications. More detailed instruction is provided on subsequent circles, but an outline of every Paradise requirement is taught by the pilgrim helpers.

That, then, is the primary or elementary course which confronts the faith-tested and much-traveled pilgrims of space. But long before reaching Havona, these ascendant children of time have learned to feast upon uncertainty, to fatten upon disappointment, to enthuse over apparent defeat, to invigorate in the presence of difficulties, to exhibit indomitable courage in the face of immensity, and to exercise unconquerable faith when confronted with the challenge of the inexplicable. Long since, the battle cry of these pilgrims became: "In liaison with God, nothing — absolutely nothing — is impossible."

There is a definite requirement of the pilgrims of time on each of the Havona circles; and while every pilgrim continues under the tutelage of supernaphim by nature adapted to helping that particular type of ascendant creature, the course that must be mastered is fairly uniform for all ascenders who reach the central universe. This course of achievement is quantitative, qualitative, and experiential — intellectual, spiritual, and supreme.

Time is of little consequence on the Havona circles. In a limited manner it enters into the possibilities of advancement, but achievement is the final and supreme test. The very moment your superaphic associate deems you to be competent to pass inward to the next circle, you will be taken before the twelve adjutants of the seventh Circuit Spirit. Here you will be required to pass the tests of the circle determined by the superuniverse of your origin and by the system of your nativity. The divinity attainment of this circle takes place on the pilot world and consists in the spiritual recognition and realization of the Master Spirit of the ascending pilgrim's superuniverse.

When the work of the outer Havona circle is finished and the course presented is mastered, the pilgrim helpers take their subjects to the pilot world of the next circle and commit them to the care of the supremacy guides. The pilgrim helpers always tarry for a season to assist in making the transfer both pleasant and profitable.

6. THE SUPREMACY GUIDES

Ascenders of space are designated "spiritual graduates" when translated from the seventh to the sixth circle and are placed under the immediate supervision of the supremacy guides. These guides should not be confused with the Graduate Guides — belonging to the Higher Personalities of the Infinite Spirit — who, with their servital associates, minister on all circuits of Havona to both ascending and descending pilgrims. The supremacy guides function only on the sixth circle of the central universe.

It is in this circle that the ascenders achieve a new realization of Supreme Divinity. Through their long careers in the evolutionary universes the pilgrims of time have been experiencing a growing awareness of the reality of an almighty overcontrol of the time-space creations. Here, on this Havona circuit, they come near to encountering the central universe source of time-space unity — the spiritual reality of God the Supreme.

I am somewhat at a loss to explain what takes place on this circle. No personalized presence of Supremacy is perceptible to the ascenders. In certain respects, new relationships with the Seventh Master Spirit compensate this noncontactability of the Supreme Being. But regardless of our inability to grasp the technique, each ascending creature seems to undergo a transforming growth, a new integration of consciousness, a new spiritualization of purpose, a new sensitivity for divinity, which can hardly be satisfactorily explained without assuming the unrevealed activity of the Supreme Being. To those of us who have observed these mysterious transactions, it appears as if God the Supreme were affectionately bestowing upon his experiential children, up to the very limits of their experiential capacities, those enhancements of intellectual grasp, of spiritual insight, and of personality outreach which they will so need, in all their efforts at penetrating the divinity level of the Trinity of Supremacy, to achieve the eternal and existential Deities of Paradise.

When the supremacy guides deem their pupils ripe for advancement, they bring them before the commission of seventy, a mixed group serving as examiners on the pilot world of circuit number six. After satisfying this commission as to their comprehension of the Supreme Being and of the Trinity of Supremacy, the pilgrims are certified for translation to the fifth circuit.

7. THE TRINITY GUIDES

Trinity guides are the tireless ministers of the fifth circle of the Havona training of the advancing pilgrims of time and space. The spiritual graduates are here designated "candidates for the Deity adventure" since it is on this circle, under the direction of the Trinity guides, that the pilgrims receive advanced instruction concerning the divine Trinity in preparation for the attempt to achieve the personality recognition of the Infinite Spirit. And here the ascending pilgrims discover what true study and real mental effort mean as they begin to discern the nature of the still-more-taxing and far-more-arduous spiritual exertion that will be required to meet the demands of the high goal set for their achievement on the worlds of this circuit.

Most faithful and efficient are the Trinity guides; and each pilgrim receives the undivided attention, and enjoys the whole affection, of a secondary supernaphim belonging to this order. Never would a pilgrim of time find the first approachable person of the Paradise Trinity were it not for the help and assistance of these guides and the host of other spiritual beings engaged in instructing the ascenders respecting the nature and technique of the forthcoming Deity adventure.

After the completion of the course of training on this circuit the Trinity guides take their pupils to its pilot world and present them before one of the many triune commissions functioning as examiners and certifiers of candidates for the Deity adventure. These commissions consist of one fellow of the finaliters, one of the directors of conduct of the order of primary supernaphim, and either a Solitary Messenger of space or a Trinitized Son of Paradise.

When an ascendant soul actually starts for Paradise, he is accompanied only by the transit trio: the superaphic circle associate, the Graduate Guide, and the ever-present servital associate of the latter. These excursions from the Havona circles to Paradise are trial trips; the ascenders are not yet of Paradise status. They do not achieve residential status on Paradise until they have passed through the terminal rest of time subsequent to the attainment of the Universal Father and the final clearance of the Havona circuits. Not until after the divine rest do they partake of the "essence of divinity" and the "spirit of supremacy" and thus really begin to function in the circle of eternity and in the presence of the Trinity.

The ascender's companions of the transit trio are not required to enable him to locate the geographic presence of the spiritual luminosity of the Trinity, rather to afford all possible assistance to a pilgrim in his difficult task of recognizing, discerning, and comprehending the Infinite Spirit sufficiently to constitute personality recognition. Any ascendant pilgrim on Paradise can discern the geographic or locational presence of the Trinity, the great majority are able to contact the intellectual reality of the Deities, especially the Third Person, but not all can recognize or even partially comprehend the reality of the spiritual presence of the Father and the Son. Still more difficult is even the minimum spiritual comprehension of the Universal Father.

Seldom does the quest for the Infinite Spirit fail of consummation, and when their subjects have succeeded in this phase of the Deity adventure, the Trinity guides prepare to transfer them to the ministry of the Son finders on the fourth circle of Havona.

8. THE SON FINDERS

The fourth Havona circuit is sometimes called the "circuit of the Sons." From the worlds of this circuit the ascending pilgrims go to Paradise to achieve an understanding contact with the Eternal Son, while on the worlds of this circuit the descending pilgrims achieve a new comprehension of the nature and mission of the Creator Sons of time and space. There are seven worlds in this circuit on which the reserve corps of the Paradise Michaels maintain special service schools of mutual ministry to both the ascending and descending pilgrims; and it is on these worlds of the Michael Sons that the pilgrims of time and the pilgrims of eternity arrive at their first truly mutual understanding of one another. In many respects the experiences of this circuit are the most intriguing of the entire Havona sojourn.

The Son finders are the superaphic ministers to the ascending mortals of the fourth circuit. In addition to the general work of preparing their candidates for a realization of the Trinity relationships of the Eternal Son, these Son finders must so fully instruct their subjects that they will be wholly successful: first, in the adequate spiritual comprehension of the Son; second, in the satisfactory personality recognition of the Son; and third, in the proper differentiation of the Son from the personality of the Infinite Spirit.

After the attainment of the Infinite Spirit, no more examinations are conducted. The tests of the inner circles are the performances of the pilgrim candidates when in the embrace of the enshroudment of the Deities. Advancement is determined purely by the spirituality of the individual, and no one but the Gods presumes to pass upon this possession. In the event of failure no reasons are ever assigned, neither are the candidates themselves nor their various tutors and guides ever chided or criticized. On Paradise, disappointment is never regarded as defeat; postponement is never looked upon as disgrace; the apparent failures of time are never confused with the significant delays of eternity.

Not many pilgrims experience the delay of seeming failure in the Deity adventure. Nearly all attain the Infinite Spirit, though occasionally a pilgrim from superuniverse number one does not succeed on the first attempt. The pilgrims who attain the Spirit seldom fail in finding the Son; of those who do fail on the first adventure, almost all hail from superuniverses three and five. The great majority of those who fail on the first adventure to attain the Father, after finding both the Spirit and the Son, hail from superuniverse number six, though a few from numbers two and three are likewise unsuccessful. And all this seems clearly to indicate that there is some good and sufficient reason for these apparent failures; in reality, simply unescapable delays.

The defeated candidates for the Deity adventure are placed under the jurisdiction of the chiefs of assignment, a group of primary supernaphim, and are remanded to the work of the realms of space for a period of not less than one millennium. They never return to the superuniverse of their nativity, always to that supercreation most propitious for their retraining in preparation for the second Deity adventure. Following this service, on their own motion, they return to the outer circle of Havona, are immediately escorted to the circle of their interrupted career, and at once resume their preparations for the Deity adventure. Never do the secondary supernaphim fail to pilot their subjects successfully on the second attempt, and the same superaphic ministers and other guides always attend these candidates during this second adventure.

9. THE FATHER GUIDES

When the pilgrim soul attains the third circle of Havona, he comes under the tutelage of the Father guides, the older, highly skilled, and most experienced of the superaphic ministers. On the worlds of this circuit the Father guides maintain schools of wisdom and colleges of technique wherein all the beings inhabiting the central universe serve as teachers. Nothing is neglected which would be of service to a creature of time in this transcendent adventure of eternity attainment.

The attainment of the Universal Father is the passport to eternity, notwithstanding the remaining circuits to be traversed. It is therefore a momentous occasion on the pilot world of circle number three when the transit trio announce that the last venture of time is about to ensue; that another creature of space seeks entry to Paradise through the portals of eternity.

The test of time is almost over; the race for eternity has been all but run. The days of uncertainty are ending; the temptation to doubt is vanishing; the injunction to be *perfect* has been obeyed. From the very bottom of intelligent existence the creature of time and material personality has ascended the evolutionary spheres of space, thus proving the feasibility of the ascension plan while forever demonstrating the justice and righteousness of the command of the Universal Father to his lowly creatures of the worlds: "Be you perfect, even as I am perfect."

Step by step, life by life, world by world, the ascendant career has been mastered, and the goal of Deity has been attained. Survival is complete in perfection, and perfection is replete in the supremacy of divinity. Time is lost in eternity; space is swallowed up in worshipful identity and harmony with the Universal Father. The broadcasts of Havona flash forth the space reports of glory, the good news that in very truth the conscientious creatures of animal nature and material origin have, through evolutionary ascension, become in reality and eternally the perfected sons of God.

10. THE COUNSELORS AND ADVISERS

The superaphic counselors and advisers of the second circle are the instructors of the children of time regarding the career of eternity. The attainment of Paradise entails responsibilities of a new and higher order, and the sojourn on the second circle affords ample opportunity to receive the helpful counsel of these devoted supernaphim.

Those who are unsuccessful in the first effort at Deity attainment are advanced from the circle of failure directly to the second circle before they are returned to superuniverse service. Thus the counselors and advisers also serve as the counselors and comforters of these disappointed pilgrims. They have just encountered their greatest disappointment, in no way differing from the long list of such experiences whereon they climbed, as on a ladder, from chaos to glory — except in its magnitude. These are they who have drained the experiential cup to its dregs; and I have observed that they temporarily return to the services of the superuniverses as the highest type of loving ministrators to the children of time and temporal disappointments.

After a long sojourn on circuit number two the subjects of disappointment are examined by the councils of perfection sitting on the pilot world of this circle and are certified as having passed the Havona test; and this, so far as nonspiritual status is concerned, grants them the same standing in the universes of time as if they had actually succeeded in the Deity adventure. The spirit of such candidates was wholly acceptable; their failure was inherent in some phase of the technique of approach or in some part of their experiential background.

They are then taken by the counselors of the circle before the chiefs of assignment on Paradise and are remanded to the service of time on the worlds of space; and they go with joy and gladness to the tasks of former days and ages. In another day they will return to the circle of their greatest disappointment and attempt anew the Deity adventure.

For the successful pilgrims on the second circuit the stimulus of evolutionary uncertainty is over, but the adventure of the eternal assignment has not yet begun; and while the sojourn on this circle is wholly pleasurable and highly profitable, it lacks some of the anticipative enthusiasm of the former circles. Many are the pilgrims who, at such a time, look back upon the long, long struggle with a joyous envy, really wishing they might somehow go back to the worlds of time and begin it all over again, just as you mortals, in approaching advanced age, sometimes look back over the struggles of youth and early life and truly wish you might live your lives over once again.

But the traversal of the innermost circle lies just ahead, and soon thereafter the last transit sleep will terminate, and the new adventure of the eternal career will begin. The counselors and advisers on the second circle begin the preparation of their subjects for this great and final rest, the inevitable sleep which ever intervenes between the epochal stages of the ascendant career.

When those ascendant pilgrims who have attained the Universal Father complete the second-circle experience, their ever-attendant Graduate Guides issue the order admitting them to the final circle. These guides personally pilot their subjects to the inner circle and there place them in the custody of the complements of rest, the last of those orders of secondary supernaphim assigned to the ministry of the pilgrims of time on the world circuits of Havona.

11. THE COMPLEMENTS OF REST

Much of an ascender's time on the last circuit is devoted to a continuation of the study of the impending problems of Paradise residence. A vast and diverse host of beings, the majority unrevealed, are permanent and transient residents of this inner ring of Havona worlds. And the commingling of these manifold types provides the superaphic complements of rest with a rich situational environment which they effectively utilize in furthering the education of the ascending pilgrims, especially with regard to the problems of adjustment to the many groups of beings soon to be encountered on Paradise.

Among those who dwell on this inner circuit are the creature-trinitized sons. The primary and the secondary supernaphim are the general custodians of the conjoint corps of these sons, including the trinitized offspring of the mortal finaliters and similar progeny of the Paradise Citizens. Certain of these sons are Trinity embraced and commissioned in the supergovernments, others are variously assigned, but the great majority are being gathered together in the conjoint corps on the perfect worlds of the inner Havona circuit. Here, under the supervision of the supernaphim, they are being prepared for some future work by a special and unnamed corps of high Paradise Citizens who were, prior to the times of Grandfanda, first executive assistants to the Eternals of Days. There are many reasons for conjecturing that these two unique groups of trinitized beings are going to work together in the remote future, not the least of which is their common destiny in the reserves of the Paradise Corps of Trinitized Finaliters.

On this innermost circuit, both the ascending and the descending pilgrims fraternize with each other and with the creature-trinitized sons. Like their parents, these sons derive great benefits from interassociation, and it is the special mission of the supernaphim to facilitate and to insure the confraternity of the trinitized sons of the mortal finaliters and the trinitized sons of the Paradise Citizens. The superaphic complements of rest are not so much concerned with their training as with promoting their understanding association with diverse groups.

Mortals have received the Paradise command: "Be you perfect, even as your Paradise Father is perfect." To these trinitized sons of the conjoint corps the supervising supernaphim never cease to proclaim: "Be you understanding of your ascendant brethren, even as the Paradise Creator Sons know and love them."

The mortal creature must find God. The Creator Son never stops until he finds man — the lowest will creature. Beyond doubt, the Creator Sons and their mortal children are preparing for some future and unknown universe service. Both traverse the gamut of the experiential universe and so are educated and trained for their eternal mission. Throughout the universes there is occurring this unique blending of the human and the divine, the commingling of creature and Creator. Unthinking mortals have referred to the manifestation of divine mercy and tenderness, especially towards the weak and in behalf of the needy, as indicative of an anthropomorphic God. What a mistake! Rather should such manifestations of mercy and forbearance by human beings be taken as evidence that mortal man is indwelt by the spirit of the living God; that the creature is, after all, divinity motivated.

Near the end of the first-circle sojourn the ascending pilgrims first meet the instigators of rest of the primary order of supernaphim. These are the angels of Paradise coming out to greet those who stand at the threshold of eternity and to complete their preparation for the transition slumber of the last resurrection. You are not really a child of Paradise until you have traversed the inner circle and have experienced the resurrection of eternity from the terminal sleep of time. The perfected pilgrims begin this rest, go to sleep, on the first circle of Havona, but they awaken on the shores of Paradise. Of all who ascend to the eternal Isle, only those who thus arrive are the children of eternity; the others go as visitors, as guests without residential status.

And now, at the culmination of the Havona career, as you mortals go to sleep on the pilot world of the inner circuit, you go not alone to your rest as you did on the worlds of your origin when you closed your eyes in the natural sleep of mortal death, nor as you did when you entered the long transit trance preparatory for the journey to Havona. Now, as you prepare for the attainment rest, there moves over by your side your long-time associate of the first circle, the majestic complement of rest, who prepares to enter the rest as one with you, as the pledge of Havona that your transition is complete, and that you await only the final touches of perfection.

Your first transition was indeed death, the second an ideal sleep, and now the third metamorphosis is the true rest, the relaxation of the ages.

[Presented by a Perfector of Wisdom from Uversa.]

PAPER 27
MINISTRY OF THE PRIMARY SUPERNAPHIM

PRIMARY SUPERNAPHIM ARE the supernal servants of the Deities on the eternal Isle of Paradise. Never have they been known to depart from the paths of light and righteousness. The roll calls are complete; from eternity not one of this magnificent host has been lost. These high supernaphim are perfect beings, supreme in perfection, but they are not absonite, neither are they absolute. Being of the essence of perfection, these children of the Infinite Spirit work interchangeably and at will in all phases of their manifold duties. They do not function extensively outside Paradise, though they do participate in the various millennial gatherings and group reunions of the central universe. They also go forth as special messengers of the Deities, and in large numbers they ascend to become Technical Advisers.

Primary supernaphim are also placed in command of the seraphic hosts ministering on worlds isolated because of rebellion. When a Paradise Son is bestowed upon such a world, completes his mission, ascends to the Universal Father, is accepted, and returns as the accredited deliverer of this isolated world, a primary supernaphim is always designated by the chiefs of assignment to assume command of the ministering spirits on duty in the newly reclaimed sphere. Supernaphim in this special service are periodically rotated. On Urantia the present "chief of seraphim" is the second of this order to be on duty since the times of the bestowal of Christ Michael.

From eternity the primary supernaphim have served on the Isle of Light and have gone forth on missions of leadership to the worlds of space, but they have functioned as now classified only since the arrival on Paradise of the Havona pilgrims of time. These high angels now minister chiefly in the following seven orders of service:

1. Conductors of Worship.
2. Masters of Philosophy.
3. Custodians of Knowledge.
4. Directors of Conduct.
5. Interpreters of Ethics.
6. Chiefs of Assignment.
7. Instigators of Rest.

Not until the ascending pilgrims actually attain Paradise residence do they come under the direct influence of these supernaphim, and then they pass through a training experience under the direction of these angels in the reverse order of their naming. That is, you enter upon your Paradise career under the tutelage of the instigators of rest and, after successive seasons with the intervening orders, finish this training period with the conductors of worship. Thereupon are you ready to begin the endless career of a finaliter.

1. INSTIGATORS OF REST

The instigators of rest are the inspectors of Paradise who go forth from the central Isle to the inner circuit of Havona, there to collaborate with their colleagues, the complements of rest of the secondary order of supernaphim. The one essential to the enjoyment of Paradise is rest, divine rest; and these instigators of rest are the final instructors who make ready the pilgrims of time for their introduction to eternity. They begin their work on the final attainment circle of the central universe and continue it when the pilgrim awakes from the last transition sleep, the slumber which graduates a creature of space into the realm of the eternal.

Rest is of a sevenfold nature: There is the rest of sleep and of play in the lower life orders, discovery in the higher beings, and worship in the highest type of spirit personality. There is also the normal rest of energy intake, the recharging of beings with physical or with spiritual energy. And then there is the transit sleep, the unconscious slumber when enseraphimed, when in passage from one sphere to another. Entirely different from all of these is the deep sleep of metamorphosis, the transition rest from one stage of being to another, from one life to another, from one state of existence to another, the sleep which ever attends transition from actual universe status in contrast to evolution through various *stages* of any one status.

But the last metamorphic sleep is something more than those previous transition slumbers which have marked the successive status attainments of the ascendant career; thereby do the creatures of time and space traverse the innermost margins of the temporal and the spatial to attain residential status in the timeless and spaceless abodes of Paradise. The instigators and the complements of rest are just as essential to this transcending metamorphosis as are the seraphim and associated beings to the mortal creature's survival of death.

You enter the rest on the final Havona circuit and are eternally resurrected on Paradise. And as you there spiritually repersonalize, you will immediately recognize the instigator of rest who welcomes you to the eternal shores as the very primary supernaphim who produced the final sleep on the innermost circuit of Havona; and you will recall the last grand stretch of faith as you once again made ready to commend the keeping of your identity into the hands of the Universal Father.

The last rest of time has been enjoyed; the last transition sleep has been experienced; now you awake to life everlasting on the shores of the eternal abode. "And there shall be no more sleep. The presence of God and his Son are before you, and you are eternally his servants; you have seen his face, and his name is your spirit. There shall be no night there; and they need no light of the sun, for the Great Source and Center gives them light; they shall live forever and ever. And God shall wipe away all tears from their eyes; there shall be no more death, neither sorrow nor crying, neither shall there be any more pain, for the former things have passed away."

2. CHIEFS OF ASSIGNMENT

This is the group designated from time to time by the chief supernaphim, "the original pattern angel," to preside over the organization of all three orders of these angels — primary, secondary, and tertiary. The supernaphim, as a body, are wholly self-governing and self-regulatory except for the functions of their mutual chief, the first angel of Paradise, who ever presides over all these spirit personalities.

The angels of assignment have much to do with glorified mortal residents of Paradise before they are admitted to the Corps of the Finality. Study and instruction are not the exclusive occupations of Paradise arrivals; service also plays its essential part in the prefinaliter educational experiences of Paradise. And I have observed that, when the ascendant mortals have periods of leisure, they evince a predilection to fraternize with the reserve corps of the superaphic chiefs of assignment.

When you mortal ascenders attain Paradise, your societal relationships involve a great deal more than contact with a host of exalted and divine beings and with a familiar multitude of glorified fellow mortals. You must also fraternize with upwards of three thousand different orders of Paradise Citizens, with the various groups of the Transcendentalers, and with numerous other types of Paradise inhabitants, permanent and transient, who have not been revealed on Urantia. After sustained contact with these mighty intellects of Paradise, it is very restful to visit with the angelic types of mind; they remind the mortals of time of the seraphim with whom they have had such long contact and such refreshing association.

3. INTERPRETERS OF ETHICS

The higher you ascend in the scale of life, the more attention must be paid to universe ethics. Ethical awareness is simply the recognition by any individual of the rights inherent in the existence of any and all other individuals. But spiritual ethics far transcends the mortal and even the morontia concept of personal and group relations.

Ethics has been duly taught and adequately learned by the pilgrims of time in their long ascent to the glories of Paradise. As this inward-ascending career has unfolded from the nativity worlds of space, the ascenders have continued to add group after group to their ever-widening circle of universe associates. Every new group of colleagues met with adds one more level of ethics to be recognized and complied with until, by the time the mortals of ascent reach Paradise, they really need someone to provide helpful and friendly counsel regarding ethical interpretations. They do not need to be taught ethics, but they do need to have what they have so laboriously learned properly *interpreted* to them as they are brought face to face with the extraordinary task of contacting with so much that is new.

The interpreters of ethics are of inestimable assistance to the Paradise arrivals in helping them to adjust to numerous groups of majestic beings during that eventful period extending from the attainment of residential status to formal induction into the Corps of Mortal Finaliters. Many of the numerous types of Paradise Citizens the ascendant pilgrims have already met on the seven circuits of Havona. The glorified mortals have also enjoyed intimate contact with the creature-trinitized sons of the conjoint corps on the inner Havona circuit, where these beings are receiving much of their education. And on the other circuits the ascending pilgrims have met numerous unrevealed residents of the Paradise-Havona system who are there pursuing group training in preparation for the unrevealed assignments of the future.

All these celestial companionships are invariably mutual. As ascending mortals you not only derive benefit from these successive universe companions and such numerous orders of increasingly divine associates, but you also impart to each of these fraternal beings something from your own personality and experience which forever makes every one of them different and better for having been associated with an ascending mortal from the evolutionary worlds of time and space.

4. DIRECTORS OF CONDUCT

Having already been fully instructed in the ethics of Paradise relationships — neither meaningless formalities nor the dictations of artificial castes but rather the inherent proprieties — the ascendant mortals find it helpful to receive the counsel of the superaphic directors of conduct, who instruct the new members of Paradise society in the usages of the perfect conduct of the high beings who sojourn on the central Isle of Light and Life.

Harmony is the keynote of the central universe, and detectable order prevails on Paradise. Proper conduct is essential to progress by way of knowledge, through philosophy, to the spiritual heights of spontaneous worship. There is a divine technique in the approach to Divinity; and the acquirement of this technique must await the pilgrims' arrival on Paradise. The spirit of it has been imparted on the circles of Havona, but the final touches of the training of the pilgrims of time can be applied only after they actually attain the Isle of Light.

All Paradise conduct is wholly spontaneous, in every sense natural and free. But there still is a proper and perfect way of doing things on the eternal Isle, and the directors of conduct are ever by the side of the "strangers within the gates" to instruct them and so guide their steps as to put them at perfect ease and at the same time to enable the pilgrims to avoid that confusion and uncertainty which would otherwise be inevitable. Only by such an arrangement could endless confusion be avoided; and confusion never appears on Paradise.

These directors of conduct really serve as glorified teachers and guides. They are chiefly concerned with instructing the new mortal residents regarding the almost endless array of new situations and unfamiliar usages. Notwithstanding all the long preparation therefor and the long journey thereto, Paradise is still inexpressibly strange and unexpectedly new to those who finally attain residential status.

5. THE CUSTODIANS OF KNOWLEDGE

The superaphic custodians of knowledge are the higher "living epistles" known and read by all who dwell on Paradise. They are the divine records of truth, the living books of real knowledge. You have heard about records in the "book of life." The custodians of knowledge are just such living books, records of perfection imprinted upon the eternal tablets of divine life and supreme surety. They are in reality living, automatic libraries. The facts of the universes are inherent in these primary supernaphim, actually recorded in these angels; and it is also inherently impossible for an untruth to gain lodgment in the minds of these perfect and replete repositories of the truth of eternity and the intelligence of time.

These custodians conduct informal courses of instruction for the residents of the eternal Isle, but their chief function is that of reference and verification. Any sojourner on Paradise may at will have by his side the living repository of the particular fact or truth he may wish to know. At the northern extremity of the Isle there are available the living finders of knowledge, who will designate the director of the group holding the information sought, and forthwith will appear the brilliant beings who are the very thing you wish to know. No longer must you seek enlightenment from engrossed pages; you now commune with living intelligence face to face. Supreme knowledge you thus obtain from the living beings who are its final custodians.

When you locate that supernaphim who is exactly what you desire to verify, you will find available *all* the known facts of all universes, for these custodians of knowledge are the final and living summaries of the vast network of the recording angels, ranging from the seraphim and seconaphim of the local and superuniverses to the chief recorders of the tertiary supernaphim in Havona. And this living accumulation of knowledge is distinct from the formal records of Paradise, the cumulative summary of universal history.

The wisdom of truth takes origin in the divinity of the central universe, but knowledge, experiential knowledge, largely has its beginnings in the domains of time and space — therefore the necessity for the maintenance of the far-flung superuniverse organizations of the recording seraphim and supernaphim sponsored by the Celestial Recorders.

These primary supernaphim who are inherently in possession of universe knowledge are also responsible for its organization and classification. In constituting themselves the living reference library of the universe of universes, they have classified knowledge into seven grand orders, each having about one million subdivisions. The facility with which the residents of Paradise can consult this vast store of knowledge is solely due to the voluntary and wise efforts of the custodians of knowledge. The custodians are also the exalted teachers of the central universe, freely giving out their living treasures to all beings on any of the Havona circuits, and they are extensively, though indirectly, utilized by the courts of the Ancients of Days.

But this living library, which is available to the central and superuniverses, is not accessible to the local creations. Only by indirection and reflectively are the benefits of Paradise knowledge secured in the local universes.

6. MASTERS OF PHILOSOPHY

Next to the supreme satisfaction of worship is the exhilaration of philosophy. Never do you climb so high or advance so far that there do not remain a thousand mysteries which demand the employment of philosophy in an attempted solution.

The master philosophers of Paradise delight to lead the minds of its inhabitants, both native and ascendant, in the exhilarating pursuit of attempting to solve universe problems. These superaphic masters of philosophy are the "wise men of heaven," the beings of wisdom who make use of the truth of knowledge and the facts of experience in their efforts to master the unknown. With them knowledge attains to truth and experience ascends to wisdom. On Paradise the ascendant personalities of space experience the heights of being: They have knowledge; they know the truth; they may philosophize — think the truth; they may even seek to encompass the concepts of the Ultimate and attempt to grasp the techniques of the Absolutes.

At the southern extremity of the vast Paradise domain the masters of philosophy conduct elaborate courses in the seventy functional divisions of wisdom. Here they discourse upon the plans and purposes of Infinity and seek to co-ordinate the experiences, and to compose the knowledge, of all who have access to their wisdom. They have developed a highly specialized attitude toward various universe problems, but their final conclusions are always in uniform agreement.

These Paradise philosophers teach by every possible method of instruction, including the higher graph technique of Havona and certain Paradise methods of communicating information. All of these higher techniques of imparting knowledge and conveying ideas are utterly beyond the comprehension capacity of even the most highly developed human mind. One hour's instruction on Paradise would be the equivalent of ten thousand years of the word-memory methods of Urantia. You cannot grasp such communication techniques, and there is simply nothing in mortal experience with which they may be compared, nothing to which they can be likened.

The masters of philosophy take supreme pleasure in imparting their interpretation of the universe of universes to those beings who have ascended from the worlds of space. And while philosophy can never be as settled in its conclusions as the facts of knowledge and the truths of experience, yet, when you have listened to these primary supernaphim discourse upon the unsolved problems of eternity and the performances of the Absolutes, you will feel a certain and lasting satisfaction concerning these unmastered questions.

These intellectual pursuits of Paradise are not broadcast; the philosophy of perfection is available only to those who are personally present. The encircling creations know of these teachings only from those who have passed through this experience, and who have subsequently carried this wisdom out to the universes of space.

7. CONDUCTORS OF WORSHIP

Worship is the highest privilege and the first duty of all created intelligences. Worship is the conscious and joyous act of recognizing and acknowledging the truth and fact of the intimate and personal relationships of the Creators with their creatures. The quality of worship is determined by the depth of creature perception; and as the knowledge of the infinite character of the Gods progresses, the act of worship becomes increasingly all-encompassing until it eventually attains the glory of the highest experiential delight and the most exquisite pleasure known to created beings.

While the Isle of Paradise contains certain places of worship, it is more nearly one vast sanctuary of divine service. Worship is the first and dominant passion of all who climb to its blissful shores — the spontaneous ebullition of the beings who have learned enough of God to attain his presence. Circle by circle, during the inward journey through Havona, worship is a growing passion until on Paradise it becomes necessary to direct and otherwise control its expression.

The periodic, spontaneous, group, and other special outbursts of supreme adoration and spiritual praise enjoyed on Paradise are conducted under the leadership of a special corps of primary supernaphim. Under the direction of these conductors of worship, such homage achieves the creature goal of supreme pleasure and attains the heights of the perfection of sublime self-expression and personal enjoyment. All primary supernaphim crave to be conductors of worship; and all ascendant beings would enjoy forever remaining in the attitude of worship did not the chiefs of assignment periodically disperse these assemblages. But no ascendant being is ever required to enter upon the assignments of eternal service until he has attained full satisfaction in worship.

It is the task of the conductors of worship so to teach the ascendant creatures how to worship that they may be enabled to gain this satisfaction of self-expression and at the same time be able to give attention to the essential activities of the Paradise regime. Without improvement in the technique of worship it would require hundreds of years for the average mortal who reaches Paradise to give full and satisfactory expression to his emotions of intelligent appreciation and ascendant gratitude. The conductors of worship open up new and hitherto unknown avenues of expression so that these wonderful children of the womb of space and the travail of time are enabled to gain the full satisfactions of worship in much less time.

All the arts of all the beings of the entire universe which are capable of intensifying and exalting the abilities of self-expression and the conveyance of appreciation, are employed to their highest capacity in the worship of the Paradise Deities. *Worship is the highest joy of Paradise existence*; it is the refreshing play of Paradise. What play does for your jaded minds on earth, worship will do for your perfected souls on Paradise. The mode of worship on Paradise is utterly beyond mortal comprehension, but the spirit of it you can begin to appreciate even down here on Urantia, for the spirits of the Gods even now indwell you, hover over you, and inspire you to true worship.

There are appointed times and places for worship on Paradise, but these are not adequate to accommodate the ever-increasing overflow of the spiritual emotions of the growing intelligence and expanding divinity recognition of the brilliant beings of experiential ascension to the eternal Isle. Never since the times of Grandfanda have the supernaphim been able fully to accommodate the spirit of worship on Paradise. Always is there an excess of worshipfulness as gauged by the preparation therefor. And this is because personalities of inherent perfection never can fully appreciate the tremendous reactions of the spiritual emotions of beings who have slowly and laboriously made their way upward to Paradise glory from the depths of the spiritual darkness of the lower worlds of time and space. When such angels and mortals of time attain the presence of the Powers of Paradise, there occurs the expression of the accumulated emotions of the ages, a spectacle astounding to the angels of Paradise and productive of the supreme joy of divine satisfaction in the Paradise Deities.

Sometimes all Paradise becomes engulfed in a dominating tide of spiritual and worshipful expression. Often the conductors of worship cannot control such phenomena until the appearance of the threefold fluctuation of the light of the Deity abode, signifying that the divine heart of the Gods has been fully and completely satisfied by the sincere worship of the residents of Paradise, the perfect citizens of glory and the ascendant creatures of time. What a triumph of technique! What a fruition of the eternal plan and purpose of the Gods that the intelligent love of the creature child should give full satisfaction to the infinite love of the Creator Father!

After the attainment of the supreme satisfaction of the fullness of worship, you are qualified for admission to the Corps of the Finality. The ascendant career is well-nigh finished, and the seventh jubilee prepares for celebration. The first jubilee marked the mortal agreement with the Thought Adjuster when the purpose to survive was sealed; the second was the awakening in the morontia life; the third was the fusion with the Thought Adjuster; the fourth was the awakening in Havona; the fifth celebrated the finding of the Universal Father; and the sixth jubilee was the occasion of the Paradise awakening from the final transit slumber of time. The seventh jubilee marks entrance into the mortal finaliter corps and the beginning of the eternity service. The attainment of the seventh stage of spirit realization by a finaliter will probably signalize the celebration of the first of the jubilees of eternity.

And thus ends the story of the Paradise supernaphim, the highest order of all the ministering spirits, those beings who, as a universal class, ever attend you from the world of your origin until you are finally bidden farewell by the conductors of worship as you take the Trinity oath of eternity and are mustered into the Mortal Corps of the Finality.

The endless service of the Paradise Trinity is about to begin; and now the finaliter is face to face with the challenge of God the Ultimate.

[Presented by a Perfector of Wisdom from Uversa.]

PAPER 28
MINISTERING SPIRITS OF THE SUPERUNIVERSES

As THE SUPERNAPHIM are the angelic hosts of the central universe and the seraphim of the local universes, so are the seconaphim the ministering spirits of the superuniverses. In degree of divinity and in potential of supremacy, however, these children of the Reflective Spirits are much more like supernaphim than seraphim. They serve not alone in the supercreations, and both numerous and intriguing are the transactions sponsored by their unrevealed associates.

As presented in these narratives, the ministering spirits of the superuniverses embrace the following three orders:

1. The Seconaphim.
2. The Tertiaphim.
3. The Omniaphim.

Since the latter two orders are not so directly concerned with the ascendant scheme of mortal progression, they will be briefly discussed prior to the more extended consideration of seconaphim. Technically, neither tertiaphim nor omniaphim are ministering spirits *of* the superuniverses, though both serve as spirit ministers in these domains.

1. THE TERTIAPHIM

These high angels are of record on the superuniverse headquarters, and despite service in the local creations, technically they are residents of these superuniverse capitals inasmuch as they are not native to the local universes. Tertiaphim are children of the Infinite Spirit and are personalized on Paradise in groups of one thousand. These supernal beings of divine originality and near-supreme versatility are the gift of the Infinite Spirit to the Creator Sons of God.

When a Michael Son is detached from the parental regime of Paradise and is made ready to go forth on the universe adventure of space, the Infinite Spirit is delivered of a group of one thousand of these companion spirits. And these majestic tertiaphim accompany this Creator Son when he embarks upon the adventure of universe organization.

Throughout the early times of universe building, these one thousand tertiaphim are the only personal staff of a Creator Son. They acquire a mighty experience as Son assistants during these stirring ages of universe assembling and other astronomical manipulations. They serve by the side of the Creator Son until the day of the personalization of the Bright and Morning Star, the first-born of a local universe. Thereupon the formal resignations of the tertiaphim are tendered and accepted. And with the appearance of the initial orders of native angelic life, they retire from active service in the local universe and become the liaison ministers between the Creator Son of former attachment and the Ancients of Days of the superuniverse concerned.

2. THE OMNIAPHIM

Omniaphim are created by the Infinite Spirit in liaison with the Seven Supreme Executives, and they are the exclusive servants and messengers of these same Supreme Executives. Omniaphim are of grand universe assignment, and in Orvonton their corps maintains headquarters in the northerly parts of Uversa, where they reside as a special courtesy colony. They are not of registry on Uversa, nor are they attached to our administration. Neither are they directly concerned with the ascendant scheme of mortal progression.

The omniaphim are wholly occupied with the oversight of the superuniverses in the interests of administrative co-ordination from the viewpoint of the Seven Supreme Executives. Our colony of omniaphim on Uversa receives instructions from, and makes reports to, only the Supreme Executive of Orvonton, situated on conjoint executive sphere number seven in the outer ring of Paradise satellites.

3. THE SECONAPHIM

The secoraphic hosts are produced by the seven Reflective Spirits assigned to the headquarters of each superuniverse. There is a definite Paradise-responsive technique associated with the creation of these angels in groups of seven. In each seven there are always one primary, three secondary, and three tertiary seconaphim; they always personalize in this exact proportion. When seven such seconaphim are created, one, the primary, becomes attached to the service of the Ancients of Days. The three secondary angels are associated with three groups of Paradise-origin administrators in the supergovernments: the Divine Counselors, the Perfectors of Wisdom, and the Universal Censors. The three tertiary angels are attached to the ascendant trinitized associates of the superuniverse rulers: the Mighty Messengers, Those High in Authority, and Those without Name and Number.

These seconaphim of the superuniverses are the offspring of the Reflective Spirits, and therefore reflectivity is inherent in their nature. They are reflectively responsive to all of each phase of every creature of origin in the Third Source and Center and the Paradise Creator Sons, but they are not directly reflective of the beings and entities, personal or otherwise, of sole origin in the First Source and Center. We possess many evidences of the actuality of the universal intelligence circuits of the Infinite Spirit, but even if we had no other proof, the reflective performances of the seconaphim would be quite sufficient to demonstrate the reality of the universal presence of the infinite mind of the Conjoint Actor.

4. THE PRIMARY SECONAPHIM

The primary seconaphim, of assignment to the Ancients of Days, are living mirrors in the service of these triune rulers. Think what it means in the economy of a superuniverse to be able to turn, as it were, to a living mirror and therein to see and therewith to hear the certain responses of another being, no matter in which universe of the superuniverse it is in and no matter where in that universe it happens to be, and to do all this instantly and unerringly. Records are essential to the conduct of the universes, broadcasts are serviceable, the work of the Solitary and other messengers is very helpful, but the Ancients of Days from their position midway between the inhabited worlds and Paradise — between man and God — can instantly look both ways, hear both ways, and *know* both ways.

This ability — to hear and see, as it were, all things — can be perfectly realized in the superuniverses only by the Ancients of Days and only on their respective headquarters worlds. Even there limits are encountered: From Uversa, such communication is limited to the worlds and universes of Orvonton, and while inoperative between the superuniverses, this same reflective technique keeps each one of them in close touch with the central universe and with Paradise. The seven supergovernments, though individually segregated, are thus perfectly reflective of the authority above and are wholly sympathetic, as well as perfectly conversant, with the needs below.

The primary seconaphim are found to incline by inherent nature towards seven types of service, and it is befitting that the first serials of this order should be so endowed as inherently to interpret the mind of the Spirit to the Ancients of Days:

1. *The Voice of the Conjoint Actor*. In each superuniverse the first primary seconaphim and every seventh one of that order subsequently created exhibit a high order of adaptability for understanding and interpreting the mind of the Infinite Spirit to the Ancients of Days and their associates in the supergovernments. This is of great value on the headquarters of the superuniverses, for, unlike the local creations with their Divine Ministers, the seat of a supergovern-

ment does not have a specialized personalization of the Infinite Spirit. Hence these secoraphic voices come the nearest to being the personal representatives of the Third Source and Center on such a capital sphere. True, the seven Reflective Spirits are there, but these mothers of the secoraphic hosts are less truly and automatically reflective of the Conjoint Actor than of the Seven Master Spirits.

2. *The Voice of the Seven Master Spirits*. The second primary seconaphim and every seventh one thereafter created incline towards portraying the collective natures and reactions of the Seven Master Spirits. Though each Master Spirit is already represented on a superuniverse capital by some one of the seven Reflective Spirits of assignment, such representation is individual, not collective. Collectively, they are only reflectively present; therefore do the Master Spirits welcome the services of these highly personal angels, the second serials of the primary seconaphim, who are so competent to represent them before the Ancients of Days.

3. *The Voice of the Creator Sons*. The Infinite Spirit must have had something to do with the creation or training of the Paradise Sons of the order of Michael, for the third primary seconaphim and every seventh serial thereafter possess the remarkable gift of being reflective of the minds of these Creator Sons. If the Ancients of Days would like to know — really know — the attitude of Michael of Nebadon regarding some matter under consideration, they do not have to call him on the lines of space; they need only call for the Chief of Nebadon Voices, who, upon request, will present the Michael seconaphim of record; and right then and there the Ancients of Days will perceive the voice of the Master Son of Nebadon.

No other order of sonship is thus "reflectible," and no other order of angel can thus function. We do not fully understand just how this is accomplished, and I doubt very much that the Creator Sons themselves fully understand it. But of a certainty we know it works, and that it unfailingly works acceptably we also know, for in all the history of Uversa the secoraphic voices have never erred in their presentations.

You are here beginning to see something of the manner in which divinity encompasses the space of time and masters the time of space. You are here obtaining one of your first fleeting glimpses of the technique of the eternity cycle, divergent for the moment to assist the children of time in their tasks of mastering the difficult handicaps of space. And these phenomena are additional to the established universe technique of the Reflective Spirits.

Though apparently deprived of the personal presence of the Master Spirits above and of the Creator Sons below, the Ancients of Days have at their command living beings attuned to cosmic mechanisms of reflective perfection and ultimate precision whereby they may enjoy the reflective presence of all those exalted beings whose personal presence is denied them. By and through these means, and others unknown to you, God is potentially present on the headquarters of the superuniverses.

The Ancients of Days perfectly deduce the Father's will by equating the Spirit voice-flash from above and the Michael voice-flashes from below. Thus may they be unerringly certain in calculating the Father's will concerning the administrative affairs of the local universes. But to deduce the will of one of the Gods from a knowledge of the other two, the three Ancients of Days must act together; two would not be able to achieve the answer. And for this reason, even were there no others, the superuniverses are always presided over by three Ancients of Days, and not by one or even two.

4. *The Voice of the Angelic Hosts*. The fourth primary seconaphim and every seventh serial prove to be angels peculiarly responsive to the sentiments of all orders of angels, including the supernaphim above and the seraphim below. Thus the attitude of any commanding or supervising angel is immediately available for consideration at any council of the Ancients of Days. Never a day passes on your world that the chief of seraphim on Urantia is not made conscious of the phenomenon of reflective transference, of being drawn upon from Uversa for some purpose; but unless forewarned by a Solitary Messenger, she remains wholly ignorant of what is sought and of how it is secured. These ministering spirits of time are constantly furnishing this sort of unconscious and certainly, therefore, unprejudiced testimony concerning the endless array of matters engaging the attention and counsel of the Ancients of Days and their associates.

5. *Broadcast Receivers*. There is a special class of broadcast messages which are received only by these primary seconaphim. While they are not the regular broadcasters of Uversa, they work in liaison with the angels of

the reflective voices for the purpose of synchronizing the reflective vision of the Ancients of Days with certain actual messages coming in over the established circuits of universe communication. Broadcast receivers are the fifth serials, the fifth primary seconaphim to be created and every seventh one thereafter.

6. *Transport Personalities*. These are the seconaphim who carry the pilgrims of time from the headquarters worlds of the superuniverses to the outer circle of Havona. They are the transport corps of the superuniverses, operating inward to Paradise and outward to the worlds of their respective sectors. This corps is composed of the sixth primary seconaphim and every seventh one subsequently created.

7. *The Reserve Corps*. A very large group of seconaphim, the seventh primary serials, are held in reserve for the unclassified duties and the emergency assignments of the realms. Not being highly specialized, they can function fairly well in any of the capacities of their diverse associates, but such specialized work is undertaken only in emergencies. Their usual tasks are the performance of those generalized duties of a superuniverse which do not fall within the scope of the angels of specific assignment.

5. THE SECONDARY SECONAPHIM

Seconaphim of the secondary order are no less reflective than their primary fellows. Being classed as primary, secondary, and tertiary does not indicate a differential of status or function in the case of seconaphim; it merely denotes orders of procedure. Identical qualities are exhibited by all three groups in their activities.

The seven reflective types of secondary seconaphim are assigned to the services of the co-ordinate Trinity-origin associates of the Ancients of Days as follows:

To the Perfectors of Wisdom — the Voices of Wisdom, the Souls of Philosophy, and the Unions of Souls.

To the Divine Counselors — the Hearts of Counsel, the Joys of Existence, and the Satisfactions of Service.

To the Universal Censors — the Discerners of Spirits.

Like the primary order, this group is created serially; that is, the first-born was a Voice of Wisdom, and the seventh thereafter was similar, and so with the six other types of these reflective angels.

1. *The Voice of Wisdom.* Certain of these seconaphim are in perpetual liaison with the living libraries of Paradise, the custodians of knowledge belonging to the primary supernaphim. In specialized reflective service the Voices of Wisdom are living, current, replete, and thoroughly reliable concentrations and focalizations of the co-ordinated wisdom of the universe of universes. To the well-nigh infinite volume of information circulating on the master circuits of the superuniverses, these superb beings are so reflective and selective, so sensitive, as to be able to segregate and receive the essence of wisdom and unerringly to transmit these jewels of mentation to their superiors, the Perfectors of Wisdom. And they so function that the Perfectors of Wisdom not only hear the actual and original expressions of this wisdom but also reflectively see the very beings, of high or lowly origin, who gave voice to it.

It is written, "If any man lack wisdom, let him ask." On Uversa, when it becomes necessary to arrive at the decisions of wisdom in the perplexing situations of the complex affairs of the superuniverse government, when both the wisdom of perfection and of practicability must be forthcoming, then do the Perfectors of Wisdom summon a battery of the Voices of Wisdom and, by the consummate skill of their order, so attune and directionize these living receivers of the enminded and circulating wisdom of the universe of universes that presently, from these secoraphic voices, there ensues a stream of the wisdom of divinity from the universe above and a flood of the wisdom of practicality from the higher minds of the universes below.

If confusion arises regarding the harmonization of these two versions of wisdom, immediate appeal is made to the Divine Counselors, who forthwith rule as to the proper combination of procedures. If there is any doubt as to the authenticity of something coming in from realms where rebellion has been rife, appeal is made to the Censors, who, with their Discerners of Spirits, are able to rule immediately as to "what manner of spirit" actuated the adviser. So are the wisdom of the ages and the intellect of the moment ever present with the Ancients of Days, like an open book before their beneficent gaze.

You can just faintly comprehend what all this means to those who are responsible for the conduct of the superuniverse governments. The immensity and the comprehensiveness of these transactions are quite beyond finite conception. When you stand, as I repeatedly have, in the special receiving chambers of the temple of wisdom on Uversa and see all this in actual operation, you will be moved to adoration by the perfection of the complexity, and by the surety of the working, of the interplanetary communications of the universes. You will pay homage to the divine wisdom and goodness of the Gods, who plan and execute with such superb technique. And these things actually happen just as I have portrayed them.

2. *The Soul of Philosophy*. These wonderful teachers are also attached to the Perfectors of Wisdom and, when not otherwise directionized, remain in focal synchrony with the masters of philosophy on Paradise. Think of stepping up to a huge living mirror, as it were, but instead of beholding the likeness of your finite and material self, of perceiving a reflection of the wisdom of divinity and the philosophy of Paradise. And if it becomes desirable to "incarnate" this philosophy of perfection, so to dilute it as to make it practical of application to, and assimilation by, the lowly peoples of the lower worlds, these living mirrors have only to turn their faces downward to reflect the standards and needs of another world or universe.

By these very techniques do the Perfectors of Wisdom adapt decisions and recommendations to the real needs and actual status of the peoples and worlds under consideration, and always do they act in concert with the Divine Counselors and the Universal Censors. But the sublime repleteness of these transactions is beyond even my ability to comprehend.

3. *The Union of Souls*. Completing the triune staff of attachment to the Perfectors of Wisdom, are these reflectors of the ideals and status of ethical relationships. Of all the problems in the universe requiring an exercise of the consummate wisdom of experience and adaptability, none are more impor-

tant than those arising out of the relationships and associations of intelligent beings. Whether in human associations of commerce and trade, friendship and marriage, or in the liaisons of the angelic hosts, there continue to arise petty frictions, minor misunderstandings too trivial even to engage the attention of conciliators but sufficiently irritating and disturbing to mar the smooth working of the universe if they were allowed to multiply and continue. Therefore do the Perfectors of Wisdom make available the wise experience of their order as the "oil of reconciliation" for an entire superuniverse. In all this work these wise men of the superuniverses are ably seconded by their reflective associates, the Unions of Souls, who make available current information regarding the status of the universe and concurrently portray the Paradise ideal of the best adjustment of these perplexing problems. When not specifically directionized elsewhere, these seconaphim remain in reflective liaison with the interpreters of ethics on Paradise.

These are the angels who foster and promote the teamwork of all Orvonton. One of the most important lessons to be learned during your mortal career is teamwork. The spheres of perfection are manned by those who have mastered this art of working with other beings. Few are the duties in the universe for the lone servant. The higher you ascend, the more lonely you become when temporarily without the association of your fellows.

4. *The Heart of Counsel.* This is the first group of these reflective geniuses to be placed under the supervision of the Divine Counselors. Seconaphim of this type are in possession of the facts of space, being selective for such data in the circuits of time. Especially are they reflective of the superaphic intelligence co-ordinators, but they are also selectively reflective of the counsel of all beings, whether of high or low estate. Whenever the Divine Counselors are called upon for important advice or decisions, they immediately requisition an ensemble of the Hearts of Counsel, and presently there is handed down a ruling which actually incorporates the co-ordinated wisdom and advice of the most competent minds of the entire superuniverse, all of which has been censored and revised in the light of the counsel of the high minds of Havona and even of Paradise.

5. *The Joy of Existence.* By nature these beings are reflectively attuned to the superaphic harmony supervisors above and to certain of the seraphim below, but it is difficult to explain just what the members of this interesting group really do. Their principal activities are directed toward promoting reactions of joy among the various orders of the angelic hosts and the lower will creatures. The Divine Counselors, to whom they are attached, seldom use them for specific joy finding. In a more general manner and in collaboration with the reversion directors, they function as joy clearinghouses, seeking to upstep the pleasure reactions of the realms while trying to improve the humor taste, to develop a superhumor among mortals and angels. They endeavor to demonstrate that there is inherent joy in freewill existence, independent of all extraneous influences; and they are right, although they meet with great difficulty in inculcating this truth in the minds of primitive men. The higher spirit personalities and the angels are more quickly responsive to these educational efforts.

6. *The Satisfaction of Service.* These angels are highly reflective of the attitude of the directors of conduct on Paradise, and functioning much as do the Joys of Existence, they strive to enhance the value of service and to augment the satisfactions to be derived therefrom. They have done much to illuminate the deferred rewards inherent in unselfish service, service for the extension of the kingdom of truth.

The Divine Counselors, to whom this order is attached, utilize them to reflect from one world to another the benefits to be derived from spiritual service. And by using the performances of the best to inspire and encourage the mediocre, these seconaphim contribute immensely to the quality of devoted service in the superuniverses. Effective use is made of the fraternal competitive spirit by circulating to any one world information about what the others, particularly the best, are doing. A refreshing and wholesome rivalry is promoted even among the seraphic hosts.

7. *The Discerner of Spirits.* A special liaison exists between the counselors and advisers of the second Havona circle and these reflective angels. They are the only seconaphim attached to the Universal Censors but are probably the most uniquely specialized of all their fellows. Regardless of the source or channel of information, no matter how meager the evidence at

hand, when it is subjected to their reflective scrutiny, these discerners will forthwith inform us as to the true motive, the actual purpose, and the real nature of its origin. I marvel at the superb functioning of these angels, who so unerringly reflect the actual moral and spiritual character of any individual concerned in a focal exposure.

The Discerners of Spirits carry on these intricate services by virtue of inherent "spiritual insight," if I may use such words in an endeavor to convey to the human mind the thought that these reflective angels thus function intuitively, inherently, and unerringly. When the Universal Censors behold these presentations, they are face to face with the naked soul of the reflected individual; and this very certainty and perfection of portraiture in part explains why the Censors can always function so justly as righteous judges. The discerners always accompany the Censors on any mission away from Uversa, and they are just as effective out in the universes as at their Uversa headquarters.

I assure you that all these transactions of the spirit world are real, that they take place in accordance with established usages and in harmony with the immutable laws of the universal domains. The beings of every newly created order, immediately upon receiving the breath of life, are instantly reflected on high; a living portrayal of the creature nature and potential is flashed to the superuniverse headquarters. Thus, by means of the discerners, are the Censors made fully cognizant of exactly "what manner of spirit" has been born on the worlds of space.

So it is with mortal man: The Mother Spirit of Salvington knows you fully, for the Holy Spirit on your world "searches all things," and whatsoever the divine Spirit knows of you is immediately available whenever the secoraphic discerners reflect with the Spirit concerning the Spirit's knowledge of you. It should, however, be mentioned that the knowledge and plans of the Father fragments are not reflectible. The discerners can and do reflect the presence of the Adjusters (and the Censors pronounce them divine), but they cannot decipher the content of the mindedness of the Mystery Monitors.

6. THE TERTIARY SECONAPHIM

In the same manner as their fellows, these angels are created serially and in seven reflective types, but these types are not assigned individually to the separate services of the superuniverse administrators. All tertiary seconaphim are collectively assigned to the Trinitized Sons of Attainment, and these ascendant sons use them interchangeably; that is, the Mighty Messengers can and do utilize any of the tertiary types, and so do their co-ordinates, Those High in Authority and Those without Name and Number. These seven types of tertiary seconaphim are:

1. *The Significance of Origins*. The ascendant Trinitized Sons of a superuniverse government are charged with the responsibility of dealing with all issues growing out of the origin of any individual, or world; and the significance of origin is the paramount question in all our plans for the cosmic advancement of the living creatures of the realm. All relationships and the application of ethics grow out of the fundamental facts of origin. Origin is the basis of the relational reaction of the Gods. Always does the Conjoint Actor "take note of the man, in what manner he was born."

With the higher descendant beings, origin is simply a fact to be ascertained; but with the ascending beings, including the lower orders of angels, the nature and circumstances of origin are not always so clear, though of equally vital importance at almost every turn of universe affairs — hence the value of having at our disposal a series of reflective seconaphim who can instantly portray anything required respecting the genesis of any being in either the central universe or throughout the entire realm of a superuniverse.

The Significance of Origins are the living ready-reference genealogies of the vast hosts of beings — men, angels, and others — who inhabit the seven superuniverses. They are always ready to supply their superiors with an up-to-date, replete, and trustworthy estimate of the ancestral factors and the current actual status of any individual on any world of their respective superuniverses; and their computation of possessed facts is always up to the minute.

2. *The Memory of Mercy*. These are the actual, full and replete, living

records of the mercy which has been extended to individuals by the tender ministrations of the instrumentalities of the Infinite Spirit in the mission of adapting the justice of righteousness to the status of the realms, as disclosed by the portrayals of the Significance of Origins. The Memory of Mercy discloses the moral debt of the children of mercy — their spiritual liabilities — to be set down against their assets of the saving provision established by the Sons of God. In revealing the Father's pre-existent mercy, the Sons of God establish the necessary credit to insure the survival of all. And then, in accordance with the findings of the Significance of Origins, a mercy credit is established for the survival of each rational creature, a credit of lavish proportions and one of sufficient grace to insure the survival of every soul who really desires divine citizenship.

The Memory of Mercy is a living trial balance, a current statement of your account with the supernatural forces of the realms. These are the living records of mercy ministration which are read into the testimony of the courts of Uversa when each individual's right to unending life comes up for adjudication, when "thrones are cast up and the Ancients of Days are seated. The broadcasts of Uversa issue and come forth from before them; thousands upon thousands minister to them, and ten thousand times ten thousand stand before them. The judgment is set, and the books are opened." And the books which are opened on such a momentous occasion are the living records of the tertiary seconaphim of the superuniverses. The formal records are on file to corroborate the testimony of the Memories of Mercy if they are required.

The Memory of Mercy must show that the saving credit established by the Sons of God has been fully and faithfully paid out in the loving ministry of the patient personalities of the Third Source and Center. But when mercy is exhausted, when the "memory" thereof testifies to its depletion, then does justice prevail and righteousness decree. For mercy is not to be thrust upon those who despise it; mercy is not a gift to be trampled under foot by the persistent rebels of time. Nevertheless, though mercy is thus precious and dearly bestowed, your individual drawing credits are always far in excess of your ability to exhaust the reserve if you are sincere of purpose and honest of heart.

The mercy reflectors, with their tertiary associates, engage in numerous superuniverse ministries, including the teaching of the ascending creatures.

Among many other things the Significance of Origins teach these ascenders how to apply spirit ethics, and following such training, the Memories of Mercy teach them how to be truly merciful. While the spirit techniques of mercy ministry are beyond your concept, you should even now understand that mercy is a quality of growth. You should realize that there is a great reward of personal satisfaction in being first just, next fair, then patient, then kind. And then, on that foundation, if you choose and have it in your heart, you can take the next step and really show mercy; but you cannot exhibit mercy in and of itself. These steps must be traversed; otherwise there can be no genuine mercy. There may be patronage, condescension, or charity — even pity — but not mercy. True mercy comes only as the beautiful climax to these preceding adjuncts to group understanding, mutual appreciation, fraternal fellowship, spiritual communion, and divine harmony.

3. *The Import of Time*. Time is the one universal endowment of all will creatures; it is the "one talent" intrusted to all intelligent beings. You all have time in which to insure your survival; and time is fatally squandered only when it is buried in neglect, when you fail so to utilize it as to make certain the survival of your soul. Failure to improve one's time to the fullest extent possible does not impose fatal penalties; it merely retards the pilgrim of time in his journey of ascent. If survival is gained, all other losses can be retrieved.

In the assignment of trusts the counsel of the Imports of Time is invaluable. Time is a vital factor in everything this side of Havona and Paradise. In the final judgment before the Ancients of Days, time is an element of evidence. The Imports of Time must always afford testimony to show that every defendant has had ample time for making decisions, achieving choice.

These time evaluators are also the secret of prophecy; they portray the element of time which will be required in the completion of any undertaking, and they are just as dependable as indicators as are the frandalanks and chronoldeks of other living orders. The Gods foresee, hence foreknow; but the ascendant authorities of the universes of time must consult the Imports of Time to be able to forecast events of the future.

You will first encounter these beings on the mansion worlds, and they will there instruct you in the advantageous use of that which you call "time," both in its positive employment, work, and in its negative utilization, rest. Both uses of time are important.

4. *The Solemnity of Trust.* Trust is the crucial test of will creatures. Trustworthiness is the true measure of self-mastery, character. These seconaphim accomplish a double purpose in the economy of the superuniverses: They portray to all will creatures the sense of the obligation, sacredness, and solemnity of trust. At the same time they unerringly reflect to the governing authorities the exact trustworthiness of any candidate for confidence or trust.

On Urantia, you grotesquely essay to read character and to estimate specific abilities, but on Uversa we actually do these things in perfection. These seconaphim weigh trustworthiness in the living scales of unerring character appraisal, and when they have looked at you, we have only to look at them to know the limitations of your ability to discharge responsibility, execute trust, and fulfill missions. Your assets of trustworthiness are clearly set forth alongside your liabilities of possible default or betrayal.

It is the plan of your superiors to advance you by augmented trusts just as fast as your character is sufficiently developed to gracefully bear these added responsibilities, but to overload the individual only courts disaster and insures disappointment. And the mistake of placing responsibility prematurely upon either man or angel may be avoided by utilizing the ministry of these infallible estimators of the trust capacity of the individuals of time and space. These seconaphim ever accompany Those High in Authority, and never do these executives make assignments until their candidates have been weighed in the secoraphic balances and pronounced "not wanting."

5. *The Sanctity of Service.* The privilege of service immediately follows the discovery of trustworthiness. Nothing can stand between you and opportunity for increased service except your own untrustworthiness, your lack of capacity for appreciation of the solemnity of trust.

Service — purposeful service, not slavery — is productive of the highest satisfaction and is expressive of the divinest dignity. Service — more service, increased service, difficult service, adventurous service, and at last divine and perfect service — is the goal of time and the destination of space. But ever will the play cycles of time alternate with the service cycles of progress. And after the service of time there follows the superservice of eternity. During the play of time you should envision the work of eternity, even as you will, during the service of eternity, reminisce the play of time.

The universal economy is based on intake and output; throughout the eternal career you will never encounter monotony of inaction or stagnation of personality. Progress is made possible by inherent motion, advancement grows out of the divine capacity for action, and achievement is the child of imaginative adventure. But inherent in this capacity for achievement is the responsibility of ethics, the necessity for recognizing that the world and the universe are filled with a multitude of differing types of beings. All of this magnificent creation, *including yourself*, was not made just for you. This is not an egocentric universe. The Gods have decreed, "It is more blessed to give than to receive," and said your Master Son, "He who would be greatest among you let him be server of all."

The real nature of any service, be it rendered by man or angel, is fully revealed in the faces of these secoraphic service indicators, the Sanctities of Service. The full analysis of the true and of the hidden motives is clearly shown. These angels are indeed the mind readers, heart searchers, and soul revealers of the universe. Mortals may employ words to conceal their thoughts, but these high seconaphim lay bare the deep motives of the human heart and of the angelic mind.

6 and 7. The Secret of Greatness and the Soul of Goodness. The ascending pilgrims having awakened to the import of time, the way is prepared for the realization of the solemnity of trust and for the appreciation of the sanctity of service. While these are the moral elements of greatness, there are also secrets of greatness. When the spiritual tests of greatness are applied, the moral elements are not disregarded, but the quality of unselfishness revealed in disinterested labor for the welfare of one's earthly fellows, particularly worthy beings in need and in distress, that is the real measure of planetary greatness. And the manifestation of greatness on a world like Urantia is the exhibition of self-control. The great man is not he who "takes a city" or "overthrows a nation," but rather "he who subdues his own tongue."

Greatness is synonymous with divinity. God is supremely great and good. *Greatness and goodness simply cannot be divorced.* They are forever made one in God. This truth is literally and strikingly illustrated by the reflective interdependence of the Secret of Greatness and the Soul of Goodness, for neither can function without the other. In reflecting other qualities of divinity, the superuniverse seconaphim can and do act alone, but the reflective estimates of greatness and of goodness appear to be inseparable. Hence, on any world, in any universe, must these reflectors of greatness and of goodness work together, always showing a dual and mutually dependent report of every being upon whom they focalize. Greatness cannot be estimated without knowing the content of goodness, while goodness cannot be portrayed without exhibiting its inherent and divine greatness.

The estimate of greatness varies from sphere to sphere. To be great is to be Godlike. And since the quality of greatness is wholly determined by the content of goodness, it follows that, even in your present human estate, if you can through grace become good, you are thereby becoming great. The more steadfastly you behold, and the more persistently you pursue, the concepts of divine goodness, the more certainly will you grow in greatness, in true magnitude of genuine survival character.

7. MINISTRY OF THE SECONAPHIM

The seconaphim have their origin and headquarters on the capitals of the superuniverses, but with their liaison fellows they range from the shores of Paradise to the evolutionary worlds of space. They serve as valued assistants to the members of the deliberative assemblies of the supergovernments and are of great help to the courtesy colonies of Uversa: the star students, millennial tourists, celestial observers, and a host of others, including the ascendant beings in waiting for Havona transport. The Ancients of Days take pleasure in assigning certain of the primary seconaphim to assist the ascending creatures domiciled on the four hundred ninety study worlds surrounding Uversa, and here also do many of the secondary and tertiary orders serve as teachers. These Uversa satellites are the finishing schools of the universes of time, presenting the preparatory course for the seven-circuited university of Havona.

Of the three orders of seconaphim, the tertiary group, attached to the ascendant authorities, minister most extensively to the ascending creatures of time. You will on occasion meet them soon after your departure from Urantia, though you will not freely make use of their services until you reach the tarrying worlds of Orvonton. You will enjoy their companionship when you become fully acquainted with them during your sojourn on the Uversa school worlds.

These tertiary seconaphim are the timesavers, space abridgers, error detectors, faithful teachers, and everlasting guideposts — living signs of divine surety — in mercy placed at the crossroads of time, there to guide the feet of anxious pilgrims in moments of great perplexity and spiritual uncertainty. Long before attaining the portals of perfection, you will begin to gain access to the tools of divinity and to make contact with the techniques of Deity. Increasingly, from the time you arrive on the initial mansion world until you close your eyes in the Havona sleep preparatory to your Paradise transit, you will avail yourself of the emergency help of these marvelous beings, who are so fully and freely reflective of the sure knowledge and certain wisdom of those safe and dependable pilgrims who have preceded you on the long journey to the portals of perfection.

We are denied the full privilege of using these angels of the reflective order on Urantia. They are frequent visitors on your world, accompanying assigned personalities, but here they cannot freely function. This sphere is still under partial spiritual quarantine, and some of the circuits essential to their services are not here at present. When your world is once more restored to the reflective circuits concerned, much of the work of interplanetary and interuniverse communication will be greatly simplified and expedited. Celestial workers on Urantia encounter many difficulties because of this functional curtailment of their reflective associates. But we go on joyfully conducting our affairs with the instrumentalities at hand, notwithstanding our local deprivation of many of the services of these marvelous beings, the living mirrors of space and the presence projectors of time.

[Sponsored by a Mighty Messenger of Uversa.]

PAPER 29
THE UNIVERSE POWER DIRECTORS

Of all the universe personalities concerned in the regulation of interplanetary and interuniverse affairs, the power directors and their associates have been the least understood on Urantia. While mankind has long known of the existence of angels and similar orders of celestial beings, little information concerning the controllers and regulators of the physical domain has ever been imparted. Even now I am permitted fully to disclose only the last of the following three groups of living beings having to do with force control and energy regulation in the master universe:

1. Primary Eventuated Master Force Organizers.
2. Associate Transcendental Master Force Organizers.
3. Universe Power Directors.

Though I deem it impossible to portray the individuality of the various groups of directors, centers, and controllers of universe power, I hope to be able to explain something about the domain of their activities. They are a unique group of living beings having to do with the intelligent regulation of energy throughout the grand universe.

Including the supreme directors, they embrace the following major divisions:

1. The Seven Supreme Power Directors.
2. The Supreme Power Centers.
3. The Master Physical Controllers.
4. The Morontia Power Supervisors.

The Supreme Power Directors and Centers have existed from the near times of eternity, and as far as we know, no more beings of these orders have been created. The Seven Supreme Directors were personalized by the Seven Master Spirits, and then they collaborated with their parents in the production of an enormous number of associates. Before the days of the power directors the energy circuits of space outside of the central universe were under the intelligent supervision of the Master Force Organizers of Paradise.

Having knowledge about material creatures, you have at least a contrastive conception of spiritual beings; but it is very difficult for the mortal mind to envisage the power directors. In the scheme of ascendant progression to higher levels of existence you have nothing directly to do with either the supreme directors or the power centers. On certain rare occasions you will have dealings with the physical controllers, and you will work freely with the supervisors of morontia power upon reaching the mansion worlds. These Morontia Power Supervisors function so exclusively in the morontia regime of the local creations that it is deemed best to narrate their activities in the section dealing with the local universe.

1. THE SEVEN SUPREME POWER DIRECTORS

The Seven Supreme Power Directors are the physical-energy regulators of the grand universe. Their creation by the Seven Master Spirits is the first recorded instance of the derivation of semimaterial progeny from true spirit ancestry. When the Seven Master Spirits create individually, they bring forth highly spiritual personalities on the angelic order; when they create collectively, they sometimes produce these high types of semimaterial beings. But even these quasi-physical beings would be invisible to the short-range vision of Urantia mortals.

The Supreme Power Directors are seven in number, and they are identical in appearance and function. One cannot be distinguished from another except by that Master Spirit with whom each is in immediate association, and to whom each is in complete functional subservience. Each of the Master Spirits is thus in eternal union with one of their collective offspring. The same director is always in association with the same Spirit, and their working partnership results in a unique association of physical and spiritual energies, of a semiphysical being and a spirit personality.

The Seven Supreme Power Directors are stationed on peripheral Paradise, where their slowly circulating presences indicate the whereabouts of the force-focal headquarters of the Master Spirits. These power directors function singly in the power-energy regulation of the superuniverses but collectively in the administration of the central creation. They operate from Paradise but maintain themselves as effective power centers in all divisions of the grand universe.

These mighty beings are the physical ancestors of the vast host of the power centers and, through them, of the physical controllers scattered throughout the seven superuniverses. Such subordinate physical-control organisms are basically uniform, identical except for the differential toning of each superuniverse corps. In order to change in superuniverse service, they would merely have to return to Paradise for retoning. The physical creation is fundamentally uniform in administration.

2. THE SUPREME POWER CENTERS

The Seven Supreme Power Directors are not able, individually, to reproduce themselves, but collectively, and in association with the Seven Master Spirits, they can and do reproduce — create — other beings like themselves. Such is the origin of the Supreme Power Centers of the grand universe, who function in the following ten groups:

1. Supreme Center Supervisors.
2. Havona Centers.

3. Superuniverse Centers.
4. Local Universe Centers.
5. Major Sector Centers
6. Minor Sector Centers
7. Galaxy Centers
8. Constellation Centers.
9. System Centers.
10. Unclassified Centers.

These power centers together with the Supreme Power Directors are beings of high will freedom and action. They are all endowed with Third-Source personality and disclose unquestioned volitional capacity of a high order. These directing centers of the universe power system are the possessors of exquisite intelligence endowment; they are the intellect of the power system of the grand universe and the secret of the technique of the mind control of all the vast network of the far-flung functions of the Master Physical Controllers and the Morontia Power Supervisors.

1. *Supreme Center Supervisors*. These seven co-ordinates and associates of the Supreme Power Directors are the regulators of the master energy circuits of the grand universe. Each center supervisor is headquartered on one of the special worlds of the Seven Supreme Executives, and they work in close association with these co-ordinators of general universe affairs.

The Supreme Power Directors and the Supreme Center Supervisors function both as individuals and conjointly with regard to all cosmic phenomena below the levels of "gravity energy." When acting in liaison, these fourteen beings are to universe power what the Seven Supreme Executives are to general universe affairs, and what the Seven Master Spirits are to the cosmic mind.

2. *Havona Centers*. Before the creation of the universes of time and space, power centers were not required in Havona, but ever since these far-distant times, one million have functioned in the central creation, each center having the supervision of a thousand Havona worlds. Here in the divine universe there is perfection of energy control, a condition not existing else-

where. Perfection of energy regulation is the ultimate goal of all the power centers and the physical controllers of space.

3. *Superuniverse Centers*. Occupying an enormous area on the capital sphere of each of the seven superuniverses are a large number of power centers of the third order. Three currents of primary energy of ten segregations each come in to these power centers, but seven specialized and well-directed, though imperfectly controlled, circuits of power go forth from their seat of united action. This is the electronic organization of universe power.

All energy is circuited in the Paradise cycle, but the Universe Power Directors direct the force-energies of nether Paradise as they find them modified in the space functions of the central and superuniverses, converting and directing these energies into channels of useful and constructive application. There is a difference between Havona energy and the energies of the superuniverses. The power charge of a superuniverse consists of three phases of energy of ten segregations each. This threefold energy charge spreads throughout the space of the grand universe; it is like a vast moving ocean of energy which engulfs and bathes the whole of each of the seven supercreations.

The electronic organization of universe power functions in seven phases and discloses varying response to local or linear gravity. This sevenfold circuit proceeds from the superuniverse power centers and pervades each supercreation. Such specialized currents of time and space are definite and localized energy movements initiated and directed for specific purposes, much as the Gulf Stream functions as a circumscribed phenomenon in the midst of the Atlantic Ocean.

4. *Local Universe Centers*. Numerous power centers of the fourth order are stationed on the headquarters of each local universe, and distributed down through the major and minor sectors, galaxies, constellations, and systems. They function to downstep and otherwise to modify the seven power circuits emanating from superuniverse headquarters. The local astronomical catastrophes of space are of passing concern to these power centers; they are engaged in the orderly dispatch of effective energy to all of the subsidiary components of a universe. They are of great assistance to the Creator Sons during the later times of universe organization and energy

mobilization. These centers are able to provide intensified lanes of energy useful for interplanetary communication between important inhabited points. Such a lane or line of energy, sometimes also called an energy path, is a direct circuit of energy from one power center to another power center or from one physical controller to another controller. It is an individualized stream of power and stands in contrast to the free space movements of undifferentiated energy.

5. *Major Sector Centers*. A large number of power centers of the fourth order are stationed in each major sector. They receive the energies from the local universe headquarters and use them throughout their sector as well as downsteping and distributing them to their respective minor sectors.

6. *Minor Sector Centers*. Power centers stationed in the minor sectors in many ways have the most difficult and challenging task of any power centers. Downstepping and distributing energies to far flung individual galaxies and out to all their local groups and galactic clusters and their organized associations, and even to groups of stars and planets not yet stabilized within any galaxy, yet within their minor sector responsibilities.

7. *Galaxy Centers*. The number of power centers assigned to any galaxy varies greatly due to the size and type of galaxy concerned and the number of organized constellations. These power centers likewise downstep and distribute energies to their respective constellations.

8. *Constellation Centers*. Ten of these living power centers are stationed in each constellation, functioning as energy projectors to the tributary local systems. From these beings there go forth the power lines for communication and transport and for the energizing of those living creatures who are dependent upon certain forms of physical energy for the maintenance of life. But neither the power centers nor the subordinate physical controllers are otherwise concerned with life as a functional organization.

9. *System Centers*. One Supreme Power Center is permanently assigned to each local system. These system centers dispatch the power circuits to the inhabited worlds of time and space. They co-ordinate the activities of the

subordinate physical controllers and otherwise function to insure the satisfactory distribution of power in the local system. The circuit relay between the planets depends upon the perfect co-ordination of certain material energies and upon the efficient regulation of physical power.

10. *Unclassified Centers.* These are the centers who function in special local situations but not on the inhabited planets. The individual worlds are in the charge of Master Physical Controllers and receive the encircuited lines of power dispatched by the power center of their system. Only those spheres of the most extraordinary energy relationships have power centers of the seventh order acting as universe balance wheels or energy governors. In every phase of activity these power centers are the full equals of those who function on the higher units of control, but not one space body in a million harbors such a living power organization.

3. THE DOMAIN OF POWER CENTERS

The Supreme Power Centers and their associates and subordinates are all in perfect synchrony and complete liaison with their Paradise progenitors, the Seven Supreme Power Directors. The power control of the grand universe is thus intrusted to the keeping and direction of the Seven Master Spirits, the creators of the Seven Supreme Power Directors.

The Supreme Power Directors and all their associates, assistants, and subordinates are forever exempt from apprehension or interference by all the tribunals of all space; neither are they subject to the administrative direction either of the superuniverse government of the Ancients of Days or of the local universe administration of the Creator Sons.

These power centers and directors are brought into being by the children of the Infinite Spirit. They are not germane to the administration of the Sons of God, though they affiliate with the Creator Sons during the later epochs of universe material organization. But the power centers are in some way closely associated with the cosmic overcontrol of the Supreme Being.

Power centers and physical controllers undergo no training; they are all created in perfection and are inherently perfect in action. Never do they pass from one function to another; always do they serve as originally assigned. There is no evolution in their ranks, and this is true of all seven divisions of both orders.

Having no ascendant past to revert to in memory, power centers and physical controllers never play; they are thoroughly businesslike in all their actions. They are always on duty; there is no provision in the universal scheme for the interruption of the physical lines of energy; never for a fraction of a second can these beings relinquish their direct supervision of the energy circuits of time and space.

The directors, centers, and controllers of power have nothing to do with anything in all creation except power, material or semiphysical energy; they do not originate it, but they do modify, manipulate, and directionize it. Neither do they have anything whatever to do with physical gravity except to resist its drawing power. Their relation to gravity is wholly negative.

The power centers utilize vast mechanisms and co-ordinations of a material order in liaison with the living mechanisms of the various segregated energy concentrations. Each individual power center is constituted in exactly one million units of functional control, and these energy-modifying units are not stationary as are the vital organs of man's physical body; these "vital organs" of power regulation are mobile and truly kaleidoscopic in associative possibilities.

It is utterly beyond my ability to explain the manner in which these living beings encompass the manipulation and regulation of the master circuits of universe energy. To undertake to inform you further concerning the size and function of these gigantic and almost perfectly efficient power centers, would only add to your confusion and consternation. They are both living and "personal," but they are beyond your comprehension.

Outside of Havona the Supreme Power Centers function only on especially constructed (architectural) spheres or on otherwise suitably constituted space bodies. The architectural worlds are so constructed that the living power centers can act as selective switches to directionize, modify, and concentrate the energies of space as they pour over these spheres. They could not so function on an ordinary evolutionary sun or planet. Certain groups are also concerned in the heating and other material necessities of these special headquarters worlds. And though it is beyond the scope of Urantia knowledge, I may state that these orders of living power personalities have much to do with the distribution of the light that shines without heat. They do not produce this phenomenon, but they are concerned with its dissemination and directionization.

The power centers and their subordinate controllers are assigned to the working of all of the physical energies of organized space. They work with the three basic currents of ten energies each. That is the energy charge of organized space; and organized space is their domain. The Universe Power Directors have nothing whatever to do with those tremendous actions of force which are now taking place outside the present boundaries of the seven superuniverses.

The power centers and controllers exert perfect control over only seven of the ten forms of energy contained in each basic universe current; those forms which are partly or wholly exempt from their control must represent the unpredictable realms of energy manifestation dominated by the Unqualified Absolute. If they exert an influence upon the primordial forces of this Absolute, we are not cognizant of such functions, though there is some slight evidence which would warrant the opinion that certain of the physical controllers are sometimes automatically reactive to certain impulses of the Universal Absolute.

These living power mechanisms are not consciously related to the master universe energy overcontrol of the Unqualified Absolute, but we surmise that their entire and almost perfect scheme of power direction is in some unknown manner subordinated to this supergravity presence. In any local energy situation the centers and controllers exert near-supremacy, but they are always conscious of the superenergy presence and the unrecognizable performance of the Unqualified Absolute.

4. THE MASTER PHYSICAL CONTROLLERS

These beings are the mobile subordinates of the Supreme Power Centers. The physical controllers are endowed with capabilities of individuality metamorphosis of such a nature that they can engage in a remarkable variety of autotransport, being able to traverse local space at velocities approaching the flight of Solitary Messengers. But like all other space traversers they require the assistance of both their fellows and certain other types of beings in overcoming the action of gravity and the resistance of inertia in departing from a material sphere.

The Master Physical Controllers serve throughout the grand universe. They are directly governed from Paradise by the Seven Supreme Power Directors as far as the headquarters of the superuniverses; from here they are directed and distributed by the Council of Equilibrium, the high commissioners of power dispatched by the Seven Master Spirits from the personnel of the Associate Master Force Organizers. These high commissioners are empowered to interpret the readings and registrations of the master frandalanks, those living instruments which indicate the power pressure and the energy charge of an entire superuniverse.

While the presence of the Paradise Deities encircles the grand universe and sweeps around the circle of eternity, the influence of any one of the Seven Master Spirits is limited to a single superuniverse. There is a distinct segregation of energy and a separation of the circuits of power between each of the seven supercreations; hence individualized control methods must and do prevail.

The Master Physical Controllers are the direct offspring of the Supreme Power Centers, and their numbers include the following:

1. Associate Power Directors.
2. Mechanical Controllers.
3. Energy Transformers.
4. Energy Transmitters.
5. Primary Associators.
6. Secondary Dissociators.
7. The Frandalanks and Chronoldeks.

Not all of these orders are persons in the sense of possessing individual powers of choice. Especially do the last four seem to be wholly automatic and mechanical in response to the impulses of their superiors and in reaction to existing energy conditions. But though such response appears wholly mechanistic, it is not; they may seem to be automatons, but all of them disclose the differential function of intelligence.

Personality is not necessarily a concomitant of mind. Mind can think even when deprived of all power of choice, as in numerous of the lower types of animals and in certain of these subordinate physical controllers. Many of these more automatic regulators of physical power are not persons in any sense of the term. They are not endowed with will and independence of decision, being wholly subservient to the mechanical perfection of design for the tasks of their allotment. Nonetheless all of them are highly intelligent beings.

The physical controllers are chiefly occupied in the adjustment of basic energies undiscovered on Urantia. These unknown energies are very essential to the interplanetary system of transport and to certain techniques of communication. When we lay lines of energy for the purpose of conveying sound equivalents or of extending vision, these undiscovered forms of energy are utilized by the living physical controllers and their associates. These same energies are also, on occasion, used by the midway creatures in their routine work.

1. *Associate Power Directors.* These marvelously efficient beings are intrusted with the assignment and dispatch of all orders of the Master Physical Controllers in accordance with the ever-shifting needs of the constantly changing energy status of the realms. Vast reserves of the physical controllers are maintained on the headquarters worlds of the local universe with local reserves in each minor sector capital, and from these concentration points they are periodically dispatched by the associate power directors to the headquarters of the major sectors, galaxies, constellations, systems, and to the individual planets. When thus assigned, the physical controllers are provisionally subject to the orders of the divine executioners of the conciliating commissions but are otherwise solely amenable to their associate directors and to the Supreme Power Centers.

The associate power directors are amazingly versatile beings, and since their local reserves are maintained on the minor sector worlds, they also serve there as instructors of all who study the sciences of the techniques of intelligent energy control and transmutation.

These directors alternate periods of executive service in the universe headquarters, or on the minor sectors, with equal periods of inspection service to the realms of space. At least one acting inspector is always present in each local system, maintaining headquarters on its capital sphere. They keep the whole vast living energy aggregation in harmonious synchrony.

2. *Mechanical Controllers.* These are the exceedingly versatile and mobile assistants of the associate power directors. Trillions upon trillions of them are commissioned in Ensa, your minor sector. These beings are called mechanical controllers because they are so completely dominated by their superiors, so fully subservient to the will of the associate power directors. Nevertheless they are, themselves, very intelligent, and their work, though mechanical and matter-of-fact in nature, is skillfully performed.

Of all the Master Physical Controllers assigned to the inhabited worlds, the mechanical controllers are by far the most powerful. Possessing the living endowment of antigravity in excess of all other beings. Ten of these controllers are now stationed on Urantia, and one of their most important planetary activities is to facilitate the departure of seraphic transports. In so functioning, all ten of the mechanical controllers act in unison while a battery of one thousand energy transmitters provides the initial momentum for the seraphic departure.

The mechanical controllers are competent to directionize the flow of energy and to facilitate its concentration into the specialized currents or circuits. These mighty beings have much to do with the segregation, directionization, and intensification of the physical energies and with the equalization of the pressures of the interplanetary circuits. They are expert in the manipulation of twenty-one of the thirty physical energies of space, constituting the power charge of a superuniverse. They are also able to accomplish much towards the management and control of six of the nine more subtle forms of physical energy. By placing these controllers in proper technical relationship to each other and to certain of the power centers, the associate power directors are enabled to effect unbelievable changes in power adjustment and energy control.

The Master Physical Controllers often function in batteries of hundreds, thousands, and even millions and by varying their positions and formations are able to effect energy control in a collective as well as an individual capacity. As requirements vary, they can upstep and accelerate the energy volume and movement or detain, condense, and retard the energy currents. They influence energy and power transformations somewhat as so-called catalytic agents augment chemical reactions. They function by inherent ability and in co-operation with the Supreme Power Centers.

3. *Energy Transformers*. The number of these beings in a superuniverse is unbelievable. There are almost one million in Satania alone, and the usual quota is one hundred for each inhabited world.

The energy transformers are the conjoint creation of the Seven Supreme Power Directors and the Seven Central Supervisors. They are among the more personal orders of physical controllers, and except when an associate power director is present on an inhabited world, the transformers are in command. They are the planetary inspectors of all departing seraphic transports. All classes of celestial life can utilize the less personal orders of the physical controllers only by liaison with the more personal orders of the associate directors and the energy transformers.

These transformers are powerful and effective living switches, being able to dispose themselves for or against a given power disposition or directionization. They are also skillful in their efforts to insulate the planets against the powerful energy streams passing between gigantic planetary and starry neighbors. Their energy-transmutive attributes render them most serviceable in the important task of maintaining universal energy balance, or power equilibrium. At one time they seem to consume or store energy; at other times they appear to exude or liberate energy. The transformers are able to increase or to diminish the "storage-battery" potential of the living and dead energies of their respective realms. But they deal only with physical and semimaterial energies, they do not directly function in the domain of life, neither do they change the forms of living beings.

In some respects the energy transformers are the most remarkable and mysterious of all semimaterial living creatures. They are in some unknown manner physically differentiated, and by varying their liaison relationships, they are able to exert a profound influence upon the energy which passes through their associated presences. The status of the physical realms seems to undergo a transformation under their skillful manipulation. *They can and do change the physical form of the energies of space.* With the aid of their fellow controllers they are actually able to change the form and potential of twenty-seven of the thirty physical energies of the superuniverse power charge. That three of these energies are beyond their control proves that they are not instrumentalities of the Unqualified Absolute.

The remaining four groups of the Master Physical Controllers are hardly persons within any acceptable definition of that word. These transmitters, associators, dissociators, and frandalanks are wholly automatic in their reactions; nevertheless they are in every sense intelligent. We are greatly limited in our knowledge of these wonderful entities because we cannot communicate with them. They appear to understand the language of the realm, but they cannot communicate with us. They seem fully able to receive our communications but quite powerless to make response.

4. *Energy Transmitters*. These beings function chiefly, but not wholly, in an intraplanetary capacity. They are marvelous dispatchers of energy as it is manifested on the individual worlds.

When energy is to be diverted to a new circuit, the transmitters deploy themselves in a line along the desired energy path, and by virtue of their unique attributes of energy-attraction, they can actually induce an increased energy flow in the desired direction. This they do just as literally as certain metallic circuits directionize the flow of certain forms of electric energy; and they are living superconductors for more than half of the thirty forms of physical energy.

Transmitters form skillful liaisons which are effective in rehabilitating the weakening currents of specialized energy passing from planet to planet and from station to station on an individual planet. They can detect currents which are much too feeble to be recognized by any other type of living being, and they can so augment these energies that the accompanying message becomes perfectly intelligible. Their services are invaluable to the broadcast receivers.

Energy transmitters can function with regard to all forms of communicable perception; they can render a distant scene "visible" as well as a distant sound "audible." They provide the emergency lines of communication in the local systems and on the individual planets. These services must be used by practically all creatures for purposes of communication outside of the regularly established circuits.

These beings, together with the energy transformers, are indispensable to the maintenance of mortal existence on those worlds having an impoverished atmosphere, and they are an integral part of the technique of life on the nonbreathing planets.

5. *Primary Associators*. These interesting and invaluable entities are masterly energy conservators and custodians. Somewhat as a plant stores solar light, so do these living organisms store energy during times of plus manifestations. They work on a gigantic scale, converting the energies of space into a physical state not known on Urantia. They are also able to carry forward these transformations to the point of producing some of the primitive units of material existence. These beings simply act by their presence. They are in no way exhausted or depleted by this function; they act like living catalytic agents.

During seasons of minus manifestations they are empowered to release these accumulated energies. But your knowledge of energy and matter is not sufficiently advanced to make it possible to explain the technique of this phase of their work. They always labor in compliance with universal law, handling and manipulating atoms, electrons, and ultimatons much as you maneuver adjustable type to make the same alphabetical symbols tell vastly different stories.

The associators are the first group of life to appear on an organizing material sphere, and they can function at physical temperatures which you would regard as utterly incompatible with the existence of living beings. They represent an order of life which is simply beyond the range of human imagination. Together with their co-workers, the dissociators, they are the most slavish of all intelligent creatures.

6. *Secondary Dissociators*. Compared with the primary associators, these beings of enormous antigravity endowment are the reverse workers. There is never any danger that the special or modified forms of physical energy on the local worlds or in the local systems will be exhausted, for these living organizations are endowed with the unique power of evolving limitless supplies of energy. They are chiefly concerned with the evolution of a form of energy which is hardly known on Urantia from a form of matter which is recognized still less. They are truly the alchemists of space and the wonder-

workers of time. But in all the wonders they work, they never transgress the mandates of Cosmic Supremacy.

7. *The Frandalanks*. These beings are the joint creation of all three orders of energy-control beings: the primary and secondary force organizers and the power directors. Frandalanks are the most numerous of all the Master Physical Controllers; the number functioning in Satania alone is beyond your numerical concept. They are stationed on all inhabited worlds and are always attached to the higher orders of physical controllers. They function interchangeably in the central and superuniverses and in the domains of outer space.

The frandalanks are created in thirty divisions, one for each form of basic universe force, and they function exclusively as living and automatic presence, pressure, and velocity gauges. These living barometers are solely concerned with the automatic and unerring registration of the status of all forms of force-energy. They are to the physical universe what the vast reflectivity mechanism is to the minded universe. The frandalanks that register time in addition to quantitative and qualitative energy presence are called chronoldeks.

I recognize that the frandalanks are intelligent, but I cannot classify them as other than living machines. About the only way I can help you to understand these living mechanisms is to compare them to your own mechanical contrivances which perform with almost intelligentlike precision and accuracy. Then if you would conceive of these beings, draw upon your imagination to the extent of recognizing that in the grand universe we actually have intelligent and living mechanisms (entities) that can perform more intricate tasks involving more stupendous computations with even greater delicacy of accuracy, even with ultimacy of precision.

5. THE MASTER FORCE ORGANIZERS

The force organizers are resident on Paradise, but they function throughout the master universe, more particularly in the domains of unorganized space. These extraordinary beings are neither creators nor creatures, and they comprise two grand divisions of service:

1. Primary Eventuated Master Force Organizers.
2. Associate Transcendental Master Force Organizers.

These two mighty orders of primordial-force manipulators work exclusively under the supervision of the Architects of the Master Universe, and at the present time they do not function extensively within the boundaries of the grand universe.

Primary Master Force Organizers are the manipulators of the primordial or basic space-forces of the Unqualified Absolute. They transmute *primordial force* (pre-energy not responsive to direct Paradise gravity) into primary or *puissant energy*, energy transmuting from the exclusive grasp of the Unqualified Absolute to the gravity grasp of the Isle of Paradise. They are thereupon succeeded by the associate force organizers, who continue the process of energy transmutation from the primary through the secondary or *gravity-energy* stage.

Upon the completion of the plans for the creation of a local universe, signalized by the arrival of a Creator Son, the Associate Master Force Organizers give way to the orders of power directors acting in the superuniverse of astronomic jurisdiction. But in the absence of such plans the associate force organizers continue on indefinitely in charge of these material creations, even as they now operate in outer space.

The Master Force Organizers withstand temperatures and function under physical conditions which would be intolerable even to the versatile power centers and physical controllers of Orvonton. The only other types of revealed beings capable of functioning in these realms of outer space are the Solitary Messengers and the Inspired Trinity Spirits.

[Sponsored by a Universal Censor acting by authority of the Ancients of Days on Uversa.]

PAPER 30
PERSONALITIES OF THE GRAND UNIVERSE

THE PERSONALITIES and other-than-personal entities now functioning on Paradise and in the grand universe constitute a well-nigh limitless number of living beings. Even the number of major orders and types would stagger the human imagination, let alone the countless subtypes and variations. It is, however, desirable to present something of two basic classifications of living beings — a suggestion of the Paradise classification and an abbreviation of the Uversa Personality Register.

It is not possible to formulate comprehensive and entirely consistent classifications of the personalities of the grand universe because all of the groups are not revealed. It would require numerous additional papers to cover the further revelation required to systematically classify all groups. Such conceptual expansion would hardly be desirable as it would deprive the thinking mortals of the next thousand years of that stimulus to creative speculation which these partially revealed concepts supply. It is best that man not have an overrevelation; it stifles imagination.

1. THE PARADISE CLASSIFICATION OF LIVING BEINGS

Living beings are classified on Paradise in accordance with inherent and attained relationship to the Paradise Deities. During the grand gatherings of the central and superuniverses those present are often grouped in accordance with origin: those of triune origin, or of Trinity attainment; those of dual origin; and those of single origin. It is difficult to interpret the Paradise classification of living beings to the mortal mind, but we are authorized to present the following:

I. *TRIUNE-ORIGIN BEINGS.* Beings created by all three Paradise Deities, either as such or as the Trinity, together with the Trinitized Corps, which designation refers to all groups of trinitized beings, revealed and unrevealed.

A. *The Supreme Spirits.*

1. The Seven Master Spirits.
2. The Seven Supreme Executives.
3. The Seven Orders of Reflective Spirits.

B. *The Stationary Sons of the Trinity.*

1. Trinitized Secrets of Supremacy.
2. Eternals of Days.
3. Ancients of Days.
4. Unions of Days.
5. Perfections of Days.
6. Recents of Days.
7. Faithfuls of Days.
8. Perfectors of Wisdom.
9. Divine Counselors.
10. Universal Censors.

C. *Trinity-origin and Trinitized Beings.*

1. Trinity Teacher Sons.
2. Inspired Trinity Spirits.
3. Havona Natives.
4. Paradise Citizens.
5. Unrevealed Trinity-origin Beings.
6. Unrevealed Deity-trinitized Beings.
7. Trinitized Sons of Attainment.
8. Trinitized Sons of Selection.
9. Trinitized Sons of Perfection.
10. Creature-trinitized Sons.

II. *DUAL-ORIGIN BEINGS.* Those of origin in any two of the Paradise Deities or otherwise created by any two beings of direct or indirect descent from the Paradise Deities.

A. *The Descending Orders.*

1. Creator Sons.
2. Magisterial Sons.
3. Bright and Morning Stars.
4. Father Melchizedeks.
5. The Melchizedeks.
6. The Vorondadeks.
7. The Lanonandeks.
8. Brilliant Evening Stars.
9. The Archangels.
10. Life Carriers.
11. Unrevealed Universe Aids.
12. Unrevealed Sons of God.

B. *The Stationary Orders.*

1. Abandonters.
2. Susatia.
3. Univitatia.
4. Spironga.
5. Unrevealed Dual-origin Beings.

C. *The Ascending Orders.*

1. Adjuster-fused Mortals.
2. Son-fused Mortals.
3. Spirit-fused Mortals.
4. Translated Midwayers.
5. Unrevealed Ascenders.

III. *SINGLE-ORIGIN BEINGS.* Those of origin in any one of the Paradise Deities or otherwise created by any one being of direct or indirect descent from the Paradise Deities.

A. *The Supreme Spirits.*

1. Gravity Messengers.
2. The Seven Spirits of the Havona Circuits.
3. The Twelvefold Adjutants of the Havona Circuits.
4. The Reflective Image Aids.
5. Universe Mother Spirits.
6. The Sevenfold Adjutant Mind-Spirits.
7. Unrevealed Deity-origin Beings.

B. *The Ascending Orders.*

1. Personalized Adjusters.
2. Ascending Material Sons.
3. Evolutionary Seraphim.
4. Evolutionary Cherubim.
5. Unrevealed Ascenders.

C. *The Family of the Infinite Spirit.*

1. Solitary Messengers.
2. Universe Circuit Supervisors.
3. Census Directors.
4. Personal Aids of the Infinite Spirit.
5. Associate Inspectors.
6. Assigned Sentinels.
7. Graduate Guides.
8. Havona Servitals.
9. Universal Conciliators.
10. Morontia Companions.
11. Supernaphim.
12. Seconaphim.
13. Tertiaphim.
14. Omniaphim.
15. Seraphim.
16. Cherubim and Sanobim.
17. Unrevealed Spirit-origin Beings.
18. The Seven Supreme Power Directors.
19. The Supreme Power Centers.
20. The Master Physical Controllers.
21. The Morontia Power Supervisors.

IV. *EVENTUATED TRANSCENDENTAL BEINGS.* There is to be found on Paradise a vast host of transcendental beings whose origin is not ordinarily disclosed to the universes of time and space until they are settled in light and life. These Transcendentalers are neither creators nor creatures; they are the *eventuated* children of divinity, ultimacy, and eternity. These "eventuators" are neither finite nor infinite — they are *absonite*; and absonity is neither infinity nor absoluteness.

These uncreated noncreators are ever loyal to the Paradise Trinity and obedient to the Ultimate. They are existent on four ultimate levels of personality activity and are functional on the seven levels of the absonite in twelve grand divisions consisting of one thousand major working groups of seven classes each. These eventuated beings include the following orders:

1. The Architects of the Master Universe.
2. Transcendental Recorders.
3. Other Transcendentalers.
4. Primary Eventuated Master Force Organizers.
5. Associate Transcendental Master Force Organizers.

God, as a superperson, eventuates; God, as a person, creates; God, as a preperson, fragments; and such an Adjuster fragment of himself evolves the spirit soul upon the material and mortal mind in accordance with the freewill choosing of the personality which has been bestowed upon such a mortal creature by the parental act of God as a Father.

V. *FRAGMENTED ENTITIES OF DEITY.* This order of living existence, originating in the Universal Father, is best typified by the Thought Adjusters, though these entities are by no means the only fragmentations of the prepersonal reality of the First Source and Center. The functions of the other-than-Adjuster fragments are manifold and little known. Fusion with an Adjuster or other such fragment constitutes the creature a *Father-fused being.*

The fragmentations of the premind spirit of the Third Source and Center, though hardly comparable to the Father fragments, should be here recorded. Such entities differ very greatly from Adjusters; they do not as such dwell on Spiritington, nor do they as such traverse the mind-gravity circuits; neither do they indwell mortal creatures during the life in the flesh. They are not prepersonal in the sense that the Adjusters are, but such fragments of premind spirit are bestowed upon certain of the surviving mortals, and fusion therewith constitutes them *Spirit-fused mortals* in contradistinction to Adjuster-fused mortals.

Still more difficult of description is the individualized spirit of a Creator Son, union with which constitutes the creature a *Son-fused mortal.* And there are still other fragmentations of Deity.

VI. *SUPERPERSONAL BEINGS.* There is a vast host of other-than-personal beings of divine origin and of manifold service in the universe of universes. Certain of these beings are resident on the Paradise worlds of the Son; others, like the superpersonal representatives of the Eternal Son, are encountered elsewhere. They are for the most part unmentioned in these narratives, and it would be quite futile to attempt their description to *personal* creatures.

VII. *UNCLASSIFIED AND UNREVEALED ORDERS.* During the present universe age it would not be possible to place all beings, personal or otherwise, within classifications pertaining to the present universe age; nor have all such categories been revealed in these narratives; hence numerous orders have been omitted from these lists. Consider the following:

The Consummator of Universe Destiny.
The Qualified Vicegerents of the Ultimate.
The Unqualified Supervisors of the Supreme.
The Unrevealed Creative Agencies of the Ancients of Days.
Majeston of Paradise.
The Unnamed Reflectivator Liaisons of Majeston.
The Midsonite Orders of the Local Universes.

No especial significance need attach to the listing of these orders together except that none of them appear in the Paradise classification as revealed herein. These are the unclassified few; you have yet to learn of the unrevealed many.

There are spirits: spirit entities, spirit presences, personal spirits, prepersonal spirits, superpersonal spirits, spirit existences, spirit personalities — but neither mortal language nor mortal intellect are adequate. We may however state that there are no personalities of "pure mind"; no entity has personality unless he is endowed with it by God who is spirit. Any mind entity that is not associated with either spiritual or physical energy is not a personality. But in the same sense that there are spirit personalities who have mind there are mind personalities who have spirit. Majeston and his associates are fairly good illustrations of mind-dominated beings, but there are better illustrations of this type of personality unknown to you. There are even whole unrevealed orders of such *mind personalities*, but they are always spirit associated. Certain other unrevealed creatures are what might be termed *mindal- and physical-energy personalities*. This type of being is nonresponsive to spirit gravity but is nonetheless a true personality — is within the Father's circuit.

These papers do not — cannot — even begin to exhaust the story of the living creatures, creators, eventuators, and still-otherwise-existent beings who live and worship and serve in the swarming universes of time and in the central universe of eternity. You mortals are persons; hence we can describe beings who are *personalized*, but how could an *absonitized* being ever be explained to you?

2. THE UVERSA PERSONALITY REGISTER

The divine family of living beings is registered on Uversa in seven grand divisions:

1. The Paradise Deities.
2. The Supreme Spirits.
3. The Trinity-origin Beings.
4. The Sons of God.
5. Personalities of the Infinite Spirit.
6. The Universe Power Directors.
7. The Corps of Permanent Citizenship.

These groups of will creatures are divided into numerous classes and minor subdivisions. The presentation of this classification of the personalities of the grand universe is however chiefly concerned in setting forth those orders of intelligent beings who have been revealed in these narratives, most of whom will be encountered in the ascendant experience of the mortals of time on their progressive climb to Paradise. The following listings make no mention of vast orders of universe beings who carry forward their work apart from the mortal ascension scheme.

I. *THE PARADISE DEITIES.*

1. The Universal Father.
2. The Eternal Son.
3. The Infinite Spirit.

II. *THE SUPREME SPIRITS.*

1. The Seven Master Spirits.
2. The Seven Supreme Executives.
3. The Seven Groups of Reflective Spirits.
4. The Reflective Image Aids.
5. The Seven Spirits of the Circuits.
6. Local Universe Creative Spirits.
7. Adjutant Mind-Spirits.

III. *THE TRINITY-ORIGIN BEINGS.*

1. Trinitized Secrets of Supremacy.
2. Eternals of Days.
3. Ancients of Days.
4. Unions of Days.
5. Perfections of Days.
6. Recents of Days.
7. Faithfuls of Days.
8. Trinity Teacher Sons.
9. Perfectors of Wisdom.
10. Divine Counselors.
11. Universal Censors.
12. Inspired Trinity Spirits.

13. Havona Natives.
14. Paradise Citizens.

IV. *THE SONS OF GOD.*

A. *Descending Sons.*

1. Creator Sons — Michaels.
2. Magisterial Sons — Avonals.
3. Trinity Teacher Sons — Daynals.
4. Melchizedek Sons.
5. Vorondadek Sons.
6. Lanonandek Sons.
7. Life Carrier Sons.

B. *Ascending Sons.*

1. Father-fused Mortals.
2. Son-fused Mortals.
3. Spirit-fused Mortals.
4. Evolutionary Seraphim.
5. Ascending Material Sons.
6. Translated Midwayers.
7. Personalized Adjusters.

C. *Trinitized Sons.*

1. Mighty Messengers.
2. Those High in Authority.
3. Those without Name and Number.
4. Trinitized Custodians.
5. Trinitized Ambassadors.
6. Celestial Guardians.
7. High Son Assistants.
8. Ascender-trinitized Sons.
9. Paradise-Havona-trinitized Sons.

10. Trinitized Sons of Destiny.

V. *PERSONALITIES OF THE INFINITE SPIRIT.*

A. *Higher Personalities of the Infinite Spirit.*

1. Solitary Messengers.
2. Universe Circuit Supervisors.
3. Census Directors.
4. Personal Aids of the Infinite Spirit.
5. Associate Inspectors.
6. Assigned Sentinels.
7. Graduate Guides.

B. *The Messenger Hosts of Space.*

1. Havona Servitals.
2. Universal Conciliators.
3. Technical Advisers.
4. Custodians of Records on Paradise.
5. Celestial Recorders.
6. Morontia Companions.
7. Paradise Companions.

C. *The Ministering Spirits.*

1. Supernaphim.
2. Seconaphim.
3. Tertiaphim.
4. Omniaphim.
5. Seraphim.
6. Cherubim and Sanobim.
7. Midwayers.

VI. *THE UNIVERSE POWER DIRECTORS.*

A. *The Seven Supreme Power Directors.*

B. *Supreme Power Centers.*

1. Supreme Center Supervisors.
2. Havona Centers.
3. Superuniverse Centers.
4. Local Universe Centers.
5. Major Sector Centers.
6. Minor Sector Centers.
7. Galaxy Centers.
8. Constellation Centers.
9. System Centers.
10. Unclassified Centers.

C. *Master Physical Controllers.*

1. Associate Power Directors.
2. Mechanical Controllers.
3. Energy Transformers.
4. Energy Transmitters.
5. Primary Associators.
6. Secondary Dissociators.
7. Frandalanks and Chronoldeks.

D. *Morontia Power Supervisors.*

1. Circuit Regulators.
2. System Co-ordinators.
3. Planetary Custodians.
4. Combined Controllers.
5. Liaison Stabilizers.
6. Selective Assorters.
7. Associate Registrars.

VII. *THE CORPS OF PERMANENT CITIZENSHIP.*

1. The Planetary Midwayers.
2. The Adamic Sons of the Systems.
3. The Constellation Univitatia.
4. The Local Universe Susatia.
5. Spirit-fused Mortals of the Local Universes.
6. The Superuniverse Abandonters.
7. Son-fused Mortals of the Superuniverses.
8. The Havona Natives.
9. Natives of the Paradise Spheres of the Spirit.
10. Natives of the Father's Paradise Spheres.
11. The Created Citizens of Paradise.
12. Adjuster-fused Mortal Citizens of Paradise.

This is the working classification of the personalities of the universes as they are of record on the headquarters world of Uversa.

COMPOSITE PERSONALITY GROUPS. There are on Uversa the records of numerous additional groups of intelligent beings, beings that are also closely related to the organization and administration of the grand universe. Among such orders are the following three composite personality groups:

A. *The Paradise Corps of the Finality.*

1. The Corps of Mortal Finaliters.
2. The Corps of Paradise Finaliters.
3. The Corps of Trinitized Finaliters.
4. The Corps of Conjoint Trinitized Finaliters.
5. The Corps of Havona Finaliters.
6. The Corps of Transcendental Finaliters.
7. The Corps of Unrevealed Sons of Destiny.

The Mortal Corps of the Finality is dealt with in the next and final paper of this series.

B. *The Universe Aids.*

1. Bright and Morning Stars.
2. Brilliant Evening Stars.
3. Archangels.
4. Most High Assistants.
5. High Commissioners.
6. Celestial Overseers.
7. Mansion World Teachers.

On all headquarters worlds of both local and superuniverses, provision is made for these beings who are engaged in specific missions for the Creator Sons, the local universe rulers. We welcome these Universe Aids on Uversa, but we have no jurisdiction over them. Such emissaries prosecute their work and carry on their observations under authority of the Creator Sons. Their activities are more fully described in the narrative of your local universe.

C. *The Seven Courtesy Colonies.*

1. Star Students.
2. Celestial Artisans.
3. Reversion Directors.
4. Extension-school Instructors.
5. The Various Reserve Corps.
6. Student Visitors.
7. Ascending Pilgrims.

These seven groups of beings will be found thus organized and governed on all headquarters worlds from the local systems up to the capitals of the superuniverses, particularly the latter. The capitals of the seven superuniverses are the meeting places for almost all classes and orders of intelligent beings. With the exception of numerous groups of Paradise-Havoners, here the will creatures of every phase of existence may be observed and studied.

3. THE COURTESY COLONIES

The seven courtesy colonies sojourn on the architectural spheres for a longer or shorter time while engaged in the furtherance of their missions and in the execution of their special assignments. Their work may be described as follows:

1. *The Star Students*, the celestial astronomers, choose to work on spheres like Uversa because such specially constructed worlds are unusually favorable for their observations and calculations. Uversa is favorably situated for the work of this colony because of its central location in higher dimensional space-time, and the fact that it exists outside of all of the four (or more) dimensional universes. These students are not in any manner organically connected with the affairs of the superuniverse; they are merely guests.

The astronomical colony of Uversa contains individuals from many near-by realms, from the central Divine universe, and even from Norlatiadek. Any being on any world in any system of any universe may become a star student, may aspire to join some corps of celestial astronomers. The only requisites are: continuing life and sufficient knowledge of the worlds of space, especially their physical laws of evolution and control. Star students are not required to serve eternally in this corps, but no one admitted to this group may withdraw under one millennium of Uversa time.

The star-observer colony of Uversa now numbers over one million. These astronomers come and go, though some remain for comparatively long periods. They carry on their work with the aid of a multitude of mechanical instruments and physical appliances; they are also greatly assisted by the Solitary Messengers and other spirit explorers. These celestial astronomers make constant use of the living energy transformers and transmitters, as well as of the reflective personalities, in their work of star study, relationships between universes, the structure of the superuniverse, and space survey. They study all forms and phases of space material and energy manifestations, and they are just as much interested in force function as in stellar and universe phenomena; nothing in all space escapes their scrutiny.

Similar astronomer colonies are to be found on the architectural capitals of the local universes and their administrative subdivisions. Except on Paradise, knowledge is not inherent; understanding of the physical universe is largely dependent on observation and research.

2. *The Celestial Artisans* serve throughout the seven superuniverses. Ascending mortals have their initial contact with these groups in the morontia career of the local universe in connection with which these artisans will be more fully discussed.

3. *The Reversion Directors* are the promoters of relaxation and humor — reversion to past memories. They are of great service in the practical operation of the ascending scheme of mortal progression, especially during the earlier phases of morontia transition and spirit experience. Their story belongs to the narrative of the mortal career in the local universe.

4. *Extension-School Instructors*. The next higher residential world of the ascendant career always maintains a strong corps of teachers on the world just below, a sort of preparatory school for the progressing residents of that sphere; this is a phase of the ascendant scheme for advancing the pilgrims of time. These schools, their methods of instruction and examinations, are wholly unlike anything which you essay to conduct on Urantia.

The entire ascendant plan of mortal progression is characterized by the practice of giving out to other beings new truth and experience just as soon as acquired. You work your way through the long school of Paradise attainment by serving as teachers to those pupils just behind you in the scale of progression.

5. *The Various Reserve Corps.* Vast reserves of beings not under our immediate supervision are mobilized on Uversa as the reserve-corps colony. There are seventy primary divisions of this colony on Uversa, and it is a liberal education to be permitted to spend a season with these extraordinary personalities. Similar general reserves are maintained on Salvington and other universe capitals; they are dispatched on active service on the requisition of their respective group directors.

6. *The Student Visitors.* From all the universes of the superuniverse a constant stream of celestial visitors pours through the various headquarters worlds. As individuals and as classes these various types of beings flock in upon us as observers, exchange pupils, and student helpers. On Uversa, at present, there are over one billion persons in this courtesy colony. Some of these visitors may tarry a day, others may remain a year, all dependent on the nature of their mission. This colony contains almost every class of universe beings except Creator personalities and morontia mortals.

Morontia mortals are student visitors only within the confines of the local universe of their origin. They may visit in a superuniverse capacity only after they have attained spirit status. Fully one half of our visitor colony consists of "stopovers," beings enroute elsewhere who pause to visit the Orvonton capital. These personalities may be executing a universe assignment, or they may be enjoying a period of leisure — freedom from assignment. The privilege of intrauniverse travel and observation is a part of the career of all ascending beings. The human desire to travel and observe new peoples and worlds will be fully gratified during the long and eventful climb to Paradise through the local, super-, and central universes.

7. *The Ascending Pilgrims.* As the ascending pilgrims are assigned to various services in connection with their Paradise progression, they are domiciled as a courtesy colony on the various headquarters spheres. While functioning here and there throughout a superuniverse, such groups are largely self-governing. They are an ever-shifting colony embracing all orders of evolutionary mortals and their ascending associates.

4. THE ASCENDING MORTALS

While the mortal survivors of time and space are denominated ascending pilgrims when accredited for the progressive ascent to Paradise, these evolutionary creatures occupy such an important place in these narratives that we here desire to present a synopsis of the following seven stages of the ascending universe career:

1. Planetary Mortals.
2. Sleeping Survivors.
3. Mansion World Students.
4. Morontia Progressors.
5. Superuniverse Wards.
6. Havona Pilgrims.
7. Paradise Arrivals.

The following narrative presents the universe career of an Adjuster-indwelt mortal. The Son- and Spirit-fused mortals share portions of this career, but we have elected to tell this story as it pertains to the Adjuster-fused mortals, for such a destiny may be anticipated by all Urantians.

1. *Planetary Mortals*. Mortals are all animal-origin evolutionary beings of ascendant potential. In origin, nature, and destiny these various groups and types of human beings are not wholly unlike the Urantia peoples. The human races of each world receive the same ministry of the Sons of God and enjoy the presence of the ministering spirits of time. After natural death all types of ascenders fraternize as one morontia family on the mansion worlds.

2. *Sleeping Survivors*. All mortals of survival status, in the custody of personal guardians of destiny, pass through the portals of natural death and, on the third period, personalize on the mansion worlds. Those accredited beings who have, for any reason, been unable to attain that level of intelligence mastery and endowment of spirituality which would entitle them to personal guardians, cannot thus immediately and directly go to the mansion worlds. Such surviving souls must rest in unconscious sleep until the judgment day of a new epoch, a new dispensation, the coming of a Son of God to call the rolls of the age and adjudicate the realm, and this is the general practice throughout all Nebadon. It was said of Christ Michael that, when he ascended on high at the conclusion of his work on earth, "He led a great multitude of captives." And these captives were the sleeping survivors from the days of Adam to the day of the Master's resurrection on Urantia.

The passing of time is of no moment to sleeping mortals; they are wholly unconscious and oblivious to the length of their rest. On reassembly of personality at the end of an age, those who have slept five thousand years will react no differently than those who have rested five days. Aside from this time delay these survivors pass on through the ascension regime identically with those who avoid the longer or shorter sleep of death.

These dispensational classes of world pilgrims are utilized for group morontia activities in the work of the local universes. There is a great advantage in the mobilization of such enormous groups; they are thus kept together for long periods of effective service.

3. *Mansion World Students*. All surviving mortals who reawaken on the mansion worlds belong to this class.

The physical body of mortal flesh is not a part of the reassembly of the sleeping survivor; the physical body has returned to dust. The seraphim of assignment sponsors the new body, the morontia form, as the new life vehicle for the immortal soul and for the indwelling of the returned Adjuster. The Adjuster is the custodian of the spirit transcript of the mind of the sleeping survivor. The assigned seraphim is the keeper of the surviving identity — the immortal soul — as far as it has evolved. And when these two, the Adjuster and the seraphim, reunite their personality trusts, the new individual constitutes the resurrection of the old personality, the survival of the evolving morontia identity of the soul. Such a reassociation of soul and Adjuster is quite properly called a resurrection, a reassembly of personality factors; but even this does not entirely explain the reappearance of the surviving *personality*. Though you will probably never understand the fact of such an inexplicable transaction, you will sometime experientially know the truth of it if you do not reject the plan of mortal survival.

The plan of initial mortal detention on seven worlds of progressive training is nearly universal in Orvonton. In each local system of approximately one thousand inhabited planets there are seven mansion worlds, usually satellites or subsatellites of the system capital. They are the receiving worlds for the majority of ascending mortals.

Sometimes all training worlds of mortal residence are called universe "mansions," and it was to such spheres that Jesus alluded when he said: "In my Father's house are many mansions." From here on, within a given group of spheres like the mansion worlds, ascenders will progress individually from one sphere to another and from one phase of life to another, but they will always advance from one stage of universe study to another in class formation.

4. *Morontia Progressors*. From the mansion worlds on up through the spheres of the system, constellation, galaxy, and the universe, mortals are classed as morontia progressors; they are traversing the transition spheres of mortal ascension. As the ascending mortals progress from the lower to the higher of the morontia worlds, they serve on countless assignments in association with their teachers and in company with their more advanced and senior brethren.

Morontia progression pertains to continuing advancement of intellect, spirit, and personality form. Survivors are still three-natured beings. Throughout the entire morontia experience they are wards of the local universe. The regime of the superuniverse does not function until the spirit career begins.

Mortals acquire real spirit identity just before they leave the local universe headquarters for the receiving worlds of the superuniverse. Passing from the final morontia stage to the first or lowest spirit status is but a slight transition. The mind, personality, and character are unchanged by such an advance; only does the form undergo modification. But the spirit form is just as real as the morontia body, and it is equally discernible.

Before departing from their native local universes for the superuniverse receiving worlds, the mortals of time are recipients of spirit confirmation from the Creator Son and the local universe Mother Spirit. From this point on, the status of the ascending mortal is forever settled. Superuniverse wards have never been known to go astray. Ascending seraphim are also advanced in angelic standing at the time of their departure from the local universes.

5. *Superuniverse Wards*. All ascenders arriving on the training worlds of the superuniverses become the wards of the Ancients of Days; they have traversed the morontia life of the local universe and are now accredited spirits. As young spirits they begin the ascension of the superuniverse system of training and culture, extending from the receiving spheres to the higher cultural spheres of the superuniverse headquarters.

As morontia ascenders studied and worked on the worlds of the local universe, so spirit ascenders continue to master new worlds while they practice at giving out to others that which they have imbibed at the experiential founts of wisdom. But going to school as a spirit being in the superuniverse career is very unlike anything that has ever entered the imaginative realms of the material mind of man.

Before leaving the superuniverse for Havona, these ascending spirits receive the same thorough course in superuniverse management that they received during their morontia experience in local universe supervision. Before spirit mortals reach Havona, their chief study, but not exclusive occupation, is the mastery of local and superuniverse administration. The reason for all of this experience is not now fully apparent, but no doubt such training is wise and necessary in view of their possible future destiny as members of the Corps of the Finality.

The superuniverse regime is not the same for all ascending mortals. They receive the same general education, but special groups and classes are carried through special courses of instruction and are put through specific courses of training.

6. *Havona Pilgrims*. When spirit development is complete, even though not replete, then the surviving mortal prepares for the long flight to Havona, the haven of evolutionary spirits. On earth you were a creature of flesh and blood; through the local universe you were a morontia being; through the superuniverse you were an evolving spirit; with your arrival on the receiving worlds of Havona your spiritual education begins in reality and in earnest; your eventual appearance on Paradise will be as a perfected spirit.

The journey from the superuniverse headquarters to the Havona receiving spheres is always made alone. From now on no more class or group instruction will be administered. You are through with the technical and administrative training of the evolutionary worlds of time and space. Now begins your *personal education*, your individual spiritual training. From first to last, throughout all Havona, the instruction is personal and threefold in nature: intellectual, spiritual, and experiential.

The first act of your Havona career will be to recognize and thank your transport seconaphim for the long and safe journey. Then you are presented to those beings who will sponsor your early Havona activities. Next you go to register your arrival and prepare your message of thanksgiving and adoration for dispatch to the Creator Son of your local universe, the universe

Father who made possible your sonship career. This concludes the formalities of the Havona arrival; whereupon you are accorded a long period of leisure for free observation, and this affords opportunity for looking up your friends, fellows, and associates of the long ascension experience. You may also consult the broadcasts to ascertain who of your fellow pilgrims have departed for Havona since the time of your leaving Uversa.

The fact of your arrival on the receiving worlds of Havona will be duly transmitted to the headquarters of your local universe and personally conveyed to your seraphic guardian, wherever that seraphim may chance to be.

The ascendant mortals have been thoroughly trained in the affairs of the evolutionary worlds of space; now they begin their long and profitable contact with the created spheres of perfection. What a preparation for some future work is afforded by this combined, unique, and extraordinary experience! But I cannot tell you about Havona; you must see these worlds to appreciate their glory or to understand their grandeur.

7. *Paradise Arrivals*. On reaching Paradise with residential status, you begin the progressive course in divinity and absonity. Your residence on Paradise signifies that you have found God, and that you are to be mustered into the Mortal Corps of the Finality. Of all the creatures of the grand universe, only those who are Father fused are mustered into the Mortal Corps of the Finality. Only such individuals take the finaliter oath. Other beings of Paradise perfection or attainment may be temporarily attached to this finality corps, but they are not of eternal assignment to the unknown and unrevealed mission of this accumulating host of the evolutionary and perfected veterans of time and space.

Paradise arrivals are accorded a period of freedom, after which they begin their associations with the seven groups of the primary supernaphim. They are designated Paradise graduates when they have finished their course with the conductors of worship and then, as finaliters, are assigned on observational and co-operative service to the ends of the far-flung creation. As yet there seems to be no specific or settled employment for the Mortal Corps of Finaliters, though they serve in many capacities on worlds settled in light and life.

If there should be no future or unrevealed destiny for the Mortal Corps of the Finality, the present assignment of these ascendant beings would be altogether adequate and glorious. Their present destiny wholly justifies the universal plan of evolutionary ascent. But the future ages of the evolution of the spheres of outer space will undoubtedly further elaborate, and with more repleteness divinely illuminate, the wisdom and loving-kindness of the Gods in the execution of their divine plan of human survival and mortal ascension.

This narrative, together with what has been revealed to you and with what you may acquire in connection with instruction respecting your own world, presents an outline of the career of an ascending mortal. The story varies considerably in the different superuniverses, but this recital affords a glimpse of the average plan of mortal progression as it is operative in the local universe of Nebadon and in the seventh segment of the grand universe, the superuniverse of Orvonton.

[Sponsored by a Mighty Messenger from Uversa.]

PAPER 31
THE CORPS OF THE FINALITY

THE CORPS OF MORTAL FINALITERS represents the present known destination of the ascending Adjuster-fused mortals of time. But there are other groups who are also assigned to this corps. The primary finaliter corps is composed of the following:

1. Havona Natives.
2. Gravity Messengers.
3. Glorified Mortals.
4. Adopted Seraphim.
5. Glorified Material Sons.
6. Glorified Midway Creatures.

These six groups of glorified beings compose this unique body of eternal destiny. We think we know their future work, but we are not certain. While the Corps of the Mortal Finality is mobilizing on Paradise, and while they now so extensively minister to the universes of space and administer the worlds settled in light and life, their future destination must be the now-organizing universes of outer space. At least that is the conjecture of Uversa.

The corps is organized in accordance with the working associations of the worlds of space and in keeping with the associative experience acquired throughout the long and eventful ascendant career. All the ascendant creatures admitted to this corps are received in equality, but this exalted equality in no way abrogates individuality or destroys personal identity. We can immediately discern, in communicating with a finaliter, whether he is an ascendant mortal, Havona native, adopted seraphim, midway creature, or Material Son.

During the present universe age the finaliters return to serve in the universes of time. They are assigned to labor successively in the different superuniverses and never in their native superuniverses until after they have served in all the other six supercreations. Thus may they acquire the sevenfold concept of the Supreme Being.

One or more companies of the mortal finaliters are constantly in service on Urantia. There is no domain of universe service to which they are not assigned; they function universally and with alternating and equal periods of assigned duty and free service.

We have no idea as to the nature of the future organization of this extraordinary group, but the finaliters are now wholly a self-governing body. They choose their own permanent, periodic, and assignment leaders and directors. No outside influence can ever be brought to bear upon their policies, and their oath of allegiance is only to the Paradise Trinity.

The finaliters maintain their own headquarters on Paradise, in the superuniverses, in the local universes, and on all the divisional capitals. They are a separate order of evolutionary creation. We do not directly manage them or control them, and yet they are absolutely loyal and always co-operative with all our plans. They are indeed the accumulating tried and true souls of time and space — the evolutionary salt of the universe — and they are forever proof against evil and secure against sin.

1. THE HAVONA NATIVES

Many of the Havona natives who serve as teachers in the pilgrim-training schools of the central universe become greatly attached to the ascending mortals and still more intrigued with the future work and destiny of the Corps of Mortal Finaliters. On Paradise there is maintained, at the administrative headquarters of the corps, a registry for Havona volunteers presided over by the associate of Grandfanda. Today, you will find millions upon millions of Havona natives upon this waiting list. These perfect beings of direct and divine creation are of great assistance to the Mortal Corps of Finality, and they will undoubtedly be of even greater service in the far-distant future. They provide the viewpoint of one born in perfection and divine repleteness. The finaliters thus embrace both phases of experiential existence — perfect and perfected.

Havona natives must achieve certain experiential developments in liaison with evolutionary beings which will create reception capacity for the bestowal of a fragment of the spirit of the Universal Father. The Mortal Finaliter Corps has as permanent members only such beings as have been fused with the spirit of the First Source and Center, or who, like the Gravity Messengers, innately embody this spirit of God the Father.

The inhabitants of the central universe are received into the corps in the ratio of one in a thousand — a finaliter company. The corps is organized for temporary service in companies of one thousand, the ascendant creatures numbering 997 to one Havona native and one Gravity Messenger. Finaliters are thus mobilized in companies, but the finality oath is administered individually. It is an oath of sweeping implications and eternal import. The Havona native takes the same oath and becomes forever attached to the corps.

The Havona recruits follow the company of their assignment; wherever the group goes, they go. And you should see their enthusiasm in the new work of the finaliters. The possibility of attaining the Corps of the Finality is one of the superb thrills of Havona; the possibility of becoming a finaliter is one of the supreme adventures of these perfect races.

The Havona natives are also received, in the same ratio, into the Corps of Conjoint Trinitized Finaliters on Vicegerington and into the Corps of Transcendental Finaliters on Paradise. The Havona citizens regard these three destinies as constituting the supreme goals of their supernal careers, together with their possible admission to the Corps of Havona Finaliters.

2. GRAVITY MESSENGERS

Wherever and whenever Gravity Messengers are functioning, the finaliters are in command. All Gravity Messengers are under the exclusive jurisdiction of Grandfanda, and they are assigned only to the primary Corps of the Finality. They are invaluable to the finaliters even now, and they will be all-serviceable in the eternal future. No other group of intelligent creatures possesses such a personalized messenger corps able to transcend time and space. Similar types of messenger-recorders attached to other finaliter corps are not personalized; they are absonitized.

Gravity Messengers hail from Divinington, and they are modified and personalized Adjusters, but no one of our Uversa group will undertake to explain the nature of one of these messengers. We know they are highly personal beings, divine, intelligent, and touchingly understanding, but we do not comprehend their timeless technique of traversing space. They seem to be competent to utilize any and all energies, circuits, and even gravity. Finaliters of the mortal corps cannot defy time and space, but they have associated with them and subject to their command all but infinite spirit personalities who can. We presume to call Gravity Messengers personalities, but in reality they are superspirit beings, unlimited and boundless personalities. They are of an entirely different order of personality as compared with Solitary Messengers.

Gravity Messengers may be attached to a finaliter company in unlimited numbers, but only one messenger, the chief of his fellows, is mustered into the Mortal Corps of the Finality. This chief however has assigned to him a permanent staff of 999 fellow messengers, and as occasion may require, he may call upon the reserves of the order for assistants in unlimited numbers.

Gravity Messengers and glorified mortal finaliters achieve a touching and profound affection for one another; they have much in common: One is a direct personalization of a fragment of the Universal Father, the other a creature personality existent in the surviving immortal soul fused with a fragment of the same Universal Father, the spirit Thought Adjuster.

3. GLORIFIED MORTALS

Ascendant Adjuster-fused mortals compose the bulk of the primary Corps of the Finality. Together with the adopted and glorified seraphim they usually constitute 990 in each finaliter company. The proportion of mortals and angels in any one group varies, though the mortals far outnumber the seraphim. The Havona natives, glorified Material Sons, glorified midway creatures, the Gravity Messengers, and the unknown and missing member make up only one per cent of the corps; each company of one thousand finaliters has places for just ten of these nonmortal and nonseraphic personalities.

We of Uversa do not know the "finality destiny" of the ascendant mortals of time. At present they reside on Paradise and temporarily serve in the Corps of Light and Life, but such a tremendous course of ascendant training and such lengthy universe discipline must be designed to qualify them for even greater tests of trust and more sublime services of responsibility.

Notwithstanding that these ascendant mortals have attained Paradise, have been mustered into the Corps of the Finality, and have been sent back in large numbers to participate in the conduct of local universes and to assist in the administration of superuniverse affairs — in the face of even this apparent destiny, there remains the significant fact that they are of record as only sixth-stage spirits. There undoubtedly remains one more step in the career of the Mortal Corps of the Finality. We do not know the nature of that step, but we have taken cognizance of, and here call attention to, three facts:

1. We know from the records that mortals are spirits of the first order during their sojourn in the minor sectors, and that they advance to the second order when translated to the major sectors, and to the third when they go forward to the central training worlds of the superuniverse. Mortals become quartan or graduate spirits after reaching the sixth circle of Havona and become spirits of the fifth order when they find the Universal Father. They subsequently attain the sixth stage of spirit existence upon taking the oath that musters them forever into the eternity assignment of the Corps of the Mortal Finality.

We observe that spirit classification, or designation, has been determined by actual advancement from one realm of universe service to another realm of universe service or from one universe to another universe; and we surmise that the bestowal of seventh-spirit classification upon the Mortal Corps of the Finality will be simultaneous with their advancement to eternal assignment for service on hitherto unrecorded and unrevealed spheres and concomitant with their attainment of God the Supreme. But aside from these bold conjectures, we really know no more about all this than you do; our knowledge of the mortal career does not go beyond present Paradise destiny.

2. The mortal finaliters have fully complied with the injunction of the ages, "Be you perfect"; they have ascended the universal path of mortal attainment; they have found God, and they have been duly inducted into the Corps of the Finality. Such beings have attained the present limit of spirit progression but not *finality of ultimate spirit status*. They have achieved the present limit of creature perfection but not *finality of creature service*. They have experienced the fullness of Deity worship but not *finality of experiential Deity attainment*.

3. The glorified mortals of the Paradise Corps of Finality are ascendant beings in possession of experiential knowledge of every step of the actuality and philosophy of the fullest possible life of intelligent existence, while during the ages of this ascent from the lowest material worlds to the spiritual heights of Paradise, these surviving creatures have been trained to the limits of their capacity respecting every detail of every divine principle of the just and efficient, as well as merciful and patient, administration of all the universal creation of time and space.

We deem that human beings are entitled to share our opinions, and that you are free to conjecture with us respecting the mystery of the ultimate destiny of the Paradise Corps of Finality. It seems evident to us that the present assignments of the perfected evolutionary creatures partake of the nature of postgraduate courses in universe understanding and superuniverse administration; and we all ask, "Why should the Gods be so concerned in so thoroughly training surviving mortals in the technique of universe management?"

4. ADOPTED SERAPHIM

Many of the faithful seraphic guardians of mortals are permitted to go through the ascendant career with their human wards, and many of these guardian angels, after becoming Father fused, join their subjects in taking the finaliter oath of eternity and forever accept the destiny of their mortal associates. Angels who pass through the ascending experience of mortal beings may share the destiny of human nature; they may equally and eternally be mustered into this Corps of the Finality. Large numbers of the adopted and glorified seraphim are attached to the various nonmortal finaliter corps.

5. GLORIFIED MATERIAL SONS

There is provision in the universes of time and space whereby the Adamic citizens of the local systems, when long delayed in receiving planetary assignment, may initiate a petition for release from permanent-citizenship status. And if granted, they join the ascending pilgrims on the universe capitals and thence proceed onward to Paradise and the Corps of the Finality.

When an advanced evolutionary world attains the later eras of the age of light and life, the Material Sons, the Planetary Adam and Eve, may elect to humanize, receive Adjusters, and embark upon the evolutionary course of universe ascent leading to the Corps of Mortal Finaliters. Certain of these Material Sons have partially failed or technically defaulted in their mission as biologic accelerators, as Adam did on Urantia; and then are they compelled to take the natural course of the peoples of the realm, receive Adjusters, pass through death, and progress by faith through the ascendant regime, subsequently attaining Paradise and the Corps of the Finality.

These Material Sons are not to be found in many finaliter companies. Their presence lends great potential to the possibilities of high service for such a group, and they are invariably chosen as its leaders. If both of the Edenic pair are attached to the same group, they are usually permitted to function jointly, as one personality. Such ascendant pairs are far more successful in the adventure of trinitizing than are the ascendant mortals.

6. GLORIFIED MIDWAY CREATURES

On many planets the midway creatures are produced in large numbers, but they seldom tarry on their native world subsequent to its being settled in light and life. Then, or soon thereafter, they are released from permanent-citizenship status and start on the ascension to Paradise, passing through the morontia worlds, the superuniverse, and Havona in company with the mortals of time and space.

The midway creatures from various universes differ greatly in origin and nature, but they are all destined to one or another of the Paradise finality corps. The secondary midwayers are all eventually Adjuster fused and are mustered into the mortal corps. Many finaliter companies have one of these glorified beings in their group.

7. THE EVANGELS OF LIGHT

At the present time every finaliter company numbers 999 personalities of oath status, permanent members. The vacant place is occupied by the chief of attached Evangels of Light assigned on any single mission. But these beings are only transient members of the corps.

Any celestial personality assigned to the service of any finaliter corps is denominated an Evangel of Light. These beings do not take the finaliter oath, and though subject to the corps organization they are not of permanent attachment. This group may embrace Solitary Messengers, supernaphim, seconaphim, Paradise Citizens, or their trinitized offspring — any being required in the prosecution of a transient finaliter assignment. Whether or not the corps is to have these beings attached to the eternal mission, we do not know. At the conclusion of attachment these Evangels of Light resume their former status.

As the Mortal Corps of the Finality is at present constituted, there are just six classes of permanent members. The finaliters, as might be expected, engage in much speculation as to the identity of their future comrades, but there is little agreement among them.

We of Uversa often conjecture respecting the identity of the seventh group of finaliters. We entertain many ideas, embracing possible assignment of some of the accumulating corps of the numerous trinitized groups on Paradise, Vicegerington, and the inner Havona circuit. It is even conjectured that the Corps of the Finality may be permitted to trinitize many of their assistants in the work of universe administration in the event they are destined to the service of universes now in the making.

One of us holds the opinion that this vacant place in the corps will be filled by some type of being of origin in the new universe of their future service; the other inclines to the belief that this place will be occupied by some type of Paradise personality not yet created, eventuated, or trinitized. But we will most likely await the entrance of the finaliters upon their seventh stage of spirit attainment before we really know.

8. THE TRANSCENDENTALERS

Part of the perfected mortal's experience on Paradise as a finaliter consists in the effort to achieve comprehension of the nature and function of more than one thousand groups of the transcendental supercitizens of Paradise, eventuated beings of absonite attributes. In their association with these superpersonalities, the ascendant finaliters receive great assistance from the helpful guidance of numerous orders of transcendental ministers who are assigned to the task of introducing the evolved finaliters to their new Paradise brethren. The entire order of the Transcendentalers live in the west of Paradise in a vast area which they exclusively occupy.

In the discussion of Transcendentalers we are restricted, not only by the limitations of human comprehension, but also by the terms of the mandate governing these disclosures concerning the personalities of Paradise. These beings are in no way connected with the mortal ascent to Havona. The vast host of the Paradise Transcendentalers have nothing whatever to do with the affairs of either Havona or the seven superuniverses, being concerned only with the superadministration of the affairs of the master universe.

You, being a creature, can conceive of a Creator, but you can hardly comprehend that there exists an enormous and diversified aggregation of intelligent beings who are neither Creators nor creatures. These Transcendentalers create no beings, neither were they ever created. In speaking of their origin, in order to avoid using a new term — an arbitrary and meaningless designation — we deem it best to say that Transcendentalers simply eventuate. The Deity Absolute may well have been concerned in their origin and may be implicated in their destiny, but these unique beings are not now dominated by the Deity Absolute. They are subject to God the Ultimate, and their present Paradise sojourn is in every way Trinity supervised and directed.

Although all mortals who attain Paradise frequently fraternize with the Transcendentalers as they do with the Paradise Citizens, it develops that man's first serious contact with a Transcendentaler occurs on that eventful occasion when, as a member of a new finaliter group, the mortal ascender stands in the finaliter receiving circle as the Trinity oath of eternity is administered by the chief of Transcendentalers, the presiding head of the Architects of the Master Universe.

9. ARCHITECTS OF THE MASTER UNIVERSE

The Architects of the Master Universe are the governing corps of the Paradise Transcendentalers. This governing corps numbers 28,011 personalities possessing master minds, superb spirits, and supernal absonites. The presiding officer of this magnificent group, the senior Master Architect, is the co-ordinating head of all Paradise intelligences below the level of Deity.

The sixteenth proscription of the mandate authorizing these narratives says: "If deemed wise, the existence of the Architects of the Master Universe and their associates may be disclosed, but their origin, nature, and destiny may not be fully revealed." We may, however, inform you that these Master Architects exist in seven levels of the absonite. These seven groups are classified as follows:

1. *The Paradise Level.* Only the senior or first-eventuated Architect functions on this highest level of the absonite. This ultimate personality —

neither Creator nor creature — eventuated in the dawn of eternity and now functions as the exquisite co-ordinator of Paradise and its twenty-one worlds of associated activities.

2. *The Havona Level.* The second Architect eventuation yielded three master planners and absonite administrators, and they have always been devoted to the co-ordination of the one billion perfect spheres of the central universe. Paradise tradition asserts that these three Architects, with the counsel of the pre-eventuated senior Architect, contributed to the planning of Havona, but we really do not know.

3. *The Superuniverse Level.* The third absonite level embraces the seven Master Architects of the seven superuniverses, who now, as a group, spend about equal time in the company of the Seven Master Spirits on Paradise and with the Seven Supreme Executives on the seven special worlds of the Infinite Spirit. They are the superco-ordinators of the grand universe.

4. *The Primary Space Level.* This group numbers seventy Architects, and we conjecture that they are concerned with the ultimate plans for the first universe of outer space, now mobilizing beyond the borders of the present seven superuniverses.

5. *The Secondary Space Level.* This fifth corps of Architects numbers 490, and again we conjecture that they must be concerned with the second universe of outer space, where already our physicists have detected definite energy mobilizations.

6. *The Tertiary Space Level.* This sixth group of Master Architects numbers 3,430, and we likewise infer that they may be occupied with the gigantic plans for the third universe of outer space.

7. *The Quartan Space Level.* This, the final and largest corps, consists of 24,010 Master Architects, and if our former conjectures are valid, it must be related to the fourth and last of the ever-increasing-sized universes of outer space.

These seven groups of Master Architects total 28,011 universe planners. On Paradise there is a tradition that far back in eternity there was attempted the eventuation of the 28,012th Master Architect, but that this being failed to absonitize, experiencing personality seizure by the Universal Absolute. It is possible that the ascending series of the Master Architects attained the limit of absonity in the 28,011th Architect, and that the 28,012th attempt encountered the mathematical level of the presence of the Absolute. In other words, at the 28,012th eventuation level the quality of absonity equivalated to the level of the Universal and attained the value of the Absolute.

In their functional organization the three supervising Architects of Havona act as associate assistants to the solitary Paradise Architect. The seven Architects of the superuniverses act as co-ordinates of the three supervisors of Havona. The seventy planners of the universes of the primary outer space level are at present serving as associate assistants to the seven Architects of the seven superuniverses.

The Architects of the Master Universe have at their disposal numerous groups of assistants and helpers, including two vast orders of force organizers, the primary eventuated and the associate transcendental. These Master Force Organizers are not to be confused with the power directors, who are germane to the grand universe.

All beings produced by the union of the children of time and eternity, such as the trinitized offspring of the finaliters and the Paradise Citizens, become wards of the Master Architects. But of all other creatures or entities revealed as functioning in the present organized universes, only Solitary Messengers and Inspired Trinity Spirits maintain any organic association with the Transcendentalers and the Architects of the Master Universe.

The Master Architects contribute technical approval of the assignment of the Creator Sons to their space sites for the organization of the local universes. There is a very close association between the Master Architects and the Paradise Creator Sons, and while this relationship is unrevealed, you have been informed of the association of the Architects and the grand universe Supreme Creators in the relationship of the first experiential Trinity. These two groups, together with the evolving and experiential Supreme Being, constitute the Trinity Ultimate of transcendental values and master universe meanings.

10. THE ULTIMATE ADVENTURE

The senior Master Architect has the oversight of the seven Corps of the Finality, and they are:

1. The Corps of Mortal Finaliters.
2. The Corps of Paradise Finaliters.
3. The Corps of Trinitized Finaliters.
4. The Corps of Conjoint Trinitized Finaliters.
5. The Corps of Havona Finaliters.
6. The Corps of Transcendental Finaliters.
7. The Corps of Unrevealed Sons of Destiny.

Each of these destiny corps has a presiding head, and the seven constitute the Supreme Council of Destiny on Paradise; and during the present universe age Grandfanda is the chief of this supreme body of universe assignment for the children of ultimate destiny.

The gathering together of these seven finaliter corps signifies reality mobilization of potentials, personalities, minds, spirits, absonites, and experiential actualities that probably transcend even the future master universe functions of the Supreme Being. These seven finaliter corps probably signify the present activity of the Ultimate Trinity engaged in mustering the forces of the finite and the absonite in preparation for inconceivable developments in the universes of outer space. Nothing like this mobilization has taken place since the near times of eternity when the Paradise Trinity similarly mobilized the then existing personalities of Paradise and Havona and commissioned them as administrators and rulers of the projected seven superuniverses of time and space. The seven finaliter corps represent the divinity response of the grand universe to the future needs of the undeveloped potentials in the outer universes of future-eternal activities.

We venture the forecast of future and greater outer universes of inhabited worlds, new spheres peopled with new orders of exquisite and unique beings, a material universe sublime in its ultimacy, a vast creation lacking in only one important detail — the presence of actual *finite experience* in the universal life of ascendant existence. Such a universe will come into being under a tremendous experiential handicap: the deprivation of participation in the evolution of the Almighty Supreme. These outer universes will all enjoy the matchless ministry and supernal overcontrol of the Supreme Being, but the very fact of his active presence precludes their participation in the actualization of the Supreme Deity.

During the present universe age the evolving personalities of the grand universe suffer many difficulties due to the incomplete actualization of the sovereignty of God the Supreme, but we are all sharing the unique experience of his evolution. We evolve in him and he evolves in us. Sometime in the eternal future the evolution of Supreme Deity will become a completed fact of universe history, and the opportunity to participate in this wonderful experience will have passed from the stage of cosmic action.

But those of us who have acquired this unique experience during the youth of the universe will treasure it throughout all future eternity. And many of us speculate that it may be the mission of the gradually accumulating reserves of the ascendant and perfected mortals of the Corps of the Finality, in association with the other six similarly recruiting corps, to administer these outer universes in an effort to compensate their experiential deficiencies in not having participated in the time-space evolution of the Supreme Being.

These deficiencies are inevitable on all levels of universe existence. During the present universe age we of the higher levels of spiritual existences now come down to administer the evolutionary universes and minister to the ascending mortals, thus endeavoring to atone for their deficiencies in the realities of the higher spiritual experience.

But though we really know nothing about the plans of the Architects of the Master Universe respecting these outer creations, nevertheless, of three things we are certain:

1. There actually is a vast and new system of universes gradually organizing in the domains of outer space. New orders of physical creations, enormous and gigantic circles of swarming universes upon universes far out beyond the present bounds of the peopled and organized creations. At present, these outer creations are wholly physical; they are apparently uninhabited and seem to be devoid of creature administration.

2. For ages upon ages there continues the unexplained and wholly mysterious Paradise mobilization of the perfected and ascendant beings of time and space, in association with the six other finaliter corps.

3. Concomitantly with these transactions the Supreme Person of Deity is powerizing as the almighty sovereign of the supercreations.

As we view this triune development, embracing creatures, universes, and Deity, can we be criticized for anticipating that something new and unrevealed is approaching culmination in the master universe? Is it not natural that we should associate this agelong mobilization and organization of physical universes on such a hitherto unknown scale and the personality emergence of the Supreme Being with this stupendous scheme of upstepping the mortals of time to divine perfection and with their subsequent mobilization on Paradise in the Corps of the Finality — a designation and destiny enshrouded in universe mystery? It is increasingly the belief of all Uversa that the assembling Corps of the Finality are destined to some future service in the universes of outer space, where we already are able to identify the clustering of at least seventy thousand aggregations of new types of space-time dimensional structures, each of which is greater than any one of the present superuniverses.

Evolutionary mortals are born on the planets of space, pass through the morontia worlds, ascend the spirit universes, traverse the Havona spheres, find God, attain Paradise, and are mustered into the primary Corps of the Finality, therein to await the next assignment of universe service. There are six other assembling finality corps, but Grandfanda, the first mortal ascender, presides as Paradise chief of all orders of finaliters. And as we view this sublime spectacle, we all exclaim: What a glorious destiny for the animal-origin children of time, the material sons of space!

[Jointly sponsored by a Divine Counselor and One without Name and Number authorized so to function by the Ancients of Days on Uversa.]

Afterword

These thirty-one papers depicting the nature of Deity, the reality of Paradise, the organization and working of the central and superuniverses, the personalities of the grand universe, and the high destiny of evolutionary mortals, were sponsored, formulated, and put into English by a high commission consisting of twenty-four Orvonton administrators acting in accordance with a mandate issued by the Ancients of Days of Uversa directing that we should do this on Urantia, 606 of Satania, in Norlatiadek of Nebadon, in the year A.D. 1934.